When should I trave

Where do I go for answ ... ns?

What's the best and easies... ...y trip?

frommers.travelocity.com

Frommer's, the travel guide leader, has teamed up with **Travelocity.com**, the leader in online travel, to bring you an in-depth, easy-to-use resource designed to help you plan and book your trip online.

At **frommers.travelocity.com**, you'll find free online updates about your destination from the experts at Frommer's plus the outstanding travel planning and purchasing features of Travelocity.com. Travelocity.com provides reservations capabilities for 95 percent of all airline seats sold, more than 47,000 hotels, and over 50 car rental companies. In addition, Travelocity.com offers more than 2,000 exciting vacation and cruise packages. Travelocity.com puts you in complete control of your travel planning with these and other great features:

Expert travel guidance from Frommer's - over 150 writers reporting from around the world!

Best Fare Finder - an interactive calendar tells you when to travel to get the best airfare

Fare Watcher - we'll track airfare changes to your favorite destinations

Dream Maps - a mapping feature that suggests travel opportunities based on your budget

Shop Safe Guarantee - 24 hours a day / 7 days a week live customer service, and more!

Whether traveling on a tight budget, looking for a quick weekend getaway, or planning the trip of a lifetime, Frommer's guides and Travelocity.com will make your travel dreams a reality. You've bought the book, now book the trip!

Frommer's

Great Outdoor Guide to Vermont & New Hampshire

Also Available:

Frommer's Great Outdoor Guide to New England
Frommer's Great Outdoor Guide to Southern New England
Frommer's Great Outdoor Guide to Southern California & Baha
Frommer's Great Outdoor Guide to Washington & Oregon
Frommer's New England
Frommer's Vermont, New Hampshire & Maine

Great Outdoor Guide to Vermont & New Hampshire

1st Edition

by Stephen Jermanok

Hungry Minds, Inc.
New York, NY • Cleveland, OH • Indianapolis, IN

About the Author

In the past decade, **Stephen Jermanok** has written more than 100 articles on Vermont and New Hampshire for such publications as ***Outside, Men's Journal, National Geographic Adventure, Outdoor Explorer, Arthur Frommer's Budget Travel Magazine,*** and the ***Boston Globe.*** Regarding books, Mr. Jermanok is a contributor to ***Lonely Planet's Guide to New England, Men's Journal's The Great Life, Discovery Channel's North American Wilderness Guide,*** and ***Discovery Channel's Paddling North America Guide.*** He's the New England outdoor expert for www.gorp.com, and many of his stories can be found on www.travelintelligence.net and on his Web site, www.activetravels.com. Mr. Jermanok's latest screenplay, ***Sally's Gamble,*** was just filmed in New Bedford, Massachusetts. He resides in Newton, Massachusetts, with his wife and two young children.

Published by:

Hungry Minds, Inc.

909 Third Ave.
New York, NY 10022
www.frommers.com

ISBN 0-02-863593-0
ISSN 1531-1600

Editor: Matthew Kiernan, Amy Lyons
Production Editor: M. Faunette Johnston
Photo Editor: Richard Fox
Design by Michele Laseau
Cartographer: John Decamillis
Production by Hungry Minds Indianapolis Production Services

Special Sales

For general information on Hungry Minds' products and services please contact our Customer Care department; within the U.S. at 800-762-2974, outside the U.S. at 317-572-3993 or fax 317-572-4002. For sales inquiries and reseller information, including discounts, bulk sales, customized editions, and premium sales, please contact our Customer Care department at 800-434-3422.

Manufactured in the United States of America.

5 4 3 2 1

Contents

List of Maps

Map Legend

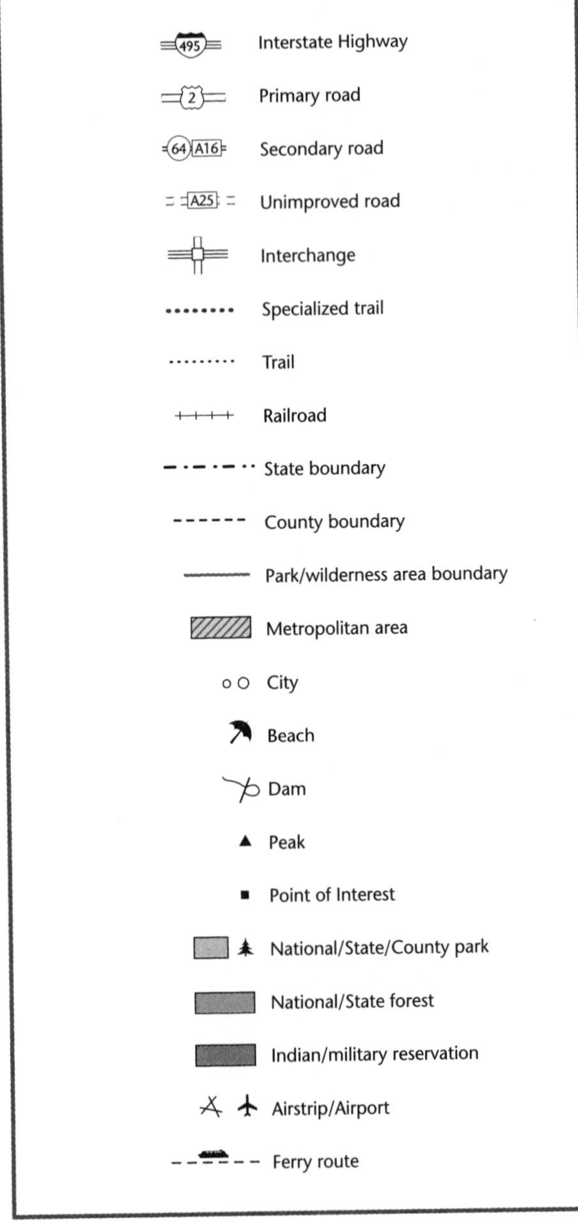
495
Interstate Highway
2
Primary road
64
A16
Secondary road
A25
Unimproved road
Interchange
Specialized trail
Trail
Railroad
State boundary
County boundary
Park/wilderness area boundary
Metropolitan area
City
Beach
Dam
Peak
Point of Interest
National/State/County park
National/State forest
Indian/military reservation
Airstrip/Airport
Ferry route

To Mom

Who never failed to take the tiller and chart her own course.

Acknowledgments

This book would never have come to fruition without the keen advice and wise guidance from the following people. First and foremost, my wife, Lisa, who accompanied me on many of these trips or took care of our children, 4-year-old Jake and 2-year-old Melanie, while I was off gallivanting in the forest. I'm grateful to my brother, Jim, who kept me laughing on numerous hiking, biking, sea kayaking, and fishing adventures; Julie, Neil, Ami, and Tali for our weeks together in Vermont; Dad, Ginny, Fawn, Jack, and Fran for their continuing support of my career.

Kudos go to my researcher, Judith Perry, who helped dwindle down those thousands of trails in Vermont and New Hampshire to that one desirable route. I'd like to thank Ian Wilker, who worked hard to make the Vermont chapters as informative as possible. The Vermont chapters also owe much of their existence to the diligent work of Emily Case. Accolades also go to Meryl Pearlstein and Larry Olmsted. In New Hampshire, many thanks to Margaret Joyce, Dick Hamilton, and Alice Pierce. Finally, I would like to thank all the park rangers, outfitters, sporting goods store owners, friends, and anonymous outdoor lovers who helped me along the way.

An Invitation to the Reader

In researching this book, we discovered many wonderful places—hotels, restaurants, shops, and more. We're sure you'll find others. Please tell us about them, so we can share the information with your fellow travelers in upcoming editions. If you were disappointed with a recommendation, we'd love to know that too. Please write to:

Frommer's Great Outdoor Guide to Vermont & New Hampshire, 1st Edition
Hungry Minds, Inc.
909 Third Avenue
New York, NY 10022

An Additional Note

Please be advised that travel information is subject to change at any time—and this is especially true of prices. We therefore suggest that you write or call ahead for confirmation when making your travel plans. The author, editors, and publisher cannot be held responsible for the experiences of readers while traveling. Your safety is important to us, however, so we encourage you to stay alert and be aware of your surroundings. Keep a close eye on cameras, purses, and wallets, all favorite targets of thieves and pickpockets.

Abbreviations

The following abbreviations are used for credit cards:

AE	American Express	DISC	Discover	JCB	Japan Credit Bank
CB	Carte Blanche	ER	enRoute	MC	MasterCard
DC	Diners Club	EC	Eurocard	V	Visa

Find Frommer's Online

www.frommers.com offers up-to-the-minute listings on almost 200 cities around the globe—including the latest bargains and candid, personal articles updated daily by Arthur Frommer himself. No other Web site offers such comprehensive and timely coverage of the world of travel.

Introduction

Feel like taking a canoe ride to see a pair of nesting bald eagles? How about biking through Vermont's 200-year-old villages and verdant countryside on a self-guided tour? Or hiking the windblown, lichen-encrusted granite summits of the White Mountains? Keep on reading. Perhaps you're wondering whether there's shoreline on the New Hampshire coast that isn't wall-to-wall people when it's 96° in the shade, whether the skiing at Mad River Glen is as tough as they say, or whether there's a deep-woods walk within an hour north of Boston. You'll find what you're looking for within these pages.

Want to locate elusive single tracks for mountain-bike rides, telemark-ski on former downhill runs, kayak with whales, or climb a sheer face of rock? Maybe you're determined to backpack the rugged Mahoosuc Range of the Whites, cross-country ski the length of Vermont on the 280-mile Catamount Trail, or sail Lake Champlain. All the information you'll need is now within your grasp. Did you know there are outfitters who'll teach you the age-old art of falconry, take you scuba diving to wrecks from the War of 1812, guide you on weekend snowmobiling excursions into the Green Mountain National Forest, and include you on weeklong inn-to-inn canoeing jaunts on Vermont's finest rivers?

Finally, there's a definitive guide to the finest outdoor activities in Vermont and New Hampshire. No longer will you have to purchase piles of books on every sport and every region in these two states. No longer will you have to make numerous phone calls to find the one outfitter ideal for you. This book covers the entirety of these two northern New England states. It includes every sport imaginable, from walking to biking to fishing to hiking to canoeing to skiing and swimming, even hang gliding, off-road driving, and llama trekking. Most important, this guide is for everyone. I don't care if you're an average Joe like me who simply yearns to play outdoors or a parent with small children, a cyclist in training for the Tour de France, or a couch potato who wishes to leave home to cool off on a hot summer's day—you'll find a long list of invigorating activities to choose from. All you need is the desire to venture outdoors into one of America's most historic and majestic regions.

The activities listed alphabetically in each of the five regional chapters fall under two categories—self-guided sporting trips and spur-of-the-moment recreation. Self-guided trips describe hiking, road biking, walking, mountain biking, canoeing, sailing, sea kayaking, and cross-country skiing adventures that I have personally experienced and highly recommend.

These paths, routes, or waterways weren't chosen at random. In 1995 I drove more than 20,000 miles around every nook and cranny of New England to write ***Frommer's Great Outdoor Guide to New England*** (IDG Books Worldwide). During the course of the year, I tried as many sporting activities as possible. But, alas, there were time restrictions, and I found the region was just too vast for the depth I wanted to plumb. I had the chance to try only two hikes in the Presidential Range of the White Mountains and barely had a chance to ride the backcountry roads of southwestern New Hampshire, where the road biking is as sublime as in Vermont. In this edition, I went back to these two states only and took my time savoring the countryside.

For the past year, I've talked to park rangers, outfitters, sporting goods store owners, high school and college coaches, sporting clubs, professional athletes, numerous family members, friends, and locals who have lived their entire lives in New England. I somehow managed, by the power of persuasion or by simply prying, to get these people to reveal their most coveted trails, fishing holes, and backcountry roads. No one could possibly know these places without living in that locale for years. Now these places appear in print for the first time.

The fun part for me, of course, was rambling my way through the region. With my treasured list of recommended activities, I tried more than 100 new bike rides, hikes, cross-country ski routes, walks, canoe jaunts, you name it, to make this book the comprehensive guide it is now. More than half of those routes never made it into this book. They were good exercise, but for one reason or another I did not feel that they were the premier trips in these two states. Thus, I can attest to the high quality of every one of the featured trails in this book. These trips are indeed the best that Vermont and New Hampshire have to offer. I have also tried to be as honest as possible so you can get a feel of what it's like to take each venture before you begin. This is not your typical guidebook where superlatives are applied liberally, opinions aren't expressed, and each trip looks remarkably similar to the last. I've given my frank opinion of each featured venture and of course have included the required directions to guide you along the way.

Spur-of-the-moment recreation pertains to sports like downhill skiing, swimming, golfing, or horseback riding where you don't need explicit information regarding trails or routes. For these sports, I listed the leading ski areas, swimming holes, golf courses, and stables as suggested to me by the knowledgeable people mentioned above.

For the outdoors person who doesn't like to go anywhere without a guide or instruction, I've included a comprehensive list of outfitters and schools both in Chapter 1 and in the specific regional chapters. Under each outfitter or school is an in-depth description of the sport and the region covered.

Whether you crave mountains and lakes, the Atlantic Ocean, ponds and rivers, or 18th-century villages in which clapboard houses and a white steeple surround a well-manicured green, there's no better time to reacquaint yourself with the splendor and rich history of Vermont and New Hampshire. According to an article that appeared in the April 1995 issue of the ***Atlantic Monthly,*** the forests that were denuded in the 1700s and 1800s for farming and timbering are regenerating at a rapid pace. Writer Bill McKibben notes that "despite great increases in the state's population, 90% of New Hampshire is covered by forest. . . . Vermont was 35% woods in 1850 and is 80% today."

I sincerely hope this book will live in the glove compartment of your car, there to help you steal away from the woes of our modern age into the quietude of nature.

—Stephen Jermanok

1

The Basics

This book is divided into five geographical regions that span Vermont and New Hampshire, from the Lake Champlain Islands in the northeast corner of Vermont to the 18-mile stretch of Atlantic coast shoreline in the southeastern region of New Hampshire. All of the regional chapters include an in-depth list of sports, categorized alphabetically from backpacking to white-water rafting. Under each sports heading, I feature specific trails, routes, and waterways that I've personally tried and that proved to be the best in these two states. These featured activities are described in detail. Time required, level of difficulty, and location are all addressed. Of course, time and level of difficulty are relative terms, but I based these quotients on the average person who works out several times a week and is in relatively decent shape. Level of difficulty varies from sport to sport. For example, I labeled all walks and rambles as easy, but a hike designated as easy is inherently more strenuous than a walk, since hikes denote a climb uphill. An easy cross-country ski trail involves far more work than say an easy flatwater canoe jaunt. I'm assuming that you've tried the sport within the last year. If you have not been on a bicycle in the past 12 months, you'll find my easy routes attainable but challenging.

At the other extreme are the bikers, hikers, and skiers who work out religiously. I guarantee that the routes I've listed as strenuous will test your abilities and stamina.

However, I'm not worried about you. I'm worried about the guy who just inhaled a box of chocolate chip cookies, smoked a couple of butts, and now wants to climb Mount Lafayette at 4 in the afternoon. Use common sense. If you haven't climbed a mountain since the Red Sox were in the World Series, don't start with Mount Adams. If a mountain climb is listed as easy, it might challenge the casual hiker who has not climbed in a long time. If a mountain climb is listed as strenuous, you better believe that this trail is unrelenting, often grueling, and goes straight up the mountain at a steep pitch.

For sports such as boardsailing, golfing, and surfing, I've listed the top courses or beaches as recommended to me by golf pros, local outfitters or owners of sporting goods stores, college sporting clubs, chambers of commerce, other writers, and friends. Also discussed under the regional sport headings are outfitters, schools, and store rentals that cater specifically to that area and to outdoor recreation. A complete alphabetical listing of outfitters and schools, as well as some helpful hints regarding options, can be found at the end of this chapter. Each regional chapter concludes with the top campsites, inns, and resorts that cater to sports enthusiasts.

This introductory section will help you plan your trip, whether it's on your own or with an outfitter. I have listed every sport found in the regional chapters, discussing in detail the equipment, logistics, and conditioning necessary to perform that particular activity. I've included the top destinations in Vermont and New Hampshire for each sport. The latter half of this chapter contains information on locating the best maps, additional reading, and an overall list of outfitters and schools.

Getting Underway

BACKPACKING

Backpacking is the perfect sport with which to begin this section, since no other activity requires more preplanning than backpacking. You have to eat and sleep for days or weeks without the luxury of a refrigerator, oven, and bed. Obviously, the first items you need are good hiking boots and a backpack. Boots these days have uppers made of either water-resistant (Nubuck) leather or a combination of leather and lighter synthetic fabric; most good boots today have a waterproof Gore-Tex lining sewn into the boot. Basically, if you're going on a short weekend hike with a fairly light load, the synthetic boots are probably okay, but for anything else you'll want the heavy-duty support and rugged durability of the leather models. Prevent blistering by wearing new boots ***before*** heading out to the trails. Preferably, you should also soak the boots and wear them till they dry to break in the leather.

As far as packs go, the debate over the merits of the old-fashioned external-frame pack and the more newfangled internal-frame pack has raged on for years. External-frame packs probably enjoy their greatest continuing popularity on the East Coast: They're generally a little cheaper; they're well-suited to carrying heavy loads on fairly straight-ahead trails like most of the Appalachian Trail (AT), the chief long-distance backpacking route in the Northeast; and experienced AT hikers pare down their loads to the point that they don't really need the carrying capacity of a big internal-frame pack.

But internal-frame packs have clearly outdistanced their rivals in most ways. They're more stable for rough going—the rock-hopping and steep-and-twisty section of the AT, for example—because they distribute the weight more evenly across your hips and shoulders and cinch more snugly to your back. They let you carry greater loads, and they're now easier to use, what with packs that have both top and front zippers, allowing easy access to the whole sack. I myself prefer internal-frame packs, which can be formed to your back.

Whichever you choose, get a pack that really fits you—don't try to fit yourself to a pack. A good pack will have plenty of padding and support, a wide, firm hip belt, and a lumbar support pad.

Now comes the hard part—trying to pare down your load so you don't feel like a beast of burden on your hike. All the essentials are listed in the "Backcountry Equipment Checklist," below. Make sure you pack enough food for at least 2 more days than you intend to be out, but go for the lightest dehydrated foods you can find. Take all food out of its bulky packaging and put it instead in resealable bags. Invest in ultralight, multipurpose outdoor clothing—and don't bring more than one change of socks, T-shirt, etc., because long-distance hiking is inevitably a business that brings people out of the woods in an incredibly fragrant, gamey condition. And don't bring Colin Fletcher's ***Complete Walker*** with you, or any other large, heavy book. Dispensing with these things will make the difference between a 30- and a 50-pound pack, which is the gap between comfort and misery.

Clothing, food, and matches should be kept in plastic bags, tubes, or waterproof stuff sacks so that they stay dry.

Being outside without a refrigerator and a house on your back is a serious impediment to gourmet cookery. Meals on the trail are a mixture of dried foods—rice, beans, lentils, pastas, dried meats, Wasa bread, plastic jars of peanut butter and jelly, cereal, dried fruits, trail mix (nuts, carobs, raisins, and so on), granola bars, salt and pepper, cookies, and pre-made meals such as Lipton's Cup-a-Soups or freeze-dried backpacker dinners. The last are kind of expensive, and I've seen more than a few hikers scoff at them, but what the hey, they're featherweight, easy-to-prepare meals that generally taste like three-star fare next to Kraft Macaroni and Cheese. I buy them all the time.

One of the crucial survival duties of every backpacking trip is to make sure you are carrying enough water to last you a while—and to know exactly where your refills along the trail are going to come. Topographical maps can help, and guidebooks to the Long Trail and Appalachian Trail will tell you where you'll find reliable springs. In addition to water, it's good to bring dried milk, tea, and hot chocolate; those new "coffee singles" (coffee bags shaped like tea bags) are, I think, the best bit of new technology for backpackers in a while, but I guess you have to hate instant coffee as much as I do. Depending on the amount of time you plan to spend away from civilization, you might need to send packages of food and fuel to friendly inns or post offices along the way.

Perusing the pages of the ***Boston Globe,*** I saw an article about an obese man who quit his job to lose weight by walking the Appalachian Trail. He was venturing from south to north and had lost 50 pounds by the time he reached the Massachusetts border. The moral of this story is that anyone can backpack (though you'll be a lot more comfortable if you're in shape). Indeed, I meet far more backpackers who start their long hikes out of shape than in shape. If you can somehow make it through the first 2 to 3 days of hiking, you should be fine for the rest of the trip. The most important task is to prevent blistering by wearing comfortable shoes and heavy socks—and more important, to do at least a week of fairly heavy walking before you hit the trail. (Of course, if you are seriously out of shape or have a medical condition, you should check with your doctor before setting out.)

Vermont's 265-mile **Long Trail** runs the length of the state from Massachusetts to Canada, and it's wonderful from top to bottom. Any number of section hikes can be made, but the reaches of the trail north of Sherburne Pass (U.S. 4) are a little less crowded. If I had to make one recommendation for a long weekend's hike, I'd say haul yourself up to the northernmost section, from **Jay Peak to State Route 15,** near Johnson. It draws the fewest hikers and has perhaps the greatest variety of really rugged terrain. Give yourself 3 to 4 weeks to walk the entire length of the trail, which is the oldest long-distance hiking trail in the nation. For additional information, contact the **Green Mountain Club,** 4711 Waterbury-Stowe Rd., Waterbury Center, VT 05677 (**☎ 802/244-7037;** www.greenmountainclub.org).

The **Pemigewasset Wilderness** between the Franconia Range and Crawford Notch and the **Mahoosuc**

Range on the Maine border offer excellent 5-day backpacking opportunities in the White Mountains. Also in the Whites are the **"High Huts,"** eight mountain huts operated by the Appalachian Mountain Club (AMC). Strung along 56 miles of the Appalachian Trail, these rustic accommodations offer two hot meals a day and bunk beds. For more information, contact the **AMC,** 5 Joy St., Boston, MA 02108 (☎ **617/523-0636;** www.outdoors.org).

BALLOONING

I haven't the slightest idea how to go up in your *own* hot-air balloon. If you plan on flying with one of the numerous outfitters across New England, all you'll need is a camera, sunglasses, and perhaps a sweater. **Boland Balloons** (☎ **802/333-9254**), in West Fairlee, central Vermont, is one of the better options.

BIRD WATCHING

With the Atlantic coast to the east and a slew of national forests and state parks to the west, birding opportunities in Vermont and New Hampshire are virtually unlimited. More than 300 species have been observed in New England in the past decade. During the last year alone, I have spied bald eagles, peregrine falcons, ospreys, every type of heron imaginable, piping plovers, warblers, snowy egrets, ibis, terns, rufous-sided towhees,

BACKCOUNTRY EQUIPMENT CHECKLIST

Below is a list of things you'll need for a backcountry trip of 2 or more days. This is more or less a backpacker's list for a 4- to 7-day summer or fall trip on a New England long-distance trail. The list will also do for canoeing, backcountry skiing, whatever—there will be a few extra items of equipment you'll want for different kinds of trips, but no matter what you're planning, you'll kick yourself at some point if you don't have nearly all of this gear with you (a few things are obviously optional):

KITCHEN

- ☐ lightweight water filter (I suggest the SweetWater Guardian)
- ☐ 2–3 Nalgene quart-size water bottles
- ☐ 5-gallon camp waterbag
- ☐ stainless-steel cookset
- ☐ wooden spoon
- ☐ backpacking stove (like MSR Whisper-Lite)
- ☐ 1.5–2 quarts of stove fuel
- ☐ kitchen matches
- ☐ biodegradable soap
- ☐ scouring pad
- ☐ washcloth/potholder/towel

PANTRY

- ☐ coffee singles or tea bags, in Ziploc bag
- ☐ breakfast foods, like instant oatmeal, in Ziploc bag
- ☐ lunch items, such as peanut butter and jelly, crackers, cheese, hard sausage
- ☐ trail snacks, like gorp (trail mix), beef jerky, dried fruit, in Ziploc bags
- ☐ dinners—mac'n'cheese, freeze-dried dinners, couscous and Knorr-brand gravy, other one-pot meals, in Ziploc bags
- ☐ spices/seasonings
- ☐ big chocolate bar (you'll thank yourself)
- ☐ Nalgene bottle o' booze (you'll thank yourself again)
- ☐ separate stuff sacks for lunch/snacks and breakfast/dinner foods

BEDROOM

- ☐ waterproof groundcloth
- ☐ tent (roomy 3-season, Moss or Sierra Designs)
- ☐ sleeping bag rated to 20°F
- ☐ cotton sleeping-bag liner
- ☐ sleeping pad (Therm-A-Rests are great)

CLOTHES CLOSET

- ☐ boots (Vasque Sundowners, Salomon 8's)

American oystercatchers, razorbill auks, black guillemots, seven different sandpipers, and numerous other birds migrating along the coast. Inland, I've seen wild turkeys, red-tailed hawks, eagles, owls, hummingbirds, cackling loons, Canada geese, wood ducks, mallards, and goldfinches with breasts as yellow as the morning sun.

The most essential piece of equipment for any bird watcher is binoculars. It's worth spending the extra money to buy a really good high-power pair, with good close-focus, sharpness of image, and contrast. On the coast, wear a hat or you might get a nasty sunburn during your outing.

Both Vermont and New Hampshire have so many special places to view birds that it's almost impossible to list them all. Due to the nature of bird watching, on any given day, one spot could be far better than the next. However, you will never go wrong with these locales:

- **Dead Creek Wildlife Management Area, Vergennes, Vermont** Dead Creek is an excellent spot for birding year-round. In warm weather, you'll see a variety of waterfowl, including great blue herons. And in winter it's one of the best places in New England to seek out a snowy owl.

- [ ] 2 pairs heavy wool socks
- [ ] polypropylene sock liners
- [ ] polypropylene long johns
- [ ] 2 pairs baggy nylon shorts, with sewn-in briefs
- [ ] baseball cap, or other sun hat
- [ ] knit wool cap
- [ ] bandanna
- [ ] water-/wind-resistant, breathable shell
- [ ] rain pants
- [ ] cotton/synthetic T-shirt
- [ ] fleece-style pullover
- [ ] fleece-style pants
- [ ] camp shoes (Tevas)
- [ ] clothes stuff sack

ALL-PURPOSE ESSENTIALS

- [ ] maps/compass
- [ ] GPS (global positioning system) device
- [ ] bug repellent
- [ ] lighter
- [ ] whistle (for bear country, or rescue)
- [ ] sunglasses
- [ ] watch
- [ ] toothbrush, razor, other toilet gear
- [ ] camera gear
- [ ] binoculars
- [ ] Mini Mag or similar flashlight
- [ ] extra batteries
- [ ] battery-powered or candle lantern
- [ ] Swiss army knife
- [ ] 75–100-foot rope, for hanging food, etc.
- [ ] toilet paper
- [ ] toilet trowel
- [ ] extra quart Ziploc bags
- [ ] extra gallon Ziploc bags
- [ ] extra stuff sack
- [ ] a good book
- [ ] notebook/pen

FIRST-AID KIT

- [ ] 2-inch-by-3-inch moleskin
- [ ] pair of small shears
- [ ] thermometer
- [ ] safety pins
- [ ] acetaminophen/ibuprofen/aspirin
- [ ] diarrhea pills
- [ ] antacid tablets
- [ ] sunscreen
- [ ] sting-relief pads
- [ ] iodine solution
- [ ] iodine ointment
- [ ] triple antibiotic ointment
- [ ] antiseptic towelettes
- [ ] single-edge razor blade
- [ ] 1-inch-by-3-inch fabric bandages
- [ ] fabric knuckle bandages
- [ ] sterile wound closure strips
- [ ] 4-inch-by-4-inch sterile gauze pads
- [ ] adhesive tape
- [ ] elastic bandage
- [ ] 5-inch-by-9-inch combine dressings
- [ ] irrigation syringe
- [ ] wire mesh splint

The highlight, however, is the more than 20,000 migrating snow geese that fly by in the spring and fall.

- **Missisquoi National Wildlife Refuge, Swanton Vermont** Near the Canadian border on Lake Champlain, this is another pit stop for migrating snow geese and waterfowl.
- **Great Bay Estuary, Durham, New Hampshire** The 5,280-acre embankment on the New Hampshire–Maine border is composed of the Piscataqua River, Little Bay, and Great Bay. Ocean tides and river runoff mix 15 miles inland to attract some 281 species of birds, including ospreys, bald eagles, cormorants, and great blue herons.
- **Umbagog Lake, Errol, New Hampshire** You'll need a canoe to go birding here, but it's worth the extra effort. Loons, Canada geese, and herons line the waters; you eventually reach a dead oak tree where a pair of nesting bald eagles is the main attraction.

BOARDSAILING

The same prevailing winds and countless bays that enchant sailors attract windsurfers, especially in the Lakes region. Under each regional chapter, I have listed the leading boardsailing locales and places that rent sailboards.

CANOEING

Whether you like to canoe the quiet water of a backwoods pond, run a leisurely float-and-paddle down a flat and mild quickwater river, or take the challenge of white-water trips, the long sinuous rivers, lakes, and hidden ponds that blanket these two New England states are among the premier canoeing destinations in the country. Tensions turn to tranquility on waters where loons replace the loonies of the city. There are hundreds of camping sites on the shores and islands, tucked between large evergreens.

Before You Go

In planning your canoe trip, you face a host of options, which lead to many questions:

1. *Should I buy or rent a canoe?*

   You really don't need to be an expert to answer this question. Purchasing a canoe will increase your canoeing options greatly. Some of the rivers and lakes I've written about are accessible only to people who own canoes. However, most waterways have rentals on the shores. If you live close to a river or lake and canoe often, you probably own a canoe already. Obviously, if you paddle only once or twice a summer, a rental will suffice.

2. *What equipment will I need for a day trip? For overnight trips?*

   For a day trip, the necessary equipment includes a canoe, paddles, life jackets, sunscreen, sunglasses, bathing suit, and water. For overnight trips, you will need the aforementioned items plus all the equipment found in the backpacking section—backpack, tent, sleeping bag, food, stove, fuel, clothes, and so on. Since you're not walking, carrying all your belongings in the canoe is much easier. That is, unless, you will be portaging. ***Portaging*** means balancing the canoe on your shoulder as you walk on land between two bodies of water. Depending on the distance overland, a portage can be a 2-second walk or a grueling 2-mile journey. Portages should be taken into account on longer trips. Take a look at the handy backcountry checklist above.

3. *Should I go with a guide or on my own?*

   Flatwater canoeists certainly don't need a guide for day trips. The advantage of having a guide or outfitter for longer flatwater canoe trips is that someone is there to assist you with your paddling, set up the tents, help cook the food, and provide you with an intriguing history of the area. It's also nice to share the experience with a large group. Obviously, the major disadvantage of hiring a guide or signing up with an outfitter is the additional cost and the lack of privacy. With a little more work, you can have the water to yourself.

White-water canoeists that are not completely confident in their skills should consider a guide for day and overnight trips. It's no fun tipping over and watching your canoe get loose and go down the river without you.

4. *Do I need instruction?*

Instruction in flatwater canoeing can only help, but is not necessary. Mastering the strokes will help you guide yourself in the proper direction without exerting more energy than is needed. For white-water canoeing, however, lessons should be mandatory. Every year, inexperienced paddlers try their luck on the rapids, only to find their canoes or bodies thrashed on the rocks. Don't be foolish. If you're not prepared, white-water canoeing can be a dangerous sport.

The Best Day Trips

Here's my list of favorite 1-day paddle trips in Vermont and New Hampshire:

- **Long Pond, Benton, New Hampshire** Tucked away in the White Mountain National Forest, the 124-acre Long Pond is entirely uninhabited and surrounded by the White Mountains.
- **Umbagog Lake, Errol, New Hampshire** New Hampshire's premier canoeing jaunt is on rivers that lead to and from Umbagog Lake.
- **The Lamoille River, northern Vermont** Weaving through Vermont's green pastures and farmland, the Lamoille is canoeable anywhere from Johnson to Lake Champlain.
- **Green River Reservoir, northern Vermont** A little-known gem surrounded by uninhabited forest.

CROSS-COUNTRY SKIING

Cross-country skiing in New England is a very broad term. With new skis and new techniques, Nordic skiers are no longer confined to the groomed trails of a ski-touring center. In fact, the distinction between downhill and cross-country skiing gets hazier every year. The touring centers are still the most popular place for cross-country skiing, with the Trapp Family Lodge in Stowe, Vermont and the Jackson Ski Touring Foundation in Jackson, New Hampshire, leading the pack. Yet, even these premier ski touring centers are devoting more and more space every year to backcountry skiing.

What is backcountry skiing? That's a good question. I tend to think of backcountry skiing as any trail that isn't groomed or track-set. This includes the thousands of miles of dirt roads and snowmobile trails that weave through upper New England; the former downhill ski slopes like the Teardrop and Bruce Ski Trails built in the 1930s but no longer in use; the hundreds of miles of hiking trails through the Green Mountain and White Mountain National Forests; and the renowned Tuckerman, the large cirque, or bowl, that sits on Mount Washington.

Within this wide web of trails that traverse mountains, skirt lakes, and overlook oceans, is one 280-mile-long route that runs the length of Vermont. Called the **Catamount Trail,** it starts in southern Vermont at Readsboro and ends at North Troy on the Canadian border. In between, lies some of the finest skiing in the East, from backcountry trails that are etched into Mount Mansfield to ski touring centers located in the Green Mountain National Forest, like Blueberry Hill and Mountain Top. The Catamount is more than 90% complete, with over 250 miles of the trail now in service.

Cross-country skiing, mountain biking, and rock climbing are the most demanding sports in this book. Some of the noted telemark trails involve climbing mountains on skis. Even the level, groomed trails at ski touring centers require that you be in relatively good shape. Many cross-country skiers work out on ski machines (Nordic Tracks) or treadmills for weeks in advance. This is good conditioning, but I find the best exercise for cross-country skiing is simply to jog outside in winter. I'm facing the elements, getting acclimated to the cold weather, and, unlike working out on the machines at the local health club, I'm propelling myself forward with my own power. To build up arm strength, simply do lightweight curls or push-ups.

If you haven't been cross-country skiing in a while, you're in for a big surprise. You now have a variety of skis with which to tackle the variety of terrain. First, there's the old touring ski, good for diagonal striding on groomed trails. Skating skis or racing skis are shorter and narrower than the traditional track skis and are used with a speed-skating technique for quickness. Backcountry skis are wider than touring skis to aid maneuverability on ungroomed trails. You'll need to purchase telemark skis and learn the telemark technique if you want to try downhill backcountry runs like Tuckerman, the Teardrop Trail, or the Bolton-Trapp Trail from Bolton Ski Touring Center to Trapp Ski Touring Center. ***Telemarking*** is a gracefully lunging, turning technique that gives freeheelers something close to the kind of control on steep slopes that alpine skiers have. The telemark ski is like a backcountry ski but has metal edges to grip hard surfaces and give you control and carving ability. It tends to be heavy and should be used only on difficult trails. Finally, there are ***randonée*** skis. These skis bridge the gap between cross-country and downhill skiing and are for the telemarker who wants to ski down both ungroomed and groomed Alpine slopes.

Away from groomed trails, you should always carry water and food in a backpack. Serious skiers also wear climbing skins and, like a biker, bring a small tool kit to fix skis or bindings. If you think getting a flat is bad on a warm summer day, just wait till your skis snap atop a blustery mountain. Climbing skins are imperative for backcountry skiers who plan to climb mountains before skiing down them. ***Climbing skins*** are strips of fabric that travel the length of the ski and stick to the snow to prevent it from sliding backward. A tool kit includes a screwdriver, screws, glue, hose clamps and aluminum flashing (to fix broken poles and skis), duct tape, and even an extra binding. Many telemarkers also wear kneepads, just in case they wipe out on a patch of ice or a rock.

Since cross-country skiing is a highly aerobic sport done in a cold climate, I want to discuss the importance of layering clothes. The simple problem with cold weather sports is that if you get too cold, you'll freeze, and if you get too warm, you'll sweat, dehydrate, and also freeze. Layering helps to alleviate this problem. I usually wear three layers of clothing. The first layer is a thin polypropylene or capilene thermal underwear that "wicks" sweat away from my body to the outer layer. The second layer is polar fleece, or pile, to keep me warm, and the final layer is a light Gore-Tex shell and pants, which both "breathe" moisture into the air and protect against harsh winds. Some of my friends also wear a long-sleeved shirt between the capilene and polar fleece jacket, but that's far too much warmth for me. I can't overemphasize how important it is that you don't sweat profusely. It's much better to be cold when you start skiing and quickly warm up within the first 5 minutes of exercise than to be overheated and perspiring excessively. Hat, mittens, and a scarf are essential.

Frankly, I have no favorite cross-country ski trails. All the ones that I feature in this book are equally exhilarating. Depending on the amount of snow and skiers, the best trails vary day to day. Under each regional chapter, I describe my favorite backcountry trails and ski touring centers. With such a wide range of routes, the important thing is to stick to your level of competence. Don't attempt to ski Tuckerman or the Bruce Trail unless you know how to telemark or downhill-ski.

DOWNHILL SKIING/ SNOWBOARDING

Vermont and New Hampshire have a long history of downhill skiing. They are the home of the first U.S. ski trail, first ski school, first tow rope, and first aerial tram (installed at Cannon Mountain, New Hampshire in 1938). From Tuckerman and Wildcat in New Hampshire to Mount Mansfield in Vermont, fearless outdoors enthusiasts in those early days would brace themselves for their quick descent on two pieces of wood. They were even foolhardy enough to compete in races.

Today, detachable quad chairlifts and high-speed gondolas whisk you to the top in record times. From there, you have an incredible number of ever-expanding options, from easy trails that wind slowly down the mountain to heart-thumping double diamonds that will have you hurtling down moguls at an electrifying pace. With increased technology, each year brings more and more trails, faster lifts, and better snowmaking.

Conditioning, equipment, and clothing for downhill skiing and snowboarding are far less complex than for cross-country skiing. Learning the skills and practicing them is more of an asset than a well-tuned body. Of course, the better shape you're in, the less you risk injury. But I've been on lifts with people who make Pavarotti look like a toothpick and who ski far better than I ever will. They know their techniques and they have taken time to hone their skills. Schooling is a very important element of this sport. You should always consider signing up for a lesson or two.

Skis range from high-performance to the much wider specialty-performance skis. High-performance skis are used by racers or other adroit skiers; specialty-performance skis help you improve your turns quickly. There are also a variety of snowboards, from the short and wide freestyle used for trick riding, to the long and narrow freeride used in deep powder for cruising. Try the different types of skis and snowboards at a rental shop before you buy.

The Gore-Tex, slimtech, and fleece jackets and ski pants are a lot warmer and more weather-resistant than they used to be. I usually wear just a turtleneck, thermal bottoms, jacket, ski pants, gloves, hat, and scarf. Unlike during cross-country skiing, the only time you really sweat is when you're peering over that double-diamond run, egged on by your buddies to follow them. Snowboarders tend to wear looser-fitting pullovers and shells for greater freedom of movement.

Skiers are so fond of their particular ski resorts that I'm inevitably going to cause a debate with my Top 10 List, but here goes:

1. Sugarbush
2. Stowe
3. Killington
4. Jay
5. Attitash
6. Mount Snow
7. Statton
8. Okemo
9. Loon
10. Mad River Glen

My top three choices for snowboarding are Stratton, Stowe, and Killington, in that order.

FALCONRY

There's nothing quite like seeing a bird of prey whip down from a tree straight toward your arm. At Manchester, Vermont's British School of Falconry, you can do just that. Guides will take you and their trained Harris hawks on a 4-hour hunt in a nearby preserve. Follow the hawks from treetop to treetop as they search for pheasant, quail, and partridge and the chase ensues. If that sounds a bit too violent, opt for the Hawk Walk.

FISHING

From the trout and landlocked salmon caught on the Battenkill to the stripers, blues, cod, and tuna found in the Atlantic, you have to try hard not to hook anything in the waters of these two northern New England states. In almost any body of water you venture to, whether it's a pond, river, lake, or ocean, you'll find an assortment of fish. There are so many places to fish and so many different techniques, from fly-fishing to surf-casting to deep-sea fishing, that it would be absurd to list my favorites. What I have done in each region is to jot down the places where the locals fish. They're not going to be happy with me, but I have exposed their coveted fishing holes—the rivers where fly-fishing anglers are knee-deep in water, the rips in the coastline where ocean stripers and blues swim to saltwater ponds and other estuaries, the small ponds that can be found only if you've lived nearby for years.

Before you break out your pole, make sure you have a fishing permit. Contact the respective state's Department of Fish and Wildlife, listed under each region. Many of these offices also publish guides offering various techniques, including catching the big one. If you don't know the area, it's always worthwhile to go with a guide who can show you around and explain which flies, hooks, and lines to use. Instruction is also beneficial, and almost mandatory when it comes to fly-fishing. Orvis in Arlington, Vermont, is one of the better fishing schools. Most important, fishing is fun for everybody, not just the ***Field & Stream*** subscriber who has been casting for the past 40 years.

GOLF

For this section, I have asked golf pros in the region what their favorite courses are—excluding the one at which they're employed. If pros in the region kept naming the same course, I included it in this book. The rest simply don't make the grade.

New England golfing varies with the landscape, from ocean courses in New Hampshire to the more-mountainous courses inland. The best courses, like the Country Club of Vermont in Waterbury, Vermont, and the Shattuck Inn Golf Club in Jaffrey, New Hampshire, take full advantage of their scenery.

HANG GLIDING

Morningside Flight Park in western New Hampshire is the most respected place to learn how to hang-glide in the Northeast. The 250-foot hill gently slopes down to a landing area.

HIKING

I've devoted more space to hiking than to any other sport in this book. That's because mountains and hills dominate the landscape of Vermont and New Hampshire. The network of trails is extensive and impressive. Footpaths climb up the verdant mountains of Vermont and slip through the granite notches of the Whites. Paths are both narrow and wide, soft and springy, rock-littered, leaf-littered, and root-studded. They cross rivers, skirt lakes, find hidden ponds, and overlook the wide blue ocean.

Since the day I climbed New Hampshire's Mount Willard as a kid, I've been attacking these hills and I haven't been bored yet. Even if I've hiked a trail several times, I still find something new—a new tree, a better view. I'm not the first hiker to be enthralled. These trails have enticed visitors since hikers were called rusticators, trampers, and trekkers. Even in the 1850s, Thoreau was a second- or third-generation hiker. People have been inscribing their names on the rocks of Mount Monadnock, the most climbed mountain in the world, since 1801.

Climbing any mountain, regardless of height, will make you sweat. However, almost anyone in reasonably fit condition will enjoy the hikes listed as easy in the regional chapters. Even some of the moderate peaks are attainable. You shouldn't try any of the strenuous climbs unless you have climbed at least two moderate mountains or have been working out on a regular basis. I don't care if you were born in the Swiss Alps, climbing a Presidential peak in the Whites will make your legs weary.

Most injuries like sprained ankles or sprained knees occur on the hike down, not up. Your legs are already tired from the ascent, and it's easy to slip when you're moving much faster. Take it slowly; if you have weak ankles or knees like me, bring an ace bandage for extra protection against the pounding. In your day pack, always bring at least one 32-ounce bottle of water. For strenuous hikes, you'll need two. Also bring nuts, raisins, or trail mix for a quick boost of energy. For longer hikes, there's no better place to have lunch than the top of a mountain. I often bring an extra T-shirt, so I'll have something dry to wear on the way down, and a light Gore-Tex jacket to keep me warm on those windy summits.

More than one-third of the hikes I went on did not make it into this book. They were decent and even challenging, offering views of the surrounding terrain, but for one reason or another were not the best. If I had to write a book called ***100 Hikes in Vermont and New Hampshire,*** I would be forced to include them and, thus, you wouldn't have any idea which trails are truly the finest. Out of the hikes that did make it into the book, these are the crème de la crème:

- **Falling Waters Trail/Franconia Ridge/Old Bridle Path** This White Mountain trail has it all, from a path along a series of waterfalls to a 1.7-mile ridge walk between 5,108-foot Mount Lincoln and 5,249-foot Mount Lafayette.
- **Mount Jefferson** The climb to the third-largest mountain in New England, 5,715-foot Mount Jefferson, happens on one of the most exhilarating loops in the Presidential Range. Almost half of the 6.5-mile hike is above the tree line, offering stunning vistas of that large glacial cirque the Great Gulf and the backside of mighty Mount Washington.
- **The Southern Presidentials** If you have an extra car to spare, this 8.5-mile one-way route is one of the finest day hikes in the Whites. You'll be hitting four of the southern Presidentials—Monroe, Franklin, Eisenhower, and Pierce—while hiking above the tree line for almost half of the trek. Not to mention you'll be on the oldest hiking trail in the country, the Crawford Path.
- **Camel's Hump via the Forestry, Dean, and Long Trails** Foot traffic might be heavy on this 7.2-mile (round-trip) trail, but deservedly so. Walk through the forest and then onto the Long Trail for an exhilarating hike up to the slab of rock known as Camel's Hump.
- **Mount Pisgah** One of Vermont's more-grueling hikes, the trail climbs swiftly above Lake Willoughby. The reward is Pulpit Rock, a small rocky platform that juts out of Pisgah's plummeting cliffs.
- **Zealand Trail** More a walk than a hike, this rambling trail through dense forests of maples, beeches, and

birches is ideal for young children. The only climb is up to the Appalachian Mountain Club's Zealand Hut, where you can have a glass of lemonade and take in the views of the Pemigewasset Wilderness.

- **Mount Hunger** More often than not, you can have this trail and the summit to yourself. Views of Camel's Hump, Mount Mansfield, and much of the Green Mountain National Forest can be seen from the rocky peak.

HORSEBACK RIDING

You don't have to venture to the Wild West to go on an overnight riding trip. **Kedron Valley Stables** in South Woodstock, Vermont, and **Vermont Icelandic Horse Farm** in Waitsfield, Vermont, offer 4- to 6-day inn-to-inn trips in the Green Mountain National Forest. You ride 4 to 6 hours a day, covering an average of 10 to 20 miles, and while the horses rest you can take in the surroundings on foot. Both these trips are for experienced riders only. Contrary to the image presented by the movie ***City Slickers,*** horseback riding is not a sport in which you ride for 4 days straight unless you don't have any idea of what it's like to sit in a saddle. Your visions of ***High Noon*** might turn into great doom, and you could be walking bowlegged for the next month.

Hundreds of stables around New England offer lessons and guided trail rides. The various sites include the steep trails of the White Mountains to the remote Northeast Kingdom of Vermont.

ICE CLIMBING

Ice climbing is not one of those activities in which you suddenly scream to your significant other in the car, "Honey, there's an icicle hanging from that mountain over there. Let's do it." No, winter mountaineering is taken very seriously in these parts. The sport involves ascending steep slopes covered with snow and ice, frozen waterfalls, and frosted-over gorges. Intensive instruction is an absolute must. You have to learn how to use an ice axe, how to wear crampons, and how to handle the many ice formations. Even with these skills, ice climbing can be a dangerous sport. It seems as if each year someone dies at Mount Washington's Huntington Ravine, the top ice-climbing destination in the East. Many of these climbers had the necessary skills, but sometimes even experience is not enough to handle winter's unpredictable weather.

Learn the sport from an expert, **Rick Wilcox,** co-owner of International Mountain Climbing School in North Conway, New Hampshire (see "Schools," below). The former head of the White Mountains' Search and Rescue Team, Wilcox is a survivor of Everest.

ICE FISHING

Along with mountain biking, sea kayaking, and backcountry skiing, ice fishing is one of the fastest-growing sports in the region. Anglers are realizing that many of the larger fish are caught during this time of the year. And, with the advent of synthetic winter clothing, you no longer have to wear wool flannel plaids and freeze. Simply drill a hole and drop a line. Many of the larger bodies of water require snowmobiles for access. Contact the respective state's Department of Fish and Wildlife for fishing permits.

LLAMA TREKKING

All right, so you can't ride a llama like a horse, but at least the furry guy helps carry camping equipment and food, allowing you to hike or walk longer distances. You get to pet him, too (when he's not in a testy mood). Each llama can carry up to 100 pounds on a full-day trek, and their padded hooves have no impact on the trails. See chapters 4 and 6 for more information.

MOUNTAIN BIKING

In the regional chapters, you'll find that over and over again I emphasize the exhilarating feeling of freedom that mountain biking gives. I hate to be redundant, but the ability to zip down a narrow mountain trail across a shallow stream, to cruise along the banks of a river on a former railroad bed, or to ride on a dirt road through the farmland of Vermont is a thrill rarely surpassed by any other sport. On most of the trails mentioned, I hardly ever came across another human, let alone another biker. More important, I never carried a map and I almost always got lost. This might sound foolish to some of you, but not knowing where you are in a New England forest is like backpacking from village to village in Europe with no destination in mind: You create your own exciting path and your own destiny on most of these rides. That's why I love New England mountain biking. Unlike the West, with its 14,000-foot peaks and vast wide-open spaces, New England's parks and forests are compact and far more gentle. If I take a wrong turn I don't risk death, nor do I spend the night howling with coyotes. Even within the larger national forests, I'm never more than 2 to 3 miles from a dirt road and civilization.

With this in mind, most of the rides featured in the regional chapters have no specific routes. I have led you to the water, now drink! Ironic as it might seem, with regard to mountain biking, this guidebook is not going to guide you at all. The worst thing I can do is give you directions. I don't want you to be clutching a map, looking at a network of single tracks spiraling in every direction and saying, "I think this is the way. No, maybe it's this one . . . or this one." Weave your own web and you'll soon find your own favorite trails to try again and again.

Single tracks, double tracks, and dirt roads dominate the mountain biker's terrain. Dirt roads are hard-packed gravel logging roads that snake through the White and Green mountains. Double tracks vary in width from snowmobile tracks to former railroad beds to old carriage paths. They are ideal trails for the beginner to intermediate biker. All experienced bikers are in search of the elusive single-track trail. These narrow trails, created by hikers or motorcross bikers, whisk you in and out of the forest, within arm's length of trees and bushes on both sides. So-called technical single-track trails are the most challenging. They wind up and down the hills, over rocks and roots and through soft mud that often feels like quicksand. On these trails, it's not uncommon to get off your bike and walk around an obstacle.

Conditioning is of the utmost importance for this sport. A 5- to 10-mile jaunt on a single-track trail is far more exhausting than the same distance on a paved road. The trail becomes even more grueling if it's too advanced for your level and you have to get on and off your bike numerous times. The best way to get in shape for mountain biking is to mountain-bike. Start with easy trails around your neighborhood and work your way up. If there are no forests or parks nearby, then opt for a road-biking route that takes you up and down hills. Any of the easy dirt roads described in the regional chapters can be tried without much advance preparation.

Bring lots of water. I can't stress this enough. Mountain biking is such a strenuous sport that even the short trips require two to three bottles (I prefer the backpack-style hydration system called a CamelBak, which can hold upward of 100 ounces of water). A spare tube and patch kit, tire lever, air pump, chain rivet tool, spoke wrench, Allen wrenches, 6-inch adjustable wrench, and small screwdriver are essential for fixing flats, broken spokes or chains, and other problems that might arise in the woods. A small first-aid kit is also advisable. You can fit all of this equipment into a backpack or fanny pack. As for the main piece of equipment, the bike, I bought a Trek 950 5 years ago and I've been riding it ever since. I added hand grips on the sides of the handlebars to help in climbing hills and also added snap-in pedals so that my biking shoes are locked in. This prevents my feet from slipping off the pedals. Most of my friends have Rockshox shock absorbers, which help absorb the constant pounding of the bike when you're on technical single tracks. Since I switch from fat knobby tires to thin slick tires when I go road biking, I don't want to put many more mountain-biking features on my Trek. But believe me, I've felt the need for these biking shock absorbers numerous times.

On a final note, I've been mountain biking with people of all ages, from 7 to 70. The preconception that this sport is for crazed kids who like to catch air off mountainous cliffs applies to only a few bikers and stunt men who do Nike and Dr. Pepper commercials. For the rest of us, the only differences between road biking and mountain biking are the tires and the terrain. My favorite trails cater to all levels:

- **Ridgepole Trail, New Hampshire** An incredibly strenuous yet thrilling trail, the Ridgepole climbs high into the Sandwich Mountain Range, with views overlooking Squam Lake. The downhill on steep single tracks will shake you like an earthquake on the San Andreas Fault.
- **Bartlett Experimental Forest, New Hampshire** Situated in the heart of the White Mountains, snowmobilers have created a vast network of trails that suit bikers well. The paths cruise up and down mountains across numerous brooks.
- **Sugar River Trail, Newport, New Hampshire** Sugar River Trail is an apt name for this sweet trail that hugs the shores of a river. Formerly part of the Boston and Maine Railroad, this rail-trail crosses more than a dozen bridges, including two large covered bridges.
- **Waitsfield, Vermont** One of the three areas in central and northern Vermont that will entice bikers. The hills on Sugarbush's slopes are laced with technical single tracks.
- **Randolph, Vermont** Orange County, the administrative district in which the city of Randolph resides, has more Class IV roads (grass or dirt trails that are impassable during the winter by a vehicle other than a snowmobile) than any other county in Vermont. Add flat valley floors, gentle rolling hills, and steep winding climbs from 500 to 2,900 feet high and you have one of the premier mountain-biking destinations in the country, accessible to all levels of riders.
- **The Kingdom Trails, Vermont** Several years ago, dedicated locals in East Burke linked together more than 150 miles of single tracks and dirt roads into a network they call the Kingdom Trails. Many of these routes were created from logging roads and former cross-country skiing trails that had been abandoned 50 to 70 years ago. They cruise through hundred-year-old dairy farms and over the rolling hills of the Northeast Kingdom.
- **Mount Snow, Vermont** The first Eastern ski resort to devote itself to mountain biking, Mount Snow now offers more than 140 miles of riding. This is a great place to take courses and train before venturing into the wild woods.

OFF-ROAD DRIVING

Presiding over a village green that evokes images of a Currier and Ives print, Manchester Village, Vermont, is one of those quintessential New England villages where you stroll between shops, play golf, and . . . go off-road driving. That's right. Land Rover opened its first year-round 4×4 Driving School in the United States in Manchester. Spend an hour or longer with one of the Land Rover's expert instructors and compress a lifetime of off-road experience into a 1-mile route.

POWERBOATING

Listings for motorboat and jet ski rentals can be found in each regional chapter.

ROAD BIKING

Vermont and New Hampshire's diversity of terrain, history, and compact size have all helped to create one of the top road-biking destinations in the country. Perhaps most significant, the landscape is manageable. The media love to harp about the spectacular beauty of the Rockies and the West—and there's no denying that beauty. However, most people do not have the leg strength to bike through the mountainous passes of Colorado. Even the most treacherous gaps in the White Mountains are no more than a 2,000-foot climb, and those will challenge the best and fittest bikers. Go East, young man and woman, and you'll find thousands of miles of roads that form hundreds of loops ranging from 10 to 110 miles long. And, contrary to what you might be thinking, car traffic is not a problem. Most of the congested roads are found around urban centers, not in the rural countryside.

The main attraction of New England biking is its stunning scenery—the white steeples that dot the rolling green hills and farmland of Vermont, the towering granite of New Hampshire's White Mountains.

The routes in this book are geared toward every type of biker imaginable. Whether you bike more than 100 miles a week or haven't been on two wheels in 2 years, whether you want a serious workout or want to go sightseeing at a slow pace, there are rides in each region at your level of biking. I have also taken into account your interests, from enjoying the spectacular scenery to learning the local lore and history, to finding a good place to picnic or have lunch. Architecture, geology, wildlife, and art history are a few of the subjects I've touched on to make each ride as intriguing as possible. Thus, if you are expecting to see only terse directions like "turn right at 15.2 miles, veer left at 18.6 miles, and so on," you're in for a surprise. The necessary directions and remarks about terrain have been sprinkled with anecdotes and history that I hope will enrich each ride. I discuss only day trips. However, in many regions, like Vermont, you can simply connect the day loops to ride around the state.

After your bike, water is the most important necessity. I always bring 32 to 64 ounces with me and usually end up stopping at a store to buy more. Drink often, especially when riding under a hot sun, because it's difficult to realize how dehydrated your body really is. My backpack or fanny pack also holds trail mix or raisins for a quick energy boost, spare tube and patch kit, tire lever, air pump, chain rivet tool, spoke wrench, Allen wrenches, 6-inch adjustable end wrench, and small screwdriver. If you think that a basic bicycle repair kit is essential only for mountain biking, you're wrong. I've had flats in the middle of cow country, where the nearest town was 10 to 20 miles away. You don't want to walk that far. On overnight camping trips, you'll need to purchase front and back panniers (packs). Believe it or not, you can fit all your belongings in these packs. Look under "Backpacking," above, for the list of essential gear needed for overnight jaunts.

For years, I wore loose-fitting T-shirts and shorts on all my rides, vowing never to wear brightly colored spandex. Then one day, after a particularly treacherous mountain-bike ride, I walked into a bike shop and bought a pair of fluorescent blue shorts. I will never wear loose-fitting shorts on a bike again. Spandex is far more supportive, and my voice is now back down to its normal tenor range.

The problem with bike riding is that it's too easy a sport to learn. Most people have been biking since the age of 5 or younger, and think they can hop on a bike and ride 40 miles on any given day. Some of you who haven't pedaled in years will attempt to ride my moderate to strenuous loops, and you might succeed. But I guarantee you won't be happy the next couple of days or during the latter part of the ride. If you are not in condition prior to a 5-day bike tour, most of your riding will be in the support van. (I'll talk about conditioning for guided overnight trips in detail under "Outfitters.") As with all sports, start slow! Prior to going on a long bike trip, I'll ride around the neighboring countryside where I live in Newton, Massachusetts, gradually building my stamina to ride 50-milers. Start with an easy bike ride and slowly work your way up to moderate and strenuous trails.

This is just a small sampling of routes featured in the regional chapters. There are many more rides where these came from:

- **Grafton, Vermont** Very few places in New England epitomize small-town charm better than the historic village of Grafton. It is the ideal starting point for a loop that ties together a wealth of rural scenery and the equally picturesque little towns of Chester, Rockingham, Saxton's River, and Cambridgeport.
- **Woodstock, Vermont** For moderate bikers only, this 25-mile ride takes you high up in the hills over Pomfret, before zipping down along the White River and coming back to Woodstock on bucolic River Road.
- **Lake Champlain, Vermont** A 27-mile ride that takes you along the southern shores of this long lake. Ride south from Vergennes past Basin Harbor and Arnold's Bay for views of the Adirondacks on the far shores and the Green Mountains to the east.
- **Waitsfield-Warren Loop** This short, 15-mile loop skirts the mountains and enters these two small villages via covered bridges.
- **Randolph, Vermont** Vermont's highly touted green meadows, cornfields, pastures, and farms are nestled in the foothills of the Green Mountains on this 36.5-mile loop. The ride is best taken during fall foliage season when the trees are ablaze in color.
- **Greensboro–Craftsbury Common Loop** This up-and-down 32.6-mile run takes you to two of my favorite villages in Vermont—Greensboro, on the pristine shores of Caspian Lake, and the mid-1850s village green of Craftsbury Common.
- **Francestown, New Hampshire** With its large Federal-style homes lining the streets, including Francestown Academy, the former school of President Franklin Pierce, Francestown makes an ideal start to any bike tour. Add a covered bridge, a state park, and a mountain to skirt and you have one of the finest loops in New Hampshire.
- **Swanzey, New Hampshire** The southwest corner of New Hampshire is a relatively flat section of woods, farmland, college towns, and, most notably, covered bridges. This 18-mile loop rides through four covered bridges on quiet country roads.

ROCK CLIMBING

Depending on the region, rock climbing can be just as accessible as mountain climbing. This is certainly the case in the White Mountains of New Hampshire, where faces of rock line the major roads. Numerous rock-climbing sites like Cathedral Ledge, Whitehorse Ledge, and Cannon Cliffs exist within the twisted and carved granite that shapes these mountains.

A good rock-climbing school will help you spot the hand and footholds in the rock face that, at first glance, may appear too smooth. You will also learn how to use your ropes and pulley to rappel down safely. The International Mountain Equipment Climbing School in North Conway, New Hampshire, is the largest and one of the most respected rock-climbing schools in the eastern United States.

SAILING

The large interior lakes of these chapters—Champlain, Winnipesaukee, and Squam—and many smaller bodies of water are popular with sailors. Within each region, I have pointed out remote and picturesque anchorages, listed the top sailing schools, and mentioned the top places to bareboat-charter. ***Bareboat-chartering*** means renting a large sailboat for day or overnight trips; you play the role of captain, in charge of navigation, provisions, and the safety of the boat. Schooling and prior sailing experience are necessary to bareboat-charter, especially on the New Hampshire coast where fog, currents, wide tidal differences, and a merciless shoreline can wreak havoc on the most-accomplished sailors and their crafts. Less-experienced sailors should consider renting Lasers, Rhodes, or Sunfishes at the rental places listed in the regional chapters.

SCUBA DIVING

Scuba diving is another sport in which schooling is not only suggested, it's mandatory. You must be certified by the National Association of Underwater Instructors (NAUI) or the Professional Association of Dive Instructors (PADI) to scuba dive. Once you have your certification or C-card, you can dive with any resort or outfitter in the world. However, some diving operators offer a 1-day resort course. I'm not sure how the sport's governing bodies justify this approach, but I don't recommend it. The dive is supposed to take place in a shallow pool to give nondivers a feel of what it's like to breathe with a self-contained underwater breathing apparatus (SCUBA) or air tank, but that's not always the case. My brother once took a so-called resort dive in Bali. Within 5 minutes of the instruction, he was diving at a depth of 60 feet with me and the other certified divers, swallowing water between large gasps of air. If you want to dive, get your certification.

Scuba diving is one of the most meditative and mesmerizing sports around. Once you get over your initial fear of breathing from an air tank and having to regulate your ears to the depth, you can relax and take in the wondrous surroundings. Coral of every fluorescent color imaginable play host to a dazzling array of sea life. Tropical fish look you in the eye, manta rays glide above your air bubbles, innocuous sharks thrill you as they swim by. This is what diving is like in the warm waters of the Caribbean and South Seas. New England diving pales in comparison. It has its share of sea life, from harbor seals to porpoises to starfish, but visibility and water temperatures are dramatically reduced. The best feature of New England diving is the 18th- and 19th-century shipwrecks that rest on the lake or ocean floor. In Lake Champlain, divers are still finding boats that were used in the Revolutionary War and the War of 1812.

Go diving in New England to sharpen your skills between trips to the Caymans, Turks and Caicos, or Fiji. I would not go out of my way to take a diving trip here, nor would I register for a course. Start off your diving career on the right foot with an intensive 4-day course in the Florida Keys or Caribbean. Once you've whet your appetite for diving, try the cold waters of New England.

SCULLING

If you ever wanted to learn the sport of sculling or if you already scull and want to perfect your stroke, northern Vermont's Craftsbury Outdoor Center is arguably the best place in the country to do just that. Opened 25 years ago, the school is run by Rutgers University's crew coach.

SEA KAYAKING

All it took was one guided trip on Maine's Frenchman Bay six summers ago and I was immediately hooked on this sport.

Paddling on the surface of the water, I was eye-to-eye with seals, porpoises, and chubby birds called black guillemots. As I kayaked around the islands of the bay, the mountains of Acadia National Park hovered above the shoreline. It was an incredible experience, one that made me wonder why I had waited so long. In fact, after that memorable day, whenever I travel along the coast or on big lakes like Champlain and Winnipesaukee, I always ask, "You wouldn't happen to know where I could rent a sea kayak?"

Don't make the same mistake I did and overlook the chance to glide over the ocean waters with the sea's myriad creatures. It's far less dangerous than you would imagine. Many of the guided trips are in bays or ocean tributaries where the surf is low or nonexistent. Even when you venture out to the open ocean, the water is usually calm once you break the crest of the waves. However, lessons are still imperative if you plan on renting a kayak on your own. You need to learn proper paddling technique and how to self-rescue. Those who have mastered this sport will treasure the New Hampshire coast and Lake Champlain. See chapters 4 and 5 for a chance to try the sport.

SNOWMOBILING

Snowmobiling in many areas of northern New England is more than a sport; it's a method of transport. Hundreds of miles of trails snake through secluded woods in Vermont, New Hampshire, and Quebec. The North Country in northern New Hampshire is consistently rated one of the top five snowmobiling destinations in the country. But you don't have to travel so far north to enjoy this exciting activity. Many of the parks in southern Vermont and New Hampshire are open to snowmobiles.

If you own a snowmobile, all it usually takes is a phone call to the local snowmobile chapter and the state Department of Parks and Recreation to find the network of trails in the region and to obtain maps. For those of you who don't own snowmobiles, I've listed places for renting them and outfitters who arrange guided trips.

SNOWSHOEING

Snowshoeing is essentially winter hiking. Many of the trails that weave through the forests of New England are ideal for snowshoeing once a blanket of white covers the ground. Simply replace your hiking boots with snowshoes. In the regional chapters, I have named stores that rent snowshoes and I've mentioned guided tours by outfitters.

SURFING

Hey, dude, this side of the country has waves, too, and we're more civilized. When I lived in Huntington Beach, California, I heard stories all the time about the lowly beginner who had the bad fortune of cutting in front of the local surfing stud on a killer wave. He often went home with fragments of his board imbedded in his scalp. In Hawaii, it can get even uglier. Thankfully, we have proper etiquette on the East Coast. If someone dares to cut a line in front of us, we yell, "Get out of the way!"

Throw on the wetsuit and surf year-round. As with cross-country skiing, it might be a little cold at first, but once you swim back from the shore a couple times, you'll warm up. Hampton Beach is the only surfing venue in this book.

SWIMMING

Wherever you venture in New England, water is always close by. Whether you're heading east to the Atlantic Coast, west to 120-mile-long Lake Champlain, or to the multitude of ponds, rivers, and large lakes that lie in between, you should never have to travel more than 30 minutes to go swimming. Your only dilemma is deciding which number of sunblock to apply to your skin.

I feel somewhat remorseful that clandestine beaches and coveted swimming holes are now public knowledge, but there's more than enough water to go around. Check each chapter to find the swimming holes where locals go in your region.

WALKS & RAMBLES

Finally, we arrive at the sports where conditioning is not necessary and your excuses for not attempting them are unconvincing. All you need is a good pair of walking shoes or sneakers, a bottle of water, and off you go. The hardest part of many of these walks is finding the trailhead, but now that problem is eliminated because in each chapter I give you directions to the described trailheads. Try these trails for starters:

- **West River Trail, Jamaica State Park, Vermont** This 5-mile (round-trip) trail is a former railroad bed on the banks of the West River. Strollers, mountain bikers, horseback riders, and joggers can all be found here on a clear summer's day.
- **Robert Frost Interpretive Trail, Ripton, Vermont** This 1-mile-long dirt path is a worthy introduction to the poet and to the woods where he summered for 39 years. Seven Frost poems are posted at regular intervals throughout the forest setting.
- **Button Bay State Park, Vergennes, Vermont** Much of Lake Champlain's shoreline is privately owned, so it's a treat to take a walk along the water. This short trail weaves through the cedars of Button Bay State Park along a crescent-shaped bay.
- **Marsh-Billings National Historical Park, Woodstock, Vermont** This park was the first unit of the National Park System to focus on the theme of conservation history. You'll find carriage-path trails through the 550-acre forest.
- **Burton Island State Park, St. Albans, Vermont** Surrounded by Lake Champlain, Burton Island is a welcome refuge from the woes of the modern world. No cars are allowed on this 250-acre island, replaced instead by the songs of birds as they scamper across beaches, meadows, and woodlands. On the North Shore Trail, the waters of this great lake are never far from your side, but occasionally you'll slip into a forest of white pines, spruce, and speckled alder.
- **Odiorne Point State Park, Portsmouth, New Hampshire** This 2-mile loop weaves around the only undeveloped shoreline on the New Hampshire coast.
- **Fox State Forest, Hillsborough Center, New Hampshire** This 1,445-acre forest, a former working farm, has more than 20 miles of well-marked trails through the woods.
- **Sabbaday Falls, White Mountains, New Hampshire** Just off the Kancamagus Highway, this 1-mile round-trip is an easy walk through a forest of maples, birches, and beeches down the stone steps to the falls.
- **Artist's Bluff and Bald Mountain, Franconia Notch, New Hampshire** For a mere 300-foot climb, Artist's Bluff and Bald Mountain reward walkers with one of the finer views in Franconia Notch.

WHALE WATCHING

Whale-watching cruises are big business along the Atlantic coast. Almost every day, from mid-April to November, boats leave the mainland in search of the biggest mammal on the planet. Many of these boats have naturalists on board to discuss the various species that you'll see and to explain their migratory patterns and the dangers that fishing nets and oil spills pose to whales' survival. The majority of these naturalists have been at their jobs for so many years that not only do they know the whales on a first-name basis, but they also know their parents, grandparents, and children.

One of the most popular whale hangouts is Stellwagen Bank, an 18-mile-long, crescent-shaped underwater mesa that's located about 25 miles southeast of the New Hampshire coast. Cruises leave daily from Rye Harbor. Bring a jacket on board, and don't make the mistake I did of venturing out to sea on an overcast day when the swells are immense. Your pallor will transform your face from its natural color to a shade of green.

WHITE-WATER KAYAKING

As Vermont's foremost white-water kayaking river, the West is also the only white-water rafting river in these two states. However, that's where the similarities end. White-water kayakers need serious instruction, practice, and conditioning, whereas white-water rafters can simply sign up for a trip and have an incredible journey down the waterway with no experience whatsoever. There's a vast difference between a large floating object you sit in with eight other people (including a guide) and a small, slender watercraft you essentially wear. Kayakers should know how to handle Class II and III rapids before attempting the West River and New Hampshire's Androscoggin River.

WHITE-WATER RAFTING

White-water rafting is a thrilling experience that everyone can enjoy regardless of age or degree of fitness. There's very little danger involved in riding these rafts, which easily handle high and rough water. Occasionally the craft will tip, but guides are experienced in assisting guests back into the boat, and everybody is required to wear a flotation device.

Rivers are rated by varying degrees of white water. Class I is calm with slow moving currents; Class II has moderate rapids or waves with relatively few obstructions; Class III is a swift current with more obstructions; Class IV is a powerful current with drops and many obstacles; and Class V is the most advanced, with series of complex rapids, drops, and challenging obstacles. There is a Class VI rating for those of you who are suicidal. However, these rivers are not considered navigable and you could easily risk death.

The West River in southern Vermont is the only place to raft in these two states. See chapter 2 for information on day trips.

Outfitters

"Yeah, yeah. All these sports, I love them, but the problem is I don't have time. I don't have time to buy a bike. I don't even have time to pedal. Listen, I get 2 weeks off a year and then it's back to the floor of the Stock Exchange. For those 2 weeks, I'd like to breathe in some fresh air while I'm outside. A nice bike trip in Vermont, hiking in the Whites, you know what I mean. And I don't want to take care of a single thing . . . no flat tires, no rentals, no accommodations, no food, nothin'. Ya got it?"

Yes, Type A, I understand your criteria. You want to participate in some sort of outdoor activity in the day and be pampered at night. You want someone to guide you on your sporting excursion, and you don't want to be bothered with equipment problems, finding a trailhead, renting a canoe, or setting up a tent and cooking over a fire. You want someone to deal with all your arrangements, but you still want to take the best trips outlined in this book. Then you'll need to find an outfitter.

The choice of outfitters in New England is overwhelming. Pick a sport, any sport. How about a 5-day bike trip in the isolated Northeast Kingdom of Vermont; an overnight winter mountaineering trip to the tallest peak in New England, Mount Washington; a week-long hiking tour of the Green Mountains; a mountain-biking camp in the White Mountains; a 3-day fly-fishing trip on Vermont's Battenkill River;

or a weekend kayaking tour of the Lake Champlain Islands? If you can't get away for that long, you can always hire a boat to go deep-sea fishing for a day off the Atlantic coast, go white-water rafting down the West River in Vermont, telemark-ski with a guide in the Mount Mansfield area, jump in a boat for a whale-watching cruise to Stellwagen Bank, or rock-climb the ledge of the Whites.

The irony is that even finding a good outfitter and trip takes time. Hopefully, I've saved you hours of researching by listing my favorite outfitters under each sport heading in the regional chapters. However, some questions should always be asked. Most are common sense. Some are related to specific sports:

1. *What's the cost and what's included in the price?*

   First and foremost, discuss the type of accommodation and whether all meals are included. Some outfitters skip lunch or an occasional dinner. Is liquor included? Ask about shuttles to and from airports, cost of rentals for bikes, skis, and so on.

2. *What level of fitness is required?*

   This is by far the most important question. Get a feeling for the tour. Is this an obstacle course better suited for Marines, a walk in the park for teetotalers, or somewhere in between? Will I be biking 20, 40, or 60 miles a day? Do I have options for each day? Can I go shopping or sightseeing one day while my wife bikes to her legs' delight?

3. *How long have you been in business?*

   Credentials are important, but not nearly as important as the answer to the next question.

4. *What are the ages and experience of the guides?*

   Outfitters in desperate financial straits may be tempted to hire young guides on the cheap. You don't want guides who have little experience in that sport or who are from an entirely different part of the country.

5. *How many people are in the group?*

   What is the guide-to-client ratio? Do I have to compete with 30 or only 5 other people for the guide's attention?

6. *Is it mostly singles or couples?*

   Guided tours are a great place to befriend other singles or couples. Make sure you find out which trip best suits your needs.

7. *What equipment is required? What type of equipment can I rent?*

   Some fly-fishing companies request that you bring your own equipment. Others will rent you their own poles. Find out what they offer, especially when dealing with bikes. Do they rent 10-speed Raleighs or 21-speed Cannondales and Treks?

8. *What happens if it rains?*

   Do you have alternative plans, or do you expect me to climb Mount Eisenhower in a downpour? How much free time do we have? Is every minute of the day accounted for, or should I bring that new novel I've been wanting to read?

9. *How far in advance do I need to book?*

   Don't miss out on a limited number of spaces by waiting till the last minute. Some of these tours are booked a year in advance.

10. *Can I bring young children?*

    Most outfitters will usually answer affirmatively to this. A buck is a buck, no matter who hikes or sits on the bike. However, you should take yourself and the other guests into account. Do you want to bike just 5 miles when you can actually bike 50? Do you really want to bring along a young child for bird watching or fly-fishing so he or she can scream and scare off all the birds and fish?

The most important question above is about the level of fitness. Depending on what shape you're in, your trip can be nirvana or a living hell, not to mention a waste of money. Don't wait until the last minute to condition. If you plan on taking a week-long bike trip, start biking or doing an aerobic activity 4 to 6 weeks in advance, three times a week. If you can work out on weights or do push-ups or pull-ups, that's even better. I'd even hire a trainer at the local health club to set up a workout schedule. A $40 to $60 investment for a 1-hour session with a trainer is far less money than the $500 or more you'll lose if you can't keep up or if hurt yourself trying.

The advantage of hiring a guide is the complete and utter lack of responsibility on your part. Most outfitters will find a way to relieve all your vacation worries, from accommodations to food to equipment. You also have a chance to make new friends. The disadvantage is the additional cost. Most of these trips can be done on your own for much less money (that's one of the reasons I wrote this book). The other disadvantage is the lack of privacy. There's no place better than a mountaintop, lonely backcountry road, or tranquil river to collect your thoughts and gain a sense of serenity. This is especially true if you live in a city as I do. On vacation, you've earned a certain amount of peace and quiet. This fragile state can easily be shattered by the loquacious woman with the shrill voice or the garrulous man with the guttural laugh. One way to eliminate this problem is to book the whole trip with a group of your friends.

The following is a list of all the outfitters found in the book that offer overnight trips. To locate the more than 100 outfitters who provide day trips, look under the specific sport and chapter.

- **Appalachian Mountain Club,** P.O. Box 298, Gorham, NH 03581 (☎ **603/466-2727;** www.outdoors.org). I can't possibly list all the overnight trips the AMC offers. Call for a catalog. A small sampling: 4-day women's canoe trip on Umbagog Lake, 8-day hike and rock-climbing trip in the White Mountains for teenagers, more than 23 guided hut-to-hut hikes in the Whites, and guided Appalachian Trail hike in southern Vermont.
- **Back of Beyond Expeditions,** Burlington, Vermont (☎ **802/860-9500;** www.backofbeyond.com). Four seasons of multisport trips, including hiking, mountain biking, canoeing, rock climbing, snowshoeing, and cross-country skiing.
- **Backroads,** 801 Cedar St., Berkeley, CA 94710-1800 (☎ **800/GO-ACTIVE;** www. backroads.com). Five-day inn-to-inn biking and walking tours throughout Vermont.
- **Battenkill Canoe, Ltd.,** U.S. 7A, Arlington, VT 05250 (☎ **802/362-2800;** www.battenkill.com). Conveniently located on the river. Two-, three-, and five-day inn-to-inn trips on Vermont's finest waterways. Daily rentals as well.
- **Bike the Whites,** Intervale, New Hampshire (☎ **800/448-3534;** www.bikethewhites.com). Inn-to-inn biking trips through the White Mountain National Forest.
- **Bike Vermont,** P.O. Box 207, Woodstock, VT 05091 (☎ **800/257-2226;** www.bikevermont.com). Celebrating their 25th anniversary this year. Operates exclusively within the borders of Vermont and offers 2-, 3-, 5, and 6-day guided tours all over the state.
- **Clearwater Sports,** State Rte. 100, Waitsfield, VT 05673 (☎ **802/496-2708;** www.clearwatersports.com). Day and overnight trips on the Winooski, Mad, and White Rivers.

- **Country Inns Along the Trail,** R.R. 3, P.O. Box 3115, Brandon, VT 05773 (☎ **802/247-3300;** www.inntoinn.com). Custom-designed self-guided hiking trips where you can walk inn-to-inn.
- **Country Walkers,** P.O. Box 180, Waterbury, VT 05676 (☎ **802/244-1387;** www.countrywalkers.com). Inn-to-inn tours, some led by natural history grad students at the University of Vermont.
- **Cycle-Inn-Vermont,** P.O. Box 243, Ludlow, VT 05149-0243 (☎ **802/228-8799**). Sets up inn-to-inn mountain-biking tours.
- **Escape Routes Adventure Tours** (☎ **802/746-8943;** www.escaperoutesoutdoors.com). Guided and self-guided mountain-biking and hiking tours around Vermont. Operates out of the Pittsfield Inn.
- **Green Mountain Rock Climbing Center,** Rutland, Vermont (☎ **802/773-3343;** www.bestclimb.com). Guided rock-climbing and ice-climbing trips around Vermont. Clinics and an indoor climbing wall, as well.
- **High Country Snowmobile Tours,** Wilmington, Vermont 05363 (☎ **800/627-7533** or 802/464-2108; www.high-country-tours.com). Guided hourly, half-day, full-day, and overnight snowmobile trips into the Green Mountain National Forest.
- **Hiking Holidays,** Bristol, Vermont (☎ **800/245-3856;** www.vbt.com). Inn-to-inn hiking and walking holidays.
- **Kayak Vermont** (☎ **888/525-3644;** www.vermontkayak.com). Trips through the Lake Champlain Islands where you sea-kayak a relaxed 3 to 8 miles by day and stay in the historic North Hero House (built in 1891) by night.
- **Kedron Valley Stables,** P.O. Box 368, South Woodstock, VT 05071 (☎ **802/457-1480;** www.kedron.com). Guided 4-day inn-to-inn horseback riding tours in southern Vermont. The horses average 15 miles a day.
- **New England Hiking Holidays,** P.O. Box 1648, North Conway, NH 03860 (☎ **800/869-0949;** www.nehikingholidays.com). Trips include 5-day hiking tours of the White Mountains or Vermont's Northeast Kingdom.
- **On the Loose Expeditions,** Huntington, Vermont (☎ **800/688-1481;** www.otloose.com). You name the sport—backcountry skiing, llama trekking, sea kayaking—and they'll guide you to those sporting areas in Vermont.
- **POMG** (Peace of Mind Guaranteed) **Bike Tours of Vermont** (☎ **888/635-BIKE;** www.pomgbike.com). Now entering their 6th year of operation. Two- to 5-day tours focusing on Plymouth, Okemo, and the Mad River Valleys. Known for affordability of trips.
- **Saco Bound Outfitters,** P.O. Box 119, Center Conway, NH 03813 (☎ **603/447-2177;** www.sacobound.com). Canoeing options include 3-, 6.4-, and 10.2-mile day trips; a 22-mile overnight jaunt to Lovewell Pond; and a 3-day, 40-mile journey to Hiram.
- **Strictly Trout,** Westminster West, Vermont (☎ **802/869-3116;** www.sover.net/~deenhome/index.html). Guided fishing service as well as overnight trips on the Connecticut River and its tributaries.
- **Vermont Bicycle Touring,** P.O. Box 711, Bristol, VT 05433 (☎ **800/245-3868;** www.vbt.com). Six 5-day biking tours and eight weekend tours to every region of Vermont.

- **Vermont Outdoor Guides Association (☎ 800/425-8747;** www.voga.com). Depending on your ability, budget, and length of stay, VOGA will develop a detailed itinerary that includes accommodations (B&Bs, youth hostels, or campgrounds), bike routes (including a map and a description of the terrain), even a bike. Remarkably, there's no charge for their consulting. This is a self-guided tour of the state, so luggage will be transported by the lodging properties and each night's accommodation will keep track of your route in case of an emergency.
- **Vermont Icelandic Horse Farm,** P.O. Box 577, Waitsfield, VT 05673 (**☎ 802/496-7141;** www.icelandichorses.com). Owner Christina Calabrese offers half- to 3-day rides in the Green Mountain National Forest on her pony-sized Icelandic horses.
- **Walking-Inn-Vermont,** P.O. Box 243, Ludlow, VT 05149 (**☎ 802/228-8799**). Specializing in self-guided inn-to-inn tours on which they shuttle your luggage to the next accommodation.
- **Wild Branch Trail Horse Adventures,** Wolcott, Vermont (**☎ 802/888-9233;** www.vermonthorseadventures.com). Short overnight horse-trekking jaunts in northern Vermont.
- **Wild Earth Adventures,** P.O. Box 655, Pomona, NY 10970 (**☎ 914/354-3717;** www.wildearthadventures.com). Author Charles Cook often leads backpacking trips through the Green Mountain National Forest.
- **Wonder Walks (☎ 802/453-4169;** www.wonderwalks.com). Owner-led walking tours through the Green Mountain National Forest and the Champlain Valley. They offer 3- to 5-night inn-to-inn trips.
- **Tracks of Vermont,** Weston, Vermont (**☎ 802/645-1938;** www.exploreVT.com). Hiking, canoeing, fly-fishing, and sculling are but a few of the sports you'll try in these women-only retreats in Vermont.

Schools

Instruction is an important aspect of outdoor recreation. For sports like sailing, scuba diving, sea kayaking, white-water kayaking, and rock climbing, schooling is imperative. Lessons in cross-country or downhill skiing, mountain biking, horseback riding, golfing, fishing, and canoeing can only improve your skills and make the sport more enjoyable.

The same questions asked above of outfitters apply to schools. Group size is extremely important. You want to be in a small group where you get personalized attention. Be blunt with your questioning. If you want to be able to bareboat-charter a sailboat in the Lake Champlain Islands or white-water kayak down a Class III river, inquire whether you'll be able to achieve those goals after the course is finished. Also ask how much time is spent in the classroom compared with time spent participating in the activity. From my years of being a swim instructor, I know that you can talk to students until you're blue in the face outside the water, but it's not until they jump into the pool that they learn anything. You retain far more by doing than listening.

Throughout the regional chapters, I have pointed out schools that cater to each activity. I have also listed these schools alphabetically below. I omitted downhill-ski areas and horseback riding stables, but obviously they, too, offer lessons.

- **Adventure Learning,** 67 Bear Hill, Merrimack, MA 01860 (☎ **800/649-9728** or 978/346-9728; www.adventure-learning.com/sea.htm). Sea-kayaking clinics off the New Hampshire coast and Cape Ann, Massachusetts.
- **Appalachian Mountain Club,** P.O. Box 298, Gorham, NH 03581 (☎ **603/466-2727;** www.outdoors.org). A long list of courses offered all over New England, from mushroom foraging to canoeing to backpacking. Call for a catalog.
- **The Battenkill Anglers,** 6204 Main St., Manchester Center, VT 05255 (☎ **802/362-3184;** www.battenkill.apexhosting.com). Fly-fishing lessons on the Battenkill River in southern Vermont.
- **The British School of Falconry,** Manchester, Vermont (☎ **802/362-4780**). One of only two falconry schools in America. Guides will take you and trained Harris hawks on a 1-hour hawk walk or 4-hour hunt in a nearby preserve.
- **Burlington Community Boathouse,** 1 LaValley Lane, Burlington, VT 05401 (☎ **802/865-3377**). Sailboat lessons on Lake Champlain.
- **Chauvin Guides International,** North Conway, New Hampshire (☎ **603/356-8919;** www.chauvinguides.com). Top-notch rock- and ice-climbing school in the White Mountains.
- **Craftsbury Outdoor Center,** P.O. Box 31, Craftsbury Common, VT 05827 (☎ **802/586-7767;** www.craftsbury.com). The place to go in the North-east for sculling and running schools.
- **Dirt Camp,** Waterville Valley, New Hampshire (☎ **800/711-DIRT;** www.dirtcamp.com). Arguably the finest mountain-biking school in the country, decade-old Dirt Camp runs clinics around the country, including the one in Waterville Valley, New Hampshire.
- **Fly Fish Vermont,** 804 S. Main St., Unit 4, Stowe, VT 05672 (☎ **802/253-3964;** www.flyfishvt.com). Fly-fishing instruction in the Mount Mansfield region of Vermont.
- **The Golf School,** Mount Snow, Rte. 100 W. Dover, VT, 05356 (☎ **800/240-2555;**www.mountsnow.com). Golf classes in Mount Snow.
- **Green Mountain Rock Climbing Center,** Rutland, Vermont (☎ **802/773-3343;** www.bestclimb.com). Rock-climbing clinics and an indoor climbing wall.
- **International Mountain Equipment Climbing School,** North Conway, New Hampshire (☎ **603/356-6316;** www.guides@ime-usa.com). The biggest ice-climbing and rock-climbing school in the East.
- **The International Sailing School and Club,** 253 Lakeshore Drive, Colchester, VT 05446 (☎ **802/864-9065;** www.vermontsailingschool.com). A membership fee entitles you to sailing workshops, clinics, and unlimited use of their sailboats and sailboards on Lake Champlain.
- **Kroka Expeditions,** Putney, Vermont (☎ **802/387-5397;** www.kroka.com). The premier wilderness education school in New England. Teaches kids of all ages how to rock-climb, white-water kayak, and canoe; also teaches orienteering, and general outdoor skills.
- **Lake Winnipesaukee Sailing Association,** Gilford, New Hampshire (☎ **603/279-8553;** www.lwsa.org). A youth sailing school.
- **Land Rover 4×4 Driving School,** Manchester, Vermont (☎ **800/362-4747**). Spend an hour or longer

with one of the Land Rover's expert instructors on an all-natural circuit and learn to off-road drive over rocks, ruts, and streams.

- **Morningside Flight Park,** 357 Morningside Lane, Charlestown, NH 03603 (☎ **603/542-4416;** www.flymorningside.com). Hang-gliding lessons in western New Hampshire.
- **Mount Snow,** Mountain Rd., West Dover, VT 05356 (☎ **800/245-SNOW;** www.mountsnow.com). Runs one of the top mountain-biking schools in the Northeast.
- **Orvis,** 1711 Blue Hills Drive, Roanoke, VA 24012 (☎ **800/235-9763;** www.orvis.com). Two- to 2.5-day fly-fishing courses taught on the Battenkill River in southern Vermont.
- **Northern Waters Canoe and Kayak Company,** Errol, New Hampshire (☎ **603/447-2177;** www.sacobound/kayak.html). White-water canoe trips and instruction on the Class II and III rapids of Androscoggin River.
- **Portsmouth Kayak Adventures,** New Hampshire (☎ **603/559-1000;** www.portsmouthkayak.com). Leads paddlers on sea-kayaking clinics off the New Hampshire coast.
- **Stratton Golf School,** R.R. 1, Box 145, Stratton Mountain, VT 05155 (☎ **802/297-4114;** www.stratton.com). Golf school in central Vermont.
- **Tudhope Sailing Center and Marina,** Vermont (☎ **802/372-5320**). Located at the foot of the Grand Isle Bridge in the Lake Champlain Islands. Sailing lessons on Lake Champlain.
- **Umiak Outdoor Outfitters,** 849 S. Main St., Stowe, VT 05672 (☎ **802/253-2317;** www.umiak.com). Canoeing and snowshoeing instruction in the Stowe area.
- **Vermont Fly Fishing School,** Quechee Inn, Woodstock, VT (☎ **802/295-7620**). Fly-fishing instruction in eastern Vermont.
- **Waterfront Diving Center,** 214 Battery St., Burlington, VT 05401 (☎ **802/865-2771**). Scuba-diving instruction on Lake Champlain.
- **Winnipesaukee Kayak Company,** 17 Bay St., P.O. Box 2163, Wolfborough, NH 03894 (☎ **603/569-9926**). Kayak lessons on the waters of Lake Winnipesaukee and other nearby lakes.
- **Winni Sailboarder's School & Outlet,** 687 Union Ave., Laconia, NH 03247 (☎ **603/528-4110**). Board-sailing lessons on Lake Opechee in western New Hampshire.

Maps

It is my intention throughout this book to guide you along trails and roads via words, without maps. However, if you're a map lover like me, you'll still want to know exactly where you started and where you're going. For that reason, I've tried to name the relevant map for each featured trip or explain how to locate the map. Many hikes simply have maps at the trailhead. Other times, I have mentioned the respective United States Geological Survey (USGS) maps—topographical maps designed by the U.S. government. Many of these maps can be found at local bookstores or retail sporting goods stores like the **Globe Corner bookstores** in Boston and Cambridge (call ☎ **617/523-6658** or 617/859-8008 in Boston, 617/497-6277 in Harvard Square). If you can't locate the map for a particular section, go to the source, **U.S. Geological Survey** Federal Center, Building 810, P.O. Box 25286, Denver, CO 80225 (www.usgs.gov).

Many of my biking routes in Vermont and New Hampshire were found by using the Atlas and Gazetteer published by **DeLorme Mapping Company.** These large-scale maps are excellent for biking and driving to hiking trailheads because they incorporate topographical maps and local logging roads. Contact DeLorme Mapping, 2 DeLorme Drive, Yarmouth, ME 04096 (☎ **800/452-5931** or 207/846-7000; www.delorme.com).

If you plan on doing any hiking or cross-country skiing in the Mount Mansfield region of Vermont or in the Whites, the maps published by Map Adventures are indispensable. The respective maps depict all the hiking trails and cross-country trails in the Stowe area and the Presidential Range. The maps can be purchased from the **Mountain Wanderer Map & Book Store** (☎ **800/745-2707;**www.mountainwanderer.com).

Another excellent mapping system in this digital age is the Terrain Navigator CD-ROM created by **Maptech** (☎ **888/433-8500;** www.maptech.com). Simply slip the disc in the computer and, depending on which disc you use (say, the White Mountain National Forest CD), you can print customized versions of USGS topographical maps, plot trails, even mark and measure distance and area with just a click of the mouse. A large database lets you zero in on a location or trail just by entering the name. Download a map for wherever your destination might be and off you go on your next adventure.

Books

During the course of my research, many books proved helpful, including guidebooks on specific sports in one region, nonfiction books on a host of subjects ranging from ecology to geology to history to anecdotal New England stories, and fiction from the likes of Nathaniel Hawthorne. Let's start with the sporting guides that I found useful.

Single-Sport Guides

Classic Back-country Skiing by David Goodman (AMC Books), ***25 Ski Tours in Vermont*** by Stan Wass (Backcountry), ***Winter Trails: Vermont and New Hampshire*** by Marty Basch (Globe Pequot), ***The Mountain Biker's Guide to Northern New England*** by Paul Angiolillo (Menasha), ***Mountain Bike! New Hampshire: A Guide to the Classic Trail*** by Jeff Faust (Menasha), ***The Best Bike Rides in New England*** by Paul Thomas (Globe Pequot), ***25 Bicycle Tours in Vermont*** by John S. Freiden (Backcountry), *Touring New England by Bicycle* by Peter Powers (Terragraphics), *Quiet Water Canoe Guide, New Hampshire, Vermont* by Alex Wilson (AMC Books), *Fifty Hikes in Vermont* by the Green Mountain Club (Backcountry), *Guide Book of the Long Trail* (Green Mountain Club), *Hiker's Guide to the Mountains of Vermont* by Jared Grange (Huntington Graphics), *Fifty Hikes in the White Mountains* by Daniel Doan (Backcountry), *Fifty More Hikes in New Hampshire* by Daniel Doan (Backcountry), and *AMC White Mountain Guide* (AMC).

General Travel Guides

The Explorer's Guide series (Countryman Press) is the most comprehensive and fact-filled collection of guides on specific New England states. The series includes ***Vermont,*** by Christina Tree and Peter Jennison, and ***New Hampshire,*** by Christina Tree and Peter Randall. Aside from small-press one-state books like those that Countryman publishes, ***Frommer's Northern New England*** (IDG Books Worldwide, Inc.), written by Mainer Wayne Curtis, is probably the best general guide to New England, giving you all the lodging, dining, and sightseeing info you'll need.

Literary Nonfiction, Natural History, Ecology, and Geology

Essays on Nature by Ralph Waldo Emerson, ***The Survival of the Bark Canoe*** by John McPhee, ***Changes in the Land*** by William Cronon, ***Hope, Human, and Wild*** by Bill McKibben, ***The Changing Faces of New England*** by Betty Flanders Thomson, ***The Sierra Club Guide to the Natural Areas of New England*** by John Perry and Jane Greverus Perry, ***A Guide to New England's Landscape*** by Neil Jorgensen, and ***Ecology of Eastern Forests*** by John Kricher and Gordon Morrison.

New England History

The Pulitzer prize-winning ***The Flowering of New England*** by Van Wyck Brooks; ***Inside New England*** by Judson Hale, a witty combination of anecdotes, history, and highly opinionated satire; ***New Hampshire: A Bicentennial History*** by Elizabeth Forbes Morison and Elting Morison; ***Vermont: A Bicentennial History*** by Charles T. Morrissey; and ***Literary New England*** by William Corbett, a guidebook to the historical literary sites of New England.

Fiction

"The Great Stone Face" by Nathaniel Hawthorne, ***Stranger in the Kingdom*** by Howard Frank Mosher.

Spas

Vermont's spas are more than mere retreats to rejuvenate your weary body or instill a healthy lifestyle. More and more spas are taking advantage of their bucolic surroundings, whisking guests outdoors to breathe in the clean, crisp air before returning them to the invigorating massage and aromatherapy rooms indoors. Considering that many of these spas are located in the mountains, it's a shrewd move. Obviously, aerobic classes, weight rooms, and other indoor services are still in place, but New England spas are finally realizing that you don't have to be in southern California to savor spectacular surroundings year-round.

- **The Equinox,** P.O. Box 46, Manchester Village, VT 05254 (☎ **800/362-4747;** www.equinoxresort.com). Body scrubs, therapeutic herbal wraps, and massages are just a few of the services offered at this prestigious 230-year-old resort. Rates per person, including all meals, facilities, one herbal wrap, one loofah salt glow scrub, and a daily short massage, cost $2,170 for a 7-night package.
- **New Life,** The Inn of the Six Mountains, Killington Rd., P.O. Box 395, Killington, VT 05751 (☎ **800/545-9407;** www.newlifehikingspa.com). As the name implies, New Life specializes in changing poor health habits through yoga, smart eating, and hiking. Rates per person, including all meals, facilities, and two 1-hour massages, range from $899 to $999 for a 5-night package.
- **Topnotch Resort & Spa at Stowe,** 4000 Mountain Rd., Stowe, VT 05672 (☎ **800/451-8686;** www.topnotch-resort.com). Catering to sports enthusiasts, Topnotch gives every client a "Fitness Profile" for planning a customized exercise regimen. Rates per person, including all meals, facilities, and one daily personal service of your choice, range from $1,505 to $2,247 for a 7-night package.

Campgrounds & Other Accommodations

Names of the top public campgrounds, inns, and resorts have been provided at the end of each regional chapter. I have personally stayed at many of these places and can attest to their high quality. Others were recommended by rangers, locals, or friends. The inns and resorts all feature outdoor activities or are situated near recreational areas.

2

Southern Vermont

Anyone who more than once or twice has driven the stretch of I-91 from Bernardston, Massachusetts, north across the state line takes it as an article of faith that an ineffable change occurs when the WELCOME TO VERMONT sign slides by on the roadside. The landscape sweetens somehow. It's not just the absence of billboards, which Vermonters outlawed long ago. Hills rise higher and undulate toward the horizon. The green that clothes them becomes greener by the mile. The hayfields seem more golden; the Holstein cows in the pastures seem to increase; and the very air seems fresher. And in winter, when every other northbound car is topped with a loaded ski rack, the snow cover gets rapidly deeper the farther north you go. The snowbanks mount ever higher, and the branches of roadside evergreens droop under their wintry burden. Travelers from other places realize they've arrived, and Vermonters know they're home.

In contrast to almost any other place in the United States, Vermont's 3 centuries of settlement seem actually to have ***enhanced*** the land's appeal. The no-billboards law is only one of the ways Vermonters have defended their sense of what their home should look like. The hundreds of tiny historic villages dotting the state look like they did a century ago, complete with white-painted Victorian homes and church steeples reaching toward the sky. At last count, there were more than 100 covered bridges still intact along lonely country roads. All in all, you'd be hard put to find another place where people and all their works fit in such harmony with the natural features of the land; so many generations have lived here in balance with the land that it's hard to say whether the land has shaped the people or the people have shaped the land.

I'd say that the reason Vermonters have behaved so well is that the hand of nature always was and always will be very insistent up here, both in its harsh, exacting demands on humans and in its willingness to reward them with livelihoods and any number of simple pleasures, from the quiet beauty of the countryside to delicacies like wild trout, game, and strawberries. Each of Vermont's seasons is forceful enough to define completely what life is like for the people who live here, from summer's alternating days of sultry heat, wild thunderstorms, and crystal-clear sunshine, to fall's brisk snap and explosion of colorful foliage; from winter's blankets of snow and frigid mornings that make your throat catch when you step outside, to the monochromatic and dreary mud season, which is followed by fast and brilliant springtime.

Vermont's pastoral look of dairy farm and cornfield is kept intact by its tiny population. Although about the same size as New Hampshire, its inverted neighbor to the east, Vermont has only a little more than half that state's population. Whereas southern New Hampshire is more or less a suburb of Boston, all of Vermont north of U.S. 4 is far enough away from the urban centers of the Northeast to hold most of the hordes at arm's length. Less than 9,000 people live in Montpelier, the nation's smallest state capital, and only a third of the state's total population lives in anything like an urban area. Add the state's strict environmental statutes, and the result is a state overrun with small villages and their signature white steeples, backcountry roads, and more farmland than you could possibly imagine.

The countrified feeling of Vermont's valleys, along with its wilder, mountainous areas, has been attracting visitors for almost 200 years. George Round opened the Clarendon Mineral Springs in 1798; his hotel soon was bringing carriage loads of "flatlanders" north to breathe the crisp fresh air and indulge in the invigorating, supposedly therapeutic waters of the springs. In many other Vermont towns, other entrepreneurial types followed suit. The most famous of these "water-cures" was created in 1845 in Brattleboro, where the spring became a rural retreat for some of the most distinguished figures among New England's literati—Harriet Beecher Stowe, Henry Wadsworth Longfellow, James Russell Lowell, and William Dean Howells. These salubrious retreats soon declined in popularity, and their patrons were replaced by pleasure-seeking summer vacationers. Mary Todd Lincoln and her son Robert first visited Manchester during Abe's presidency in 1863. Robert would later build an estate called Hildene, where he summered ever year until he died in 1925.

These summer visitors weren't always appreciated by the locals. Vermonters, understandably proud of their state and their way of life, have a longstanding reputation for being prickly, laconic, and sometimes downright cranky toward their southern countrymen. A fellow named Matthew Buckham, who would later reign as president of the University of Vermont, provided an early record of the mischievous nature of the Vermont Yank when he unleashed this long-winded article in an 1867 issue of the ***Vermont Historical Gazetteer:***

> ***Let us do all we can to keep up the notion among our city cousins, that to live "away up in Vermont," is the American equivalent for being exiled to Siberia.***
>
> ***Not that we do not think very highly of our city cousins, especially when we see them in the city. But when they come with their long baggage-train of trunks and band-boxes, and take possession of a country village, bringing their livery and their minister with them, occupying all the finest building sites, ordering all their groceries and toggery from the city, and importing into industrious communities the seductive fashion of doing nothing and doing it elegantly, they turn the heads of the young, demoralize the whole tone of society, convert respectable villages into the likeness of suburban Connecticut and New Jersey, and for all these losses do not compensate by***

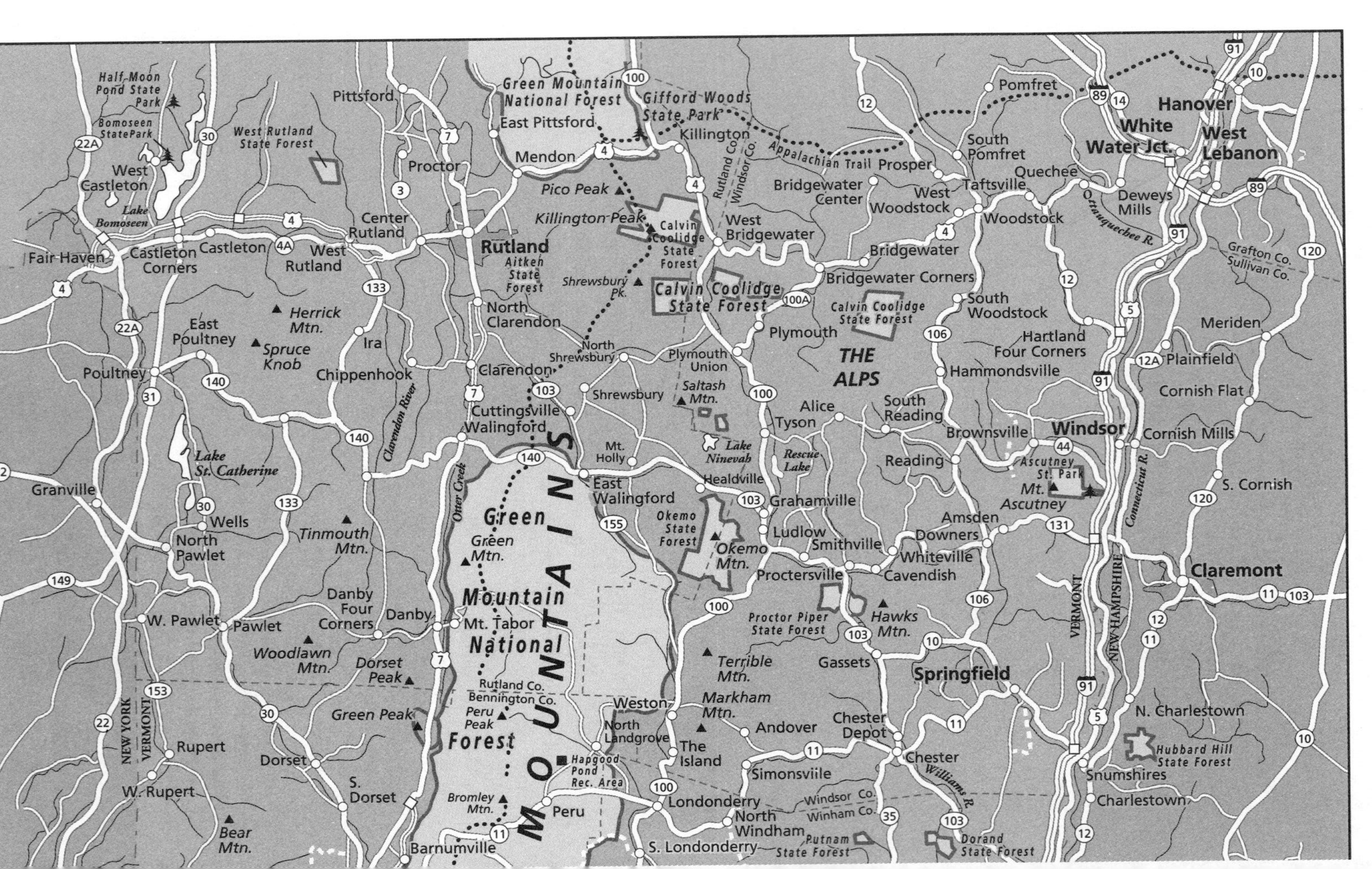
Green Mountain National Forest
Gifford Woods State Park
Half-Moon Pond State Park
Bomoseen State Park
Lake Bomoseen
West Castleton
Fair Haven
Castleton Corners
Castleton
West Rutland
West Rutland State Forest
Pittsford
Proctor
Center Rutland
Rutland
Aitken State Forest
East Pittsford
Mendon
Pico Peak
Killington Peak
Killington
Calvin Coolidge State Forest
Shrewsbury Pk.
North Clarendon
Clarendon
North Shrewsbury
Shrewsbury
Cuttingsville
Walingford
Herrick Mtn.
Spruce Knob
East Poultney
Poultney
Ira
Chippenhook
Clarendon River
Lake St. Catherine
Granville
Wells
North Pawlet
W. Pawlet
Pawlet
Tinmouth Mtn.
Danby Four Corners
Danby
Woodlawn Mtn.
Dorset Peak
Green Peak
Dorset
S. Dorset
Rupert
W. Rupert
Bear Mtn.
NEW YORK
VERMONT
Otter Creek
Green Mtn.
Mt. Tabor
Rutland Co.
Bennington Co.
Peru Peak
Green Mountain National Forest
MOUNTAINS
Bromley Mtn.
Barnumville
Hapgood Pond Rec. Area
Peru
Rutland Co.
Windsor Co.
Appalachian Trail
West Bridgewater
Plymouth Union
Saltash Mtn.
Mt. Holly
East Walingford
Lake Ninevah
Healdville
Okemo State Forest
Okemo Mtn.
Weston
North Landgrove
The Island
Londonderry
S. Londonderry
North Windham
Windsor Co.
Winham Co.
Putnam State Forest
Plymouth
Tyson
Alice
Rescue Lake
Grahamville
Ludlow
Proctersville
Smithville
Terrible Mtn.
Markham Mtn.
Andover
Simonsville
Chester Depot
Chester
Williams R.
Dorand State Forest
Gassets
Proctor Piper State Forest
Hawks Mtn.
Cavendish
Whiteville
Downers
Amsden
Springfield
Bridgewater Center
Bridgewater
Bridgewater Corners
Prosper
West Woodstock
Woodstock
South Pomfret
Pomfret
Taftsville
Quechee
THE ALPS
South Woodstock
Hartland Four Corners
Hammondsville
South Reading
Reading
Brownsville
Windsor
Ascutney St. Park
Mt. Ascutney
Ottauquechee R.
Deweys Mills
White River Jct.
Hanover
West Lebanon
Grafton Co.
Sullivan Co.
Meriden
Plainfield
Cornish Flat
Cornish Mills
Connecticut R.
S. Cornish
Claremont
VERMONT
NEW HAMPSHIRE
N. Charlestown
Hubbard Hill State Forest
Snumshires
Charlestown

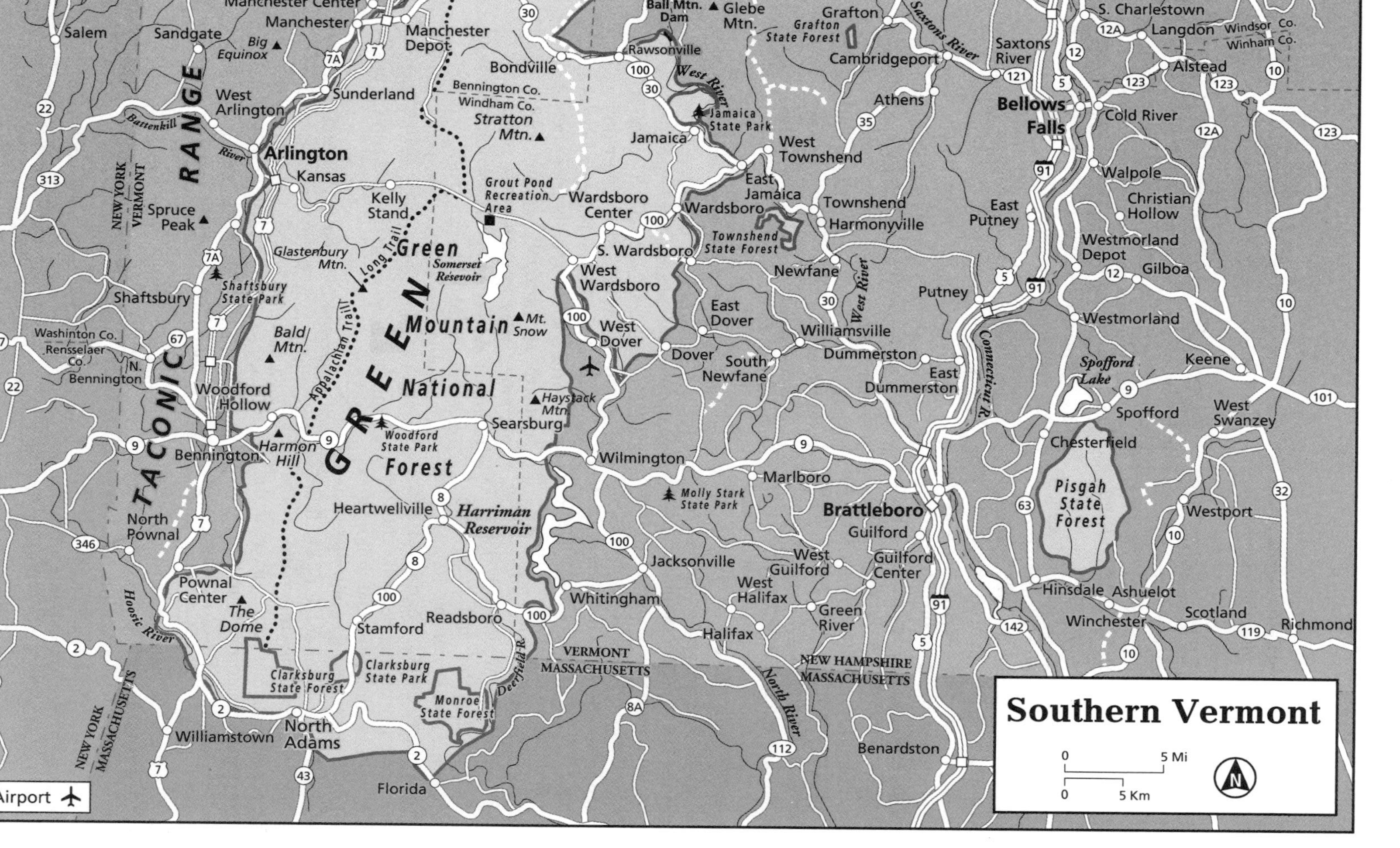
Southern Vermont
0
5 Mi
0
5 Km
N
Airport
TACONIC RANGE
GREEN Mountain National Forest
Manchester Center
Manchester
Manchester Depot
Salem
Sandgate
Big Equinox
Sunderland
West Arlington
Arlington
Kansas
Kelly Stand
Battenkill River
NEW YORK
VERMONT
Spruce Peak
Shaftsbury
Shaftsbury State Park
Glastenbury Mtn.
Long Trail
Appalachian Trail
Bald Mtn.
Washinton Co.
Rensselaer Co.
N. Bennington
Woodford Hollow
Bennington
Harmon Hill
Woodford State Park
North Pownal
Pownal Center
The Dome
Hoosic River
Heartwellville
Harriman Reservoir
Stamford
Readsboro
Clarksburg State Forest
Clarksburg State Park
Monroe State Forest
Deerfield R.
Williamstown
North Adams
Florida
MASSACHUSETTS
Bondville
Bennington Co.
Windham Co.
Stratton Mtn.
Grout Pond Recreation Area
Somerset Resevoir
Mt. Snow
Haystack Mtn.
Searsburg
Ball Mtn. Dam
Glebe Mtn.
Rawsonville
West River
Jamaica
Jamaica State Park
Wardsboro Center
S. Wardsboro
West Wardsboro
West Dover
Wilmington
Whitingham
VERMONT
MASSACHUSETTS
Grafton
Grafton State Forest
Cambridgeport
Athens
West Townshend
East Jamaica
Wardsboro
Townshend
Harmonyville
Townshend State Forest
Newfane
East Dover
Dover
South Newfane
Williamsville
Dummerston
East Dummerston
Molly Stark State Park
Marlboro
Jacksonville
West Guilford
West Halifax
Halifax
Green River
North River
Saxtons River
Saxtons River
Bellows Falls
East Putney
Putney
Connecticut R.
Brattleboro
Guilford
Guilford Center
NEW HAMPSHIRE
MASSACHUSETTS
Benardston
S. Charlestown
Langdon
Windsor Co.
Winham Co.
Alstead
Cold River
Walpole
Christian Hollow
Westmorland Depot
Gilboa
Westmorland
Spofford Lake
Keene
Spofford
West Swanzey
Chesterfield
Pisgah State Forest
Westport
Hinsdale
Ashuelot
Winchester
Scotland
Richmond
22
313
7A
7
67
9
346
2
43
8
100
8A
112
30
35
121
5
91
12
12A
123
10
101
63
142
119
32

adding any appreciable amount to the circulating capital or to public improvement.

However, Vermonters soon learned to live with the increasing numbers of tourists; there was room enough for all in the green hills. The locals confined their jibes against New Hampshirites and the city folk to the occasional dig and turned their wit to appreciating all that Vermont had given them. In a 1905 ***Chicago Tribune*** article, a reporter asked a Vermont politico how he got his start in life. "I was born on a hillside farm in Vermont," said the statesman with a twinkle, "and at an early age I rolled down."

The state government did its best to encourage tourism. In 1891, it established the first state-operated publicity service in the nation. Anglers flocked to the rivers and hunters took to the forests, where they were soon joined by hikers and skiers. In 1930, the Green Mountain Club cleared the last stretches of the Long Trail, which runs continuously along the ridges of the Green Mountains from the Massachusetts border all the way to Canada. Five years later, a Ford Model T engine in Clinton Gilbert's pasture in Woodstock powered the first alpine-skiing rope tow in America. By 1975, the state had 78 downhill and cross-country ski areas, fully ready for the 1970s boom in cross-country skiing. Legions of vacationers took up biking as well, and the gently undulating roads that follow the contours of the Vermont countryside have earned a reputation as some of the finest road-biking terrain in the nation. The hundreds of trails that entice hikers in the summer are transformed in wintertime into easy woodland Nordic-skiing trails and major backcountry skiing challenges. In short, there is far more to this small state than the annual leaf-peeping auto caravans that clog its roadways every October. There's just no excuse for restricting your experience of the Vermont outdoors to a view through the glass windowpanes of your car.

The Lay of the Land

One reason why the southern Vermont countryside is so pleasing to the eye is that the scale of the landscape neither overwhelms nor is overwhelmed by the farms, roads, and communities scattered across it. The Green Mountains are imposing, but not to the point that they render the villages in the valleys at their feet ant-sized by comparison. The valleys are commonly just wide enough to support an operation like a small family farm, and the homes you see on individual hillsides east of the mountains seem to complement the view rather than blemish it. Everything seems to fit into its place.

Drive east to west in Vermont and you'll inevitably run into the high barrier of rising ridges called the **Green Mountains.** This sturdy backbone, whose width varies from 20 to 36 miles, marches the whole length of the state and on into Canada. In southern Vermont, the mountains roll along in one distinct ridge, whereas at Sherburne Pass, the border between southern and central Vermont (for our purposes), they split into three ridges: the Hogback Range, which runs north from Brandon; the Main Range, which continues on and is the route of the Long Trail; and the Lowell Mountains in the east, which start at Stockbridge and run on up toward Morrisville.

As suggested by their fairly gentle contours, these are old mountains, created 450 millions years ago by a running fold in the earth's crust. They contain rock that is among the oldest on the continent—more than a billion years old. The official state rock, green metamorphic schist, is the building block of the Green Mountains; its brilliant green coloring reflects the presence of the mineral chlorite.

In some spots, the continental folding was so strong that huge slabs of rock toppled from the heights of the Green

Mountains to create other mountain ranges, such as the **Taconic Mountains** in Vermont's southwestern corner. Mount Equinox, standing just west of Manchester, is the highest peak in the Taconics at 3,816 feet.

The remoter parts of the Green Mountain National Forest are the best places in southern and central Vermont to gain a fleeting encounter with Vermont's abundant wildlife. Moose, black bears, beavers, gray foxes, and otters all do quite well in the backcountry, and white-tailed deer are so common everywhere that they rival snow and ice as the state's chief driving hazards. Maybe you'll be the lucky one to catch the definitive glance of the fabled catamount; pessimists think the species has long since deserted the Northeast, but the faithful continue to see the golden, long-tailed big cat out of the corner of their eye (or, at least, imagine that they do). Birds are everywhere, as well, including such species as wild turkeys, great horned owls, yellow-bellied sapsuckers, peregrine falcons and numerous kinds of hawks, eastern kingbirds, huge flocks of snow geese and Canada geese, great blue herons, and snowy egrets. There are also warblers, thrushes, and many other species of waterfowl and songbirds too numerous to mention.

Between the southern Green Mountains and the Taconics on the border with New York State is the **Valley of Vermont,** the narrow southern extension of the broad Champlain Valley. It's only a mile wide in places, and is the corridor along which the picturesque villages of southwestern Vermont—Bennington, Arlington, Manchester, Dorset, and Danby, beehives of tourism all—are located.

Streams, rivers, ponds, and lakes abound in southwestern Vermont and the Green Mountain National Forest, from the Hoosic River in the far southwestern corner, to Somerset and Harriman reservoirs just east of the Green Mountains, to the famed Battenkill River and to Otter Creek, which runs north into Lake Champlain. East of the mountains, narrow streams tumble down hillsides into ponds, rivers, and lakes, eventually draining into the Connecticut River on Vermont's eastern border. The part of Vermont's Connecticut River watershed that begins on the eastern slope of the Green Mountains and extends from Brattleboro in the south all the way up to the Northeast Kingdom (see chapter 4, "Northern Vermont") is called the **Vermont Piedmont.** The Piedmont is among the prettiest areas of the state, still given over to dairying for the most part, and consisting of an endless succession of modest rolling hills, narrow settled valleys, a spider web of dirt and frost-heaved paved roads, and villages that greet the world with signs like EAST RANDOLPH, POP. 216.

Although skiers and road bikers make their presence loudly felt in the state, let's face it: The big hoo-ha, which every town uses as its pitch to tourists, is the fall foliage season. In September and October, the leaves transform the landscape into a vibrant, ever-changing kaleidoscope of color. The leaves on the white birches turn yellow; aspens display a copper-coin color; sugar maples offer a combination of yellow, green, orange, and red (depending on how much sugar is trapped in the leaf); white ashes become the color of ripe plums; and oak leaves turn into a warm, dark brown. This is not news to most of us. Indeed, "Autumn in Vermont" has become a cliché.

In southern Vermont, peak season usually occurs during the last week in September and the first two weeks in October. Columbus Day weekend is absolute madness. It seems as if the entire population of New York and Boston is behind the wheels of rental cars, congesting New England's roadways with Jersey Turnpike traffic. There's a basic problem with the usual autumn driving trip—one of you has to drive. Prime leaf-watching soon becomes tiresome road-watching. Your significant other keeps prodding you to look, but you barely get a glimpse of that purple-leafed tree, suffering severe neck strain in the process—thus, the reason I have written this book. Hike away from the crowds on trails where you can slow down, stop easily, and appreciate Mother Nature wearing her most flamboyant dress. The Department of Travel in Vermont maintains a foliage hotline (☎ **800/VERMONT**) updating the conditions of the leaves.

As for the rest of the year, summer days can be hot and humid, cooler at night. January temperatures are below freezing most of the time, with snowfall averaging 55 inches in the valleys to over 120 inches on high elevations. Call ☎ **802/464-2111** or 802/773-8056 for current weather conditions in southern Vermont.

Orientation

This chapter covers all of the southern part of the state of Vermont. It took some hard thinking to decide where to draw the line between southern and central Vermont, mainly because no one agrees on where the one ends and the other begins. Vermont's state tourism office breaks things down according to county lines, calling southern Vermont everything in Bennington and Windham Counties, and central Vermont everything in Rutland, Windsor, Orange, Addison, and Washington Counties. I've gone a very different route, trying to balance the natural topographic divisions between Vermont's areas with the way visitors and residents tend to travel through and use the land. Roughly speaking, I've decided to define southern Vermont as everything from the Massachusetts border north to the area immediately surrounding U.S. 4.

To me, the border between southern and central Vermont is drawn more by the much greater numbers of visitors in the south than by any feature of the landscape. From the Massachusetts border north through all of the areas covered here, both east and west of the ridge of the Green Mountains, southern Vermont is by and large the stuff of postcards and the magazine covers of ***Yankee***—long-settled rolling hills and valleys, with the soft, green, but massive, contours of the mountains looming up wherever you look. The forest-and-farmland countryside is broken up frequently by the historic small towns, lonely farmhouses, and covered bridges that give Vermont that harmonious rural feel for which it is justly famous.

The combination of a still unruly natural beauty with this rustic, well-lived-in quality makes Vermont an awfully appealing place to visit, and southern Vermont has been drawing tourists in droves for over a century. It's not that there aren't other parts of the state with this kind of appeal—the Northeast Kingdom is an incredibly lovely place, for example—but that the other parts of the state are just that much farther away from the big cities. Looking at a difference of several hours of tedious driving between central Vermont and southern Vermont, most "flatlanders" happily settle for a southern destination like Manchester, Bennington, or even the area up around Killington, rather than spend more of their precious weekend time traveling all the way to areas such as central Vermont's Mad River Valley.

The impact of tourism gives the two regions a subtle difference in character. Southern Vermont still has the little white villages with the ubiquitous church steeples, but it's more aggressively "open for business" than central Vermont. Look closely under the rustic veneer of places like Brattleboro, Bennington, and especially Manchester, and you'll find all the hallmarks of the affluent, sophisticated communities around Boston or New York. In Manchester, for example, there are as many Mercedes sedans as there are pickup trucks, and for every old-fashioned general store (not too many of the authentic kind are left around here), there's an Armani or Anne Klein outlet store. Southern Vermont has simply been cashing in on its old-time New England character for more years and with more efficiency than has central Vermont.

Southern Vermont's primary north-south corridor on the western side is **U.S. 7,** which passes through **Bennington, Arlington, Manchester,** and eventually **Rutland,** and is more commercially developed than any route east of the Green Mountains. A far more bucolic north-south route is **State Route 100,** which might simply be called Ski Country Road. Running just east of the main ridge of the Green Mountains, Route 100 is rural—there's nothing remotely like a city along its entire length from the Massachusetts border nearly to Canada—but all the state's major ski resorts are either right on it or within a few miles of it. From south to north, you'll pass the signs for **Mount Snow/Haystack, Stratton Mountain, Bromley, Okemo,** and the **Killington** area. Passing through fairly narrow valleys between the green-swathed mountains, Route 100 is thick with the cozy inns and B&Bs, beautiful small towns, antiques shops, small lakes and rivers, and "gulfs"—wild, forested, steep-walled gorges that twist through mountainous areas—that are the very picture of Vermont's lure for tourists.

Along the Connecticut River runs **I-91,** the fast lane for travel from the south or east to any part of the state east of the main mountain chain. If you're coming from New York and are bound for a town along U.S. 7, you're probably better off taking the Adirondack Northway (I-87) instead. For Bennington/Manchester, change to N.Y. 7 north of Albany and follow it into Vermont, where it becomes State Route 9 and intersects with U.S. 7 at Bennington. (Don't confuse N.Y. 7 and U.S. 7; they're two different highways.) For the Rutland/Killington area, take the Northway to Glens Falls, New York, change to U.S. 4, and follow it on up into the Vermont mountains. If you're coming from the Boston area to any point in Vermont, you'll be taking I-91 up from the Mass Pike (I-90) to whatever point in Vermont at which you need to turn west again.

The east and west sides of the Green Mountains offer distinctly different recreational menus: On the east, between the mountains and I-91, is a seemingly endless amount of hilly, rural country and lonely road that's perfect for both road and mountain biking as well as cross-country skiing. All the feeder streams of the Connecticut River offer good trout fishing, and some of them have runable white water, notably the West River. West of the mountains, the heavier traffic of U.S. 7 and State Route 7A makes road biking a little less inviting, but then again you've got world-class trout fishing on the Battenkill, bass and perch fishing and boating on nice big lakes like St. Catherine, and an easygoing canoeing river in Otter Creek.

In either case, you're never more than a short drive from the main attraction, the Green Mountains. If I-91 and slow-moving U.S. 7 are the sidepieces to a ladder running north up the length of southern Vermont, it's the Green Mountain **gaps** that are the crosspieces. Cut through natural breaks and gorges in the otherwise impassable ridge of the mountains, these are usually the most beautiful, and hairiest, roads in the state. Narrow, steep, and replete with hairpin turns around blind curves, they can pose a considerable challenge to even four-wheel-drive vehicles in snowy weather, and some are closed in winter. All of them provide access to the Green Mountain backcountry, the best place in southern Vermont to do many of the things you'll want to do outdoors. The least precipitous is the southernmost, **State Route 9,** which connects Brattleboro and Bennington. From south to north, the others are **Kelley Stand Road,** between West Wardsboro and Arlington, which provides access to some of southern Vermont's most pristine country and is closed in winter; **State Route 11,** which runs from Manchester to Londonderry and on to Springfield; **Green Mountain National Forest Road No. 10,** another remote dirt road closed in winter, which connects North Landgrove with Danby; **State Route 140,** the Wallingford Gulf Road; **State Route 103,** the Rutland–Bellows Falls Highway; and **U.S. 4,** which connects Glens Falls, New York, and Rutland with Woodstock and I-89, and which is also the access road for the Pico Peak and Killington Ski Areas, near Sherburne Pass.

Parks & Other Hot Spots

I've tried to round up the places in southern Vermont that come up again and again in the sports section as great spots for different kinds of outdoor recreation.

Connecticut River

235 miles along the Vermont–New Hampshire border. Access: State-owned public boating access sites in southern Vermont include Old Ferry Rd. Access Area (Brattleboro, off U.S. 5); Putney Landing Area (Putney-Dummerston town line, off U.S. 5); Hoyt Landing Access Area (Springfield, off I-91); and Hammond Cove Access Area (Hartland, off U.S. 5). Bird watching, canoeing, fishing, wildlife watching.

The lower half of Vermont's Connecticut River is not nearly as pristine as the northern half, but it's still a decent place to fish—for trout, walleye, pike, bass, and shad—or canoe. In fact, you can make a small-scale Huck Finn journey on the Connecticut, canoe camping at points along its shores. There are, however, a few unrunnable sections of the river, near Bellows Falls being one example. If you're interested in more than a day trip on the Connecticut, you'll need a river guide such as the ***AMC River Guide: New Hampshire/Vermont*** (AMC Books, 1989), or the ***Connecticut River Guide*** (available from Connecticut River Watershed Council, 125 Combs Rd., Easthampton, MA 01027).

The Connecticut is also a good spot for birding and wildlife watching, with river otters, muskrats, beavers, bitterns, bank swallows, and other birds.

Vernon Black Gum Swamp

Contact **Vernon Town Clerk** for more information, R2, P.O. Box 525, Vernon, VT 05354-0116 (☎ **802/257-0292**). Picnic area, no developed facilities. Access: 4 miles south of Brattleboro on State Rte. 142; turn east onto Pond Rd. about 1.25 miles south of Vernon; proceed 1.2 miles and turn right onto Huckle Hill Rd.; proceed 1.3 miles; then turn right onto Basin Rd., following it to parking lot at road's end. Map: USGS 7.5- × 15-min. Brattleboro; 7.5-min. Bernardston. Bird watching.

The Vernon Black Gum Swamp is an unusual place to find as far north as Vermont—its namesake trees are far more commonly found a considerable distance to the south, as are the mountain laurel and Virginia chain fern that also grow here. Marked trails in the swamp take you past gnarled, weirdly shaped 400-year-old black gums and offer good birding—flickers, thrushes, cedar waxwings, wood ducks, and other species frequent the swamp.

Molly Stark State Park

On State Rte. 9 in Wilmington, 3 miles east of junction with State Rte. 100. ☎ **802/464-5460.** 34 campsites, lean-tos, wheelchair-accessible rest rooms, picnic area. Camping, fishing, hiking.

A 158-acre preserve with hiking trails that include one to the expansive views from the fire tower atop 2,145-foot Mount Olga. The park also offers cold-water fishing on Beaver Brook and good camping.

Harriman Reservoir

Public boating access from State Rte. 9 west of Wilmington; access also from Whitingham at south end of reservoir, off State Rte. 100. For information: **Green Mountain National Forest,** 231 N. Main St., Rutland, VT 05701 (☎ **802/ 747-6700**), or **U.S. Generating Co.,** P.O. Box 218, Harriman Station, Readsboro, VT 05350 (☎ **802/423-7700**). Picnic areas; marked trails for biking, hiking, cross-country skiing. Contact **Vermont Department of Forests, Parks, and Recreation,** R.R. 1, P.O. Box 33, North Springfield, VT 05150 (☎ **802/ 886-2215**), for more information on Atherton Meadow Wildlife Management Area at southern end of reservoir. Map: USGS 7.5-min. Readsboro. Camping, canoeing, cross-country skiing, fishing, mountain biking, sailing, swimming, wildlife watching.

One look at a map will show you that this huge reservoir is situated in the closest thing to truly remote country you'll find in southern Vermont. The place is teeming with wildlife—there are bears, loons, moose, and other icons of the northern wilds around here, and deer and wild turkeys are abundant. Harriman is prime fishing, cross-country skiing, mountain biking, canoeing, and even sailing country. There are swimming beaches off Castle Hill Road a mile from Wilmington Village and off State Route 100 near Flame Stables; and the Harriman Trail, following the west shore of the lake from State Route 9 to Harriman Dam, passes numerous relics of abandoned settlements along the shore—old stone walls and ruined foundations.

The reservoir is owned by the New England Power Company, which permits day use only. However, at the Whitingham end of the lake is the Atherton Meadow Wildlife Management Area; it has a large and lively marsh, and primitive camping is permitted.

The Green Mountain National Forest/ South Half

For information: **U.S. Forest Service,** Green Mountain and Finger Lakes National Forest, 231 N. Main St., Rutland, VT 05701 (☎ **802/747-6700**). Map: USGS Green Mountain National Forest/South Half. Cross-country and downhill skiing, fishing, hiking, mountain biking.

Since the outer boundaries of the Green Mountain National Forest's southern half contain within them at least half of the best spots in southern Vermont for getting outside, this is necessarily a kind of umbrella listing. Within its boundaries are cold streams and beaver ponds famous for brook and rainbow trout fishing; the Long Trail, a tramper's treasure; a latticework of remote forest roads and old logging roads, all perfect for mountain biking, cross-country skiing, or simple scenic drives; and the major ski areas of southern Vermont—Mount Snow, Stratton, Bromley, Okemo, and Killington.

With a total of 325,534 acres, the Green Mountain National Forest occupies half of all the publicly owned land in Vermont. The boundaries of the southern half of the forest encircle the entire southwestern corner of the state. From around U.S. 7 to the western border it's settled, if clearly rural, country, characterized by small picturesque hamlets like Danby, larger towns such as Bennington and Manchester, and dairy farms and hay fields everywhere in between. Most of this land is in private hands. The quintessential experience of the Green Mountain National Forest, however, begins when you leave settled areas along U.S. 7 or State Route 100 and begin winding up one of the "gaps" into the rugged spine of the Green Mountains. Your car labors up ever-steeper grades and around ever-tighter hairpin curves; your ears pop; the scenery outside the window changes from settled farmland to hardwood forest to high-country spruce and fir; the air temperature drops 10°. And then you see the sign, gold paint on brown wood, that says NOW ENTERING THE GREEN MOUNTAIN NATIONAL FOREST. You've entered the wild side of Vermont, a place very different from the sweet, rolling countryside of the valleys; here you see Moose Crossing signs, it snows three times as much as in the valleys, and you can really imagine that wild catamounts still roam unseen.

The forest-service headquarters functions as a clearinghouse of recreational information, and it publishes the most useful maps. The South Half map is a good overall topographical map; if you want more detailed small-scale topos to specific areas of the forest, you can write or call for an index. The service's "Winter Recreation" map is a few years out of date but remains an indispensable guide to ferreting out the best cross-country and backcountry skiing.

The Long Trail

For information and maps: **Green Mountain Club,** State Rte. 100, P.O. Box 650, Waterbury Center, VT 05677 (☎ **802/244-7037;** www.greenmountainclub.org). Hiking.

The Long Trail, Vermont's long-distance, high-country hiking trail, is the oldest such trail in the nation. And it's still as its founders intended it to be—a narrow, unforgivingly rugged "footpath in the wilderness" that winds through all the best parts of Vermont's unassumingly rich and beautiful country. By all means, go whole hog and devote the four weeks or so necessary for an end-to-end hike; it will be an unforgettable experience. I once met a man on the trail who'd walked from Massachusetts to Canada, found himself so loathe to leave the trail that he retraced his steps to Massachusetts, and was on his third rebound when we shared a lean-to for a night. Maybe he was a little crazy, but I can understand the impulse.

If, however, you can't afford to drop out of the world for that long, the many roads that carve through the mountains make perfect trailheads for day hikes or overnights to the parts of the mountains you most want to see. "The Long Trail," later in this chapter, fills in the details on using the trail.

Woodford State Park

State Rte. 9, 10 miles east of Bennington. ☎ **802/447-7169.** 103 campsites, public phone, picnic area. Map: USGS 7.5-min. Woodford. Canoeing, cross-country skiing, hiking, swimming.

This 400-acre area is centered around Adams Reservoir, a good swimming hole. Rowboats and canoes are available. There's a great network of backcountry cross-country ski trails here, too. Near Harriman and Somerset reservoirs, a Long Trail access point (see "Hiking and Backpacking," below, for details on the climb to Harmon Hill), and Bennington.

Shaftsbury State Park

State Rte. 7A, 10.5 miles north of Bennington. ☎ **802/375-9978.** Day use only, wheelchair-accessible rest rooms, picnic area. Bird watching, canoeing, hiking, swimming.

The lake here is a good spot to cool off on a hot afternoon or explore lazily in a canoe. Shaftsbury has one outstanding feature—its nature trail. It's a short jaunt around the 26-acre lake, but the trail passes through a lot of different little "natural zones"; there's a swampy area with cottonwood trees, a diverse hardwood forest (oaks, hornbeams, maples), and great bird watching. The trail also passes atop a glacial ***esker***—a weird, narrow ridge in the middle of an otherwise fairly flat area. Check in at the park entrance for a good nature guide to the trail.

Somerset Reservoir

Vehicle access: From State Rte. 9, 6 miles west of Wilmington, turn north onto Somerset Rd.; drive 9 miles. For information and maps: **Green Mountain National Forest,** 231 N. Main St., Rutland, VT 05701, (☎ **802/747-6700**), or the **U.S. Generating Company,** P.O. Box 218,

Harriman Station, Readsboro, VT 05350 (☎ **802/423-7700**). Picnic areas; boat ramp; marked trails for biking, hiking, cross-country skiing. Camping, canoeing, cross-country skiing, fishing, hiking, mountain biking.

Like Harriman Reservoir, this large lake is a great place to fish or canoe. It's a popular ice-fishing spot in wintertime, although it might be difficult to get here. Trails at the south end, where there's direct road access, are a little scant, but Somerset is also accessible off Kelley Stand Road, the access point for a mother lode of trails, backwoods ponds, and old logging roads. It's a walk of a little under a mile from the Grout Pond parking lot to the reservoir. As at Harriman, you can't camp on land right near the lake (the power company forbids it), but the forest service can give you a map showing the public lands where primitive camping is permitted.

Grout Pond Recreation Area

South off Kelley Stand Rd. (Arlington–West Wardsboro Rd.), 8 miles from Arlington, 7 miles from West Wardsboro. For information and maps: **U.S. Forest Service,** Manchester Ranger District, 2538 Depot St., Manchester, VT 05255 (☎ **802/362-2307**). Boat ramp; picnic area; campsites; lean-tos; rest rooms; marked trails for mountain biking, hiking, and cross-country skiing. Map: USGS 7.5-min. Stratton Mountain. Canoeing, cross-country skiing, hiking, mountain biking.

This might be my choice of venues if I just wanted to spend a week in the woods doing a variety of different things—and be a long way away from people while I was at it. Kelley Stand Road cuts right through the Green Mountains at one of their more intractable points, meaning that there's a lot of land here that will never see development. A slew of nearby trails (including the good old Long Trail) makes all sorts of multiday loop hikes an option. My suggestion for a 3- or 4-day ramble would be a Stratton Mountain–Stratton Pond–Bourn Pond–Branch Pond loop, beginning and ending right here at Grout Pond. A wonderful spot for canoeing and cross-country skiing as well.

Battenkill River

Accessible at various points, especially all the bridges, from State Rte. 7A or 313 in Manchester or Arlington. For information: **Manchester and the Mountains Chamber of Commerce,** R.R. 2, P.O. Box 3451, Manchester Center, VT 05255 (☎ **802/362-2100**). Canoeing, fishing, swimming.

Hallowed ground among fly anglers, the upper Battenkill is considered Vermont's best wild trout stream. Both Orvis, one of the top fly-fishing schools in the country (see "Fishing," below), and Manchester Village's **American Museum of Fly-Fishing** (☎ **802/362-3300**) are located nearby. The Battenkill is also one of the best rivers in southern Vermont for activities such as canoeing, swimming, and tubing.

West River/Jamaica State Park

From Jamaica, head 0.5 mile north on the town road. ☎ **802/874-4600.** 59 campsites, lean-tos, wheelchair-accessible rest rooms, public phone, picnic area, canoe/kayak access. Camping, cross-country skiing, fishing, hiking, kayaking, swimming.

The West River has what's arguably Vermont's best white water, after water releases from Ball Mountain Dam; the river is used to host national kayaking championship races. The upper reaches of the stream are runnable only by experts, while further down toward the Connecticut River the stream widens and slows. Good swimming holes and fishing are found at various points all along the West. Jamaica State Park offers campsites right on the river, a classic Vermont swimming hole, and a network of hiking/cross-country skiing trails.

Hapgood Pond Recreation Area
From Peru, head 1.75 miles northeast on Hapgood Pond Rd. ☎ **802/824-6456.** 28 campsites, picnic area, rest rooms. Camping, fishing, mountain biking, swimming.

The campsites are slightly removed from the pond, but the pond itself is a blessed place to take the kids swimming on a hot day. Good fishing for brookies and rainbows, nearby access to a rough but beautiful section of the Long Trail, and a lot of dirt roads and faded old logging roads that beckon mountain bikers.

Emerald Lake State Park
Off U.S. 7 near North Dorset. ☎ **802/362-1655.** Campsites, lean-tos, picnic area, wheelchair-accessible rest rooms, canoe/boat access, marked trails. Bird watching, canoeing.

This state park lies deep in the narrowest part of the Valley of Vermont, an area that separates the Taconics from the Green Mountains. Emerald Lake makes for serene canoeing, and Otter Creek picks up at the south end of the lake. Good birding on the open water, in the marshes, and on the woodland trails, which lead through a beautiful ash and hickory forest.

Lake St. Catherine State Park
Located 3 miles south of Poultney on State Rte. 30. ☎ **802/287-9158.** 61 campsites, lean-tos, public phone, wheelchair-accessible rest rooms, picnic area, canoe/boating access, marked trails. Camping, fishing, swimming.

The campsites are ideally located on the shores of this 7-mile-long lake. Sandy beaches make for good swimming, and there's small- and largemouth bass, perch, pike, and walleye fishing in the lake. Big Trees nature trail rambles through meadows and woodlands that sport some true giants of the woods—maples, eastern white pines, and several enormous red oaks.

Calvin Coolidge State Park
From the junction of State Rte. 100 and 100A in Plymouth, head 2 miles north on State Rte. 100A. ☎ **802/672-3612.** 60 campsites, lean-tos, public phone, wheelchair-accessible rest rooms, picnic area, marked trails. Hiking.

A network of hiking trails traverses this large 16,165-acre preserve, and not too far away is the trail up Shrewsbury Peak, one of the few lofty Green Mountain peaks that the makers of the Long Trail didn't feel compelled to include on their route.

Ascutney State Park
From U.S. 5 between Windsor and Ascutney, take State Rte. 44A north 1 mile to Mount Ascutney Rd. The park is about a mile up this road to the left. ☎ **802/674-2060.** Campsites, lean-tos, public phone, wheelchair-accessible rest rooms, picnic area, marked trails. Bird watching, camping, hiking.

Located near the base of knoblike Mount Ascutney, this park has excellent camping. A day hike up Ascutney is a popular outing, offering expansive views from the summit and good hawk-watching.

What to Do & Where to Do It

BIRD WATCHING

Old, clunky, and more than a little heavy, my trusty pair of binoculars can seem less and less essential when I'm stuffing my pack for a backcountry trip. But I can't bear to leave them behind when I head for the Green Mountains: More than 270 species of birds have been documented in the state, and I never know when I'll be graced by the sight of a golden eagle or peregrine falcon wheeling above the crag ahead, an egret or heron stoically picking through a marsh, or the silent shadow of a great horned owl blacking out the moon on a frosty night.

I won't have space here to do much more than run through the kinds of birds you're likely to see through the seasons in the wetland areas, northern hardwood and boreal forests, and Alpine summits of southern Vermont—these are the "life zones," as biologists like to say, that make up the great part of Vermont's lands.

Up in the hills or down in the valleys, you'll find spring and fall the richest seasons for birding. The two lowland corridors that bracket the state—in the east, the Connecticut River Valley, and in the west, the Valley of Vermont (between the Taconics and the southern Green Mountains) and the broad Champlain Valley—are major conduits of the Atlantic Flyway, the aerial superhighway along which migratory birds pass on their way between southern wintering grounds and breeding grounds in the Arctic.

Marshes, bogs, and calm inshore waters draw abundant **waterfowl,** including mallards, black ducks, wood ducks, huge numbers of ring-billed gulls, Canada and snow geese, blue- and green-winged teal, great blue herons, black-crowned night herons, and many other birds. New England's bogs and swamps also are popular with birders for the many **songbirds** that nest in them almost exclusively, including Nashville warblers, black-backed woodpeckers, and olive-sided flycatchers. Two places in southern Vermont to check out are the **West Rutland Marsh,** off State Route 4A (you can walk the gravel roads or canoe through the marsh; go to the West Rutland Town Hall, at Marble and Main Streets, ☎ **802/438-2263,** for more information) and the fascinating pitcher-plant, sphagnum moss, and black spruce environment of the **North Springfield Bog** (State Route 11 west from Springfield; first right onto Fairground Road; park at the sand pit next to the town garage). The marshes at the junction of many feeder streams and rivers and the **Connecticut River** are also prime birding spots; you might see great blue herons, bitterns, and spotted sandpipers. And the **Black Gum Swamp,** in the town of Vernon in the far southeast corner of the state, with its rare stands of centuries-old black gum trees, is a spot for varied forest- and wetlands-dwelling birds (right onto Pond Road about a mile south of Vernon off State Route 142; 1 mile, then right onto Huckle Hill Road; 1 mile, then right onto Basin Road and park at road's end; call Vernon's town clerk, ☎ **802/257-0292,** for more information).

The open waters draw diving species like buffleheads, goldeneyes, and ring-necked ducks. And although loons are much more common in northern Vermont, New Hampshire, and especially Maine, pairs of these birds—whose maniacal laughing call is one of the most unforgettable sounds of a summer night in the wilderness—nest as far south as the **Somerset Reservoir.**

An event to plan around is the migration in March and October of tens of thousands of **snow geese**—sometimes as many as 20,000 in a flock. The Champlain Valley is the best place to watch this spectacle, but you'll have plenty of opportunity around the lakes of southwest Vermont.

Hardwood forests—a mix of maples, beeches, birches, aspen, and occasional stands of softwood white pine and hemlock that dominate the wooded landscape—are being infiltrated more and more by seed- and nut-bearing hickories, various species of oaks, and hop hornbeams in southern Vermont, particularly in the Taconics. Here and throughout the forested areas of southern Vermont, you might see yellow-bellied sapsuckers, more than a dozen species of warblers, flycatchers, hermit thrushes—Vermont's state bird—and year-round residents such as black-capped chickadees, blue jays, ruffed grouse, white-breasted nuthatches, and woodpeckers, along with turkeys.

Other good hardwood-forest birding spots in the area include the nature and hiking trails in **Lake St. Catherine State Park** (see "Road Biking," below); the trails around **Big Equinox** and **Equinox Pond** (a map is available at the Equinox Hotel on State Route 7A in Manchester); the **Healing Springs Nature Trail** at **Shaftsbury State Park** (a mix of oak forest and marsh—watch for herons and cedar waxwings; located on State Route 7A, 4 miles south of Arlington; pick up a trail guide at the park concession); the **Wantastiquet Mountain** hike that leads to an overlook of Brattleboro (trailhead off Bridge Street just across the Connecticut River in New Hampshire); and the **Springweather Nature Area,** a really fine and varied birding area (State Route 106 north from Springfield; right on Reservoir Road at 2.5 miles; nature area will be on your left).

Up above 3,000 feet in the Green Mountains, in the spruce and fir **boreal forests,** spring and summer bring great numbers of warblers, Swainson's and other thrushes, spruce grouse, scarlet tanagers, sapsuckers, flycatchers, and rose-breasted grosbeaks, among others. And on Vermont's highest peaks, those nearing or exceeding 4,000 feet, the last tortured-looking stunted balsam firs (called "krummholz") give way to an **arctic/Alpine region** of bare rock, lichens and mosses, and low shrubs (only Camel's Hump and Mount Mansfield further north support true "Alpine tundra" plant communities). This is a very difficult environment for life to maintain a foothold in, but it is still home to nesting ravens and dark-eyed juncos, gray-cheeked thrushes, and blackpoll warblers. Hike up into the boreal forest on any of the biggest peaks of the southern Greens, such as **Killington Peak, Shrewsbury Peak, Bromley Mountain,** and **Stratton Mountain** (all accessible from the Long Trail), as well as **Mount Equinox** near Manchester (accessible either by the Sky Line Drive toll road, off State Route 7A about 6 miles south of Manchester, or by a strenuous day hike from Burr & Burton Seminary, just off State Route 7A in Manchester Village via Seminary Avenue). You can get up into the mountains by chairlift in summertime and during foliage season at **Mount Snow,** Stratton, and Killington, as well as under your own steam.

Any open summit is also, of course, a good place to station yourself for fall **hawk migrations.** Sharp-shinned, broad-winged, Cooper's, red-winged, and red-shouldered hawks, goshawks, ospreys, and the occasional golden eagle, bald eagle, or peregrine falcon (master of the 175-m.p.h. bullet dive) are all seen aloft from early September to the end of November. The best spots in Vermont are the isolated peaks, such as **Mount Ascutney** in the Connecticut River Valley—they create an updraft that makes flying easy for the birds. (A paved road and hiking trail ascend to the summit from Ascutney State Park; left off U.S. 5, north of Ascutney.) Peregrines, once nearly extirpated from New England, are nesting again in a few of the steep crags they've historically occupied in Vermont, including **Hawk Ledge** (also great for watching its namesake) on Birdseye Mountain near West Rutland (2.5 miles west of town in Birdseye Mountain Park on the south side of State Route 4A; North Peak Trail 1.5 miles to Castle Peak Trail, Castle Peak Trail just under 1 mile to Hawk Ledge; contact **Bird Mountain WMA** at ☎ **802/483-2314** for closings to protect birds).

My personal favorites among New England's birds are **owls.** Great horned owls are all over the woods, while screech owls are found in hardwood forests and aren't uncommon in residential parts of towns. Saw-whet owls live in stands of coniferous woods (especially pine and eastern hemlock), and snowy owls are particularly fond of wide, open fields. The amazing thing about owls is their responsiveness to calls; you can go out with a flashlight and a tape player and a recording of owl calls (make an edited recording of the owl calls from Roger Tory Peterson's ***Field Guide to Bird Songs of Eastern and Central North America,*** Cornell University, 1983) or nothing but your own imitations of owl hoots. If you're game for the latter, try ***hoo-hoo-hoo, hoooo-hoooo***—the call of the great horned owl—with the last two hoots descending a little in pitch. On a clear, cold, and calm moonlit night in November or December, just drive along one of the dirt roads that proliferate all over the state. Stop here and there and play or sing the calls, keeping an eye peeled for the silhouette of your owl. It can be an amazing experience.

Another cold-weather birding highlight is the annual ritual of the National Audubon Society's **Christmas Bird Counts** (CBC). Within a week or two on either side of the holiday, local chapters of the society venture out into the frigid Vermont winter for an entire day of counting the different species and individual numbers of birds they can find within their area. I've never done it, but it sounds like one of those activities that offers an esprit de corps and unique sense of the wild that more than makes up for the hardship of dealing with the elements. CBCs are currently held in southern Vermont in Rutland, Bennington, Brattleboro, Saxton's River, and Springfield; contact the Vermont office of the **National Audubon Society** (**☎ 802/434-3068**) for info on how to get involved.

See the other Vermont chapters in this book for other nearby birding opportunities, and check the section on birding in chapter 1 for various local organizations and guidebooks. Serious birders can get a complete checklist of species observed in Vermont from the **Vermont Department of Fish and Wildlife,** 103 S. Main St., 10 South, Waterbury, VT 05671-0501 (**☎ 802/241-3700;** www.anr.state.vt.us/fw/fwhome/index.htm).

CANOEING

Vermont's three great canoeing waterways—the Missisquoi, Lamoille, and Winooski rivers—are up north, but the southern third of the state has a lot of good paddling nevertheless. The **West River** in springtime is probably the best white-water run Vermont has to offer. There's good and fairly long novice and intermediate paddling runs on the **Connecticut River, Otter Creek,** and the **Battenkill.** And I found a couple of unspoiled ponds that offer interesting, varied shorelines and perfect spots for primitive camping—the locals are going to kill me for revealing these!

Quiet Water

Grout Pond

West of Stratton. Access: Take Grout Pond Rd. 1 mile south off Kelley Stand Rd. (Arlington–West Wardsboro Rd.); 12 miles east of Arlington, 7 miles west of West Wardsboro. Primitive camping permitted.

Seeing ghostly mists over glass-smooth water become suffused with early morning sun, or listening to an amphibian choir warm up at twilight—these are the serene and magical experiences that you find at an undeveloped backwoods pond. Grout Pond is deep in one of the wildest and loveliest parts of the Green Mountain National Forest; although small, it's a perfect place to retreat for a day or two in the woods. Make this your last paddle of the year and you'll be treated to the kaleidoscopic fall colors. Strung around the shoreline are tent sites with fire rings, as well as several lean-tos and a cabin. It's a beautiful place to fish—sunnies, yellow perch, some bass; on the small side but all good eating. Paddle down toward the south end of the pond in the early morning or evening and you'll undoubtedly see beavers hard at work. There are lots of good hiking trails around, too, including a loop around the pond, a walk south from the pond to the north end of Somerset Reservoir, a precipitous climb up Stratton Mountain, and the Long Trail, accessible a couple miles west along Kelley Stand Road.

Branch Pond

East of Arlington. Access: Take Branch Pond Rd. 2 miles north off Kelley Stand Rd. (Arlington–West Wardsboro Rd.); 8 miles east of Arlington, 13 miles west of West Wardsboro. 0.25-mile carry to pond from parking area. Primitive camping permitted.

Much the same kind of place as Grout Pond (see above), but even more remote and smaller (a mere 40 acres compared with 86 acres). There are some really nice tent sites here, but you'll be happier in late summer or early fall if you're camping—I was eaten alive by mosquitoes here in June. The general bogginess of the pond, which makes paddling the shoreline so interesting, probably has a lot to do with the bug situation.

Gale Meadows Pond

North of Bondville. Access: Take River Rd. north of Bondville, turning left 0.8 mile later onto Gale Meadows Rd. Follow this road for 0.9 mile until you see a fork in the road. Bear left and follow until you reach a small parking lot and boat launch area.

Rare is the day when you'll find other humans on the waters of Gale Meadows. In their place are nesting wood ducks. Nestled within a forest of hardwoods and ferns, this 210-acre pond is a perfect spot for bird watching and fishing. Brownies, yellow perch, and largemouth bass are a few of the fish found in the pond.

Quick Water

Otter Creek, North Dorset to Rutland

31 miles, mostly quick water; portages at South Wallingford (Class III ledges) and Wallingford (dams, Class II rapids). Best put-ins at North Dorset, east off U.S. 7, 1 mile north of Emerald Lake onto dirt road; and at northernmost bridge in Wallingford. Last take-out in Rutland, River St. Bridge—dam is not far beyond. Maps: USGS 15-min. Wallingford, 7.5-min. Rutland.

Otter Creek's best paddling sections are a bit farther north, but even here, close to the creek's source, you can have yourself a fine afternoon's run. It's runnable only in late spring, and then it's still quite narrow, with an occasional fallen log to contend with. Probably the most consistently runnable section (and the way to avoid any portages) is from just north of Wallingford where Otter Creek is joined by the Mill River, and up to Rutland.

Battenkill River, Manchester to New York State Line

10.5 miles. Mostly flat and quick water, with some small rapids. No portages, but very possibly you'll need to carry or paddle your canoe around fallen trees; there's a washed-out dam at second bridge in Arlington. Put-in: east on Union St. from town square in Manchester about 0.75 mile; enter water below bridge. Take-outs: State Rte. 313 bridge in Arlington; any of the bridges from Arlington to state line. Maps: USGS 7.5-min. Manchester, Sunderland, Arlington.

The Battenkill comes close to exemplifying every pastoral stereotype people have about Vermont: swimmin' holes and cold waters ("invigorating" for the hardy) that are heaven-sent when the mercury climbs in August; wild, wise old brown trout and brookies, and the requisite fly anglers hell-bent on landing them; silos and Holsteins seemingly everywhere you look; and, when it's really hot, a lot of unusual watercraft competing for current with you—enormous inner tubes, rafts, floating chaise lounges, and the like.

The Manchester-Arlington section of the Battenkill is fairly narrow for the most part, and you may have to line around fallen trees here and there. At the mouth of Roaring Branch are some Class II rapids around which you can carry on the right bank if you want. The river widens out a bit as it departs Arlington, and from then on it's smooth, fast sailing all the way to the border.

Connecticut River, Bellows Falls to Brattleboro

17 miles. Easy; flat and quick water. No portages. Put-in: below dam at Bellows Falls. Take-out: Rte. 9 bridge to Keene, N.H., just above Brattleboro. Maps: USGS 15-min. Bellows Falls, Keene, Brattleboro.

An effortless paddle through Hallmark-perfect farming country. Good bass and pike fishing. Bring along some floatin' music—Hoagy Carmichael is just about the right speed. You could continue on, through deadwater for the most part, to Vernon Dam, but then you'll have to take-out within sight of Vermont Yankee, a nuke plant that I've been terrified of since I was a kid.

White Water

The few good white-water runs in southern Vermont are found on tributaries of the Connecticut River; among them are the **Black River** near Cavendish, the **Williams River** from Chester to Brockways Mills, **Saxton's River** from Grafton to Saxton's River Village, and the **Winhall River** and **Wardsboro Brook,** two tributaries to the West River. All of these are runnable for just a few weeks in spring, and they can be sufficiently treacherous that only truly competent paddlers and those under a guide's supervision should attempt them. See "Outfitters," below, if you're looking for a guide.

The **West River** is the most consistently navigable and most famous of southern Vermont's white-water streams—it's well known for the races it hosts on dam-release weekends in spring and fall. The lower sections are fairly safe for intermediate paddlers.

West River, Townshend Dam to Connecticut River

19 miles. Quick water and Class I and II rapids (mostly the former). No portages. Put-in: below the dam on east (town) side of river, between dam and covered bridge. Take-out: under I-91 bridge at State Rte. 30. Maps: USGS 15-min. Brattleboro.

I'll leave the pulse-raising upper reaches of the West—where lurk ornery Class III and IV rapids such as the Londonderry Ledges and the Dumplings below Ball Mountain Dam—to the experts, who already know about this place, and to those of you who want to take on white-water challenges under the watchful eye of outfitters and instructors. The lower section of this river is neither as scenic nor as daunting, but it is an excellent place to practice technique in fast currents and moderate rapids. Water levels are optimal during the Ball Mountain Dam releases and fairly rainy periods. The rapids that take the most concentration here are those right underneath the West Dummerston covered bridge—stay to the right.

The spring and fall releases from the Ball Mountain Dam, just upstream from Jamaica, usually occur during the last weekends of April and September. Call the **Department of Forests, Parks & Recreation** in North Springfield for more information, ☎ **802/886-2215.**

Outfitters

Battenkill Canoe, Ltd. U.S. 7A, Arlington, VT 05250 (☎ **802/362-2800;** www.battenkill.com), located on the river, offers daily rentals. They also feature 2-, 3-, and 5-day inn-to-inn trips on Vermont's finest waterways.

Canoe the lower Connecticut with **North Star Canoes,** N.H. 12A, Cornish, NH (☎ **603/542-5802**), situated just across the river from Windsor, Vermont. The check-in desk is in the owner's barn. They offer full- and half-day trips.

Both **Crabapple Whitewater, Inc.,** HC 63 Box 25, The Forks, ME 04985 (☎ **800/553-RAFT;** www.crabappleinc.com), and **North American Whitewater Expeditions,** Rte. 201, West Forks, ME 04985 (☎ **800/RAPIDS-9;** www.nawhitewater.com), offer guided rafting trips down the West in late April and September (think foliage). The day trip costs $90 and includes a hearty cookout lunch. Minimum age is 12 years old and minimum weight is 90 pounds.

CROSS-COUNTRY SKIING

Vermont, of course, goes way back with cross-country skiing—Nordic skiing first took hold in the United States on trails through the valleys and woods of the Green Mountain State, and legends such as the Von Trapp family and Olympic medalist Bill Koch made their names here.

But let's cut to the chase: Vermont has an unbelievable wealth of cross-country opportunities, including dozens of Nordic skiing centers offering traditional striding tracks and groomed skating trails; lift-serviced areas where numerous telemarkers make their elegant lunges amid all the Lycra-clad mogul-bashers. There is limitless challenge and variety on snow-covered trails and unplowed forest roads criss-crossing the Green Mountains; the Catamount Trail, a long-distance trail that will soon stretch continuously from Canada to Massachusetts (see chapter 4, "Lake Champlain, the Northern Green Mountains & the Northeast Kingdom," for details); and finally, a huge network of marked trails overseen by VAST (Vermont Association of Snow Travelers). The latter are primarily for snowmobiles (one of which every self-respecting Vermont teenager simply must own), but they're great for skiing, too. Sure, Vermonters go to the ski-touring centers, but sometimes picking out your own route among the "snowmachine" tracks and bushwhacks available just beyond your backyard is the most satisfying thing you can do on skis.

In the Backcountry

The network of trails that guide hikers through the Green Mountain National Forest in the summer entices backcountry skiers come snow time. Miles and miles of trails leave you at serene ponds or atop small summits rarely visited in the winter. Backcountry skiing is a chance to soothe your soul on skis in a pastoral setting far away from the crowds who cruise downhill or venture to Nordic skiing centers. A helpful guide is the **"Winter Recreation"** map of the **Green Mountain National Forest,** 231 N. Main St., Rutland, VT 05701 (☎ **802/747-6700**). There is also a **cross-country ski report** available by phone, recorded every Thursday (☎ **802/828-3239**). Contact the **Catamount Trail Association,** P.O. Box 1235, Burlington, VT 05402 (☎ **802/864-5794;** www.catamounttrail.together.com), for a map of the 200-mile Catamount Trail (see chapter 4 for more information). For trail and membership information about 3,500 miles of groomed snowmobile trails, contact the **Vermont Association of Snow Travelers,** P.O. Box 839, Montpelier, VT 05601 (☎ **802/229-0005;** www.vtvast.org).

Worth a special mention here is the **Merck Forest & Farmland Center,** located in Rupert, not far from the New York border, between Rutland and Manchester. The miles of rolling farmland and stands of sugar maples are home to a slew of ungroomed cross-country trails. There's a trail map available at the parking area. This is a great place to try your hand at winter camping. To get there from the junction of State Route 30 and State Route 315 in East Rupert, take State Route 315 west for 2.6 miles. Turn left and drive a half-mile to the parking lot and visitor center. (For more information on the Merck Forest, see "Hiking & Backpacking," below.)

The four tours below are all on or near the spine of the Green Mountains and are listed from south to north.

Harriman Reservoir

Allow 2–4 hr. Moderate; logging road with gradual ascent. Access: From Wilmington, take State Rte. 9 west for 3 miles until you spot a bridge on the left. Cross over it, take another left, and drive for 0.2 mile. You'll see a blue Catamount X-C Skiing diamond hanging from a tree. Parallel-park on the left side of the road. Map: GMNF Winter Recreation map.

This old logging road owned by the New England Power Company is the southernmost portion of the Catamount Trail. The trail runs alongside the Deerfield River before swerving right and going uphill, providing vistas high above the Harriman Reservoir. You can continue on this trail the whole length of the reservoir to Readsboro if you like.

On the cold day on which I set forth on this trail, the Deerfield River looked positively arctic. Steam rose from the rushing rapids as the dark blue waters carved through a mix of ice and hard snow. I glided alongside the river, taking in the arresting sight before the trail took a sharp right and headed uphill. Ascending gradually past several dilapidated houses and old logging operations, I started to think that the trail was turning into a dud. But soon the path leveled off and the rusted RVs were replaced by magnificent views of the reservoir. Through the barren maples, oaks, and birches, I could see ice anglers standing on the frozen lake.

I turned around at the point where a spit of land juts eastward, but you might feel like going considerably farther, which is certainly possible. If not, it's an easy downhill glide back to the Deerfield River and your car.

Woodford State Park

Loop trail; allow 1.5 hr. Easy to moderate; rolling terrain. Access: From Wilmington, take State Rte. 9 west for 9.6 miles. Parking is located on a side road 0.2 mile past the country store on the right side of State Rte. 9. Parallel park on the side road. Carefully walk across Rte. 9. The trail starts behind a gate on the left side of the road. Map: GMNF Winter Recreation map.

The Vermont license plates on cars parked across State Route 9 from Woodford State Park say it all—this is a trail that only locals know about and one I'm sure they would prefer to keep to themselves. It's a loop through beautiful winter scenery,over frosted ponds, and under dense evergreens. If you're in southern Vermont for only a day or two, this is a good trail to take.

One bit of winter magic that every Vermonter is aware of is the way snow levels seem to rise the minute you begin ascending into the Green Mountain National Forest. There certainly was more than enough accumulation on the paths of Woodford State Park on the day my wife and I tried the trail. We began by cruising down a short hill before crossing iced-over Adams Reservoir. At Campsite 23, we veered right and started our loop around the park. It was early morning; sunlight glistened off branches heavy with snow. The only sound we heard was the rapid patter of a woodpecker overhead. You'll have a lot of options for miniloops as you glide along, and the main trail coasts up and down short hills and over rushing brooks before returning you to the starting point.

Somerset Reservoir

4 miles round-trip; allow 2–3 hr. Easy; evergreen/hardwood forest and open meadows; mild rolls in pitch. Access: From West Wardsboro on State Rte. 100, turn west at the West Wardsboro store and continue for 7 miles on Kelly Stand Rd. (Arlington–West Wardsboro Rd.). There's a parking area at the end of the plowed section. Map: GMNF Winter Recreation map.

In a region of the Green Mountain National Forest known for its wealth of cross-country skiing trails, Somerset Reservoir is one of the finest. The 4-mile round-trip trail straddles a brook before crossing an open meadow that leads to the large body of water. Vistas of Mount Snow's North Face ski trails carved into the mountain can be seen on the far shores.

When I pulled into the parking lot here early on a Saturday morning, there was already a buzz in the air. Unfortunately, the noise came from numerous snowmobilers whipping down Kelly Stand Road. It sounded like the Indianapolis 500. I quickly threw on my skis and headed across the street to the start of the trail, hurrying toward peace and quiet. Several vigorous strides later, I began to breathe fresh air instead of fumes. The noise faded, replaced by the singing of birds. It seems few snowmobilers use this choppy but relatively flat trail, even on busy weekends.

The trail wound along a small brook known as the East Branch of the Deerfield River. The creek was barely visible beneath its blanket of snow, except for several holes where I could see water rushing by. Mountain ash and snow-laden evergreens lined the trail, with branches so burdened I had to duck many times to avoid being decapitated—remember to watch your head out here.

As I reached the point where the East Branch opens into the Somerset Reservoir, I found with some dismay that the buzz was back. Groups of snowmobilers were cruising on the iced-over waters, but the view was so majestic that I didn't care. You can follow the snowmobilers and ski on Somerset to get a closer view of Mount Snow—I skied over to where the stone levees stood before turning around.

If you want to extend the trip, go back to where you veered right onto Somerset and simply continue straight ahead. This 2.8-mile loop leads you to Grout Pond—one of the more serene and unspoiled little lakes I know of—and then back to the middle of the Somerset trail.

Mount Tabor Road Trail

Loop trail; allow 2.5–3 hr. Moderate to strenuous; narrow, occasionally steep trails through deep woods. Access: From Manchester, take State Rte. 11 east. Keep left through the village of Peru and continue 4.5 miles until you reach the Landgrove Town Hall. Turn left and drive for 0.7 mile before you take another left where the road forks. Cross a brook and take your first right onto Forest Rd. 10. Parallel park on the right-hand side of the road, avoiding the plowed turnaround area. Map: GMNF Winter Recreation map.

The Mount Tabor Road Trail has a misleading name: You ski on this unplowed road for only 5 minutes before veering left onto a winding narrow path that sweeps up and down short hills. Once you get the hang of this roller-coaster ride, the trail suddenly climbs steeply up the side of a mountain ridge, leaving you high atop the Green Mountain National Forest. Several logging roads intersect the trails, making an already complicated route even more so—you'll do well to get the map. The trail is a good workout through pretty wild country.

The day I set out on this trail was accompanied by steady snowfall. By the time I parked my car in this remote region of southern Vermont, 6 inches of powder covered the ground, with the flakes still coming down. My diagonal stride felt as smooth and effortless as a Fred Astaire dance. I took Mount Tabor Road (Forest Road 10) for less than 0.2 mile and then made a left onto the Utley Brook Trail, marked with the diamond for "most dangerous." A better name would have been the Hallucinogen Trail, because whoever designed this path must have been on some serious drugs. The trail weaves up and down slopes and turns sharply left or right without warning. It's also extremely narrow—only wide enough, mostly, for one svelte skier. Don't daydream or you might end up impaled on the trunk of an evergreen.

I was dizzy by the time I found myself looking up at the ridge of Pete Parent Peak. Instead of following the trail's blue diamonds and attacking the uphill climb, I took a left and followed another skier's tracks rapidly disappearing under the new snow. They brought me straight to the backdoor of his farmhouse. I guess I was destined to climb the 400 feet up Utley Brook Trail. I learned a valuable lesson—stick to the blue diamonds.

I climbed past a family of yellow birches and numerous uprooted oaks before reaching the top of the ridge, where a pair of black-capped chickadees congratulated me. A left onto Little Michigan Trail and another quick left brought me to the Stone Place Trail. Speeding downhill, I heard rustling in the branches of an evergreen and suddenly two wild turkeys appeared, flying to the lead.

From here the trail is quite an orienteering challenge: Continuing on Stone Place Trail, I veered right at a road and left across Griffith Brook. One mile later, the trail curves left onto Jones Brook Trail, a sweeping path that gently slopes downhill across fields of short brush and dense forests of hardwoods. I was just beginning to have fun when Jones Brook Trail abruptly ended at another logging road. A left turn brought me to a steep downhill, at which point I had to take off my skis and walk through a gracious farmer's backyard. A left and a quick right back to Forest Road 10 brought me to my snowed-in car.

Nordic Skiing Centers

In Vermont, it seems like every inn has its own network of Nordic trails. There are literally thousands of miles of trails crisscrossing the state, and the **Catamount Trail** has taken advantage of it, weaving trails from many Nordic skiing centers into the state-long run.

The task of choosing one Nordic skiing center above the rest can be daunting, given the limitless array of choices. However, you won't go wrong with any of the centers listed below, in south-to-north order.

The **White House Touring Center,** 178 Route 9 East, Wilmington (☎ **802/464-2136;** www.whitehouseinn.com), located in the foothills of Mount Snow and Haystack Mountain, offers 45 kilometers (28.1 miles) of trail and a base elevation of 1,573 feet (high enough to mean fairly reliable snow). The White House is a hundred-year-old classical mansion that is now a bed-and-breakfast (see "Inns & Resorts," below). Trails tend to cater to intermediates.

Prospect Ski Mountain, State Route 9, Woodford, 05201 (☎ **802/442-2575;** www.prospectmountain.com), on the Bennington side of State Route 9, is an old ski hill that now offers 50 kilometers (31.25 miles) of scenic and well-maintained groomed trails, with an emphasis on wide skating lanes. It also is a jumping-off point for a nearly unlimited number of backcountry ski trails.

If you're lucky enough to be staying in the Old Tavern in Grafton (see "Inns & Resorts," below), don't miss the opportunity to cross-country ski at **Grafton Ponds Cross-Country Ski Center,** Grafton (☎ **802/843-2400;** www.old-tavern.com), just down the road. A 30-kilometer (18.75-mile) trail system starts from the center's log cabin, winding through the forested hillside and over long meadows that offer good views of the historic village. There's another 30 kilometers (18.75 miles) of backcountry trails behind Bear Mountain. Five kilometers (3.1 miles) of snowmaking help to overcome its low elevation in the valley floor.

Situated on the outskirts of the Green Mountains' Lye Brook Wilderness Area, **Viking Center,** Little Pond Road, R.R. Box 70, Londonderry (☎ **802/824-3933;** www.vikingnordic.com), is one of the oldest New England Nordic skiing centers. The 40 kilometers (25 miles) of trails (30km—18.75 miles—of which are groomed) have been challenging all levels of skiers for over 30 years. Open fields and gentle trails are ideal for beginners; experts will find long winding runs in the hills in the outer trail system.

Located in a remote part of the Green Mountain National Forest, the elegant **Landgrove Inn,** Landgrove (☎ **800/669-8466** or 802/824-6673; www.landgroveinn.com), is better known for its food and lodging than skiing. The 15 miles of groomed trails can often feel like a maze, but that won't matter once you get back to the fireplace in your room (see "Inns & Resorts," below).

Close by, **Wild Wings Ski Touring Center,** Peru, VT 05152 (☎ **802/824-6793**), offers 25 km of groomed trails in the Green Mountain National Forest. There's usually snow here when there isn't much elsewhere—elevations are up around 2,000 feet. The touring center is an old converted horse barn, the atmosphere is decidedly low-key and family-friendly.

Downhill Skiing/Snowboarding

Alpine skiing is right up there with leaf-peeping as one of the pursuits that put Vermont on the tourism map. Vermont's been synonymous with skiing since 1934, when a Ford Model T engine was installed on a hill near Woodstock to power the nation's first rope tow (little Suicide Six now occupies the spot). As recently as 10 years ago, there were still rope tows here and there, along with other Stone-Age relics such as J-bars, poma lifts, all-natural snow, and grizzled, flannel-clad mountain men on skis. But two decades of frantic work to keep pace with Rocky Mountain skiing have changed the face of Vermont skiing. Now we have trams and detachable quads, 100% snowmaking coverage, grooming on even the steepest of steeps, and grizzled, flannel-clad snowboarders. Every year there are more trails, more lifts, more lines, more condos, more people. What keeps 'em coming? And what has all this development meant to the quality of the skiing?

Well, the big draw is Vermont's mountains: They're ***big*** mountains by almost anyone's standards—there are 10 ski areas here with vertical drops of 2,000 feet or more, second only to Colorado's 16. The mountains themselves may not be the 12,000-footers you'd find in the Rockies or the Alps, but ski areas here take full advantage of what they've got. This means long runs and an amazing diversity of terrain. From windblown summits offering huge views and steep drops through gnarled fir trees; to glade skiing through spruce or hardwood forest; to wide-open cruising boulevards and bump runs that always have snow and can seem like a fashion runway; to alarmingly narrow, unpredictable trails that rarely have adequate cover—even after a big snow.

The big drawback of all the development, as far as I'm concerned, is the slow disappearance of the latter type of trail—the classic stuff of New England skiing—as ski areas widen and groom more and more trails. You'll still find plenty of these narrow, quirky trails farther north, at places like Stowe, Sugarbush, and Mad River.

Another reason the skiers keep coming is that Vermont's ski area operators become ever more wily in their annual battle against the elements, maintaining good machine-made snow cover on a variety of terrain through the most depressing of January thaws. Of course, there's nothing like natural snow; the excitement a big snowstorm sparks in eastern skiers is something to behold. The rare big powder day brings out hot skiers from all over the hills; and when you head up the mountain in the morning, the whoops and hollers you hear from people making first tracks below remind you how much fun skiing can be.

Southern Vermont, relatively close to Boston and New York, has ski hills that are very different from those you'll find in central and northern Vermont. The big areas here—Mount Snow, Stratton, Okemo, and Killington—are now thoroughly built up; there are scores of restaurants, bars, condos, and other resort standbys clustered around the base lodges. The skiing itself has been tailored to give huge numbers of intermediate skiers as much cruising satisfaction as they could ask for: much wider trails and more snowmaking than you'll find farther north, intense grooming that leaves trails buffed to a sheen every morning, generally a gentler pitch on the slopes, and both high lift capacity and a lot of skier traffic.

Ski Areas

The ski areas below are listed south to north, starting from the bottom of the state and driving straight up State Route 100—the carotid artery of Vermont ski area access, which runs east of the ridge of the Green Mountains.

Maple Valley

Rte. 30, West Dummerston, VT 05357. ☎ **802/254-6083;** www.skimaplevalley.com. 16 trails (37% beginner, 43% intermediate, 20% expert); 3 lifts including 2 triples. Full-day tickets: $28.

When Maple Valley decided to reopen in 1998 after being dormant for 3 years, Vermonters rejoiced at the opportunity to bring their kids to the same place where many of them first skied. Everything got an upgrade, including lifts, trails, night-skiing lights (the only resort in southern Vermont to offer night skiing), snowmaking, and the base lodge so that the resort could once again provide the type of family service for which it had been known for over 30 years. Without the lines and attitudes of the mega-resorts, Maple Valley, just outside of Brattleboro, provides the ideal slopes for young families. It also offers introductory snowboard lessons.

Mount Snow/Haystack

West Dover, VT 05356. ☎ **802/464-3333;** www.mountsnow.com. Snow report: ☎ 802/464-2151. 135 trails (20% beginner, 60% intermediate, 20% expert); 26 lifts including 3 quads, 10 triples, and 6 doubles; 1,700-ft. vertical drop. Full-day tickets $54.60 weekends/holidays, $51.45 weekdays.

For years Mount Snow has had a rep as a sort of magnet for singles from the cities; these days it's trying to attract more families. If you want a day of effortless high-speed cruising—on skis or on a snowboard—this is the place for you. Nearly the whole front face of the mountain is one broad, groomed, and well-covered boulevard after another, none of which will trouble you with difficulties beyond the optional jump or two. (I've never seen so many people seemingly obsessed with getting air—sometimes Mount Snow can look as if a huge herd of jackrabbits is hopping its way down the mountain.)

Mount Snow has an entire area reserved for neophytes, and anyone with a few days' confidence can comfortably handle all those extra wide intermediate trails. Experts will find some genuinely steep pitches on the North Face, but in my opinion all the grooming and snowmaking does an injustice to them—man-made snow on steep slopes seems to inevitably establish a base of rocklike hardpack, and on the steeps I'd rather pick my way down a nice, well-established line through big moguls than scrape and rattle across concrete. Home to the 2000 and 2001 ESPN Winter X Games, Snow is starting to attract more of the freestylers and hard-core snowboarders. The resort features two halfpipes and five terrain parks for all abilities.

Stratton

Stratton Mountain, VT 05155. ☎ **802/297-2200;** www.stratton.com. Snow report: ☎ 802/297-4211. 9 trails (35% beginner, 37% intermediate, 28% expert); 14 lifts including a 12-passenger gondola, 2 high-speed 6-passengers, 3 quads, 1 triple, and 2 doubles; 2,003-ft. vertical drop. Full-day tickets $59 weekends, $55 weekdays.

Get those spanking new outfits ready for Stratton, a mountain known for its Day-Glo dress code. It's a groomed, cruiser's mountain but with a little more variety than Mount Snow. It's also the birthplace of snowboarding—Jake Burton, founder of Burton Boards, did his experimenting here and is still king of the East as far as snowboarding is concerned. The halfpipe is perfectly maintained, and carving through Stratton's long boulevards is as good as it gets. In the past two years, the ski area spent over $17.5 million on improvements to snowmaking, trails, and lifts, and several years back it opened the new snowboard park on Suntanner. Tripled in size, the halfpipe has runs for both carvers and freeriders. They even have benches to give your frozen butt a break. Stratton also hosts North America's largest snowboarding contest, the U.S. Open.

Stratton has a new 10-trail "Learning Park" that's perfect for both first-timers and intermediates looking to bone up on the finer points of carved turns and bump skiing. And there's easy skiing from the summit at Stratton, a rare commodity that lets novices get the good snow and big-mountain views that they otherwise might have to write off with a rueful "Wait till next year." (No Red Sox pun intended, really.) Intermediates will like Supertrail, a wide avenue that has more going on than meets the eye. And yes, there are good moguls at Stratton—try Upper Middlebrook, Upper Spruce, and Free Fall.

Bromley
P.O. Box 1130, Manchester Center, VT 05255. ☎ **802/824-5522;** www.bromley.com. 42 trails (35% beginner, 34% intermediate, 31% expert); 9 lifts including 2 quads and 4 doubles; 1,334-ft. vertical drop. Full-day tickets weekends $47 adults, $40 teens, $31 juniors; weekdays $36 adults, $31 teens, $26 juniors.

Not nearly as overwhelming as the other Vermont ski resorts, Bromley is one of the oldest in the country. Lift lines are shorter, and people are more down-to-earth. Don't let the seemingly even distribution of terrain across the skill levels fool you—this is a novice and intermediate area with a good ski school and plenty of slowpoke and cruising terrain, but there's not much to keep the ambitious challenged. One secret about Bromley: If you've rolled all the way up from the city to find your family ski weekend caught in the deep freeze of a Vermont cold snap, this is the place. It faces ***south,*** and a little sun on such days really is the difference between misery and a good time.

Magic Mountain
Londonderry, VT. ☎ **802/824-5645;** www.magicmtn.com. 33 trails (30% beginner, 30% intermediate, 40% expert); 3 lifts including 1 quad and 1 triple; 1,600-ft. vertical drop. Full-day tickets $38 weekends, $28 weekdays.

This ski resort is loved by New Englanders who hate lift lines. Indeed, most of Magic's runs use nearly all of the 1,600-foot vertical drop, so you'll have top-to-bottom skiing on everything from the gentle Magic Carpet Trail to the steep glades of Twilight Zone. Views of the Greens, affordable lift tickets, and easy parking at the base lodge are added bonuses.

Okemo
77 Okemo Ridge Rd., Ludlow, VT 05149. ☎ **802/228-4041;** www.okemo.com. Snow report: ☎ 802/228-5222. 98 trails (25% beginner, 50% intermediate, 25% expert); 13 lifts including 7 quads and 3 triples; 2,150-ft. vertical drop. Full-day tickets $54 weekends, $49 weekdays.

On a day when you had to look ***really*** hard to find a dirty patch of snow on a Vermont hill, I went skiing at Okemo and finally learned that machine-made snow really could be a godsend. The snowmaking and grooming are so good here I'm half-surprised it doesn't stay open year-round. Intermediates always have loved and will continue to love Okemo. It's got tons of good cruising terrain, and the area will let moguls form from time to time on runs down the main face of the mountain that are pitched just right to give a learner a little bit of slack. Even Okemo's black and mogul runs are challenging yet doable for intermediate skiers. If I lose control, there's ample room to wipe out on the spacious trails without decapitating other skiers with my poles.

The black-diamond skiing used to be a little disappointing, but recent additions to South Face have produced some genuine white-knuckle trails. Still, if it's terror you want, Killington is more inspiring.

Ascutney Mountain

State Rte. 44, Brownsville, VT 05037. ☎ **802/484-7000;** www.ascutney.com. 49 trails (26% beginner, 39% intermediate, 35% expert); 4 lifts including 3 triples and 1 double; 1,530-ft. vertical drop. Full-day tickets $41 weekends, $36 weekdays.

Like nearby Bromley and Suicide Six, Ascutney Mountain is a great place to ski with the kids for a day or a week. This monadnock has plenty of easy skiing on which first-timers can get their footing, and there are meandering intermediate runs and a few shortish mogul trails to challenge the upwardly mobile.

Killington/Pico

4763 Killington Rd., Killington, VT 05751. ☎ **802/422-3333;** www.killington.com. Snow report: ☎ 802/422-3261. 200 trails (34% beginner, 33% intermediate, 33% expert); 30 lifts including two 8-passenger gondolas, 12 quads, 4 triples, and 5 doubles; 3,150-ft. vertical drop. Full-day tickets $52 all week.

With seven interconnected mountains and seven base lodges, Killington isn't just big, it's massive. After a week of skiing far more trail than you can keep track of, you still find yourself saying, "Oh yeah, I forgot all about *that* chairlift."

This can be both good and bad. You can get lost at Killington as easily as you might on the tangle of freeways through eastern New Jersey; the trail map might qualify as a one-volume encyclopedia; and when you do screw up, you may be looking at a skate over a quarter-mile flat to the nearest lift. Even with all those lifts and trails, you'll still run into some awful lift lines and bottlenecks on the hill. And watch out for the teenybopper hotdoggers who think they own the mountain. In short, this is just not the place to go if you're looking for skiing that has that sense (like all the best of Vermont) of the hand of humankind working in wholesome concert with the hand of nature.

Now for the good news: You'll simply never run out of skiing here, no matter what your level. Beginners and novices should take advantage of one of the best ski schools anywhere, a landmark learning hill in Snowshed, and good novice cruising runs in the Rams Head and Snowdon areas. Rams Head is relatively serene for Killington and has excellent intermediate cruisers as well—and check out Swirl if you're feeling particularly strong. Skye Peak has an avalanche of moderate to strong intermediate terrain—and even more skier traffic. The Glades and South Ridge chairs also have lots of intermediate cruisers. And speaking of glades, Killington, like several other eastern areas, is trying to take better advantage of the one thing the East has that the treeline-and-up areas of the Rockies and Sierra Nevada don't always have—trees. Killington has about 100 acres of tree-skiing they call the "fusion zones."

Onward to the steeps. Bear Mountain was probably the most-hyped ski-area improvement in Vermont history, and Outer Limits indeed has the buffalo-sized moguls and gut-wrenching pitch every Type-A bump freak dreams of. Hundreds of thoughtless onlookers on the chair and sidelines are dying to see you eat it—go ahead, prove them wrong. Me, I'm happier on the Killington Peak black diamonds like Cascade and Down Draft, the lesser lights on Bear Mountain, and East Fall and Royal Flush near the Snowdon area, all of which will tax you plenty.

The Skye Peak trails, Snowdon, and Glades—Killington abounds in good snowboarding possibilities. But take extra care to avoid those darn flats. Read those trail maps. And one last tip: If you're here on one of the busy weekends, park at the Sunrise Mountain Base Lodge off State Route 100, not the main Killington Base

Southern Vermont Ski & Winter Sports Shops

City	*Shop*	*Location*	*Telephone*	*Additional Services*
Brattleboro	Burrows Sports Shop	105 Main St.	802/254-9430	repairs; alpine-ski rentals (monthly or seasonal rentals only); in-line skating rentals
Mt. Snow	Bonkers Board Room	Dover Retail Center, Rte. 100, West Dover	802/464-2536	repairs; alpine-ski and snow-board rentals; snowboard demos
	World Class Ski Experts	Rte. 100, Brookhouse Complex, West Dover	802/464-8852	alpine-ski rentals and demos
	Equipt Sport	Mt. Snow Access Rd., West Dover	802/464-2222	repairs; alpine-ski, snowboard, snowshoe rentals; alpine-ski demos
Manchester	Manchester Sports	Rte. 7A	802/362-2569	repairs; cross-country ski rentals
Stratton/ Winhall	Equipe Sport	Junction 30 & 100, Rawsonville	802/297-2847	repairs; alpine-ski, cross-country ski, snowboard, and snowshoe rentals; alpine-ski demos
	North House	Rte. 30, Bondville	802/297-1755	repairs; alpine-ski, cross-country ski, ice skate, snow shoe, and snowboard rentals; alpine-ski demos
Okemo/ Ludlow	Sports Odyssey	Okemo Market Place	802/228-2001	repairs; alpine-ski, snowboard, and snowshoe rentals
	Totem Pole	16.5 Pond St.	802/228-8447	repairs; alpine-ski, snowboard, and snowshoe rentals; alpine-ski demos
	Northern Ski Works	10 Main St.	802/228-3344	repairs; alpine-ski, snowboard, bike, and in-line skating rentals; alpine-ski and snow board demos
Killington/ Pico	Dark Side Snow Board Shop	Killington Rd.	802/422-8600	repairs; snowboard rentals and demos
	Peak Performance	Killington Rd.	802/422-9447	repairs; alpine-ski rentals and demos
Rutland	The Great Outdoors Trading Company	219 Woodstock Ave.	802/775-9989	repairs; alpine-ski rentals and demos

Lodge; you'll save yourself a little time, as well as the sensation of being in a herd of neon-clad cattle.

Pico, next door, is now part of Killington. It offers a good breather and then some from wrestling that monster, especially on a powder day. The resort, opened way back in 1938, is a little short on true beginning terrain, but it has lots of fairly easy and interesting cruisers, peaking in difficulty with Pike and Forty-Niner. There's some tricky terrain at Pico, including bump runs like Summit Glade, Upper Giant Killer, and Sunset '71. Pico was one of the first Vermont hills to go snowboard-friendly, and it still draws a lot of stick-riders.

As for the après ski scene, Killington will always reign supreme for Eastern party-goers. The party rages from Friday night when Bostonians and New Yorkers arrive late, to Sunday afternoon when they crawl into their cars for the trek back home. To unwind after your day on the mountain, have a couple of drinks at Killington's base lodge. Then you can practice your pickup lines at Pickle Barrel's shoulder-to-shoulder dance floor or Wobbly Barn's downstairs bar. A little rusty? Make a last ditch effort to meet the love of your life at the late-hour private parties at ski houses. Hangovers and other extracurricular activities keep many ski bums off the slopes on Sunday until late morning.

FALCONRY

Reputed to be the oldest sport in the world (ca. 2000 B.C.), falconry was once a necessity as hunters needed to catch their prey for the evening meal. Even though supermarkets have replaced the need to venture out with hawks for sustenance, you can still enjoy this thrilling adventure in Manchester at the **British School of Falconry (☎ 802/362-4780)**, one of only two falconry schools in America. Guides will take you and their trained Harris hawks on a 4-hour hunt in a nearby preserve. Follow the hawks from treetop to treetop as they search for pheasant, quail, and partridge and the chase ensues.

I decided to forego the hunt and instead chose a 1.5-hour Hawk Walk with instructor Rob Waite. We took our two hawks and our leather gloves to a nearby dairy farm. Wearing a glove to protect my left hand from any scratches, I paid close attention as Rob showed me how to "cast" the hawk in a rolling motion of my out-stretched arm. The bird gracefully flew to a nearby tree branch. Atop his perch, the fidgety raptor was always on the lookout for prey, eyeing chipmunks or field mice. Its keen sight is said to be three times the eyesight of humans, so the hawk can always find something roaming around the Vermont fields. When I wanted the bird to return, I raised my hand and the hawk swiftly flew back to my arm. Being trained, the bird knows full well that a treat awaits—raw beef that Rob had put atop my glove. If you get excited when your dog comes to you at your call, just wait until you see a bird of prey quickly flying back to your arm. If you keep your arms down while walking, the hawks will follow you from tree to tree. If they find something scurrying, they make a beeline for the brush to try to capture it. A Hawk Walk is a wonderful introduction to these majestic creatures.

FISHING

The waters of southern Vermont harbor all the major sport fish you'll find elsewhere in the state. Wild cold-water species such as brook and rainbow trout are found in the upper watersheds of most of the big rivers (with "brookies" or "square-tails," as everyone calls them, particularly common in the purest, coldest streams and mountain ponds; and rainbows common in white water). The notoriously finicky brown trout is found (along with rainbows) in the middle part of these rivers and sometimes in the warmer waters downstream. Warm-water lakes and big rivers are rich fisheries for large- and smallmouth bass, landlocked salmon, lake trout, walleye, northern pike, yellow perch, sunfish, and smelt.

The 27-mile-long **Battenkill River** is famous for its wild trout fishing. It runs from Manchester Village south to Arlington, and then west into New York. In Vermont, its clear, cold waters harbor brown and brook trout. The trout are known for their elusiveness, perhaps due to the large population of anglers and the abundance of natural food. Most of the fly-fishing situations can be handled with a fly rod that takes a 6-weight line. However, if you have a rod that will take a 5- or 4-weight line, you have an even better chance of hooking a fish. The fishing season on the river extends from the second Saturday in April to the last Sunday in October. The fall months can provide some of the best fishing of the year—trout feed heavily as they sense the lean times of winter coming on. Other southern Vermont streams with wild trout include the tributaries and mid- to upper sections of the **Hoosic, Walloomsac, Green, Mettawee, Poultney** (try the stretch from Poultney to East Poultney for brookies; the upper river for brookies and rainbows), **Mill,** and **Castleton Rivers,** all west of the Green Mountains, and the **Deerfield, West, Saxton's,** and **Williams Rivers** east of the mountains.

The **Connecticut River's** fishing gets short shrift, considering the variety and health of its recreational fishery. Anglers try to hook yellow perch, walleye, smallmouth bass, pike, and pickerel—as well as shad, which are beginning to reestablish themselves after a long absence from the Connecticut, with more and more fish using the Vernon and Bellows Falls fish ladder every year. An Atlantic salmon run may not be far behind.

North of the Battenkill, **Lakes Bomoseen** and **St. Catherine** are replete with bass, lake trout, northern pike, and perch. **Otter Creek** is a warm-water stream good for northern pike and smallmouth bass. Many of the bigger fish, 15-inch rainbows and 13-inch browns, are stocked in the Danby area. In the large, still-unspoiled wild areas of the Green Mountain National Forest in the central south, the **Somerset** and **Harriman Reservoirs** offer exemplary trout, bass, pike, and perch fishing year-round.

If you're looking for more information, contact the **Vermont Fish and Wildlife Department,** 103 S. Main St., Waterbury, VT 05671-0501 (☎ **802/241-3700;** www.anr.state.vt.us/fw/fwhome), and ask for a "Vermont Fishing Kit." The kit includes the new "Fish Vermont Map & Guide" as well as fishing rules and a license application. Nonresident fishing licenses good for the entire year cost $38 for adults, $15 for anglers 15 to 17 years old. Anyone under 15 does not need a license. Temporary licenses are $11 for 1 day, $18 for 3 days, and $25 for 7 days.

DeLorme Mapping Company, P.O. Box 298, 2 DeLorme Drive, Yarmouth, ME 04096 (☎ **800/452-5931** or 207/846-7000; www.delorme.com), publishes the *Vermont Atlas & Gazetteer,* which has a profusion of detail on fishing, in both text and maps. Also, the guides and bait-and-tackle stores listed below will provide the most up-to-date handle of all on stream and river conditions and what the fish are hitting.

Trout lovers will want to look at the incredibly informative Web site **caddis.middlebury.edu/trout/** for listings of all the trout rivers in Vermont, plus bait info and good reading materials.

Trips

The Battenkill

It was the middle of May, the time of the year when our guide Bob Young spends his early mornings taking people out for wild turkey hunting and his afternoons fly-fishing for the elusive trout. Bob prefers to take anglers out to the Mattawee or Walloomsac Rivers, but my brother, Jim, and I stubbornly insisted on trying the legendary Battenkill. Challenging is the word most people use to describe the fishing on the Battenkill. Fortunate might be more apropos. On the Vermont side of the river, the state refuses to stock the water, leading to a diminishing number of wild trout that are overfished and undermanaged. Thus, fly anglers who have spent years casting on this gorgeous river say that, in the last decade, the scarce and skittish fish in the Battenkill no longer offer the superior angler a fair challenge.

Bob grew up outside of Arlington on the Battenkill, so few people know the river better than he does. Since he began guiding in the mid-1980s, he says that droughts and overfishing have hurt the river severely, but he still has faith that the allure of the Battenkill can return with proper management. Bob took us to the lower Battenkill across the New York State line where the river is stocked. That stocking was evident almost immediately after we put-in near the Battenkill Sports Quarters in Cambridge, New York. A helicopter from New York's DEC flew overhead and dropped some 150 to 200 trout through a chute into the water right in front of us. We thought if we can't hook a fish in the water, maybe we'll catch one out of the sky.

Conditions weren't the best for fishing—the water level was low, the sun hot, and the color of the water yellow green. Bob noted that the fish bite better when the water's brown. We would float some 7 miles over 4 hours. Bob passed out Hendricksons and mahogany spinners for flies, and we started to cast in that meditative, rhythmic motion. Jim soon caught a beautiful 12-inch brown trout. Little did we know it would be the only fish we'd catch that day on the river. Much of the shoreline is undeveloped, offering a slow ride through pristine forest. Casting behind large rocks, we got several bites but no takers. Nonetheless, it proved to be a wonderful afternoon on a renowned river. I recommend giving this spot a try—just don't have high expectations. **Bob Young** can be reached at ☎ **802/375-9313.**

Instruction, Bait-and-Tackle Shops & River Guides

Manchester and the Battenkill River are home to **Orvis,** one of the top fly-fishing schools in the country (Historic Rte. 7A, Manchester, VT 05254, ☎ **800/235-9763;** www.orvis.com). The 2- to 2.5-day courses are taught on the river and on Orvis's own casting ponds. The classes run twice a week from early April to mid-July, then on weekends only through August. Orvis also offers parent/child and women-only weekends. The **Battenkill Anglers,** 6204 Main St., Manchester Center, VT 05255 (☎ **802/362-3184;** www.battenkill.apexhosting.com), provides private instruction or tours for one or two people.

In the eastern part of the state, **Strictly Trout** in Westminster West (☎ **802/869-3116;** www.sover.net/~deenhome/index.html) offers guided service as well as overnight trips on the Connecticut River and its tributaries.

Larry Leonard sells fishing equipment near the Harriman Reservoir. He can be reached at Delar Depot, ☎ **802/464-5391.**

GOLF

Only four states—Rhode Island, Delaware, Montana, and Alaska—have fewer venues than Vermont, but of the state's 63 courses only 6 are private. Consistently rated one of the top golf courses in the state, the Gleneagles Golf Course is located on the historic grounds of the **Equinox Resort** in Manchester Village on State Route 7A (☎ **800/362-4747** or 802/362-4700; www.equinoxresort.com). Avoid the loathsome "Snake Pit," a gaping hole of sand and scrub carved out of the hilltop green at the 13th hole. Locals also refer to it as the "Volcano Hole" because it has caused the eruption of scores and tempers. There's also a fair number of watery ditches bisecting the fairways.

Stratton Mountain's (☎ **802/297-4114;** www.stratton.com) 27-hole course, composed of the 9-hole Lake,

Mountain, and Forest courses, is at the base of the ski resort. It's a combination of long and short holes, with the main hazard being the mountain stream that wanders through the course. For **golf instruction,** your best bets are Stratton, which offers 1- to 4-day sessions on its 22-acre training facility, ranked as one of the best in New England; and the **Golf School at Mount Snow** (☎ **800/240-2555;** www.mountsnow.com), which offers 2-day weekend or midweek courses, starting at $595 per person, including accommodations. The featured hole here is the par-four 4th, a downhill approach to the green bordered by a marsh and two sand traps.

HIKING & BACKPACKING

Trying to pick a mere handful of trails from the vast web of footpaths that criss-cross southern Vermont borders on the absurd. In addition to the many unforgettable stretches of the Long Trail that are perfect for an afternoon's walk or a 3-day section hike, there are dozens of summits (in the Taconics, west of the Greens, as well as east of the main ridge of the Green Mountains) that have well-marked and maintained day-hiking trails. There are trails rolling through the foothills to backcountry beaver ponds, and trails to low summits offering views of the Green Mountains and New Hampshire's White Mountains, with verdant farmland spread out in between. The sound of the wind, the sweet air and smell of evergreen, and all the other subtle intricacies of Vermont's wilder lands were meant to be experienced at a hiker's pace.

Vermont's mountains can seem unrelenting. Very few of the hikes here are slow and steady. You start climbing from the trailhead and don't stop till you reach the summit. The soft-soil trails are usually hidden within a deep forest, the perfect place to lose yourself and others for a few hours.

A helpful overall guide is the USGS Green Mountain National Forest/South Half map, available from the **Green Mountain National Forest,** 231 N. Main St., Rutland, VT 05701 (☎ **802/747-6700**). If you're game for tramping in the Vermont hills and your interest is whetted by what space allows me to list here, I suggest first of all that you buy ***The Long Trail Guide*** (Green Mountain Club, 1996). A model of what a trail guide should be; it includes a lot of side trails connecting to the Long Trail. The publication ***50 Hikes in Vermont*** (Countryman Press, 1997) is selective and thus has good armchair trip-planning value, and the ***Day Hiker's Guide to Vermont*** (Green Mountain Club, 1987) has more hikes *off* the Long Trail than 10 people could walk in a lifetime.

Day Hikes

Harmon Hill

3.4 miles round-trip. Allow 4 hr. Very steep, difficult climb from State Rte. 9; then a rambling lark on a high meadow. Access: On the Long Trail near Bennington; take Rte. 9 5.2 miles west, take the Long Trail south. Map: USGS 7.5-min. Woodford, Stamford.

It's an arduous trip up, but come at the right time of year and a big payoff awaits you. Harmon Hill's open summit is the result of an old burn that's maintained by the forest service to keep the views intact—and what views they are: To the west, Bennington spreads out below, along with the Bennington Battle Monument, with Mount Anthony rising on the far side. To the north, you can spy Glastenbury and Bald Mountains. I once sneaked a night's camp up here (although Harmon Hill is within national forest boundaries, camping is officially ***verboten;*** it must lie on private land) and was treated to a long evening watching the sun sink and the lights of Bennington beginning to twinkle.

But for my money, the real treat here is the berry picking. An absolute mother lode of wild strawberries, blueberries, raspberries, and blackberries come to fruition up here every year in their respective seasons. The latter two, my favorites, ripen in mid- to late summer. Happy eating! And when it's time to go back down, maybe you'll have the chance, as I did, to tell a troop of miserable-looking Boy Scouts being forced up the hill that there really is a reason to get to the top.

Merck Forest & Farmland Center

Over 26 miles of forest trails, including this dirt road. Allow as much time as you want; you can camp here if you like. Easy, rolling farmland and forest trails. Access: From the junction of State Rte. 30 and 315 in East Rupert, take State Rte. 315 west for 2.6 miles. Turn left and go 0.5-mile to the parking lot and visitors center. Map: available at the visitors center.

It was New Year's Day in Vermont, and there was less than an inch of snow on the ground; instead of going skiing, I opted for a walk in the Merck Forest & Farmland Center, located northwest of Manchester near the state line. The former home of George Merck, president of Merck Pharmaceuticals, this 2,800-acre farm is now run by a nonprofit organization dedicated to education and preservation. I parked my car at the visitors' center, grabbed a map, and walked through the gate onto Old Town Road. My first stop was an old red barn where horses grazed on leftovers from summer, which seemed a long time ago on that frigid day. Bearing right and heading uphill, Old Town Road eventually reaches Spruce Lodge, a picnic spot overlooking Mount Antone and the other mountains of the Taconic Range (trails run up both Mount Antone and Spruce Peak, offering some grand pastoral vistas). I skirted Birch Pond and found numerous yellow sugar ties in the woods, a signal that I had arrived at the sugarhouse. Climbing a ladder, I poked my head inside the old wooden structure. During early spring, the sugarhouse is in full operation and manufactures over 200 gallons of syrup a year. The syrup can be purchased at the visitors center. Once my curiosity was satisfied, I returned to the parking lot via the same route. I slipped and fell on my butt when I tried to walk down icy Old Town Road. Who said walking in the wintertime isn't as challenging as skiing?

White Rocks Trail

1.6 miles round-trip. Allow 1–1.5 hr. Easy; short switchbacking ascent to summit. Access: From the junction of State Rte 7 and 140 in Wallingford, follow State Rte. 140 east for 2.1 miles. Turn right and less than 0.1 mile later veer right again. You'll see a clearly marked sign for the White Rocks Picnic Area. 0.4 mile later, you'll reach the parking lot. Map: GMNF Summer Recreation map.

A short drive south of Rutland, the hike to White Rocks Cliff and the Ice Beds is a geologist's dream come true. Rocks of every size and shape blanket the hillside, the result of an ancient retreating ice cap. From the parking lot, follow the blue blazes along the pine-strewn Ice Beds Trail. The springy path is soon replaced by moss-covered rocks as you ascend a hogback. At impressive White Rocks Cliff, look out across Otter Creek Valley where a slope of white rocks careens down to the forest floor. Peregrine falcons and red-tailed hawks are often observed hovering in the skies above. From here, the blue-blazed trail is hard to follow as you walk through the dark forest down to a brook. Cross the creek several times to get a close-up view of the Ice Beds, a boulder slide where shattered quartzite rock flows like a river down the hill. If you mistakenly lose the blue-blazed trail on the return trip, don't worry. Veer right on the dirt road and right again on the paved road to reach the parking lot.

Stratton Mountain

6.8 miles round-trip. Allow 5–6 hr. Moderate; long 1,910-ft. rise to the summit. Access: From Rte. 100 in West Wardsboro, drive 7.1 miles west on the Arlington–West Wardsboro Rd. to the Long Trail parking lot. Begin your hike north along the white-blazed Long Trail. Map: GMNF Londonderry SW.

THE LONG TRAIL

Vermont's crowning achievement for hikers is the Long Trail (LT), a 265-mile-long footpath that runs the rugged length of the Green Mountains from Massachusetts to Canada. It was the country's first long-distance hiking trail, and Vermonters take great pride in its claim to precedence and the endless variety of hiking along its narrow, rough, unspoiled route. All the special backcountry places you can find elsewhere in the state—high-country boreal bogs; many different kinds of hardwood and evergreen forests; rocky, windblown summits; ice-cold streams and beaver ponds; mountain meadows covered with wild strawberries and blueberries; and so on—you'll also happen upon during a traverse of the Long Trail. And there are places on the LT's route that are unique in Vermont: in particular, the tufts of Alpine/Arctic tundra and top-of-the-world feeling of Camel's Hump and Mount Mansfield.

The founders of the Green Mountain Club (GMC) began cutting their "path through the wilderness" along the ridge of the Green Mountains in 1910, and by 1931, the trail ran continuously along the ridge of the Green Mountains from border to border. Even during these early years, the GMC had committed itself to providing primitive shelters along the trail. Today, the GMC has approximately 7,500 members who maintain the trail system, which totals 440 miles if you include the 175 miles of side trails. A little less than half of the trail is located in the two sections of the Green Mountain National Forest, in southern and central Vermont; the rest of the trail is on either privately or state-owned land.

From the Massachusetts border, the trail heads north and joins the **Appalachian Trail** for more than 100 miles. The trail gets used much more heavily on this stretch, with AT through-hikers and the generally greater numbers of people in southern Vermont (locals and tourists alike) getting out on the trail. The trail thus tends to be a little wider and less wild, and you'll definitely run into more hikers than you would up north. And although this seems like splitting hairs to me, the southern sections are a little flatter than the northern ones—like the absolutely brutal sections fore and aft of Camel's Hump and Mansfield. But there are still climbs up 3,000-foot-plus peaks like Glastenbury Mountain (unrelentingly steep), Bromley, and the mighty Killington Peak, along with steep dips down into the gulfs that occasionally pierce the ridge. Make no mistake: Sections of the LT are certainly easygoing enough to be suitable for a family going on a day hike, but any multiday hike on this trail will take you over terrain that will challenge anyone's endurance. The 265 miles of the Long Trail are very long indeed. The trail climbs up a peak and descends steeply into a gap before ascending another peak, which is the reason why many Vermonters call the LT the "Up-and-Down" Trail.

At Sherburne Pass (U.S. 4), the AT veers east toward New Hampshire, while the Long Trail winds north into one of its most pleasurable sections. The Green Mountains from Sherburne Pass all the way through Appalachian Gap consist primarily of a narrow ridge that falls off sharply toward the Champlain Valley on the west side, and a little less regularly toward the White River and Mad River valleys on the east. The ridge-walking of this section, rising up to and descending down from greater and lesser summits, is wonderful high-altitude hiking. The forests range from mixed hardwood and evergreen transition forest to gnarled balsam-fir krummholtz on the high peaks. The trees give way to grand views of the valleys, and on overcast days you hike through clouds that lend everything an ominous gloom—and always, the wind rushes through the trees. The ridge is narrowest—and steadiest—on the Lincoln Gap to Appalachian Gap stretch, one of my favorite walks anywhere. The views from Mount Abraham, Lincoln Peak, and Mount Ellen are unforgettable.

With Camel's Hump, Mount Mansfield, and Smuggler's Notch on the itinerary, the next section is spectacular—and is also the most popular day-hiking trail in the state. After the Appalachian Gap, the LT descends gradually to its lowest elevation (on the Winooski River) before beginning its sternest test, the Bolton Mountain–Mount Mansfield–Whiteface Mountain stretch. This is unrelentingly steep, up-and-down hiking on rocky terrain, but hikers are rewarded with fantastic views and a rarefied feeling of having spent a number of days up where the eagles live.

From State Route 15, near Johnson, the LT begins its last push, to Canada. This is by far the most remote, least-traveled section of the trail, which passes through a great variety of interesting terrain. Meandering through quiet forests of firs and spruce, many through-hikers find this section a fitting finale to the trail.

For shelter, the Green Mountain Club maintains more than 60 lodges, camps, and lean-tos. This is one of the really special aspects of the trail. Hikers can easily walk from one shelter to the next in a day since they're set at 5- to 7-mile intervals. The shelters are generally warmer and drier than tents, and you'll make fast friends with the other hikers who share your shelter. Many LT end-to-enders—including myself—actually omit a tent from their pack, although it's not necessarily advisable to do so. You might be that one unfortunate who arrives late at a shelter, only to find it full, in which case you'll be glad if you do have a tent. The lodges are usually built of logs and hold up to 32 bunks. The camps are cabins with bunks and sleep 8 to 12 people. Both the lodges and camps can be almost luxurious, with indoor tables, windows, and even wood stoves. The lean-tos are the most common and the simplest accommodation, sleeping 6 to 8 people.

My favorite time to walk the Long Trail is midsummer to early fall, when the bugs are gone (they can be murder in early summer), the berries are ripe (I must have consumed a ton of heavenly blackberries and raspberries on my hikes), and the trails are generally drier. Keep in mind that nights on the mountains, even in August, can be *really* cold; pack appropriately. Good rain gear and a reliable backpacking stove are always essential. It will take three to four weeks to cover the entire LT, and you'll need to spend at least that much time planning your trip. If you're planning to spend more than 3 or 4 days on the trail, and especially if you want to go whole hog and do an end-to-end trip, the GMC's *Long Trail Guide* is indispensable. Also recommended is the GMC's *Long Trail End-to-Ender's Guide,* which is packed with nitty-gritty details on equipment sales and repairs, mail drops, and B&Bs that provide trailhead shuttle services. Two well-known food drops are the Inn at Long Trail, between Rutland and Killington on Route 4, and the Jonesville Post Office, east of Burlington on Route 2.

Many of the day hikes I describe in the hiking sections of the Vermont chapters are on the Long Trail. And in truth, it's in day hikes and weekend trips that most of us will get to sample the LT. The passes that cut through the Green Mountains make convenient trailheads; for day hikes all you'll need for an up-and-back jaunt is a jug of water, binoculars, and a really sturdy pair of boots. For section hikes it's ideal to go with another person and take two cars—you can drop one at the endpoint you've chosen for the hike and park the other at your starting point, thus leaving yourself wirh a ride when you finish. Vermont is also one of the few places in the country where hitchhiking hasn't become an impossibility—there are plenty of people who know that the unkempt backpacker near a Long Trail access point isn't likely to be a scary drifter type, and will stop and gladly drive you all the way back to wherever your car is parked. All they'll ask in return is that you tell them some good trail stories.

For more information, contact the **Green Mountain Club,** State Route 100, P.O. Box 650, Waterbury Center, VT 05677 (☎ **802/244-7037;** www.greenmountainclub.org).

It was atop Stratton Mountain in 1909 that James P. Taylor conceived the idea of linking all the Green Mountain summits together on a "long trail." With views of Somerset Reservoir and Mount Snow to the south, Mount Equinox and the backbone of the Taconic Mountain range to the east, and Mount Ascutney to the northeast, it's easy to have grandiose ideas atop Stratton. This meandering trail quickly enters the woods before arriving at a beaver dam around 0.7 mile later. The ascent begins here, soon passing stone walls and apple trees on an old farm site. At 1.7 miles, the trail climbs steeply over roots and rocks through the forest. You'll hike along the ridgeline with views of Mount Snow's slopes, eventually going on switchbacks through spruce and birch to finally reach the 3,936-foot summit. Climb the fire tower, one of the earliest built in the state, for exceptional views of southern Vermont. You'll quickly realize why James P. Taylor wanted more.

Bald Mountain

3.5-mile loop. Allow 2–3 hr. Moderate; a 1,100-ft ascent on the trail; an even steeper descent. Access: Drive 2 miles north of Townshend on Rte. 30 to the Townshend Dam. Turn left and left again when the road reaches a T. Bear right at the covered bridge, and continue along the West River until you reach the park entrance. Map: USGS 15-min. Saxton's River.

If you're in the Grafton area, this is a good nearby mountain to climb. The 1,680-foot peak is located in the middle of Townshend State Park. Follow the blue-blazed trails from campsite #25, to the right of the park building, following a brook. You'll soon bear toward an old road and start your ascent along the hillside. You'll pass a large boulder 1.1 miles from the trailhead and you'll cross a brook. From here, the trail climbs steeply through a thicket of old oak trees to the summit. You'll be treated to views of Mount Monadnock to the south, Stratton and Bromley to the north, and the bucolic West River valley sandwiched in between. Continue on the blue-blazed trail to the right of the overlook to begin your steep descent. The narrow path forges downward through the forest, becoming more gradual as you pass a maple grove lined with ferns. Once you reach campsite #6, follow the road back to your car. You've earned a dip in the West River.

Mount Ascutney

5.2 miles one-way. Allow 3–4 hr. Moderate; a good climb to the summit where you can leave your second car. Access: Take Exit 8 off I-91 and follow Rte. 5 North to Rte. 44 West. Ascutney State Park will be on the left side of the road. Park one car in the camping area parking lot, the second at the summit.

It was a perfect day in mid-May when my brother, Jim, and I ascended Mount Ascutney. The 3,144-foot-high Monadnock had just awakened from its winter slumber and, being Vermont, was putting on a new layer of green. We started on the Futures Trail as it gradually snaked through a spindly forest of maples, oaks, and pines. The dry path was littered with pine needles, cones, roots, and rocks. The quartz rock that formed this peak became more prevalent as we reached our first vista at the mile-mark. Huge boulders looked out over the rolling pasture, bordered by brooks and rivers. A half-mile later we descended into a col where the dark woods were replaced by a green wonderland—the new leaves of spring were welcoming our arrival. The trail remained relatively level, showing us how broad Ascutney's girth is. At the 3-mile mark, we started the real ascent along a cascading brook. We clambered up the steep rocky path, soon rewarded at the 3.7-mile mark with a shady forest of firs, spruces, silver birches, and mossy rocks. Yet another shade of green. The last half-mile is on the narrow Winter Trail through an alpine forest of dwarf pines and other twisted trees. From the summit's observation tower, we could see the slopes of Okemo and Killington, the Connecticut

River, the White River, and all the farmland tucked in between. After savoring the view, we climbed down 0.7 mile to our second car.

Overnights

Stratton Pond

7.8 miles round-trip. Allow 4–5 hr. Easy to moderate ascent on wide, fairly smooth trail. Access: From State Rte. 100 in West Wardsboro, take the Arlington–West Wardsboro Rd. west for 8.2 miles, until you reach the intersection of Forest Rd. 71. There's a small parking lot due south of the intersection. A wooden sign marks the trailhead. Map: GMNF Summer Recreation map.

Stratton Pond is the largest body of water on the Long Trail. According to ***The Long Trail Guide*** (Green Mountain Club, 1996), "the pond receives the heaviest overnight use of any location on the trail, accommodating over 2,000 hikers between Memorial Day and Columbus Day." Once you've hiked to this hidden gem in the wilderness, you'll easily understand why: It's an idyllic dream of a backwoods beaver pond, with pure water, lush forest on its shores, water lilies dotting its surface, and an abundance of wildlife—birds, deer, frogs and salamanders, perch, sunnies, and brookies in the water.

The 3.9-mile (one-way) Stratton Pond Trail meanders through a young forest of beeches and ferns, before descending slightly into a thicket of white birches. At the 2.3-mile mark, you cross an old road and begin a gradual climb through the dense woods. A mile and a half later, hop from stone to stone over the small brook and then turn left on an old logging road to reach the junction of the Long Trail. Most of the LT through-hikers have just arrived from Stratton Mountain, 2.6 miles away. The pristine shores of Stratton Pond soon come into view. If you feel like adding another 1.4 miles to your hike, you can continue around the perimeter of the pond; it's beautiful if somewhat difficult walking, all green moss and slippery tree roots, with the brackish shallows of the pond alongside. I've spent some memorable nights here, listening to the chorus of peepers and waking to the sight of a ghostly mist spread across the pond. If you want to do the same, tent at one of the designated sites and pay the Green Mountain Club caretaker-in-residence the overnight fee, which is just a few dollars. Otherwise, enjoy the picnic spot and then retrace your steps back to the trailhead.

Little Rock Pond and Clarendon Gorge

14.4 miles. Allow 2 days, 1 night (4–5 hr. of hiking each day). Easy to moderate portion of the Long Trail that's perfect for the first-time or young backpacker. Access: Place your first car at the end of the trek, at the Clarendon Gorge parking area. It's located on Rte. 203, 2.1 miles east of the junction of Rte. 7 and 203. Then drive the second car to the beginning of your hike. Take Rte. 7 to Danby and turn east on Forest Rd. 10 for 3.5 miles to the Long Trail parking area.

This wonderful section of the Long Trail leads you to Little Rock Pond and the suspension bridge over Clarendon Gorge. The hike starts along the waters of Little Black Brook, which you cross 0.6 mile later. At 1.8 miles, you reach the Lula Tye Shelter and soon the waters of Little Rock Pond come into view. A good place to spot beaver, the pond is also known for its fishing and is stocked with brook trout. It's also the perfect spot to have lunch and go for a swim. Continue north on the trail, and you'll pass the Little Rock Pond Shelter before heading across Homer Stone Brook. The trail turns upward along the slopes of White Rocks Mountain, leading to good vistas of the region atop White Rocks Cliff. Make the descent down to Greenwell Shelter, where, at 7.2 miles, you'll spend the evening. The lean-to sleeps eight and there are a few tenting sites just behind the shelter.

Day two, head down from the shelter through a pasture and turn left on Sugar Hill Road. You cross the road at the junction of Forest Road 19 and enter the woods once again. Cross Roaring Brook and continue on to the summit of Button Hill at the 3.5-mile mark. The descent leads past the Minerva Hinchey Shelter, up a hardwood ridge, and into a large meadow called Spring Lake Clearing. Another hike up a ridge at 6.2 miles leads up Airport Lookout to the west. We saved the best for last as you cross the suspension bridge high above Clarendon Gorge and then make your way down to the water. You've earned a bath in one of the finest swimming holes in Vermont!

Outfitters & Inn-to-Inn Tours

Country Walkers, P.O. Box 180, Waterbury, VT 05676 (☎ **802/244-1387;** www.countrywalkers.com), offers inn-to-inn tours, some led by natural history grad students from the University of Vermont. **Walking-Inn-Vermont,** P.O. Box 243, Ludlow, VT 05149 (☎ **802/228-8799**), specializes in self-guided inn-to-inn tours where they shuttle your luggage to the next accommodation. Last but not least, **Country Inns Along the Trail,** R.R. 3, P.O. Box 3115, Brandon, VT 05773 (☎ **802/247-3300;** www.inntoinn.com), will custom-design self-guided hiking trips where you can walk inn-to-inn.

HORSEBACK RIDING

Horseback riding in Vermont isn't confined to an hour-long ride around a farmer's backyard. The state has an extensive network of trails weaving through the forests and meadows, and—much as you can on foot, skis, or bicycle—you can actually go on 4-day inn-to-inn riding tours.

On the eastern side of the Green Mountains, perhaps the best-established of all Vermont's stables is **Kedron Valley Stables,** State Route 106, South Woodstock (☎ **802/457-1480;** www.kedron.com). Owner Paul Kendall will guide you through secluded woods and historic villages like South Woodstock, Weathersfield, and Windsor. Get used to your saddle because you'll be on it for 5 to 6 hours at a stretch during a 4-day inn-to-inn jaunt. The horses average 15 miles a day.

A typical itinerary is to arrive at the inn on Sunday, be introduced to your horse on Monday, and then ride through the countryside to Echo Lake Inn in the small hamlet of Tyson. Tuesday, you'll follow centuries-old stone fences to Crown Point Road, built by a British general in 1759. You'll spend the evening at the Inn at Weathersfield. The next day, you'll ride along the Black River following the slopes of Mount Ascutney to the Juniper Hill Inn in Windsor. Thursday, it's a gallop through farmland back to the Kedron Valley Inn. The inn also offers riding lessons and short trail rides.

Close to the Bromley and Stratton areas, **Horses for Hire,** on South Road in Peru (☎ **802/824-3750**), is just east of the ridge of the Green Mountains. Owner Debra Hodis accompanies all levels of riders on scenic trails in the Green Mountain National Forest. She also offers winter riding.

A little farther south and not too far from Putney, the **West River Lodge and Stable,** on Hill Road in Brookline (☎ **802/365-7745**), has been offering guided rides and instruction since 1930. Trail rides commonly last the entire day. In nearby Newfane are the **West River Stables** (☎ **802/365-7745**), offering riding instruction and trails.

West of Brattleboro you'll find **Flame Stables,** State Route 100, Wilmington (☎ **802/464-8329**), offering Western saddle trail rides.

In the southwest corner of the state, **Valley View Horses & Tack Shop,** located on Northwest Hill Road in Pownal (☎ **802/823-4649**), offers trail rides and lessons; and **Kimberly Farms,** on Myers Road in Shaftsbury, about 10 miles north of Bennington (☎ **802/442-4354**), is known for sunset trail rides and cookouts.

If you're in the Killington/Rutland area, **Mountain Top Stables** in Chittenden (☎ **802/483-2311**) offers guided trail and pony rides.

ICE FISHING

Judging by the increasing number of snowmobiles on southern Vermont's largest lakes, ice fishing is becoming nearly as popular as fishing in summer. Take a drive on southern Vermont's Route 9 during the winter, and you'll undoubtedly see numerous snowmobilers whipping across the ice of Harriman Reservoir. They're not out for a joy ride. These hearty souls eventually find a spot to stop and put up their shanties before getting out their small poles and jigging for fish. Just outside of Wilmington and the Mount Snow region, Harriman is one of the best ice fishing holes in New England. Expect to find browns (29-pounders are not unheard of), brookies, rainbows, landlocked salmon, perch, and pickerel.

Delord Depot in Wilmington (☎ **802/464-5391**) sells jigs, poles (22- to 26-inch poles are the norm), and fresh bait (minnows), and they can order ice shanties ($200 to $300) for you. Some of the old-timers are so adept at ice fishing that they now outfit their shanties with generators and TVs.

Somerset Reservoir is a popular smelt and perch pond. Smelt, northern pike, and perch are found in the waters of the western lakes—**Dunmore, St. Catherine,** and **Bomoseen.** For maps and additional information, contact the **Vermont Fish and Wildlife Department,** 103 S. Main St., Waterbury, VT 05671-0501 (☎ **802/241-3700;** www.anr.state.vt.us/fw/fwhome).

MOUNTAIN BIKING

There's just no end to the old logging roads, primitive dirt roads, and even cowpaths that lace through southern Vermont. Your best source for up-to-the-minute local finds is going to be the area's bike shops (see below); an invaluable resource will be USGS 7.5-minute and 15-minute map series to the area (see chapter 1, "The Basics," for information on acquiring these maps).

Back-Roads Rides

Bennington-Pownal Loop

14 miles. Moderate climbing; stretches of pavement fore and aft with a lot of dirt road in between. Access: Park at the Bennington Museum, on State Rte. 9 in Old Bennington, west of Bennington Village. Map: USGS 7.5-min. Bennington, Pownal, North Pownal.

This ride is like Bucolic Vermont 101—it's got the hayfields, the hundred-year-old roadside maples, apple orchards, old Victorian farmhouses, and an actual Revolutionary War battle site, marked by the Bennington Battle Monument, which commemorates the battle fought on August 16, 1777. Follow State Route 9 west for about 2 miles; then turn left onto Mount Anthony Road—there's a dairy farm right across from this intersection. After a half mile of gradual climbing, the pavement gives way to dirt. A flat stretch is followed by the major climb of the route as the road slowly and obliquely skirts the western slope of Mount Anthony, which rises to your left. There are classic rural views to your right and, shortly after you begin rolling downhill again, long views to the south toward Massachusetts. From here on, all you need to remember is to keep left; the mound of Mount Anthony is the hub around which these back roads revolve. Right where the road becomes paved again is the aforementioned monument, all of 306 feet high. When you hit U.S. 7, dodge back into the quiet again by taking a sharp left; this road will take you all the way back to State Route 9 and your starting point, located a half mile to the east.

Green Mountain National Forest Road No. 10

10 miles (20 miles round-trip). Moderate; gradual elevation gain over dirt and gravel road. Access: Since the roads around Landgrove get a bit complex, come at this one from the west end; turn east off U.S. 7 at Danby and drive the short way to the

village of Mount Tabor. In Mount Tabor, just after you enter the Green Mountain National Forest, you'll see a parking lot on the right. Map: USGS 7.5-min. Mount Tabor.

Impassable in winter, this little-traveled forest-service road rolls along above 2,000 feet through archetypal Green Mountain scenery, connecting the hamlets of Mount Tabor and North Landgrove. Brooks babble alongside for nearly its entire length, and you'll have an opportunity to make this a sort of backwoods triathlon—about 1.5 miles east of the village of Mount Tabor is a Long Trail access point, and a 2-mile walk north will bring you to Little Rock Pond, a fine cold swimming hole if ever there was one. If you want to add some serious technical single track to this otherwise undaunting ride, see "Mount Tabor Road Trail" under "Cross-Country Skiing," above; the complex network of logging roads and narrow track here is equally inviting in warm weather.

Grafton Ponds Mountain Bike Center

3.5 miles. Allow 1 hr. Moderate; gradual elevation over double tracks and single tracks. Access: south of the Old Tavern at Grafton on Townshend Rd. ☎ **802/843-2300.**

A cross-country skiing center come winter, Grafton Ponds is a small network of good fat-tire biking in the summer. There was absolutely no one else on the trails on a sunny Sunday afternoon in mid-July when I went for a spin. Out of the parking lot, I turned left on the Main Trail to the Village Overlook. Below the waves of hillside, Grafton stood nobly in its white-steeple splendor. At the end of the Lee Wilson loop, I turned right, then a quick left onto Big Bear Trail. Up and up and up I went past the Grafton Overlook, where light shimmered through the dense woods. Dark and primordial, the woods made me feel as if a big bear could easily lumber out of the forest to greet me on Big Bear Trail. Big Bear Shelter, a log cabin high up on the hills, is a good place to take a breather before you go screaming downhill on a thrilling single track. Jumping over roots and rocks, I cruised down Big Bear, Little Bear, and Chivers Trails back to the Village Overlook and the Main Trail. If you happen to be in the historic village of Grafton and have had your fair share of cheese, this is a great way to get lost in the woods for an hour.

Rail Trails

Delaware and Hudson Rail Trail—Northern Section

9.2 miles. Easy; surface is hard-packed cinder and gravel. Access: From Rutland, take Rte. 4 West to Route 4A and continue heading west to Castleton. Take a left at South St., which leads to the State College at Castleton. Parking is available near the security office.

Jay Gould, Cornelius Vanderbilt, and other entrepreneurs of the Industrial Revolution would be dismayed if they knew what some of their railroad lines are used for today. At the turn of the last century, the United States went on the greatest railroad-building spree in history. Indeed, by 1916, this country had the largest railroad system in the world, with almost 300,000 miles of track. Well, we all know what happened after that. Henry Ford and the Wright Brothers brought about a faster, sexier means of transportation, leading to eventual decline of the iron horse. Railroad companies went bankrupt and left behind more than 160,000 miles of unused trail. Some rail corridors became roads, but most have remained vacant, the dead tracks becoming rust collectors.

In the early sixties, however, a small group of locals in southwestern Wisconsin decided to do something creative with their stretch of abandoned railroad. They opened a 32-mile thoroughfare between Elroy and Sparta and designated it a recreational path for bikers and walkers. Thirty-five years later, rail trails have become a mecca for outdoor enthusiasts and a focal point of urban renewal across the country. Far away from the maddening congestion on inner-city streets or the noise of rural highways, these trails offer gentle grades and easy access for walkers, bikers, in-line skaters, and cross-country skiers. Over 1,000 rail trails are now open for public use, and close to 1,800 additional projects are underway. To find the rail trail nearest you, call the **Rails-to-Trails Conservancy** at ☎ **202/331-9696.**

Of Vermont's five rail trails, four are on hard-packed cinder and gravel. Like the carriage path trails in Acadia National Park, these fairly level trails are a great introduction to mountain biking and the feel of riding through the forest unencumbered by car traffic. The Delaware and Hudson (D&H) line was once a busy railroad corridor that carried purple, red, and green roofing slate to markets throughout New York and the Northeast. Known as the "slate picker" line, the D&H moved some 170,000 squares of slate in 1890. Eventually, trucks became more popular than the railroad for hauling slate, and in 1983 the line shut down. In the early 1990s, the Vermont Association of Snow Travelers began converting the line into a rail trail.

Head south from Castleton and you'll immediately be surrounded by dairy farms and meadows rising to the foothills of the Green Mountains. White pines, red oaks, and sugar maples line the trail, with hemlock and beech trees occasionally mixed in. At the 6.5-mile mark, you enter Poultney, a poster child for small-town Americana. This is a good place to stop for lunch. The trail continues across a 100-foot-long bridge, reaching the New York border at 9.2 miles. The New York side of the rail trail is not open at this time, and the southern section of Vermont's D&H Trail resumes 15 miles south of Poultney (see below).

Delaware and Hudson Rail Trail—Northern Section

10.6 miles. Easy; surface is hand-packed cinder and gravel. Access: From Manchester, take Rte. 30 north to Rte. 153, then Rte. 315 into West Pawlet. When the road comes to a T, turn right and the trail will be on your right. Park in the small lot next to a depot.

Meadows of wildflowers and fields of corn line the southern half of the D&H Trail. As you head south of West Pawlet, the trail parallels Route 153 all the way into West Rupert and the New York border. Go as far as you like and then head back to the car.

Mountain Biking Centers

Downhill ski areas are perfectly set up to provide a taste of mountain biking; they've got a pre-established trail network, of course, as well as lifts—which means you can take the laborious climbing out of the picture if you want. The **Killington Mountain Bike Center** (☎ **802/422-6232**) and **Stratton Mountain Resort** (☎ **802/297-2200**) rent bikes and have knowledgeable staffs that can set you up with everything from easy rides through meadows to very technical single track. Mount Snow, however, was the first ski area to cater to fat-tire enthusiasts, and it still reigns supreme.

Mount Snow Resort Mountain Biking Center

Mountain Rd., just off State Rte. 100 in West Dover. ☎ **802/464-3333.**

If you decide to venture to a ski resort to bike, Mount Snow is by far the best in the state. It was the first large ski resort to devote itself to mountain biking and now has 140 miles of rides to challenge everyone from first-timers to world champions. This number doesn't even take into account the miles of rides in the outlying country. Maps of the entire network are available in the base lodge. Grueling uphill single and double tracks suddenly start their descent for mile-long exhilarating runs through secluded woods and bare mountain ski trails. If you want downhill thrills without lung-busting climbs, ride the chairlift to the 3,556-foot

ALL ABOARD

The small strip of pavement formed a straight line into the horizon. Bordered on both sides by purple wildflowers, flowering dogwood, and small maples where red-winged blackbirds and bright yellow goldfinches nested, the trail had few hills to tackle and no motorized traffic. The only obstacles before me were runners, clumsy in-line skaters, and other leisurely bikers. In Orleans, we hopped off our bikes and took that quintessential New England snapshot of fishing boats bobbing in the harbor. Soon we were in the shade of Nickerson State Park, pedaling straight through Brewster to a series of swimming holes with names like Seymour, Long, and Hinckley Ponds. We were riding on the 25-mile Cape Cod Rail Trail on a corridor that, until 1937, was used to ship cranberries aboard the Old Colony Railroad. Today the trail is a placid retreat that has quickly become one of the most popular destinations in the Northeast. It's a relatively level and easy path used by people of all ages for biking, hiking, strolling, jogging, and in-line skating.

Like so many of these paths proliferating across the United States, the Cape Cod Rail Trail was for many decades an abandoned railroad line. Converting it into a rail trail was no easy feat. Local recreation lovers faced a complex assortment of issues, most important of them, who owned this land. Many railroad companies leased their property from federal and state governments and even from private landowners whose homes were adjacent to the trail. Thus, on any given 5-mile corridor, there could be a patchwork of 20 to 100 owners, none of whom were the bankrupt railroad company. Adding to this tangled web was the question of who's going to own and manage these trails when they cross political jurisdictions.

Thankfully, Congress intervened in 1983 and passed the rail-banking law. The bill says that, upon abandonment, if some group steps forward and maintains the trail, the Interstate Commerce Commission would put the trail in a *rail bank*—a bank for future railroad use with interim use as a recreational trail. With rail-banking, Congress reasoned that the land was once again being used for railroad purposes, alleviating the problem of entitlement. So far, 3 of the 900-plus rail trails have converted back to railroad lines after the passage of this law.

About the same time Congress passed the rail-banking law, David Burwell, a lawyer from the National Wildlife Foundation, and Peter Harnik, the Director of Environmental Action, began discussing the idea of a national organization dedicated to preserving abandoned railroad corridors for recreational use. Burwell knew firsthand the struggles encountered when trying to convert railroad lines to rail trails. In Falmouth, Massachusetts, Burwell's hometown, his mother was involved in creating the scenic Falmouth Shining Sea Trail.

summit. Mount Snow also has numerous dirt roads to challenge mountain bikers who are new to the sport.

Rentals, Schools, Outfitters & Inn-to-Inn Tours

Mount Snow (**☎ 802/464-3333;** www.mountsnow.com) rents bikes, gives 2-, 4-, and 7-hour tours, and runs one of the top mountain biking schools in the Northeast. The 2-day program is offered every weekend from June 20 through October 4. The $132 price includes 12 hours of instruction, guided tours, unlimited lift access, and lunch both days.

In the Lower Connecticut River Valley, the **Brattleboro Bike Shop** (**☎ 802/254-8644**) and Putney's **West Hill Shop** (**☎ 802/387-5718**) rent fat-tire bikes and are the nexus of local biking information.

Ludlow's **Cycle-Inn-Vermont,** P.O. Box 243, Ludlow, VT 05149-0243 (**☎ 802/228-8799**) sets up inn-to-inn tours.

In Bennington, you can rent mountain bikes from **Cutting Edge North,** 160 Benmont Ave. (**☎ 802/442-8664**).

"I was in Little League when the project first got underway," says Burwell. "I was in law school when it was finally completed."

Lengthy conversion times were a major problem that Burwell faced when he and Harnik opened the Rails-to-Trails Conservancy in Washington, D.C., in 1985. Prior to opening this nonprofit foundation, the average conversion time was 12 years. It is now 3 to 4 years. The success rate has gone from a dismal 10% in 1985 to a staggering 70 to 80% in 1997. Here's another intriguing statistic. From 1965 to 1985, only 1,000 miles of trail were opened. That's exactly the number of trails that were opened in the last 10 months. There are currently more than 10,000 miles of rail trails open in every state in the contiguous United States.

The conservancy acts as a central brain in Washington, assisting groups around the country who want to transform railroad corridors into trails. They publish a guide, "Secrets of Successful Rail Trails," that answers all the basic questions relevant to ownership, management, and design.

"We're here to hold people's hands so they won't have to reinvent the wheel each time," says Burwell, adding that "We're simply passing along tips that have helped other communities succeed in the creation of these beautiful corridors."

There are currently 100,000 members and donors in the conservancy, but the bulk of the money for owning and managing these trails has come from the federal government. In 1991, Congress passed a new transportation bill stipulating that 10% of federal gas tax money would be used for so-called enhancement projects—preserving historic railroad depots, landscaping greenways and river corridors, and, yes, funding rail trails. Since 1991, more than $300 million has been spent on this rapidly expanding movement, but a lot more money is still needed.

"There are 1,200 projects underway totaling 17,000 more miles," Burwell states.

The conservancy's goal is to eventually link up all of these smaller rail trails and create one continuous trail system across the country. In fact, Burwell's lifetime goal (he's now 52) is for people to get on the Minuteman Trail in Boston and get off at the Burke-Gilman Trail in Seattle. All the trails open across the country are free. Only 30% are paved, and most of those trails are in urban areas. For rural trails like eight of the nine rail trails in Vermont and New Hampshire, you'll have to switch to mountain-bike tires to ride on the packed gravel.

OFF-ROAD DRIVING

Presiding over a colonial green that evokes images of Currier and Ives prints, Manchester Village is one of those quintessential New England villages where you stroll between shops, play golf, and . . . go off-road driving. That's right. Land Rover opened its first year-round **4×4 Driving School** in the United States at the Equinox (☎ **800/362-4747**) in Manchester. Spend an hour or longer with one of the expert instructors on an all-natural circuit, not a man-made obstacle course in the middle of a field (the school is open to the public, not just guests at the Equinox). The sinuous trails climb through thick woods and scratching brush, over rocks, ruts, and streams to compress a lifetime of off-road experience into a 1-mile route.

I took a short class with Nate Larson at the Driving School and learned to value a self-recovery winch (if you're stuck in a bog, simply attach the device to a tree or anchor in the sand and pull yourself out). He taught me to go as slow as possible and as fast as necessary (you'll need to take it slow in an off-road vehicle to overcome obstacles); to go uphill in third gear and downhill in first, taking your foot off the brake (let the engine compress or brake for you). I learned to go with gravity on a side-tilt (when the car tilts all the way over on one side, say, cresting a hill); and to go over logs one wheel at a time. More than 50% of the people who take the course own a Land Rover and want to play with it off-road. For experienced off-roaders, there is a 10-hour trail that goes from Manchester to Woodstock on the back roads.

POWERBOATING

Fishing boats and motorboats can be rented at **Lake St. Catherine State Park** (☎ **802/287-9158**) and on the lower Connecticut River from **Green Mountain Marine,** Rockingham (☎ **802/463-4973**). For a complete listing of all motorboat, sailboat, and canoe rentals, contact the **Vermont Department of Travel,** 134 State St., Montpelier, VT 05602 (☎ **800/VERMONT**), for the "Vermont Boating, Rentals & Marinas" publication.

ROAD BIKING

There are four reasons why Vermont biking is the best in the East and possibly the finest in the country. First, although the state is mostly rural and has a relatively small population, it's thoroughly settled country. The dozens of backcountry roads connecting scenic little hamlets make for a web of ideal road-biking terrain, all with very little traffic. Second, the state is compact enough to create hundreds of 20-, 30-, 40-, 50-, and 100-mile loops. Third, the landscape is neither flat nor dauntingly hilly. Rolling hills challenge the experts but also allow the novice to feel a sense of accomplishment.

It's really the scenery that makes a bike trip in Vermont so appealing. Around every bend, there's another meadow greener than the last, another freshly painted white steeple piercing the clouds overhead, and another Green Mountain standing tall in the distance. Strict environmental statutes prohibit roadside billboards and other eyesores. In their place stand small signs advertising pure maple syrup or categorizing the type of cows found on a farm—Holstein, Hereford, or Jersey. This state was meant to be seen at a slow pace.

Rides

Grafton Loop

A 25-mile loop. Allow 3 hr. Moderate; one steep hill, otherwise rolling terrain. Access: Start and finish in Grafton, south of Chester via State Rte. 35 or west of I-91 via State Rte. 121. Map: USGS 7.5- × 15-min. Saxton's River, but most any state map will do.

Very few places in New England epitomize small-town charm better than the historic village of Grafton. It is the ideal starting and ending point for a number of different bike trips; this loop ties together a wealth of rural scenery and the equally picturesque little towns of Chester, Rockingham, Saxton's River, and Cambridgeport.

The well-appointed old houses and churches in Grafton testify to a prosperous past. Indeed, Grafton's history is pretty characteristic for Vermont: In the mid-1800s, Grafton was populated by 1,500 people—and 10,000 sheep. The woolen textile industry was supplemented by active soapstone quarries and by mills that turned the quarries' output into stoves, sinks, and foot warmers. (Foot warmers?) By the end of the century, Grafton's historic Old Tavern (see "Inns and Resorts," below) had hosted such luminaries as Emerson, Thoreau, Rudyard Kipling, Ulysses S. Grant, and Teddy Roosevelt.

However, the village soon took a turn for the worse. Sheep farmers moved west to find new land, and the mills shut down as the owners left in search of cheaper labor farther south. By the end of the Great Depression, the population had shrunk to less than 100 and most of the houses were up for sale. If it hadn't been for the generosity of Pauline Dean Fiske and the foresight of her nephews, Dean Mathey and Matthew Hall, the exquisite homes would have been torn down and turned into pasture. With their aunt's money, the two nephews founded the Windham Foundation in 1963 and proceeded to restore the entire town, including the Old Tavern. The turnaround was dramatic. The village now looks as it did a century and a half ago, replete with white steeple, sparkling white clapboard homes, and a country store.

Start this 25-mile loop at the Old Tavern, and proceed over the bridge, turning left (north) immediately onto Chester Road (State Route 35). For the first half mile, the tree-lined road rises sharply before leveling off. For the next 5 or 6 miles, the road cruises downhill, finally arriving at the houses and inns of Chester. Veer right onto State Route 11 East and continue straight onto State Route 103 South. There's a large shoulder, but be wary of traffic as you roll up and down the hills through town; 6.4 miles from the junction of State Route 35, leave the modern world behind as you bear right onto Pleasant Valley Road. You'll pass grazing horses and dilapidated barns. When the road ends, turn right onto State Route 121 West. Saxton's River soon appears on your left as you follow the winding road past the ever-present cow pastures and cornfields. The pastoral landscape never leaves your side as you pedal through Cambridgeport all the way back to Grafton.

Arlington

12.1 miles. Allow 1.5–2 hr. Access: From the intersection of Rte. 7A and 313 in Arlington, head west on Rte. 313 for 0.2 mile. There's a public parking area on the right next to the river.

This easy 6-mile out-and-back loop runs along that famous fly-fishing river, the Battenkill, twisting and turning along with the bends of the river on State Route 313 heading west. At 5.8 miles, cross the Battenkill and head back east on River Road. Two miles later, turn left onto Covered Bridge Road for a slight detour to see the West Arlington Covered Bridge. This is a good place to picnic or go swimming in the hole beside it. Return to River Road, and at the 11.6-mile mark cross the Battenkill once again and turn left to get back to your car.

Lake St. Catherine

A 24-mile loop. Allow 2–3 hr. Moderate; rolling terrain. Access: From Rutland, take Rte. 7 to State Rte. 140 West. 9 miles later, you'll reach the Middletown Springs Village Green. Park anywhere. Map: USGS 7.5-min. Wells and Poultney, but most any state map will do.

Verdant Vermont meets Victorian Vermont on this loop through a rarely visited portion of the state. The ride starts in Middletown Springs, known in the early 19th century as a resort town because of its iron and sulfur springs. From the village green, proceed on State Route 133 South beyond the Victorian homes and wraparound verandas. The road heads straight into a lush green valley. Mountains fringe the pastures on the left. Bear right at the 4.9-mile mark toward Wells, passing numerous dairy farms along the way. The road becomes dirt for a half mile but soon turns to pavement as you cruise downhill. Wave after wave of gently undulating hills fade into the horizon, as green as the Irish countryside. In the village of Wells, turn right at the library onto State Route 30 North and follow the road as it rolls alongside a forest. Less than 3 miles later, the waters of Lake St. Catherine come into view, with New York's Taconic Range standing on the far shores. You'll soon pass the Lake St. Catherine State Park on the left, a good place to stop and picnic. At the 15.9-mile mark, turn right at the fork and head uphill toward East Poultney. A tall white steeple welcomes you to the town square. Just past a country store, turn right on State Route 140 East and bike along a stream; you'll re-enter Middletown Springs 6.6 miles later.

Overnights

Bike Vermont Weekend Tour, Proctorsville, Vermont offers a 39-mile loop on Saturday and a 21-mile loop on Sunday.

Pedaling at a leisurely pace and being pampered at an inn that evening is a perfect way to see this rural state. That's exactly what my brother, Jim, and I decided to do last May. We chose one of Bike Vermont's weekend rides that centered around Proctorsville. Early Saturday morning, we rose from our beds at the Golden Stage Inn, dined on a gluttonous breakfast of blueberry pancakes and sausage, jumped on our bikes, and off we went. The first 4.2- mile section was a sweet downhill run through Proctorsville Gulf (Route 103 South), surrounded by forest on both sides of the road. We turned left on Route 10 and followed this lightly traveled road alongside a brook and pasture. After veering off on several smaller roads, we came to our first great vista at North Springfield Dam. Mount Ascutney stood tall in the background, reflected off the waters of the reservoir. A left turn after the dam brought us to one of those unnamed Vermont roads that only a bike tour operator who's explored the state for more than 20 years could find. It was a 4-mile rolling road through undeveloped land where waterfalls skirted down moss-covered rocks and the air was fresh and crisp.

We continued north on State Route 106 to the small town of Reading, where we had lunch near a waterfall along the north branch of the Black River. The bikers in our group included a couple from Minneapolis who ride some 3,000 miles a year and have taken bike trips all over the country, from the Smokies to the Big Island; and a UPS driver from Cornwall, New York, who hadn't been on a bike in 20 years. He never finished the ride that day. Around the 30-mile mark, he was looking at some cows and fell into a ditch. He chipped his tooth, scraped his knees, and sliced his chain in two. Moral of story: Train ahead of time for a bike tour if you haven't ridden in a while.

The route continued south into Downers, a side trip to a scenic swimming hole at the Stoughton Pond Recreation Area, and across Downer's Covered Bridge, built in 1840. The last 8 miles of the trip were on Route 131 along the Black River. Around every bend, you felt like you were near the end of the ride, only to be fooled by another stretch of river and another angler, wading in the water, trying to hook a bass. We made it back to Proctorsville, some 7 hours after we started, exhilarated by the day's ride and our accomplishment.

That night, we earned our dinner of salmon with carrot-ginger syrup and went to bed around 10pm, sleeping like rocks. The next morning, our ride started on Twenty Mile Stream Road past old barns, stone walls, and farmland. We stopped at Happy Acres Maple Sugar Farm to sample and buy the three grades of syrup that owners Jim and Sandy Peplau produce from the more than 3,500 taps on their property. The quick sugar buzz helped us up the hill. We turned left past Colby Pond and then swept downhill for 2.5 miles past undeveloped forest. A left turn onto Route 100 South brought us into Ludlow and the slopes of Okemo. It was early spring and there were still patches of snow on the hillside. Route 103 brought us back into Proctorsville, where we finished around 1pm. The weekend went far too quickly.

Rentals, Outfitters & Inn-to-Inn Tours

Bikes for the Grafton loop can be rented at the **Old Tavern** (☎ **802-843-2231**). For the Lake St. Catherine loop, you can rent bikes in Manchester at **Battenkill Sports Bicycle Shop** (☎ **802/362-2734**).

In Bennington, you can rent road bikes from **Cutting Edge North,** 160 Benmont Ave. (☎ **802/442-8664**).

Bike Vermont, P.O. Box 207, Woodstock, VT 05091 (☎ **800/257-2226;** www.bikevermont.com), operates exclusively within the borders of the state. They are celebrating their 25th anniversary this year. Guided tours of 2, 3, 5, and 6 days are offered all over the southern part of Vermont, from Lake St. Catherine to the Connecticut River Valley to the outskirts of Robert Frost's Breadloaf Wilderness.

Arguably, one of the best deals in the state is provided by **VOGA,** the **Vermont Outdoor Guides Association** (☎ **800/425-8747;** www.voga.com). Depending on your ability, budget, and length of stay, VOGA will develop a detailed itinerary that includes accommodations (B&Bs, youth hostels, or campgrounds), bike routes (including a map and a description of the terrain), and even a bike. Remarkably, there is no charge for their consultation. This is a self-guided tour of the state, so luggage will be transported by the lodging properties, and each night's accommodation will keep track of your route in case of an emergency. Take a week's tour in the affordable and majestic Northeast Kingdom of Vermont, for example, and your total cost including bike rental, inns, and food will be in the $500 to $600 range. If you prefer to camp and want to bring your own bike, the weekly price plummets to somewhere near $150.

POMG (Peace of Mind Guaranteed) Bike Tours of Vermont (☎ **888/635-BIKE;** www.pomgbike.com) is now entering its sixth year of operation. POMG's 2- to 5-day tours focus on Plymouth, Okemo, and the Mad River Valleys, and they're known for their affordability. Weekend trips including 2 nights at B&Bs, dinners, and breakfasts start at $319.

Backroads, 1516 Fifth St., Berkeley, CA 94710-1740 (☎ **800/GO-ACTIVE;** www.backroads.com), features a 5-day inn-to-inn tour through Woodstock, Weathersfield, and Grafton.

SNOWMOBILING

The **Vermont Association of Snow Travelers** (VAST) is a group of more than 200 local snowmobile clubs that maintain over 3,000 miles of groomed trails. The trails extend from the Massachusetts border to Canada, and from the Connecticut River to Lake Champlain. Eighty-five percent of the land is located on private property; and without the work of volunteers, the use of this land would not be possible. For detailed maps, route suggestions, and information about guided tours, contact VAST at P.O. Box 839, Montpelier, VT 05602 (☎ **802/229-0005;** www.vtvast.org). A "Winter Recreation" map is also available from the **Green Mountain National Forest,** 231 N. Main St., Rutland, VT 05701 (☎ **802/747-6700**).

In Wilmington, **High Country** (☎ **800/627-7533** or 802/464-2108; highcountry-tours.com) arranges guided hourly, half-day, full-day, and overnight trips into the national forest.

For a complete list of snowmobile tours and rentals in the state, get a copy of the "Vermont Winter Guide" from the **Vermont Department of Travel,** 134 State St., Montpelier, VT 05602 (☎ **800/VERMONT**).

SNOWSHOEING

Stratton has expanded its network of backcountry trails at the summit and in the Sun Bowl area. The well-marked system features loops for all levels. Regularly scheduled guided hikes and backcountry treks include a moonlight tour to the Pearl Buck Cottage for a cup of hot chocolate by the fireplace and a high-elevation hike to the summit fire tower near the birthplace of the Long and Appalachian Trails. Stratton has also teamed up with Tubbs Snowshoes to establish a 12-week winter fitness program that begins with a low-intensity snowshoe tour and evolves into strenuous workouts on Stratton's adventure course. Lastly, they feature a Tubbs Family Snowshoe Festival once a year, which includes a kids' obstacle course, 5k/10k competitions, backcountry treks, and snowshoe demos. Contact the **Nordic Center** at ☎ **802/297-4114** for more information.

Other excellent self-guided hikes include the 2.5-mile trail to the summit of Bald Mountain, just outside Townshend. The trail ascends through stands of birch, pines, hemlock, and alder swamp, before leaving you at the peak with good vistas of Stratton Mountain to the west. If you've never climbed a mountain on snowshoes before, this is a great introduction. To reach the trailhead, take State Route 30 for 2 miles north of the junction with Route 35, and turn left into Townshend State Park.

The West River Trail in Jamaica State Park was once a railroad bed until the tracks were torn up in 1939 (see "Walks & Rambles," below). Now it's a 2.3-mile (one-way) jaunt along a rushing river where you can learn local ecology and history at nine nature stops. The white water of the West River is always by your side as you meander through the fern-lined trail into a forest of birches, hemlocks, spruce, ash, and maples. There are numerous benches to rest and have lunch. To get here from Jamaica, turn on Depot Street and follow it 0.5 mile until you reach a small plowed-out parking area on the left side of the street.

In East Dorset, you can hike to the Freelyville Quarry, an immense cavelike formation that's a perfect spot for a winter fire and picnic. From Route 7A, take Mad Tom Road approximately 1.5 miles and turn left onto Dorset Hill Road. Drive another 4 miles and you'll see the trail on the left. In Bondville, Gale Meadows is a wonderful 2-hour walk around the perimeters of a frozen pond with views of Bromley and Stratton. Simply take River Road from Bondville and head 2 miles, turning left before the iron bridge.

In Plymouth, take the hour-long Ice Age Trail as a mountain stream trickles beside you. The trail is popular with wildlife. Take Route 100 for 8 miles north of Ludlow, and turn right at Hawk Mountain Resort. Go to the recreation center for a snowshoe map and rentals. For a more arduous trail at Hawk Mountain, take the 2-mile Rim Run Trail to the Lakeview Observation Point. Your reward is a breathtaking view of Okemo mirrored in a chain of lakes.

At the Merck Forest and Farmland Center in East Rupert, try the 4-mile Spruce Peak Trail. Then warm up with a hot drink at the visitors' center. For directions to Merck, see "Day Hikes," above. If you want to go pond hopping on the Long Trail in the dead of winter, opt for the Wallingford Pond Loop to Little Rock Pond. The 4.4-mile trail crosses over several bridges before ending at the peaceful pond. The trail is 5 miles from Wallingford via USFS Road 20.

SWIMMING

With hundreds of lakes, rivers, and ponds in southern Vermont, you'll never be far from a cool, refreshing body of water. The most obvious choices are the parks on **Emerald Lake, Lake St. Catherine, Half Moon Pond, Jamaica State Park,** and **Townshend Lake Recreation Area.** However, locals tend to keep their precious swimming holes as a clandestine destination. Crash the party at the following places:

- The section of the **West River** under the covered bridge on State Route 30 in West Dummerston
- The **Rock River** about a mile north on State Route 30
- The **Dorset Quarry** off State Route 30 on Kelly Road between Dorset and Manchester
- **Grout Pond** (see "Quiet Water," under "Canoeing," above)
- **Hapgood Pond** in Peru
- **Buttermilk Falls,** on State Route 103 north of its junction with State Route 100 in Ludlow

TENNIS

The highly regarded **Killington School for Tennis** (☎ **800/451-6108;** www.cortinainn.com/tennisschool.htm) offers 2-, 3-, and 5-day programs on their eight outdoor courts.

WALKS & RAMBLES

You don't have to kill yourself to get a taste of the Green Mountain outback. Many of the parks listed above under "Parks & Other Hot Spots" have wonderful nature trails, often with interpretive signs. The **Healing Springs Nature Trail** at Shaftsbury State Park north of Bennington, the **Emerald Lake Nature Trail,** and the **Big Trees Nature Trail** at Lake St. Catherine State Park are all excellent. **Merck Forest & Farmland Center** (see "Hiking & Backpacking," above) has an endless variety of walking over Vermont countryside. See "Bird Watching" and "Snowshoeing," above, for more walks and easy hikes through very interesting country.

West River Trail

5 miles round-trip. Allow 3 hr. Easy walking alongside the white water of the West River. Access: in Jamaica State Park, off State Rte. 30.

Very few things are as crowd-pleasing as a big waterfall. Hamilton Falls, on the West River, tumbles and pools spectacularly down 125 feet of granite ledges, making it Vermont's highest waterfall. The riverbank trail follows an old railroad bed that was built in 1881 and long ago lapsed into decay. If you come here during spring or fall, when water is being released from the Ball Mountain Dam upriver, the park is likely to be crowded; however, you'll get to see white-water paddlers take on the challenge of The Dumplings, a set of enormous boulders about a mile up the trail that were left in the river when the glaciers of the last ice age retreated. At all other times during the summer, expect to find walkers, horseback riders, mountain bikers, and joggers enjoying the level trail. And if it's a warm afternoon, down by the parking lot you can take a dip in Salmon Hole, a perfect example of a Vermont swimmin' hole.

Wilgus State Park

0.6 mile round-trip. Allow 30 min. A good break from driving on I-91. Access: Take the Ascutney exit off I-91 and follow Rte. 5 south for approximately 1.5 miles. The park entrance will be on your left. Turn right into the picnic area parking lot, the trailhead for a riverside nature trail.

What better way to stretch your legs than to take a short stroll along the Connecticut River. You can have your picnic in the company of towering white oak, white pine, and yellow birch trees.

Campgrounds & Other Accommodations

CAMPING

There are 94 campsites scattered across the **Green Mountain National Forest,** available on a first-come, first-served basis for a small fee. Free camping is also permitted anywhere on national forest land. For more information, contact the Green Mountain National Forest, 231 N. Main St., Rutland, VT 05701 (☎ **802/747-6700**).

The **Department of Forests, Parks, and Recreation** maintains 35 campgrounds in the state. For a brochure, contact the Department of Forests, Parks, and Recreation, 108 S. Main St., Waterbury, VT 05676 (☎ **802/241-3655;** www.state.vt.us/anr/fpr/).

Molly Stark State Park

From the junction of State Rte. 100 and 9 in Wilmington, head east on State Rte. 9 for 3 miles. ☎ **802/464-5460.** 34

sites, no hookups, wheelchair-accessible rest rooms, flush toilets, showers, picnic tables, fireplaces, wood, and ice.

The sites here are located in a 158-acre preserve with hiking trails leading to the summit of 2,145-foot Mount Olga.

Woodford State Park
From Bennington, head 10 miles east on State Rte. 9. ☎ **802/447-7169.** 103 sites, no hookups, public phone, flush toilets, showers, picnic tables, fireplaces, wood, playground, and boat ramp.

This 400-acre area is centered around Adams Reservoir, a good swimming hole where motorized boats are prohibited. Campsites are east of the reservoir, set deep in the forest.

Jamaica State Park
From Jamaica, head 0.5 mile north on the town road. ☎ **802/874-4600.** 59 sites, no hookups, public phone, flush toilets, showers, picnic tables, fireplaces, wood, ice, and playground.

Camp by the West River in this densely forested park. Kayak or raft down the West during dam releases in the last weeks of April and September, take the walk to Hamilton Falls (see "Walks & Rambles," above), or go for a dip in the Salmon Hole. During the French and Indian War, British soldiers were ambushed by Frenchmen and Native Americans here.

Hapgood Pond Recreation Area
From Peru, head 1.75 miles northeast on Hapgood Pond Rd. ☎ **802/824-6456.** 28 sites, no hookups, pit toilets, tables, fire rings, grills, wood.

Set in the Green Mountain National Forest, this is a perfect spot to get lost in the wilderness. Wooded, secluded sites are slightly removed from the pond. Down at the water, there's a beach for swimming and a boat launch for your canoe.

Lake St. Catherine State Park
Located 3 miles south of Poultney on State Rte. 30. ☎ **802/287-9158.** 61 sites, no hookups, public phone, wheelchair-accessible rest rooms, showers, limited grocery store, picnic tables, fireplace, wood, and boat rentals.

The campsites are ideally located on the sandy shores of this 7-mile-long lake. A great place to swim, canoe, or fish for bass, perch, pike, and walleye.

Calvin Coolidge State Park
From the junction of State Rte. 100 and 100A in Plymouth, head 2 miles north on State Rte. 100A. ☎ **802/672-3612.** 60 sites, no hookups, public phone, wheelchair-accessible rest rooms, showers, ice, picnic tables, fireplaces, wood, and playground.

A network of hiking trails traverses this large 16,165-acre preserve, including a route to Shrewsbury Peak, northwest of Plymouth. The campsites are hidden in a forest of firs, spruce, hemlock, birches, and sugar maples.

INNS & RESORTS

It's almost an absurd proposition to list the best inns in southern Vermont. The competition is fierce, forcing many innkeepers to cut cross-country ski trails, shuttle hikers or canoeists, or be affiliated with a golf course if they want to survive. You rarely come across an accommodation that doesn't feature some sporting activity. These are simply my own personal favorites.

The White House
Off State Rte. 9, Wilmington, VT 05363. ☎ **802/464-2135** or 800/541-2135. www.whitehouseinn.com. Rates start at $59 per person, including breakfast.

Set on a hill overlooking the town of Wilmington, the stately White House is a sight that's hard to miss from State Route 9. Built as a summer home for a wealthy lumber baron in 1915, this Colonial Revival mansion displays a facade of white pillars, two-storied terraces, and French doors. The inn is known for its continental cuisine and 45 kilometers

(28.1 miles) of groomed cross-country ski trails that start from the back porch. It is also located near Mount Snow.

West Mountain Inn

State Rte. 313, Arlington, VT 05250. ☎ **802/375-6516.** www.westmountaininn.com. Rates start at $155, double, including breakfast and dinner.

If you hook old tires instead of trout on the Battenkill, the West Mountain Inn will undoubtedly cheer you up. The inn is set high in the valley overlooking the mountains of the Taconic range. There are 5 miles of hiking and cross-country trails leading from the back porch and a great bike ride to the West Arlington Covered Bridge (see "Road Biking," above).

The Equinox

State Rte. 7A, Manchester Village, 05254. ☎ **802/362-4700** or 800/362-4747. www.equinoxresort.com. Rates start at $189 double.

Once a fashionable summer retreat in the late 1800s for rich Northeasterners and presidents, The Equinox continues to captivate guests who yearn for the elegance of yesteryear coupled with today's finest amenities. Step out of the modern world onto the marble sidewalks of 19th-century Manchester Village, and enter through the Equinox's stately columns and rambling white veranda. Inside the lobby, velvet chairs and marble tables are set around a Federal-style fireplace. The inn sits at the base of 3,816-foot Mount Equinox. Go golfing on one of the finest courses in the state, cross-country skiing on 20 kilometers (12.5 miles) of groomed trails, alpine skiing at nearby Bromley or Stratton, or simply take a stroll through the inn's backyard gardens of tulips and azaleas. You'll feel like you just stepped out of an Edith Wharton novel.

The Old Tavern

Grafton, VT 05146. ☎ **802/843-2231** or 800/843-1801. www.old-tavern.com. Rates start at $135 and include breakfast.

Renting a room at the Old Tavern in Grafton is like renting a historic hamlet for the weekend. This former stagecoach stop has 66 rooms, cottages, and guest houses scattered about the quaint village. All have been meticulously restored to their 19th-century splendor. The Old Tavern's tennis courts and 40-kilometer (25-mile) cross-country trail system are just down the road. This is also the start of the Grafton Bike Loop (see "Road Biking," above).

The Landgrove Inn

P.O. Box 215, Landgrove, VT 05148. ☎ **802/824-6673** or 800/669-8466. www.landgroveinn.com. Rates start at $95 per room. B&B.

Set in the small village of Landgrove on the outskirts of the Green Mountain National Forest, the 18 rooms branch out from the original 1820 house. The inn is within close proximity to Bromley and Stratton, and offers 15 miles of groomed cross-country trails. The inn is known for its romantic sleigh rides.

Inn at Windsor

106 Main St., Windsor, VT 05089. ☎ **802/674-5670** or 800/754-8668. www.bbonline.com/vt/innatwindsor/index.html. Rates start at $105 and include a 7-course breakfast.

Passion and history seep from the walls of this inn. The passion stems from the owners, Larry Bowser and his wife Holly Taylor, who have spent the last 17 years painstakingly restoring this Georgian-style house. Built in 1791 for apothecary Dr. Issac Green, the gracious house remained in the family until being sold to the Knights of Columbus in 1963. The owners have carefully peeled away the 20th-century facade to re-create the historic charm of yesteryear. The three-room inn is located near the banks of the Connecticut River and the slopes of Mount Ascutney. Larry and Holly's exuberance over their inn is contagious. Catch it while you can.

3

Central Vermont

I'm going out to clean the pasture spring;
I'll only stop to rake the leaves away
(and wait to watch the water clear, I may):
I sha'n't be gone too long.—You come too.
I'm going out to fetch the little calf
That's standing by the mother. It's so young
It totters when she licks it with her tongue.
I sha'n't be gone too long.—You come too.

—Robert Frost, *"The Pasture"*

Robert Frost is so closely associated with rural Vermont that it seems incongruous that he lived in San Francisco until he was 11 and then in Lawrence, Massachusetts, throughout his middle and high school years. It was not until he married his high school sweetheart, Elinor White, that the future poet laureate would turn to farming and move to New England. Whether or not Frost chose to be a farmer because he expected the profession to provide him with poetic images and metaphors is not fully known. But when he moved to Ripton, near Middlebury College, in 1920, he chose a pastoral landscape that would suit him well. Bordering the Green Mountains, near the Middlebury Gap, Ripton is a patchwork of farm buildings, old stone walls, and, yes, emerald pasture.

Bordering Lake Champlain to the west and the Connecticut River to the east, Ripton and the lowlands of central Vermont are about as green as this state gets. From Addison to Randolph, Pittsfield to Waitsfield, the middle chunk of the state feels like one rolling farm, with interchangeable steeples and small country stores. The only break in pasture comes with the ridge of the Green Mountains that head south to north. You can overcome this obstacle and head east to west on four majestic gap roads—Brandon, Middlebury, Lincoln, and Appalachian.

With such an abundance of water, mountains, and rolling ribbons of road, and an absence of any major urban area, central Vermont's major attraction is the great outdoors. Road bikers snake through the backcountry roads with little traffic, hikers hit the Long Trail, mountain bikers venture to the hills around Randolph and Waitsfield, and anglers can fish in an almost countless number of rivers, lakes, and ponds. Come winter, Route 100 leads from Killington to Sugarbush and Mad River Glen and there are top-notch cross-country skiing centers from Blueberry Hill in Goshen to the Woodstock Ski Touring Center.

The Lay of the Land

North of Route 4, the individual peaks of the **Green Mountains** are more prevalent, more rugged, and higher. Here, Mount Killington, Mount Ellen, and Camel's Hump all tower above 4,000 feet. To the west, the Taconics end and the valley widens out into the broad lowland occupied in part by Lake Champlain. About 1,500 feet lower than the mountains, the rocks under the valley are rich in limestone and marble. Indeed, beneath the valley floor from Dorset northward to Brandon lies virtually all of New England's commercial marble deposits. Vermont is the second largest marble producer in the nation, and large quarries are still in operation in Danby, West Rutland, and Proctor.

Aside from Champlain, other large bodies of water in the valley include Lake Bomoseen and Lake Dunmore. The Ottauquechee and White Rivers slice through the eastern part of the state as they head toward the Connecticut River. Just like the southern section of the state, the **Vermont Piedmont** continues along the Connecticut River in an even more remote fashion. More dairy farms, more rolling hills.

Large wildlife, like deer, moose, and bear, are most prevalent in the Green Mountain National Forest. Good birding locales include the **Dead Creek Wildlife Management Area** in the Champlain Valley. Migrating waterfowl, herons, and snowy owls are some of the birds spotted.

Orientation

This chapter covers the territory north of U.S. 4 as far as I-89 from South Burlington to the Montpelier/Barre area and U.S. 302 from Barre to Wells River on the Connecticut River side. For coverage of Burlington, the Green Mountains north of I-89, and the Northeast Kingdom, turn to chapter 4, "Lake Champlain, the Northern Green Mountains & the Northeast Kingdom."

Whatever the season, Killington siphons off so much of the tourist traffic that it makes U.S. 4 the natural boundary between southern and central Vermont. North of here and east of the mountains, especially off the ski-country corridor of Route 100, the landscape and atmosphere are different from that of southern Vermont. Tourist-related businesses are scarce (excepting Woodstock), and there are far fewer B&Bs and inns. All the recreational areas, including the ski areas (**Sugarbush, Mad River, and** the **Middlebury College Snow Bowl**), have a stronger local flavor. The outdoors people around here tend to be Vermonters or those who have had a long association with the state. Places like Mad River and Camel's Hump are only a short shot away from Burlington, Vermont's one true city. And aside from the area right around the Green Mountains, central Vermont really remains cow country. Dairy farming and other agricultural enterprises such as maple sugaring are in evidence everywhere, and the tiny towns, like **Bethel, Randolph, Chelsea,** and **Thetford,** still have a genuine rural-crossroads feel.

I-91 continues on up the eastern border of the state toward the Northeast Kingdom, but **I-89** cuts northwest up the White River Valley, through the heart of central Vermont. It's one of the few interstate highways that truly qualifies as a scenic route. All around is rolling farmland—granite bluffs poke out of the divider between the north- and southbound lanes, and occasionally you'll be stunned by the sight of the distinctive rocky summit of Camel's Hump peeking out above the surrounding mountains. The three branches of the White River have swimming holes and crafty trout galore; if you can't find what you're looking for here, ask at the local general store. To the east and west of the interstate are beautiful country roads like **State Routes 110, 14, 12,** and **12A.** All but Route 14 are nearly desolate, though it would seem odd to me to say that Route 14 has much traffic—it really doesn't. These roads seem tailor-made for a road-biking trip. In winter, snow machine trails are found almost everywhere, the trails constituting the locals' Nordic-skiing centers—who really needs groomed trails that you have to pay for when it's this good right outside your back door?

At the northerly end of central Vermont is the **Barre-Montpelier area,** central Vermont's closest approximation to an urban zone. Montpelier is a pretty town that's gained an arty/intellectual gloss in the last decade or so. In Onion River Sports, it has a good outdoor-sports shop; in the Inn, a truly fine New England hostelry; and in Bear Pond Books, a great bookstore strong on nature writing and local writers, among other things. Barre is a more workmanlike town, famous for its granite quarries. It's not much to look at, but go to a bar here and you're guaranteed to hear a real Vermont accent in all its glorious oddness.

As in southern Vermont, the gaps through the mountains are the most beautiful drives of all and offer access to what's probably my favorite stretch of Green Mountain backcountry (not an easy thing to settle on). The first of these drives north of Sherburne Pass is **Brandon Gap,** State Route 73, connecting Rochester and Brandon. Next up are the three must-sees—three roads that have more of a high-country feel than anyplace else in Vermont: **Middlebury Gap** (State Route 125, connecting Ripton and Hancock); **Lincoln Gap** (Lincoln-Warren Highway, closed in winter); and **Appalachian Gap** (State Route 17). The forested Lincoln Gap is gorgeous and offers access to a prime stretch of the Long Trail, and the view west from Appalachian Gap is unforgettable.

Parks & Other Hot Spots

Bomoseen State Park

Follow U.S. 4 west from Rutland to State Rte. 30/Castleton Corners exit. South on State Rte. 30 to State Rte. 4A; then west on State Rte. 4A and right (north) onto road to West Castleton/West Shore of Lake Bomoseen. ☎ **802/265-4242.** 66 campsites, public phone, wheelchair-accessible rest rooms, picnic area, large boat access, marked trails. Boating, camping, fishing, hiking, water skiing.

Lake Bomoseen is a large, very long body of water ringed by summer houses and cabins. It gets heavy recreational use—lots of powerboaters and waterskiers rip to and fro across its surface. If it's lakeside camping and waterborne recreation you're looking for, however, Bomoseen is a good place for it. There's excellent fishing on the lake, and the Slate History Trail meanders through the leftovers of the 19th century's booming slate quarries and mills. The campsites are set slightly back from the shores of the lake in a wooded refuge.

Half Moon Pond State Park
Follow U.S. 4 west from Rutland to State Rte. 30/Castleton Corners exit. South on State Rte. 30 to State Rte. 4A; then west on State Rte. 4A. Right (north) onto road to West Castleton/West Shore of Lake Bomoseen. Continue for about 7 miles on this road to Half Moon State Park. ☎ **802/273-2848.** Campsites, wheelchair-accessible rest rooms, picnic area, canoe access, marked trails. Bird watching, fishing, swimming.

A small pond with a pretty state park that gets fairly crowded on summer weekends. Half Moon's facilities make it a good place to take young children. This is wild turkey country—you're as likely to encounter a gobbler on the nearby nature trail (see "Bird Watching," below) as anywhere in southern Vermont. The pond has trout, bass, and pike fishing; a good swimming beach; and some beaver activity.

Chittenden Reservoir
Follow U.S. 4 east of Rutland to Mendon; then turn north on East Pittsford/Chittendon Rd. Keep right and road will end at boating access. For information, contact the Green Mountain National Forest, 231 N. Main St., Rutland, VT 05701 (☎ **802/747-6700**). Fishing, snowmobiling.

Stocked with trout, bass, perch, and salmon, Chittenden Reservoir is a little like the Somerset and Harriman reservoirs to the south—remote, but crowded with anglers year-round who are in on the secret. In the winter, you'll see the snowmobiles and the large holes drilled in the ice. Come summer, the waters are filled with drifting boats.

Silver Lake State Park
From Barnard, head 0.25 mile north on Town Rd. ☎ **802/234-9451.** 47 sites, no hookups, public phone, wheelchair-accessible rest rooms, sewage disposal, tables, fire rings, grills, wood. Swimming.

Located on the eastern side of the state, the park is known for its swimming.

Camel's Hump Forest Preserve
Contact the Department of Forests, Parks, and Recreation, 103 S. Main St., Building 10, Waterbury, VT 05671-0601 (☎ **802/241-3655**). Hiking.

One of Vermont's most popular day hikes is the climb up Camel's Hump. The distinctive 4,083-foot bare rock summit can be seen from almost the entire western part of the state.

What to Do & Where to Do It

BALLOONING

Boland Balloon offers early-morning, sunset, and champagne flights over Lake Fairlee, the Connecticut River Valley, and the foothills of the Green Mountains. Brian Boland can be reached at the Post Mills Airport (☎ **802/333-9254**).

In conjunction with Boland Balloon, the **Silver Maple Lodge,** P.O. Box 8, Fairlee, VT 05045 (☎ **800/666-1946** or 802/333-4326), offers Balloon Inn Vermont. The package includes 1 to 3 nights at the Silver Maple Lodge and a 1-hour champagne balloon ride. Purchase that engagement ring and propose to her up in the clouds.

BIRD WATCHING

The habitats in central Vermont are not very different from those you'd find in southern Vermont—take a look at "Bird Watching," in chapter 2, for lots of general information on what kinds of birds you should expect to see and where. You can see **hawks** above the Green Mountains and the monadnocks of the Connecticut River Valley; **vireos, thrushes, owls,** and **ruby-throated hummingbirds** throughout the hardwood forests; **bitterns, egrets,** and **bank swallows** on the Connecticut River; and high up on the

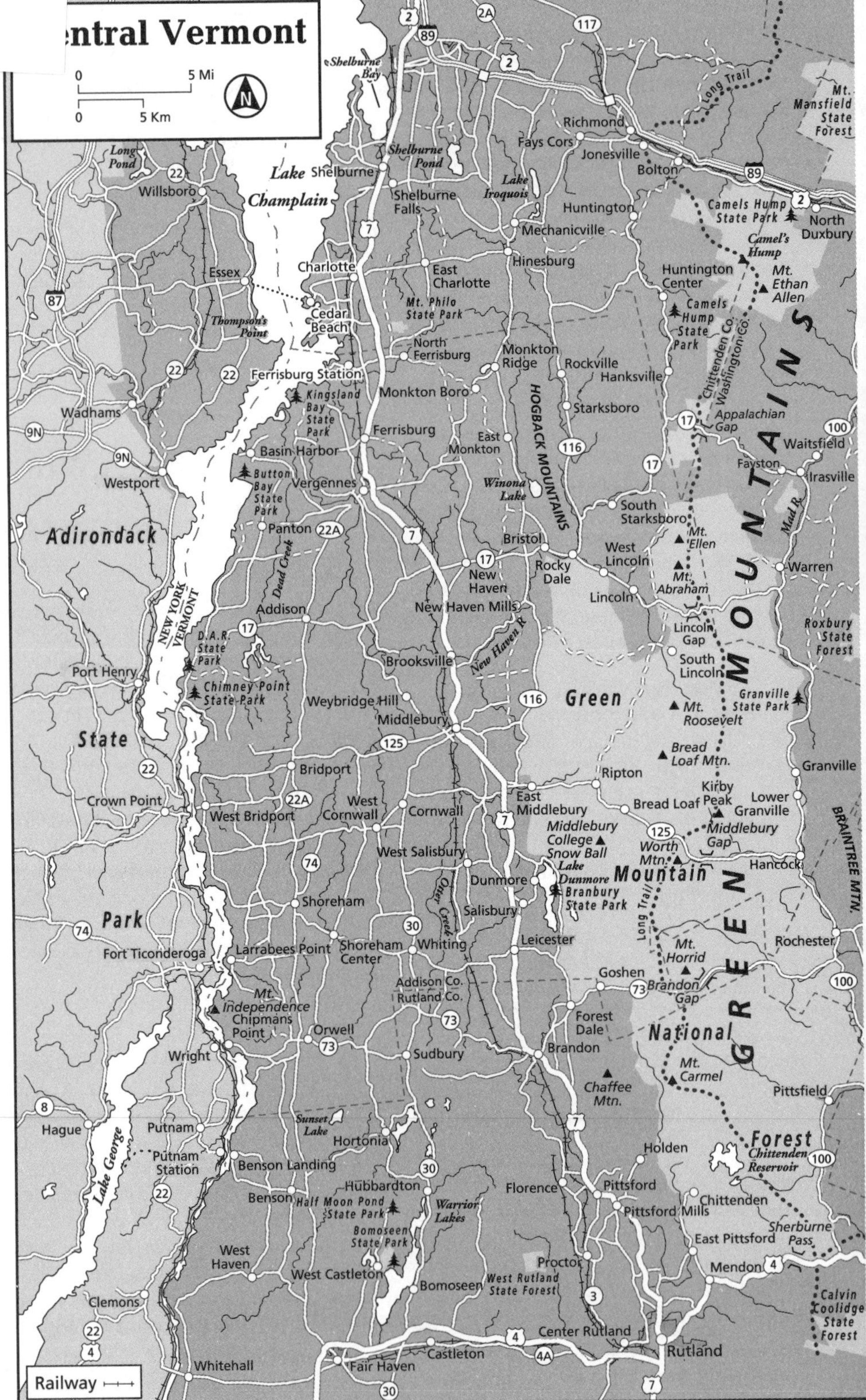

entral Vermont
0
5 Mi
0
5 Km
N
Lake Champlain
Shelburne
Shelburne Falls
Charlotte
East Charlotte
Cedar Beach
Essex
Willsboro
Wadhams
Westport
Ferrisburg Station
Ferrisburg
Vergennes
Basin Harbor
Panton
Addison
Port Henry
Crown Point
Fort Ticonderoga
Hague
Putnam
Putnam Station
West Haven
Clemons
Whitehall
Fair Haven
Castleton
West Castleton
Bomoseen
Center Rutland
Rutland
Proctor
Pittsford
Pittsford Mills
Florence
Brandon
Forest Dale
Leicester
Salisbury
Dunmore
Middlebury
Bristol
New Haven
New Haven Mills
Brooksville
Weybridge Hill
Bridport
West Bridport
West Cornwall
Cornwall
West Salisbury
Shoreham
Shoreham Center
Whiting
Larrabees Point
Orwell
Sudbury
Hubbardton
Benson
Benson Landing
Hortonia
Richmond
Jonesville
Bolton
Fays Cors
Huntington
Huntington Center
Mechanicville
Hinesburg
Monkton Ridge
Monkton Boro
East Monkton
North Ferrisburg
Rockville
Hanksville
Starksboro
South Starksboro
West Lincoln
Lincoln
Rocky Dale
South Lincoln
Lincoln Gap
Ripton
East Middlebury
Bread Loaf
Goshen
Holden
Chittenden
East Pittsford
Mendon
Pittsfield
Rochester
Hancock
Granville
Lower Granville
Warren
Waitsfield
Fayston
Irasville
North Duxbury
Adirondack State Park
Green Mountain National Forest
GREEN MOUNTAINS
HOGBACK MOUNTAINS
BRAINTREE MTN.
NEW YORK
VERMONT
Long Trail
Appalachian Gap
Middlebury Gap
Brandon Gap
Sherburne Pass
Mt. Mansfield State Forest
Camels Hump State Park
Camel's Hump
Mt. Ethan Allen
Mt. Ellen
Mt. Abraham
Mt. Roosevelt
Bread Loaf Mtn.
Kirby Peak
Worth Mtn.
Mt. Horrid
Mt. Carmel
Chaffee Mtn.
Mt. Independence
Chipmans Point
Wright
Middlebury College Snow Bowl
Branbury State Park
Kingsland Bay State Park
Button Bay State Park
D.A.R. State Park
Chimney Point State Park
Mt. Philo State Park
Half Moon Pond State Park
Bomoseen State Park
West Rutland State Forest
Calvin Coolidge State Forest
Roxbury State Forest
Granville State Park
Chittenden Co.
Washington Co.
Addison Co.
Rutland Co.
Chittenden Reservoir
Shelburne Bay
Shelburne Pond
Lake Iroquois
Long Pond
Thompson's Point
Winona Lake
Dead Creek
New Haven R.
Otter Creek
Mad R.
Lake Dunmore
Sunset Lake
Warrior Lakes
Lake George
Railway

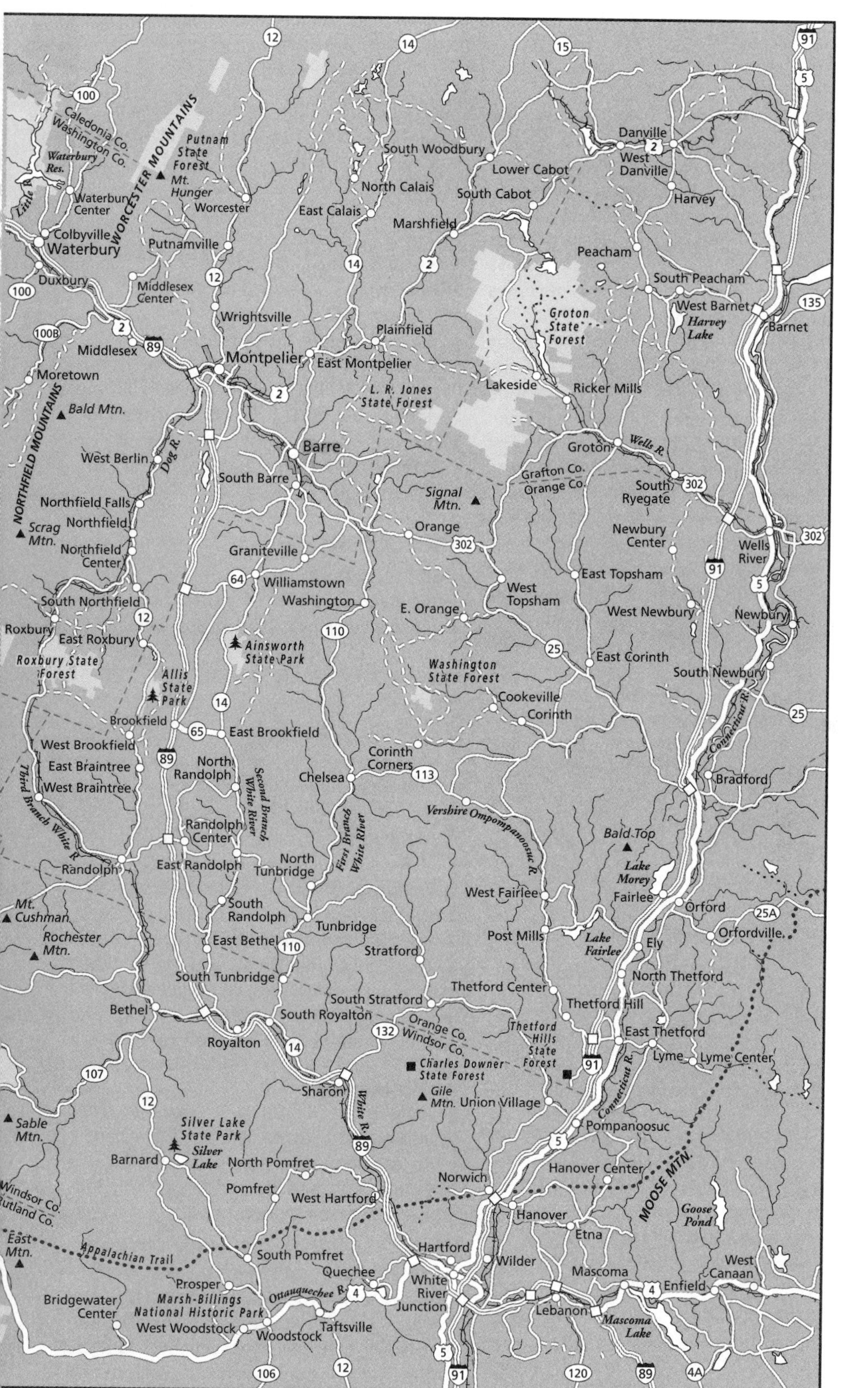

WORCESTER MOUNTAINS
NORTHFIELD MOUNTAINS
MOOSE MTN.
Caledonia Co.
Washington Co.
Waterbury Res.
Little R.
Waterbury Center
Colbyville
Waterbury
Duxbury
Putnam State Forest
Mt. Hunger
Worcester
Putnamville
Middlesex Center
Wrightsville
Middlesex
Moretown
Montpelier
East Montpelier
Plainfield
South Woodbury
North Calais
East Calais
Marshfield
Lower Cabot
South Cabot
Danville
West Danville
Harvey
Peacham
South Peacham
West Barnet
Harvey Lake
Barnet
Groton State Forest
L. R. Jones State Forest
Lakeside
Ricker Mills
Groton
Wells R.
Bald Mtn.
West Berlin
Dog R.
Barre
South Barre
Grafton Co.
Orange Co.
Signal Mtn.
South Ryegate
Northfield Falls
Northfield
Scrag Mtn.
Northfield Center
Orange
Graniteville
Newbury Center
Wells River
Williamstown
Washington
West Topsham
East Topsham
South Northfield
E. Orange
West Newbury
Newbury
Roxbury
East Roxbury
Ainsworth State Park
East Corinth
Roxbury State Forest
Allis State Park
Washington State Forest
South Newbury
Cookeville
Corinth
Connecticut R.
Brookfield
East Brookfield
West Brookfield
East Braintree
West Braintree
North Randolph
Second Branch White River
Corinth Corners
Chelsea
Bradford
Third Branch White R.
Randolph Center
Vershire
Ompompanoosuc R.
First Branch White River
Bald Top
Randolph
East Randolph
North Tunbridge
Lake Morey
West Fairlee
Fairlee
Orford
Mt. Cushman
South Randolph
Rochester Mtn.
Tunbridge
Post Mills
Lake Fairlee
Ely
Orfordville
East Bethel
Stratford
North Thetford
South Tunbridge
Thetford Center
Thetford Hill
South Stratford
Bethel
South Royalton
Orange Co.
Windsor Co.
Thetford Hills State Forest
East Thetford
Royalton
Lyme
Lyme Center
Charles Downer State Forest
Sharon
White R.
Gile Mtn.
Union Village
Sable Mtn.
Silver Lake State Park
Silver Lake
Pompanoosuc
Barnard
North Pomfret
Hanover Center
Norwich
Pomfret
West Hartford
Hanover
Goose Pond
Windsor Co.
Rutland Co.
East Mtn.
Appalachian Trail
Etna
Hartford
South Pomfret
Wilder
Quechee
Mascoma
West Canaan
Prosper
White River Junction
Enfield
Marsh-Billings National Historic Park
Ottauquechee R.
Bridgewater Center
Lebanon
Mascoma Lake
West Woodstock
Woodstock
Taftsville
100
12
14
15
91
5
2
100B
89
135
302
64
110
25
65
113
25A
132
107
4
106
120
4A

hillsides of the Green Mountains in the red spruce/balsam fir boreal forest, **spruce grouse, black-capped** and **boreal chickadees, Swainson's thrushes,** and numerous vernal **warblers.** High-country beaver ponds are a likely spot for birding, and there's usually activity around them; keep an ear open for a **loon's** whinnying call.

Wild turkeys can be found gobbling away in the oak-hickory forest of the **Glen Lake Trail** where it passes through **Half Moon State Park.** (Directions: From intersection with State Route 30, go west on State Route 4A for 1.3 miles. Make a right turn at sign for Lake Bomoseen, West Shore. After about 5 miles, near the entrance to Lake Bomoseen State Park, turn where you see the sign for Half Moon State Park and follow Moscow Road for 3 miles. Park on the shoulder at the first open meadow. Across the road from the meadow, look for the trail heading off into the woods.)

One of the most remarkable birding events in the Champlain Valley is the spring and fall stopovers of tens of thousands of migratory **snow geese. Dead Creek Wildlife Management Area** (☎ **802/878-1564**) is one hot spot. Seeing 20,000 large, shrieking white birds take to the air is a natural spectacle of a rare order. Dead Creek is an excellent spot for birding year-round; in warm weather you can canoe its calm marshes, where you'll see all varieties of migratory waterfowl, including **great blue herons.** And in winter it's one of the best places in New England to seek out a **snowy owl.** Drive around for a while and you're nearly guaranteed to spot one, stoically posed on a fence post or some such perch.

The **Vermont Institute of Natural Science & Raptor Center,** Church Hill Rd., Woodstock, VT 05091 (☎ **802/457-2779;** www.vinsweb.org), is a fascinating place for birders to visit. Bald eagles, peregrine falcons, owls, and hawks are 4 of the more than 25 species seen in the outdoor flight cages.

A "Check List for Birds of Vermont" is available from the **Green Mountain Audubon Society,** P.O. Box 33, Burlington, VT 05401. A similar checklist that also covers all manner of fauna observed in Vermont is available from the **Vermont Department of Fish and Wildlife,** 103 S. Main St., Waterbury, VT 05676 (☎ **802/241-3700;** www.anr.state.vt.us/fw/fwhome/index.htm).

It's a little out of the way, but if you drop your binoculars off Camel's Hump (ouch), the **Wild Bird Center,** on Williston Road east of Burlington (☎ **802/878-4400**), ought to be able to help you out.

CANOEING

Half Moon Pond

Hubbardton County, north of West Castleton. Access: Take U.S. 4 west from Rutland to State Rte. 30/Castleton Corners exit. South on State Rte. 30 to State Rte. 4A; then west on State Rte. 4A. Right (north) onto road to West Castleton/West Shore of Lake Bomoseen. Continue for about 7 miles on this road to Half Moon State Park. Over 60 campsites and lean-tos on the pond's shores.

A small pond with a pretty state park that gets fairly crowded on summer weekends, Half Moon is a good place to take young children. There's a worthwhile nature trail (see "Bird Watching," above); good trout, bass, and pike fishing; and some beaver activity on the pond.

Lefferts Pond

Northeast of Chittenden. Access: Take Mountain Top Rd. to Wildcat Rd. About 1 mile later, continue past the CVPS Access Rd. until you see the pond on your left. There's a small launch here.

Even though the much larger Chittenden Reservoir has motorboats—and often a stiff headwind to contend with—the 55-acre Lefferts Pond is a far better alternative for canoeing. Just off the southeast point of the Reservoir, Lefferts is surrounded by tall hemlocks, balsam fir, and spruces, and, in the distance, the slopes of Killington Ski Resort. It's a placid retreat not only for paddlers, but also for wildlife. River otters, beavers, wood ducks, herons, and even loons have been spotted here. If you feel like going for a hike, there's a great trail that loops around the pond and reservoir and you have access to the Long Trail. Unfortunately, the Central Vermont Public Service Corporation, which owns the reservoir, does not permit camping on its shores.

Dead Creek Wildlife Management Area

Southeast of Vergennes. Access: 2.4 miles south of where Rte. 22A crosses Otter Creek, turn right on West Rd. The road ends at Dead Creek, where there's ample parking. From here, canoers should head south on Dead Creek to Rte. 17. You can camp at nearby D.A.R. State Park on the shores of Lake Champlain.

Just off the southern shores of Lake Champlain and due east of the Green Mountains is a swath of Vermont farmland that's so green and fertile that you can't help but envy those lucky farmers who toil on this land. The rolling pastures are home to grazing cows, rows of corn, and tall silos. Dead Creek cuts right through this farmland on a 6-mile (round-trip) route that guarantees to leave you as relaxed as a lounging Holstein. Paddle with the geese, herons, and ducks (see "Bird Watching," above), or throw a line over the canoe to catch bass, perch, and pike. It's a great way to see this agrarian state close up.

Winona Lake

North of Bristol. Access: West of Bristol, turn right off Rte. 17 across from where Rte. 116 heads south. Drive north on this paved but unmarked road for 3.6 miles and then turn right at a sign marked BRISTOL POND. You paddle south into the lake on the gently flowing Pond Brook.

You're apt to find local anglers at this coveted gem hidden on the backside of the Hogback Mountains. The 234-acre lake is home to yellow perch, northern pike, and pickerel. Since there is no development on the lake, expect to find marshy shoreline, thick with cattails and heath. There are several islands on the western shores to cruise around, but mostly you'll be paddling on the wide open lake.

Lower White River/Connecticut River

7–8 miles. 3 hr. Easy. Access: Put-in at West Hartford off Rte. 14. Take-out is at the North Hartland Rapids, before Sumner's Falls. You'll see a large sign for the portage trail.

Marty Banak came to Vermont at the age of 26, and 19 years later he hasn't left. As the owner of Wilderness Trails, an outfitter located in the back of the Quechee Inn at Marshland Farm, Banak has plenty of activity to keep him busy. In winter, Banak leads cross-country skiers and snowshoers on 18 kilometers (11.25 miles) of groomed trails throughout the neighboring farmland to the Quechee Gorge. Come summer, Marty's in his prime, heading the Vermont Fly Fishing School at the Woodstock Inn and Resort, renting out mountain and road bikes and guiding canoers to the nearby rivers and ponds. Along with renting canoes across the street on 50-acre Dewey's Mills Pond (great for bass fishing), Banak brings experienced canoers to the Upper White River to try their luck on Class I and II water or to the Lower White for a scenic quiet-water paddle.

On a sunny spring day last summer, Marty took my brother and me on a three-river, two-state paddle. We started in West Hartford on the Lower White River, which Marty said was great for bass and trout fishing. We paddled past rope swings where kids plunge into the deep, clean water. A mile later, we merged at the real White River Junction with the murky tea water of the Connecticut River heading south from the cedar swamps of the

Northeast Kingdom. Little ripples on the White guided us smoothly under three bridges onto the Connecticut. We bore right and were greeted by Jersey cows and that sweet smell of manure. Big logs and branches lined the shores, the work of beavers. Marty has also seen the bald eagles that nest 2 miles upstream at the Wilder Dam on the Connecticut.

We stopped on one of the primitive islands and watched Marty bring out his beloved fishing pole. In late September, this section of the Connecticut, bordered by a forest of maples, is aflame in colorful fall foliage. With a graceful flick of the wrist, Marty put his fly out there on the river. Two minutes later, a beautiful brook trout was on the end of the line. We're easily convinced that this is prime fishing country. We continued on past the ripples of the Ottauquechee River and took out a mile later at the portage trail.

Outfitters

Wilderness Trails, Clubhouse Rd., Quechee (☎ **802/295-7620;** www.scenesofvermont.com/wildernesstrails/), is located in a red barn in the back of Quechee Inn at Marshland Farms. It's a 10-minute drive from the intersection of I-89 and I-91. Reserve in advance and Marty can have you off the highway and in the water in less than 20 minutes. Canoe trips, including drop-off and pickup, cost $45 to $50. Trips range from 4 to 12 miles, and you have the option of white or calm water. Also ask about Marty's full-moon paddles—champagne included.

CROSS-COUNTRY SKIING

What a bonanza! Every one of the cross-country centers listed here has a tremendous variety of skiing and a charming setting. You'll find well-established backcountry skiing trails throughout central Vermont's half of the Green Mountain National Forest; for a map, contact the forest service at ☎ **802/747-6700** and ask for their "Winter Recreation" map or, failing that, their regular map to the north half of the forest. Finally, almost anywhere you find yourself in central Vermont, there's spectacular backcountry skiing right outside your door. The intricate network of snowmobile trails is a crucial thoroughfare but also a tremendous aid for do-it-yourself Nordic touring—the trails wind through every cow pasture, up every hill, and through sugarbushes. The cross-country crowd may dislike a snowmachine's noise, but I've never met the skier who wasn't grateful for the machine's trail-breaking power on days when the snow wasn't that easy to negotiate.

Although the **Catamount Trail**—the planned border-to-border cross-country trail network from Massachusetts to Canada—is overall a little spotty, central Vermont has some of its best backcountry skiing. The **Catamount Trail Association,** 1 Main St., Burlington, VT 05401-5291 (☎ **802/864-5794;** www.catamounttrail.together.com), publishes a comprehensive guidebook.

In the Backcountry

Chittenden Brook

5.5 miles. Allow 3–4 hr. Moderate; some steep climbs and downhills. Access: 12.5 miles east of Brandon on State Rte. 73; 8 miles west of Rochester on State Rte. 73. The parking lot and large sign are located on the south side of the highway. Map: USGS 7.5-min. Rochester, Mount Carmel.

It was St. Patrick's Day and the terrain of central Vermont was dressed up for the occasion—the ground was green wherever you looked. Not to fear, I was at Blueberry Hill, one of the most respected cross-country skiing centers in New England. Owner Tony Clark, an inveterate cross-country skier, knows this neck of the forest as a bee knows honey. He directed me to one of his favorite spots, an area of the Green Mountain National Forest called Chittenden Brook.

Chittenden has a northeast exposure, which keeps the trail white long after the rest of central Vermont starts to thaw. I parked my car, walked through the gate, and skied uphill to the start of the trail, 0.6 mile away. At trail intersection number 2, the path bordered a rushing brook. The early warm spell created high, raging waters, which I continued to hear throughout the day. Three bridges and numerous birches and white pines later, I arrived at intersection 3. The trail started to climb steeply into the rolling hills of the forest. By the time I reached intersection 4, I was high above the brook. A short 0.1-mile detour brought me to Beaver Pond, where locals often find an occasional moose slurping water by the shore.

From intersections 4 to 7 to the campground is the exciting part of the loop. The trail narrows as it sweeps downhill back to the brook. This part is recommended only for skiers who can turn on a dime while cruising downhill. Otherwise, you might end up in the brook and have to water-ski back to your car. I had lunch at the campground before taking a left onto unplowed Forest Road 45. A quick 2.3 miles down the curving road and I was back at Route 73 faster than you can say, "Let it snow, let it snow, let it snow!"

Widow's Clearing

6.4 miles. Allow 3 hr. Moderate; some climbs and a nice downhill. Access: 3.5 miles east of Ripton on Rte. 125, turn right on Forest Rd. 67. A little less than a mile later, you'll see a small parking lot for the Widow's Clearing Trail on the left. Map: USFS Middlebury Ranger District Winter Sports Trails.

Connecting Blueberry Hill with the Rickert Ski Touring Center, Widow's Clearing is a 3.2-mile run that leaves you at Forest Road 32. The start of the trail is fairly steep as you head upward through a thicket of red pines. To your right, you'll begin to see the Bread Loaf Campus of Middlebury College. Follow the blue blazes into an open field, before twisting back into the woods. The trail starts to switch back as you cross over a bridge. Keep your speed under control, or you might end up in the brook. You'll spend most of your time in the hardwood forest until you cruise downhill past evergreens into Widow's Clearing. The blue blazes on posts will point you to Forest Road 32. From here, do an about-face and return home.

Texas Falls/Hancock Branch Brook

3 miles round-trip. Allow 3–4 hr. Moderate to difficult; backcountry trails that may or may not have defined tracks, and your choice as far as taking on steep parts. Access: From State Rte. 100 in Hancock, go west on State Rte. 125 for 1.2 miles; turn north (right) onto Texas Falls Forest Service Rd. Park where the plowed road ends. Map: USGS 7.5-min. Hancock.

Texas Falls and its sylvan surroundings, which by virtue of its photogenic qualities and roadside access can be a mob scene in summertime, might actually be a better place to visit in the dead of winter. With maybe 4 inches of new snow, the falls and the trails upstream along Hancock Branch Brook take on an otherworldly look; the water is mostly frozen over, and where it isn't there's still rimy, blue-green snow and ice choking it. From the car park, follow the forest road until you reach a fork. To the right is the Texas Gap Trail and to the left is the Hancock Branch Brook Trail. I took a left and began a moderate climb up the forest road, which follows and repeatedly crosses the brook. You'll face some directional choices as you go; take what looks most inviting because you really can't go wrong here.

Nordic-Skiing Centers

With all the buzz over snowboarding and shaped skis and the increasing popularity of snowshoeing, cross-country skiing seems to have been left in the snow dust. Not true. Here in the state where cross-country was reborn in the 1960s, the sport is alive and well. In fact, it's better, thanks to the same technological improvements that have helped alpine skiing—better grooming, snowmaking, and improved gear. Vermont has over 40 ski touring centers that, if stretched end-to-end, would total around 2,000 miles of trails. Here are some of the finest.

Located at the Woodstock Country Club, the **Woodstock Ski Touring Center,** State Rte. 106, Woodstock (☎ **802/457-2114;** www.woodstockinn.com), has 58 kilometers (36.25 miles) of groomed trails that ring the base and then climb Mount Tom and Mount Peg—don't miss the classic woodland trails of the former. The base lodge is well equipped with rentals, rooms, showers, a restaurant, and a lounge with fireplace. The touring center also has maps for the 6.3-mile Skyline Trail, which goes from the Suicide Six downhill skiing area to Amity Pond. This is a great backcountry route.

The Three Stallion Inn, on Stock Farm Road, left off State Route 66 just before Randolph Village, is home to the **Green Mountain Touring Center,** Randolph, VT (☎ **802/728-5575;** www.3stallioninn.com). From the Victorian farmhouse, 35 kilometers (21.9 miles) of groomed trails branch out to the fields and forests below.

There could hardly be a more picturesque site for a ski center than that enjoyed by the **Green Trails Inn** in Brookfield (☎ **802/276-3412;** www.greentrailsinn.com). Hard right by the Floating Bridge, Green Trails has 35 kilometers (21.9 miles) of groomed trails through Brookfield's wooded high country.

Opened in 1971, **Mountain Meadows** (☎ **800/221-0598;** www.webk.com/mtmeadowsxc) is set high in a mountain hollow at 1,400 feet near the slopes of Killington. Of the 57 kilometers (35.6 miles) of trails, the ones around Kent Lake are ideal for novices. The sweeping Pond Plunge or Orchard Trails are popular with experienced skiers, who twist through the woods past old apple tree groves. The ski center is known for its exemplary ski school run by former U.S. Olympics coach Mike Gallagher. The rental shop is also one of the best in the state, with lots of high-end demos and gear for sale.

Another perfect spot for gliding in almost-guaranteed snow is the **Mountain Top Cross Country Ski Resort** in Chittenden (☎ **802/483-2311**). The first commercial cross-country ski center in the state, Mountain Top offers 85 kilometers (53.1 miles) of meticulously groomed trails through the woods and fields, with picturesque views of Chittenden Reservoir and the main ridge of the Green Mountains.

With a remote locale and an abundance of trails, **Blueberry Hill** in Goshen (☎ **802/247-6735** or **800/274-6535;** www.blueberryhill.inn.com/ski) easily deserves its reputation as one of Vermont's finest ski touring centers. Its 50 to 75 kilometers (31.25 to 46.88 miles) of groomed trails are nestled in the Green Mountain Forest, offering unparalleled tranquility. The eight-room inn is known for its gourmet cooking and delectable chocolate chip cookies.

The **Carroll and Jane Rikert Ski Touring Center** is located at the Bread Loaf Campus of Middlebury College. Through the forest made famous by Robert Frost's poems weave 42 kilometers (26.25 miles) of trails, actually skirting his farm as they wind through spruce forests and fields, beaver meadows, and old country lanes. A coveted Middlebury College secret, Rikert's is located 1,400 feet up Middlebury Gap, ringed by 3,000-foot peaks. Contact Middlebury College, Middlebury (☎ **802/443-5418**).

The **Inn at Round Barn,** E. Warren Rd., Waitsfield (☎ **802/496-2276;** www.innatroundbarn.com), features 23 kilometers (14.38 miles) of track-set trails that weave through the 85 acres of meadows on Mad River Valley. Good views of Sugarbush and Mount Abraham can be seen to the west.

Also in the Mad River Valley is **Ole's Cross-Country Center** (☎ **802/496-3430**). Ole Moseson, the Norwegian owner, lays out a network of 47 kilometers (29.4 miles) of skating and traditional diagonal-stride trails on the snowed-under Warren Airport and the surrounding woods.

DOWNHILL SKIING

I was actually at Killington, in what I've called southern Vermont, when I first guessed that certain Vermont skiers constitute their own unique breed. It was a mediocre day for skiing, not long after the snowpack had hardened to a bricklike consistency after a January thaw. We decided to go where the snowmaking was, and so the five of us—four native Vermonters and lifelong skiers and one New Yorker—piled into a van for the trip south to Killington.

All was fine at first. We got the blood moving with some warm-up runs on manicured intermediate trails, all of us cutting fine, fast figures as we carved our way down the hill. A suggestion that we hit the hard stuff was heartily assented to by all—and thus I found myself, on the kind of day that separates the proverbial men from the boys, about 30 yards below the topmost lip of Cascade, with one ski loose above me and the other skidding away below. A patch of blue ice had made short work of me; I could see a lot more like it ahead and knew it was going to be a long way down. Resigning myself, I trudged about, fetching my equipment; I waved off my friends' inquiries and watched them nimbly pick their way down the trail without major mishap, like mountain goats.

My bump technique, like most people's these days, was high energy, rubber legged, and on the edge of control—and absolutely useless on snow like this. Vermonters, however, have a long tradition of never skiing as if the snow's going to be easy and forgiving; on the contrary, they make it look hard and unpredictable, a force to be warily respected. The way they ski makes you understand what "knowing the mountain" really means. It's knowing everything about how a particular trail is skiing on a particular day—what the workable lines are, where the hazards are, and so forth. It's interacting with the mountain and taking what it gives you, rather than forcing your style on it.

The central Green Mountains are the breadbasket for this kind of skier. All the areas here—from south to north, the Snow Bowl, Sugarbush, Mad River Glen, on up to Stowe and Smuggler's Notch—are bastions of the narrow, erratic, traditional New England ski trail. And skiing well on these kinds of trails is more than simply blasting down a wide groomed or moguled boulevard; it's a head game. If you've skied here before, you'll know what I mean. If you haven't, your first ride up the Castlerock chair at Sugarbush or the Single chair at Mad River on a powder day will show you examples. Look for the bearded, unfashionably clad gent linking turn after perfect turn down the hill without once pulling up, utterly in control, and maybe taking some air from time to time with an unselfconscious holler.

Reverting to the practical, there are simpler reasons to ski in central Vermont, not least among them is the generally less-crowded, lower-key atmosphere on the slopes and in the lodges. Many ski shops in the area have knowledgeable staffs and lots of good deals on both sales and rentals. But it's really the overall quality of the skiing that keeps me coming back—great terrain, good skiers, and more natural snow, for some reason, than most places within a few hundred miles.

Ski Areas

Suicide Six

Woodstock, VT 05091. ☎ **802/457-1666;** www.woodstockinn.com. Snow report: ☎ 802/457-1100. 22 trails (30% beginner, 40% intermediate, 30% expert); 3 lifts including 2 double chairs; 633-ft. vertical drop. Full-day tickets $29.50 weekends, $16 weekdays.

Suicide Six is the tiny hill where Vermont skiing was born over 60 years ago. Now part of the Woodstock Inn and Resort, it's a cheap, great place to take the kids or to learn to ski. There are some genuinely difficult runs in The Face and to its left—though the name is a lot more frightening than the skiing in general. You won't find the fluff you get at upper elevations on the bigger mountains because the summit here is only a modest 1,200 feet high.

Middlebury College Snow Bowl

State Rte. 125 between Hancock and Ripton (mail: Middlebury, VT 05753). ☎ **802/388-4356.** 15 trails (33% beginner, 34% intermediate, 33% expert); 3 double chairs; 1,020-ft. vertical drop. Full-day tickets $28 weekends, $22 weekdays.

A small, unassuming place that can't help but get lost in the shadows of its much more ambitious neighbors to the north and south, the Snow Bowl has charms that sneak up on you. Its trails are short and there are hellishly long flats here and there, but everything—the skiing included—has an unhurried, old-time New England glow. The summit chair passes over a forested crag I never tire of looking at, then finishes with a painfully long haul over a flat that's invariably blasted by arctic winds. Warm up by skating down the flat to the left of the chair and you'll be ready for the classic multiple fall-line steeps of Ross and Allen. Or wind down the backside of the mountain on Youngman, my personal favorite. There's a snowboard park here now, as well.

The Snow Bowl has beefed up its snowmaking, but anytime machine-made snow is the surface you don't want to be here. The time to come to the Snow Bowl is within a few days of a snowstorm—I don't know why, but when other places get 10 inches this place will get a legit 14 inches. Tip: State Route 125 is ***really*** steep, and you'll be blessing your four-wheel drive if you have it. Lastly, the Snow Bowl is the only place I know of with a ***morning*** half-day ticket—$15 weekdays and $20 weekends to ski from 9 am to 12:30 pm.

Sugarbush

Sugarbush South Access Rd. runs W off State Rte. 100 south of Waitsfield; Sugarbush North access is via State Rte. 17, which runs west off State Rte. 100 in Waitsfield (mail: Warren, VT 05674). ☎ **802/583-2381;** www.sugarbush.com. Snow report: ☎ 802/583-SNOW. 115 trails (23% beginner, 48% intermediate, 29% expert), 18 lifts including 7 quads, 3 triples, and 4 doubles; 2,650-ft. vertical drop. Full-day tickets $53 all week.

I've been skiing in the Mad River Valley since the days when Sugarbush North was known as Glen Ellen, and to my mind Sugarbush has always been at or near the top of Vermont's ski areas. It begins with two beautiful, rugged, and huge mountains—3,975-foot Lincoln Peak to the south and 4,135-foot Mount Ellen to the north. I'll always remember riding the Castlerock chair on an early spring day when the mountain was beginning to wake up from winter's sleep—a warm wind hissing through the waving evergreens, the brown-green skin of mud and underbrush peeking through the dirt-streaked moguls, and the air filled with the piney, raw-earth smell of a mountain thaw.

The North and South ski areas—finally united in 1995 by a superfast high-speed quad that gets you from one mountain to the next in minutes—are both totally satisfying for any skier at the intermediate level or higher. The dozens of perfectly pitched cruisers always seem to have great snow, and the bump trails range from ideal mogul-skiing practice runs to hair-raising steeps. Sugarbush also has more of those true challenges of New England skiing—flying down serpentine trails around corners, down quick dips, through tight slots, always in the company of trees. On the best trails, you'll be surrounded by the woods as you whiz by a rolling tapestry of maple, oak, birch, spruce, pine, and balsam. Paradise, Castlerock, and the backcountry runs in between braid through the forest like a crazed snake. Here, you're forever in search of the elusive fall line as you skim across windblown snow, get dumped into a basin of waist-deep snow, and somehow squirt into a glade around the next turn. Choose the wrong direction and you'll get far too intimate with a chunk of bark. This is the way we ski powder in the East—deep, steep, and tree-cluttered. Three new tree skiing/snowboarding areas were added to the map in the 1999/2000 season to add to the pleasure.

Sugarbush is also a great place to learn to ski; it has one of the older, more respected ski schools in Vermont, and both mountains have beginner and novice terrain that's genuinely interesting skiing, instead of the bland bunny slopes you find most places.

Here's the skinny for the more advanced, beginning with Sugarbush South: There's more intermediate skiing at the other hill, but Murphy's Glades/Lower Organgrinder, Moonshine, and Domino (a favorite that is overlooked by most skiers) are all terrific strong-intermediate trails. The Snowball/Spring Fling combo is an ultrawide cruiser made to be taken at a rocketlike pace, but it's also one of the most congested parts of the mountain. Stay away on crowded weekends, unless temperatures are frigid or there's not much snow—you'll always have plenty of snowmaking and sunshine here.

Strong skiers won't find a better array anywhere in the Northeast. Moguls, moguls, and more moguls: Stein's Run, The Mall, and Twist (often forgotten) off the Gatehouse chair; Upper Organgrinder and Spillsville (best lines) off Heaven's Gate; Castlerock Run and Middle Earth off the Castlerock chair. (Stay off Ripcord; except on the very edges, it's usually a horrifically broad sheet of ice.) Then there's the luminous trio at the very top: Paradise off Heaven's Gate, Lift Line off Castlerock, and sliver-thin Rumble. Don't even look for this last one unless you can confidently say you've had your way with the rest of the mountain; I made this mistake once and had a painfully close encounter with a spruce tree. I think it's the toughest trail in New England. The new gladed area includes Stein's Run down to Lower Organgrinder, the Sleeper Woods off of Hotshot in the Gatehouse area, and the woods between Organgrinder flats and Lower Downspout (by the base of Heaven's Gate).

Over at North, perfect intermediate trails abound, with Rim Run and especially Elbow being my favorites. The truly tough skiing is a little thinner but still very good. Black Diamond and Bravo are splendid bump runs; Exterminator is a nice trail with a skewed fall line, but it's no double-black diamond by this mountain's otherwise-lofty standards; and Tumbler is the most fun of all when there's lots of snow. As for the much-talked about F.I.S., it's a shorter version of Killington's Outer Limits—very steep, to be sure, but nary a good line to be found in the whole wide swath.

North is the place to go after a thaw, because the layout there doesn't bottle up skier traffic too badly when the mountain is only partly open. South, on the other hand, is the ticket when the wind's up and after a big snowstorm, when Stein's, Paradise, and the Castlerock trails can be truly sublime.

Mad River Glen

State Rte. 17, Waitsfield, VT 05673. ☎ **802/496-3551;** www.madriverglen.com. Snow report: ☎ 802/496-2001. 44 trails (30% beginner, 30% intermediate, 40% expert) plus 800 acres of boundary-to-boundary off-piste access. 4 lifts, including 3 doubles and the country's only surviving single chairlift (riding this is even scarier than skiing the trails); 2,037-ft. vertical drop. Full-day tickets $29 weekday, $36 weekend.

Rustbucket Subaru wagons with Vermont license plates often have a bumper sticker offering the following dare: "Mad River Glen, Ski It If You Can." No lie. Mad River

MORE ON LESS

Snow gently falls outside the windows of Les Otten's office in Bethel, Maine, landing on a vast network of ski trails. Indoors, Otten is rummaging through a mound of papers in the same way an adroit skier tackles a mogul—swiftly, with determination. Handsome, with salt and pepper hair, a Pierce Brosnan chin, and expressive eyes that would be poorly suited for bluffing at poker, Otten nevertheless looks haggard. He has just returned from his tenth cross-country flight in the month of December. Less than 12 hours ago, he was outside of Salt Lake City to commemorate the opening of The Canyons, one of his newest ski resorts.

Snow or, more precisely, the enjoyment of snow is Les Otten's life. In the 1980s, he took over a small struggling ski resort called Sunday River and guided it from the brink of bankruptcy to the second-most-popular ski area in the East. Not content to rest on his laurels, he ventured over the Maine border to the White Mountains, where he acquired Attitash Mountain in January 1994. A year later, he picked up Sugarbush in the small rural community of Warren, Vermont. Then in February 1996, he stunned the Eastern ski establishment when he made a bold deal to buy S-K-I Ltd., a publicly traded operating company twice the size of his own privately held LBO Resort Enterprises. Vermont's Killington and Mount Snow/Haystack, Sugarloaf USA in Maine, and New Hampshire's Waterville Valley were now part of Otten's growing empire, renamed the American Skiing Company (ASC). The Justice Department demanded that Otten sell Waterville Valley to maintain competition in the East, but this didn't stop his feeding frenzy: He now looked to the West.

In July 1998, the brash 48-year-old purchased The Canyons, formerly known as Wolf Mountain and ParkWest. Next, he finalized a deal for Colorado's Steamboat and California's Heavenly ski areas, reportedly worth $288 million. On November 5, 1998, American Skiing Company went public, offering 14.75 million shares at an initial price of $18, to help offset the cost of Heavenly and Steamboat.

Otten is not particularly concerned with the other skiing conglomerates—Vail Associates who own Vail, Beaver Creek, Arrowhead, Keystone, and Breckenridge resorts in Colorado; and Intrawest, proprietors of ski resorts all over North America, including Whistler in British Columbia, Stratton in Vermont, and Mount Tremblant in the Laurentians.

"Right now we're competing very successfully with the cruise lines, Disney World, and large hotel chains. These are our main competitors," he says. "I think all three of our companies own very significant assets, and we all believe that the demand on recreation is going to be increasing dramatically in the next decade." Otten knows that attendance at ski resorts has been relatively flat in the past 10 years, but he has also studied population trends as carefully as a researcher at the *Almanac.*

"There's a new baby boom; and when these kids become of ski age, the industry will take off. We're looking at a full 15 years of increased attendance," says Otten. But skiing is only a part of the equation. Real estate development at these ski areas could be far more lucrative than any number of lift tickets sold. Otten's expansion would bring what he sees as the best of the East and take it westward, and vice versa. The large resorts so common in the West are beginning to bulge at the bases of his New England areas, and his very structured frequent-skier programs are making their debut in the freewheeling West. The question is, What kind of welcome will he receive from dyed-in-the-wool skiers on both coasts?

Like most people lured to the skiing world, Les Otten is a former ski bum. But unlike most dreamers who develop small ski resorts, Otten has defied the skeptics and succeeded in a business where one warm winter can shut your lifts down permanently and have you looking for another kind of work. Overcoming adversity is nothing new to the brash entrepreneur or to his family. Born in New Jersey, Otten was the only child of a 63-year-old German businessman whose

4,000-acre steel mill was snatched from him by the Nazis. The elder Otten was arrested and later released in Switzerland, from where he eventually made his way to Canada and then Teaneck, New Jersey.

The Ottens didn't ski, but the family next door did; and when they introduced 7-year-old Les to the sport, he was hooked. At Ithaca College, in upstate New York, where Otten happily admits he was "an undistinguished C student," he taught skiing 3 nights a week at nearby Greek Peak. Already intrigued by the idea of owning a ski resort, he and two buddies tried to build their own ski area at Danby Mountain. They managed to get the land under option, but the deal never panned out. Instead, Otten turned his dream into a term paper for which he got an A+.

Otten graduated in 1971 and entered the ski industry against his father's wishes, though he believes the elder Otten was pleased just to see his son employed. "His main goal in life was to make sure I got out of college and didn't become a burden to him," Otten says. One of Otten's friends had told him about a management training program at Killington. But when he arrived there, all four slots for the position had already been filled. By the time Otten left the office at Killington, there was a fifth.

His tasks at Killington were menial—splicing chairlift cables, painting lift towers—all for $2.25 an hour. But he also was curious to see how long it took for lift parts to wear out, and he ended up writing a program to service those parts before that date arrived. Another paper written by Otten discussed how the 30 employees at the guest check-in could be reduced to 8. Management was impressed with his initiative; as a reward, a year later he was assigned to help run a tiny, neglected ski area the company owned in the backwoods of Maine. When Otten arrived, the Sunday River Skiway had three T-bars and one chairlift. By 1975, he had risen to the position of general manager, but the owners refused to pour any more money into their souring investment. So, in 1980 Les Otten, at the age of 30, put together a deal to buy Sunday River, even borrowing money from the parent company. People in the industry thought he was writing his own death certificate. His 93-year-old father was the worst skeptic of all.

"He offered me $100,000 not to buy the business and take on the risk of $1.2 million in debt," says Otten. "That motivated me even more to make the purchase. It was very sad, but we didn't speak for at least 6 months afterwards."

Sunday River posted a $235,000 loss against total sales of $541,000 that year, attracting just 40,000 skier visits. But Les Otten was an avid skier; and like an actor who finally gets his chance to direct, Les Otten was ready to transform Sunday River into a skier's mountain. He had more than ample terrain to expand, and the nearby Sunday River provided an abundance of water for snowmaking. For the first 6 months, he had to stave off bankruptcy. To raise initial capital, he sold off scraps of metal that had been lying around for 20 or so years—old bulldozer blades left in the woods, abandoned wiring, anything that wasn't nailed down. Then he went to work, implementing ideas that he has since used at every ski resort he owns. With debtors calling, he wasn't about to wait around for Mother Nature to drop her load. He installed new snowmaking technology that would run night and day, becoming the first ski-area operator to fully capitalize on the importance of snow quality. He tore down the archaic T-bars and replaced them with the fastest lifts of the time. Finally, he created new trails, doubling the terrain and then doubling it again.

Word of mouth spread far too slowly for Otten, so he used a little marketing savvy to push it along. He sent snowballs to TV weather forecasters, dumped snow on Boston Common during a drought, and brought press up to the mountain to see what was going on. In 1988 when White Heat, the legendary bump run, opened, he deleted the commas in an advertising slogan to claim that Sunday River had the "longest steepest widest" trail in the East. Of course, with commas, it was neither the longest, nor the steepest, nor the widest mogul run in New England. Otten also created the first learn-to-ski-in-one-day program and founded an innovative skiing course called the Perfect Turn. By 1993, Sunday River had 450,000 skier visits, second only to mighty Killington. Otten had accomplished everything he possibly could at Sunday River and now was growing restless.

The following year, he purchased Attitash and in 1995, acquired Sugarbush. "I was looking for expanding opportunities in the East and they were available," says Otten.

The drive north on Vermont's Route 100 to the base of Sugarbush encompasses one of the most bucolic stretches of road in New England—a mix of rolling hills, farmland so fertile you feel like jumping out of the car and digging your hands in the soil, and anonymous towns with their ubiquitous white steeples. Then you reach the small village of Warren and, shortly thereafter, Waitsfield, the twin communities Sugarbush hovers above. You drive through their respective covered bridges to find one-road towns where nothing seems to change. And that's the way locals prefer it.

This is especially true of their beloved ski areas, Sugarbush and Mad River. Mad River still has a chairlift for single skiers, and both mountains feature the New England skiing of yore, a time when trails were cut by hand so they weren't much wider than a hiking path. In Les Otten's growing empire, Sugarbush is an anomaly. Its challenging terrain is not well suited for families, for whom Mount Snow is a better choice; the rural setting offers no raging après-ski scene like Killington; and it's not a remote mountain getaway like Sugarloaf in the middle of Maine. Sugarbush borders the spine of the Green Mountains on a well-traveled route that connects Okemo and Killington ski areas in the south to Stowe and Jay Peak in the north.

Indeed, Sugarbush has always been far more popular with locals than with tourists. The locals include some of the most renowned skiers in the country, such as John Egan, an extreme skier who can be seen on many of Warren Miller's films flying down the side of an uncharted mountain or volcano, and Peter Oliver, contributing editor to *Skiing* magazine for the past decade and one of the foremost experts on skiing the East (he's also author of Frommer's *Great Outdoor Guide to Southern New England*). Both of these snow aficionados live to slither down the narrow trails of Sugarbush's legendary Castlerock Peak. So when Otten purchased Sugarbush, the locals, afraid that he might widen these old-style trails, began the rallying cry, "Less Otten, More Rock." Otten, a shrewd businessman, didn't touch the Rock.

"He listens to people," says Egan. "He didn't mow down the mountain terrain and make it a big, flat, wide western area. That's pretty impressive." Peter Oliver concurs: "He's politically pretty astute. When he came into Sugarbush, he understood that Castlerock is special and he kept it special within this community. Instead, he's taken snowmaking and fast lifts, his winning technique for building Sunday River, and adapted that to Sugarbush."

One of those lifts is the Slide Brook Express, a breathtaking 10-minute chairlift ride that connects Sugarbush with neighboring Mount Ellen. Seeing the ridge of the Green Mountains sloping down to the valley and rivers of central Vermont is alone worth the price of admission. Few people in the region thought Otten could pull it off, since the lift travels over bear habitat. Otten managed to allay the fears of environmentalists and just recently exchanged 3,000 acres of bear habitat on Killington for 1,000 acres of state land. "We thought it was a great trade," says Vermont's governor, Howard Dean. Otten needed the land to connect Killington with neighboring Pico.

Now that American Skiing Company owns nine ski resorts, critics are worried that all the areas will become homogenous, and they term the conglomerates "McSkiing." Mel Allen, longtime editor of *Yankee* magazine and an avid skier who first visited Sunday River in 1970, says that's not possible. "I don't think anyone can take away from a mountain's personality. It's formed by geography and tradition to some extent. Sugarloaf is not going to appeal to the same person Mount Snow appeals to." Otten rebuts his McSkiing critics by saying that his resorts are similar only in respect to "quality service and the quality of the snow." Peter Oliver adds, "You have to have differentiation between ski areas. If not, what's the point of people traveling an extra hour past Killington to go to Sugarbush or past Sunday River to visit Sugarloaf?"

Oliver and the people in the Sugarbush community are far more concerned about cookie-cutter real estate developments. Otten's plans for a hotel there have finally been accepted, but Oliver points out that the first design was essentially the same hotel as the ones being built at all the other resorts. "This is a reluctant resort community. People want to have the benefit of Sugarbush but not necessarily the character of a resort, which has already happened at Mount Snow or Killington. That's why it's important that we have something that fits in here and not just something that fits into the ASC plan," says Oliver. Regardless of design, Governor Dean states that it's essential these large-scale hotels be built to attract more clientele. "Basically, Vermont was a leader in the ski industry until the late 1960s. Colorado leapfrogged us and showed that you really have to have a four-season resort with beds right on the slopes to make it work. That's what Les is doing."

Otten has also implemented several marketing schemes, like a Frequent Skier Program called The Edge and a Magnificent 7 card that offers skiers the chance to ski any seven resorts in the ASC umbrella for $299. "Mag 7 sales are already up 100% from the same time last year," says Otten. "A lot of that has to do with the fact that the deal is usable coast-to-coast." Mel Allen, father of two sons whose great passion from Thanksgiving to April is throwing themselves down a mountain, thinks the Magnificent 7 card is a wonderful concept. "It gives people a sense of power. Instead of being locked into one mountain, you can now ski all these various peaks. You receive a different trail map at each ski area, and it gives you a sense of entering a new country for a day." Still, Otten says it would be bold to expect Westerners to head East. "I see Californians going to Steamboat and The Canyons, or vice-versa, more Easterners heading west, and Europeans heading to both coasts."

Otten seems particularly excited about the European market. He has been advertising heavily in Great Britain over the past several years, and it seems to be working. Last season, ASC recorded some 40,000 skier visits from the British market alone. "We believe that America is a more service-oriented ski destination than Europe, and that's why we're seeing an increase of European skiers coming here." Not to mention the exchange rate is far more favorable for Europeans. "I rode a chairlift the other day at Sugarloaf with a man from England," says Mel Allen. "He was able to fly from England to Bangor, rent a car, drive to Sugarloaf, get a week at the hotel, with all meals and skiing included, for £500 ($800). He couldn't come close to doing that in Europe."

The jury is still out on whether Otten has improved the slopes for skiers, but pundits admire what Otten has done to get people up on the mountains. "There are a lot of naysayers out there saying how impersonal the [Sugarbush] ski area is now, but I'll tell you, a bankrupt closed-down ski area is a lot more impersonal than one that's running with hordes of people around," says John Egan. Mel Allen agrees: "People will probably thank Les Otten for saving mountains that would have either gone under or been bought out by absentee owners."

No one in the ski industry will be surprised if Les Otten and ASC continue to acquire more ski resorts around the country. As their stock prospectus states: "The Company intends to consider acquisitions of large, well-established destination resorts." Otten also harbors a secret desire to work in the role of public service, but not as an elected politician. "Either through volunteerism or being appointed, I'd like to contribute to a wide range of subjects I'm interested in—education, the environment, and business and economic issues," says Otten. But for now, he has more flights to catch. Otten's back to The Canyons in 2 days, and then he's meeting his wife and three children at Steamboat for a vacation. It's a tossup as to which card gets more use—his Frequent Skier Card or his Frequent Flyer Card.

Glen is the nastiest lift-served ski area in the East, a combination of rocks, ice, trees—and snow, of course. It's truly a place where skiing seems little removed from a mountain's gnarled, primeval state.

Think you're tough enough? Start with Grand Canyon, a steep mogul trail where the bumps are perfectly spaced. Next up are Fall-Line and Chute from the summit, two of the most precipitous, obstacle-strewn, yet perfect mogul runs you'll ever find. And for the finale—drum roll, please—a trail that's not even on the map, Paradise. Don't let the name fool you; it should be called Hell. Barely a trail, Paradise stumbles over rocky ledges and an enormous frozen waterfall to reach the bottom. Have fun trying to hold an edge.

Mad River pales against Sugarbush as far as easy skiing, snowmaking, and lift capacity are concerned. (Its sole summit lift remains the venerable Single chair.) Save Mad River for a day when there's deep, fresh powder, and you're feeling feisty. That way you'll give yourself a chance to experience the place at its best. You'll feel privileged to be among so many world-class skiers, all feeling as if they're in heaven's playground.

Keeping to its retro appeal, Mad River is the only major eastern ski area that does not allow snowboarding. Yet, its uncrowded natural snow trails and rugged terrain offer some of the best lift-served telemark skiing anywhere. It is the longtime home of the North American Telemark Festival, usually held the second week in March. The festival is the country's oldest and largest gathering of telemark skiers. Mad River rents telemark equipment and is known for its excellent instruction.

FISHING

The slogan for central Vermont anglers is, "when the weather is hot, the fishing is not." Trout fishing peaks from mid-May to early June when numerous hatches and water levels keep the fish active all day. Once water temperatures reach about 65°, the fish get lethargic except, perhaps, in early morning and late evening. Thus, the summer months can be pretty slow.

That said, central Vermont trouters will find some of Vermont's best fishing—spooky rainbows, brookies, and browns—on the watersheds and feeder streams of the White and Winooski Rivers. Wait for one of those characteristic central Vermont flash rainstorms, and the fish seem to drop their objections to just about anything.

Central Vermont Ski & Winter Sports Shops

City	*Shop*	*Location*	*Telephone*	*Additional Services*
Sugarbush/ Mad River Area	Vermont North	Sugarbush Access Rd., Warren	802/583-2511	repairs; alpine/cross-country ski rentals, snowshoe rentals; alpine-ski demos
Montpelier	Onion River Sports	20 Langdon St.	802/229-9409	cross-country ski, snowshoes sales/rentals
Suicide Six/ Ascutney Area	Sitzmark Ski Shop	Rte. 44, Windsor	802/674-6930	alpine-ski, cross-country ski, snowboard rentals
	The Dartmouth Co-op	25 S. Main St., Hanover, NH	603/643-3100	cross-country/alpine skis
	Wilderness Trails, Inc.	Clubhouse Rd., Quechee	802/295-7620	cross-country ski, snowshoe, ice skating

In the lower part of the region, the **Ottauquechee** along U.S. 4, the **Ompompanoosuc River** around Thetford, and the First, Second, Third, and Main Branches of the **White River** are the hot spots. One of the best spots on the White is in Stockbridge, near the intersection of State Routes 100 and 107; rainbows and browns can also be hauled in along the reach from Bethel to Royalton. Another good spot is the branch of the White from Lower Granville to Hancock. It's popular with fly anglers searching for small brook trout and rainbows.

Around Middlebury, check out the **New Haven River** way upstream from Bristol to the Bartlett Falls in Lincoln. You'll find brownies and small to midsize rainbows. For bass and pike fishing in midsummer, go with the boaters to **Winona Lake,** just north of Bristol. The **Middlebury River** is not fished as heavily as the New Haven, but it's also not stocked as much. **Silver Lake** is fished heavily from the shores, but if you canoe in, you're bound to get some bites. It's a great spot to take the kids out fishing for sunnies and pumpkinseeds (see "Parks & Other Hot Spots," above). Nearby, large **Lake Dunmore** always gets its fair share of 16-inch **Atlantic Salmon** each year. It's also stocked with **bass, northern pike,** and **perch. Lewis Creek** in Starksboro is stocked with brookies averaging 8 inches. Farther south, **Baldwin Creek** also gets stocked.

A little more north, check out the **Mad River** in the Warren-Waitsfield area where you might catch all three kinds of trout in a morning. Also, stop by the **Dog River** along State Route 12A from Roxbury to Northfield, where rainbows 10 inches and up, along with trophy-class brookies, are not uncommon; and the **Winooski River,** especially around its confluence with the **Little River** near Waterbury—huge browns can be had here if you're lucky.

One of the best things about the Winooski is its recreational versatility—in addition to fly-fishing for brown trout, the river's great in summertime for smallmouth bass, from around Middlesex all the way to Lake Champlain. The big-water Winooski is also one of Vermont's three great canoeing waterways, navigable for 78 miles. And central Vermont is home to most of the best of the **Connecticut River**'s warm-water fishing—smallmouth and largemouth bass, pickerel, walleye, and bullhead are everywhere. See "Canoeing," above, for good access points along both the Connecticut and the Winooski. To the east, closer to the Connecticut River and I-91 and between the villages of Fairlee and Thetford, are lakes **Fairlee** and **Morey;** these are sizable bodies of water with good bass, pike, and panfish angling.

Bass anglers head to the shallow shores off Champlain to hook smallies and largemouth. Try the area around Basin Harbor and the mouth of Little Otter Creek. Did I forget to mention that Lake Champlain is stocked with more than 250,000 trout and salmon?

Guides & Bait-and-Tackle Shops

The **Vermont Fly Fishing School,** situated at the Quechee Inn at Marshland Farm (**☎ 802/295-7620**), offers instruction and guided trips. Learn to cast in a clear Vermont trout stream. Owner Marty Banak has three rivers—the White, Ottaquechee, and Connecticut—to choose from within a 10-minute drive (see "Canoeing," above).

The Paiges of **Green Mountain Outdoor Adventures,** HCR 32 Box 90, Montpelier, VT 05602 (**☎ 802/229-4246**), will help you find the best trout holes on the Winooski.

GOLF

Two Robert Trent Jones courses, the **Woodstock Country Club** (**☎ 802/457-2112**) and the **Sugarbush Golf Club** (**☎ 802/583-6725**) in the Mad River Valley, are the long-established class operations of central Vermont golf. The verdant Woodstock course, through which the Kedron Brook comes into play on 11 holes, is probably the nicer, while the arduous Sugarbush course not only plays hard but also might qualify as a "hike," considering all the elevation changes. The nicest view is from the seventh tee, from which you can see the Stowe area.

Other noted courses in central Vermont include the **Basin Harbor Golf Club (☎ 802/475-2309)**, the 700-acre resort in Vergennes on Lake Champlain, and the **Rutland Country Club (☎ 802/773-3254)**, built in 1902. Far from the genteel golf scene, a local favorite is Randolph's almost-earthy **Montague Golf Course (☎ 802/728-3806)**. It's old, cheap, and doesn't put on any airs. Plus, there's just something unusual about carrying on the standard waiting-for-tee-time small talk about the evil golf god with the guys scheduled to follow you—and hearing them speaking in an untamed Vermont accent. ***Aah-yaaup.*** (The ***p*** is silent, by the way; say the word as if you were going to speak it, and then cut your voice dead just before.)

HIKING & BACKPACKING

I can't say enough about hiking in the central Green Mountains. Maybe the White Mountains are higher and more spectacular, but there's something innately appealing about the way things are knit together on the ridge of the Greens. Rising and descending along the Long Trail, you pass through richly varied ecologies, from the hardwood trees and ferny understory of the lower reaches, to transitional forests mixing conifers, aspen, and birches, to upcountry meadows overrun by blackberry and raspberry thickets, and finally up toward the treeline, where things start to look as though they came out of C. S. Lewis's ***Chronicles of Narnia.*** One of the day hikes follows a stretch of the Long Trail from Lincoln Gap to Appalachian Gap that's as magical as any trail I know of, anywhere. Nearly its whole length is atop a ridge so narrow you feel a slight vertigo; both sides fall away steeply not 20 feet from the trail. The Sunset Ridge walk is less popular but is nonetheless a magnificent hike. And hiking Camel's Hump—one of the two mountains in Vermont that supports patches of genuine Alpine/arctic tundra on its summit, holdovers from the last ice age—is a rite of passage for Vermonters. It's not so much that the hike is unusually difficult but that it's hard to feel like a "real" Vermonter without having stood upon that odd hummock in the clouds, surveying your land.

Mount Tom

3.2 miles round-trip. Allow 2 hr. Easy; only a short 550-ft. climb to the top. Access: The trail originates in Faulkner Park on Mountain Ave. in Woodstock.

If you want a pleasant hike the entire family can enjoy—mom, dad, grandpa, grandma, 9-year-old, 7-year-old—take them up Mount Tom. The yellow-blazed Faulkner Trail is a gentle series of switchbacks that gradually make their way to the 1,250-foot peak. Here, you can picnic with views of Woodstock and nearby Killington.

Mount Independence

2.5 miles round-trip. Allow 1.5–2 hr. Easy; only a short 200-ft. rise on this historic site. Access: Take Rte. 22A west of Orwell and turn west on Rte. 73. At 0.3 mile, veer left off Rte. 73. At 5.2 miles, turn left onto Catfish Rd. and park in the lot on the top of the hill. Map: available at gate.

Across Lake Champlain from New York's Fort Ticonderoga, Mount Independence was once the site of a Revolutionary War fort. Now part of the Fort Ticonderoga Association, Mount Independence is open from Memorial Day to Columbus Day. Perched above the water and surrounded by cliffs on three sides, it's a scenic spot to explore and learn a little about Vermont's history. From the gate, go straight through the pasture and take the

Orange Trail. You soon reach the top of Mount Independence and your best views of the lake. Logs indicate where the fort was once placed. A nearby well is believed to have existed during the Revolutionary War period. The trail continues through the woods to a clearing where blacksmiths and wheelwrights once worked. Nearby, a horseshoe-shaped battery was the site of cannons pointed toward Fort Ticonderoga. You'll next descend to the spot where a floating bridge once connected Mount Independence with Fort Ticonderoga. The Orange Trail then leaves the lake and loops back to the beginning.

Snake Mountain

3.6 miles round-trip. Allow 2.5 hr. Easy to moderate; only a 950-ft. climb to the summit where views of Lake Champlain and the Adirondacks await. Access: From Middlebury, take Rte. 125 west to Rte. 22A north. 4.5 miles later, turn right on Wilmarth Rd. and park alongside the shoulder of Mountain Rd. Map: USGS 7.5-min. Port Henry.

Off-the-beaten Long Trail, Snake Mountain is nestled in the fertile farmland of Addison County. Follow the blue blazes behind the gate and continue on the pleasant woods road. At 0.6 mile, turn left as the road zigzags through the oak forest to the 1,287-foot summit. From the concrete pad atop the peak (someone once attempted to build a house here), you have views of Lake Champlain and the Adirondacks to the west and, a little closer, the bird-watching mecca of Dead Creek Wildlife Management Area. You might see some birds yourself—ravens lurking on the cliffs. Return on the same route.

Mount Horrid

1.25 miles round-trip. Allow 1–1.5 hr. Moderate; only a short 630-ft. climb but can ascend steeply at parts. Access: Take Rte. 73 to the top of the Brandon Gap where you'll see a parking lot. Hike north on the white-blazed trail across the street. Map: USGS 7.5-min. Mount Carmel.

Grab your lunch and head to a perfect picnic spot atop 2,800-foot Mount Horrid. But first you'll have to earn it. Part of the white-blazed Long Trail, the route is basically a ridge climb on rock steps through a mix of hardwoods. At 0.6 mile, you'll be standing atop the "Great Cliff" looking down on a beaver pond and surrounding cliffs. Please note that the trail is slippery when wet and could be closed when peregrine falcons nest on the "Great Cliff." Hike back down on the same trail.

Worth Mountain

5.8 miles round-trip. Allow 3—4 hr. A moderate climb with superb views of the Middlebury Gap section of the Long Trail. Access: From the junction of Rte. 100 and 125 in Hancock, bear west on Rte. 125 for 8.2 miles. Turn left on Forest Rd. 67. At 1.4 miles, turn right at the fork. 2.7 miles later, the road ends at a small parking lot. Map: USGS 7.5-min. Bread Loaf.

Worth Mountain is a worthy climb in the Middlebury Gap section of Vermont. The 3,234-foot summit offers fine views of the Greens as they head both north and south. Start on the blue-blazed Sucker Brook Trail, which is nothing more than an old logging road. Don't despair. One mile later, you'll be heading north on the white-blazed Long Trail pass the Sucker Brook Shelter. Ascend through the birch-laden forest until you reach a ledge with good views. At 2.4 miles, you'll start to climb log stairs, shaded by tall spruce and fir, soon arriving at the summit. Take the same trail back down after enjoying the panorama.

Texas Falls

1.2-mile loop. Allow 1hr. Easy nature loop that will get you out of the car breathing that crisp Vermont air. Access: From the junction of Rte. 100 and 125 in Hancock, bear west on Rte. 125 for 3 miles. When you see a sign for GMNF TEXAS FALLS RECREATION AREA, turn right on the access road and into a small parking lot on the left. Map: USGS 7.5-min. Bread Loaf.

What better way to learn about the Green Mountain National Forest than to take a short interpretive hike. The trail begins at Texas Falls, where water plummets down the stone steps into the deep ravine. Cross the bridge, and follow the steps up to the box where a pamphlet will help you around this self-guided trail. The Lower and Upper Trails connect to make the 1.1-mile loop. As you meander through the forest, you'll learn that evergreens are "ever green" because their leaves are more efficient at obtaining water in the harsh winter months. Also enjoy the old aspen tree and the fern-covered banks that crest a hill. But, most important, take deep breaths and savor that fresh forest air.

Sunset Ledge

2.2 miles (round-trip). Allow 1–2 hr. Easy-to-moderate hiking without too much abrupt elevation gain; ideal for young children. From either Lincoln, to the west, or Warren, to the east, follow Lincoln Gap Rd. up into the mountains until you see a parking lot on the left side of the road. Map: USGS 7.5-min. Lincoln.

My car had a far more rigorous workout getting to the trailhead than I did walking the Sunset Ledge path. Lincoln Gap Road is a mountainous pass that climbs steeply into the heart of the Green Mountains. I parked high atop the hill and continued on foot, south on the Long Trail toward the Middlebury Gap; 0.4 mile later, the leaf-littered trail turned rocky as the eastern slopes of the mountains came into view. The trail continued steadily uphill for another 0.7 mile until I reached Sunset Ledge. It was late September, and the rocky promontory overlooked a forest of fall foliage in orange and red. Views of the Adirondacks could be seen to the west, far beyond the meadows and farms of Vermont. To the north, a turkey vulture hovered over Mount Abraham. For such a small amount of effort, the rewards were great.

Mount Abraham

5.2 miles round-trip. Allow 4 hr. Moderate to difficult. Access: From either Lincoln, to the west, or Warren, to the east, follow Lincoln Gap Rd. up into the mountains until you see a parking lot on the left side of the road. Map: USGS 7.5-min. Lincoln.

South of Camel's Hump and Mount Mansfield, Mount Abraham is another one of Vermont's popular 4,000-foot-plus ascents. Since you begin high atop Lincoln Gap on the Long Trail, the actual climb is only 1,700 feet. The 2.6-mile (one-way) trail starts gradually across the parking lot, weaving its way over tree roots and small rocks. Bring all your belongings with you; this parking lot is a notorious hunting ground for thieves. At 1.2 miles, you pass The Carpenters, two large boulders named after stalwart trail workers, not the singing duo. A little more than a half mile later, the path passes the Battell Trail and a small shelter of the same name—a Green Mountain Club (GMC) lean-to that sleeps six to eight people. This hike gets such heavy use that the GMC keeps a caretaker here, something they do for only a very few of their shelters and lodges. I pity this individual in comparison to the plush natural spots that caretakers at Sterling Pond or Stratton Pond have as their lookout.

From here, the going gets rough, and you'll find yourself scrambling over large, slippery slabs of rock until you reach the open summit. The views are supposedly stunning from the top, though I wouldn't know, the mountain having been socked in by clouds both times I took this hike. Nevertheless, watching the clouds roil around, and literally walking right through them, was an experience worth the loss of the vista. All I could see on the bare rock summit were red squirrels scurrying through the krummholz, Labrador tea plants, and other high-altitude vegetation. Be cautious of slipping on the smooth rocks on the way down, especially if they're wet.

Lincoln Gap to Appalachian Gap

11.6 miles one way. Allow 8–9 hr. Moderate to difficult; one of the best high-elevation hikes in Vermont. Access: Put the first car on Rte. 17, 6 miles west of Waitsfield. This is the Appalachian Gap. The second car goes to the same place as the one described for the start of the Mount Abraham hike: From either Lincoln, to the west, or Warren, to the east, follow Lincoln Gap Rd. up into the mountains until you see a parking lot on the left side of the road. Map: USGS 7.5-min. Lincoln.

High atop the Mad River Valley, this hike leads to the peaks of Mount Abraham (see above) and continues north on the Long Trail to the Appalachian Gap. Along the way, you'll summit Mount Ellen (4,083 ft.) and General Stark Mountain (3,662 ft.). You can shorten this hike by leaving cars at the Sugarbush or Mad River Ski resorts and descending down to their bases. This also makes for a nice overnight if you want to spend the evening at the Mount Ellen Lodge, just north of Mount Ellen's peak. After making it to the top of General Stark, it's another 2.5 miles to your car on Route 17.

Camel's Hump

7.2 miles. Allow 5–6 hr. Moderate to difficult. Access: From the junction of U.S. 2 and State Rte. 100, east of Waterbury (across from the Feed Bag), take State Rte. 100 south for 0.2 mile. Turn right on Main St. for 0.1 mile and veer right again onto River Rd. for 4.9 miles. Turn left on Camel's Hump Rd. and continue 3.1 miles to a fork where you bear right. The last 0.3 mile to the parking lot is on a horrible dirt road. Be very careful. There are several approaches to Camel's Hump; this one is via the Forestry, Dean, and Long Trails. Map: USGS 7.5-min. Waterbury.

On every Vermonter's list of favorite hikes is the climb up the distinctive mass of rock known as Camel's Hump. Standing 4,083 feet tall, the summit can be seen from Burlington all the way to Jay Peak and Mount Pisgah across the state. My wife, Lisa, and I decided to make our ascent from the eastern slopes of the mountain on a relatively clear and crisp autumn day. By the time we arrived in the late morning, the parking lot was already full.

We began our walk on the Forestry Trail. Lined with ferns and strewn with yellow leaves, the soil was soft to the sole as we wandered deeper and deeper into the dark forest. At 1.3 miles, we veered left onto the Dean Trail, crossing over Hump Creek, where there is a small campground. The trail climbed ever so gradually to a boreal forest where the air became cooler and resonant with the sweet smell of firs. Sun started to seep into the woods when we approached a small but stunning pond. Trees with leaves the shade of Van Gogh's yellow fringed the shores. In the background stood our ultimate destination, the Hump, towering over a ridge of rock.

One mile from the intersection of the Forestry Trail, we turned right on the Long Trail for a rigorous 1.7-mile climb. The narrow trail winds steeply up a face of rock before leveling off at an overlook. Below us was the pond surrounded by a sea of orange, red, and yellow leaves. We climbed through a glacial morass, following the rocky trail upward. The large boulders would be a good hideout for people on the lam. Every so often, views of the Hump would tease us—for, as we continued forward, it felt as if we weren't making any ground. Finally, we descended into a col where the massive peak stood directly above us. We proceeded to hike slowly up the sharply rising trail, stopping to look at the hundreds of hilltops that encircled us under a layer of marshmallow clouds. At the bare summit, the wind was howling, but that didn't deter us from having lunch and taking in the views of Lake Champlain, Mount Mansfield, the White Mountains, and the Adirondacks.

We chose the Alpine Trail for the first 0.7 mile of our descent. Halfway down the path, we saw a wing from an airplane. It was here on October 16, 1944, that a B-24J bomber crashed and nine crew members died. The Alpine Trail eventually connects with the Forestry Trail. We veered right and continued for 2.5 miles to the trailhead and parking lot, weary yet invigorated by our day's accomplishment.

Green Mountain Audubon Nature Center

0.7 mile for the Hires Trail, 0.5 mile for the Sensory Trail. Allow 1–2 hr. Easy. Excellent trails for young children or hikers with disabilities. Access: Take Exit 11 off I-89 and turn left onto Rte. 2. Drive 1.6 miles and turn right at the traffic light onto Bridge St. toward Huntington. At 6.7 miles, you'll see a sign for the nature center. Turn right into the parking lot.

Part of the National Audubon Society, this 230-acre center offers a handful of easy trails that families or hikers with disabilities can enjoy. On the Hires Trail, you climb upward for some 200 feet to Lookout Rock, hiking through a hardwood forest lined with birches. Here, your children are rewarded with views of Camel's Hump and Mount Mansfield. The unique Sensory Trail is a half-mile loop through the woods where rope is strung between signposts. Not only is this a guide for the visually impaired, but an excellent opportunity to close your eyes, hang on to the rope, listen to the sounds, and breathe in the redolent aromatic delights of the forest.

HORSEBACK RIDING

A jaunt into central Vermont will take you to Waitsfield's **Vermont Icelandic Horse Farm (☎ 802/496-7141;** www.icelandichorses.com). In a state known for the imposing Morgan horse, these small pony-size horses are a special treat. Icelandics move at a very steady pace without much rocking—it's like driving a car with good shock absorbers. Owner Christina Calabrese offers half- to 5-day rides. A typical 5-day ride will take you, on average, 15 miles a day through the woods of Mad River Valley and on country roads. You'll stop overnight at inns in Waitsfield, Warren, and Fayston.

In the foothills of the Greens, **Firefly Ranch (☎ 802/453-2223)** in Bristol offers riding and a cozy place to stay. Hearty dinners and breakfasts are included in the price. **Autumn Harvest Inn (☎ 802/433-1355)** in Williamstown features 3 hours of trail riding, 2 nights' stay for two, and dinners and breakfasts for as low as $380. Located just 15 minutes from Hanover and Dartmouth College, **Hoofbeats of Vermont (☎ 802/785-HORSE;** www.hoofbeatsvermont.com) offers daily rides through meadows and along streams. Seven miles north of Killington on Route 100, **Riverside Farm Riding Stables (☎ 802/746-8544;** www.riversidefarm.com) offers hourly rides, including a sunset dinner ride. In the White River Valley is Brookfield's **Birch Meadow Trail Rides (☎ 802/276-3156)**.

ICE FISHING

It takes very little to get started in ice fishing. The basic piece of equipment is called a "tip-up," a spool of fishing line suspended in the water with a little trip mechanism when a fish takes the bait. They can be purchased for a little over $10 each, with live bait running $3 to$5 a dozen. Stick to flannel shirts and wool sweaters like the locals, instead of the far warmer polypro and polar fleece stuff, and you'll save hundreds of more dollars.

Many of the local lakes like **Dunmore, Bomoseen,** and **Chittenden,** open to ice fishing the third week of January. On Champlain, ice fishing is allowed for several species, including trout, salmon, pike, walleye, and perch. For a moderate fee, you can rent a shanty, be driven by truck out onto the ice, and be supplied with all the bait and equipment you need. You may legally keep up to 75 perch a day.

ICE SKATING

At Silver Lake, the snow is cleared away for ice skating. This almost laughably Norman Rockwell-like setting is found in Barnard off State Route 12.

MOUNTAIN BIKING

Trying to locate the best mountain biking trails in Vermont was turning into a grueling exercise in futility. Looking around the forested rolling hills, I knew that there were riches out there, but no one was giving up their secrets. Many of the rides are on private lands owned by farmers who only let the local contingent bike there. Downhill and cross-country ski resorts have taken up the slack, especially in northern Vermont, but riding on numbered trails will never provide the thrill that biking out in the wild does. On the verge of giving up, I did what every good writer does who has a book to finish—I groveled like an idiot and begged a local for his coveted knowledge.

Waitsfield

Allow 3–6 hr. Moderate; technical single-track and double-track riding. Access: Park at John Egan's Big World, located on State Rte. 100, between Waitsfield and Warren. Map: Dream on!

The daunting task of finding good mountain biking in Vermont finally came to an end when I was taken to an incredible network of single-track trails on the outskirts of Waitsfield. Having been told by bikers in Burlington, Stowe, and Jeffersonville in northern Vermont that the best riding is on private lands, cross-country ski centers, or large dirt roads, I was extremely frustrated by the time I sat down and had dinner with John Egan at his Big World restaurant in the Sugarbush area. No worries. By the time I'd finished my "Extreme" beer, John had told me about the extensive riding possibilities in the Waitsfield-Warren area and introduced me to his chef and co-owner, Jerry, an avid biker. Chef Jerry invited me to go biking with him the following morning and I accepted.

It wasn't until the next morning, when the alcohol wore off, that I realized who I was riding with—friends of John Egan, the crazed skier seen in many of Warren Miller's ski films skillfully maneuvering down the bumpy slopes of an incredibly steep and uncharted mountain. Maniacal John Egan, whose hobby is collecting rocks from volcanoes that have never been skied on before. Indeed, Egan has skied more than 50 virgin slopes, most recently in Greenland, where he was hired to map and name the slopes he survived. My fears were intensified when I finally saw Jerry without his chef's smock. His legs were the size of a professional running back's. However, it was too late to turn back; plus, I had this book to write.

"Mountain biking is a lot like extreme skiing," Egan explained. "You get dumped in the woods, find your own line through the trees, and somehow make your way out." Well, here goes nothing.

From Egan's restaurant and hotel, we crossed Route 100 and climbed Tucker Hill Road to reach the start of the recently carved Millbrook Trail. Within moments, I was jumping logs and pedaling through small streams on this root-studded, rock-littered technical single track. I bounced from obstruction to obstruction, like a kangaroo with one wobbly leg, wiping out on several occasions, only to find Egan waiting patiently for me at the end of the half-hour trail.

"Nice little warm-up, huh?" said the Maniac. "It's just the tip of the iceberg."

He should know. He's probably skied one.

I followed Egan and Jerry up one of the umpteenth hills we climbed that day to reach the Sugar Trail. This "deep-in-the-woods" set of rutted double tracks is part of the state-long cross-country ski corridor known as the Catamount, a 280-mile journey from Readsboro in the south to North Troy on the Canadian border. We rode under tall pines and beeches, where the work of a black bear's claws could be seen etched into the bark, as the bear climbed higher onto the slopes of Waitsfield's Sugarbush South. At last, we reached high ground and found the trees that made Vermont famous: maples. In every direction, waves of color illuminated the hills. For the remainder of the day, we wove up and down the remote slopes of Sugarbush through a kaleidoscopic tunnel of reds, yellows, and oranges, as if we had just biked into a Monet painting. It's no wonder my smile was starting to overtake my face.

By the time our jaunt was finished, I had flown over my handlebars twice, fixed a flat tire after slamming into a rock, sucked down every drop of water in my trusty 90-ounce CamelBak, and had cramps in my legs. Yet there I was with a mud-eating grin, the same adrenaline-induced expression that had been pasted on my face for the past 6 hours.

Green Mountain Stock Farm

Allow as much time as you need. Moderate to experienced; single-track and double-track riding. Access: Park at Three Stallion Inn, located off Rte. 12 in Randolph.

Vermonters are used to seeing herds of Holsteins, Jerseys, and Herefords holding up traffic as their owners lead them across the road from pasture to barn. In the past several decades, locals have also become accustomed to seeing flocks of bikers huddled together on long routes while they're riding from inn to inn. But judging from the astonished faces of the people we met in Randolph, Vermont, one fine September morning, no one is quite ready to find a group of bikers riding on mountainous trails that cows might find a tight squeeze.

Yet, there we were, 23 riders in all, ages 8 to 61, sweeping by bemused farmers on their land. We had made our way up high in the hills above Randolph along a ridge where the spine of the Greens could be seen in the distance. Soon we were coasting downhill on a narrow trail past fertile farmland and rows of yellow cornstalks ready to be cleared. Like good soldiers, we followed our tour leader deep into a forest of evergreens, crossing a shallow stream before finding ourselves on a sinuous dirt road that lined a branch of the White River.

It was early autumn and the maples and birches were starting their yearly light show. As we continued our descent, red, yellow, and orange leaves whizzed by in a colorful blur. Exhilarated by the view, the scent of the pines, and the exercise, I knew I would never again go on another fall foliage driving trip. Who needs neck strain from trying to see a purple-colored tree out of a car window when I can see those same leaves brushing against my legs as I whip down a mountain on two wheels?

This 15-mile route, known as the Quarry Ride, was one of the many guided loops being offered at the New England Mountain Biking Festival. The festival, which is held on the grounds of the historic 1,300-acre Green Mountain Stock Farm, offers more than 50 kilometers (31.25 miles) of cross-country trails weaving through the woods. The festival has attracted more than 4,000 participants each year, coming from as far away as Colorado and Montana. The event, sponsored by ***Mountain Biking*** and ***Bicycling*** magazines, Jeep, and Pedro's, a Newport, Rhode Island, manufacturer of vegetable-based chain lubricants and other "environmentally cool" bike products, has helped the small town of Randolph garner a reputation as the "Mountain Biking Capital of the East."

Remarkably, the festival and the numerous loops that line Randolph were all created largely by one person, Paul Rea. Rea grew up near Randolph but left the state to attend the University of Wyoming. In Wyoming, he mountain-biked to his legs' content on miles and miles of narrow trails called single tracks. When he returned to Randolph in 1994 to open a sporting goods store called Slab City, he continued to mountain-bike, but, more often than not, he was trespassing on private land. Unlike Wyoming, which has large tracts of public land, 88% of Vermont is privately owned. Thanks to Rea, much of that private land is now open to the public to ride.

At the same time Rea opened Slab City, he founded the White River Valley Trails Association. By creating well-designed routes and an efficient management plan, the organization was eventually granted permission by private landowners to link together bike loops. "We already had a well-developed system of trails for mountain bikers to use," says Rea, "including 242 miles of Class IV roads. All we needed to do was to knock on doors and beg." Class IV roads are nothing more than grass or dirt trails that are impassable during the winter by a vehicle other than a snowmobile. Created by farmers or timber companies many years ago, they are ideal for mountain bikers. Orange County, the administrative district in which the city of Randolph resides, has more of these roads than any other county in Vermont. Add flat valley floors, gentle rolling hills, and steep winding climbs from 500 to 2,900 feet high and you have one of the premier mountain biking destinations in the country, accessible to all levels of riders.

The next day, I once again weaved through the grounds of the Green Mountain Stock Farm. Giving my trusty Trek 950 mountain bike a rest, I took a test ride on one of the Schwinn Moabs with front-wheel suspension, a feature designed to cushion some of the bumps when you roll over, say, a log. Perhaps I'm a bit nostalgic for my youth when everyone rode a Schwinn 10-speed or envied those who did. Now Schwinn is making a comeback with its mountain bikes, and I was looking forward to seeing if the grand old company still had that magic touch.

I biked past hundreds of tents onto a wet trail that led me high into the hills. The route was lined with dense firs and maples, occasionally lowering their branches to let a glimmer of light into this shaded forest. Soon I passed a dilapidated sugar shack, a remnant of this former farm's rich history. In existence since 1796, the Green Mountain Stock Farm grew to prominence during the Civil War as a stock-breeding establishment. Its purebred Jerseys and Morgan horses were renowned throughout the region. In the early 1900s, the farm was regarded as one of the top Jersey breeders in the entire Northeast, and it developed an elite market for high-class butter, selling only to hotels and steamship lines. However, during the course of the 20th century, the farm changed ownership numerous times, eventually disbanding in 1962. In September of that year, more than 3,000 people, including actor James Cagney and Vermont's poet laureate, Robert Frost, attended an auction where the farm's prized Morgans and equipment were sold.

After sweeping up and down on one trail, I found myself on a set of wider grassy trails that led out of the woods into the hot sun of a cloudless fall day. There was no one around except me and my Schwinn, which easily passed the challenging test ride. The only sounds heard were the birds chirping above and the squirrels scurrying by.

I hopped off the bike, sat down on a large boulder, and stared at the valley of Randolph below. My body was covered in dirt. A pale yellow leaf was stuck to the top of my shoe. I pulled it off, thinking of the poor souls who were battling traffic on Route 7, trying to convince themselves that they were enjoying their congested ride through Vermont's legendary fall foliage. Then I jumped back onto my bike and continued to savor my good fortune.

For more information on the **New England Mountain Biking Festival,** visit www.pedrosfest.com. The trails at the Green Mountain Stock Farm are open to the public year-round.

Mud Pond Loop

Allow 2 hr. Moderate; hilly terrain. Access: Start at Slab City on Rte. 12 in Randolph. Map: available from Slab City Bike & Sports.

Paul Rea, owner of Randolph's Slab City Bike & Sports shop, took me on the 12-mile Mud Pond Loop, a perfect Vermont ride past lost farmland and cornfields. Most of the riding was on grassy double tracks and dirt roads.

From Rea's store, we veered left and then right onto Brigham Hill Road, climbing high in the hills above Randolph along a ridge where the spine of the Greens could be seen in the distance. Patches of bright red and yellow dotted the countryside. We continued on double tracks through a deep dark forest, finally reaching Mud Pond, a hidden watering hole where moose are often sighted. Sunlight splintered between the tall trees to illuminate sections of the blackened water.

Soon we were on dirt roads again, passing small-town steeples, and longstanding farmsteads where vintage pickups and tractors shared the front yard with lounging cows. I took my last deep breaths of crisp Vermont air, a symphony of scents ranging from the pungent smell of manure to the sweet aroma of the maple leaves that crunched under my wheels. Within hours, I'd be on four wheels, driving to Boston. At least I'd be leaving with an invigorated body splattered with Vermont's finest souvenir: mud.

Maple Ridge Sheep Farm

Allow 2 hr. Moderate; hilly terrain. Access: From Slab City, bear left and follow State Rte. 12 North through East Braintree. At 5.2 miles from Slab City, you'll see a cemetery on the left side of the road and a sign pointing toward West Brookfield. Turn left and go up the dirt road until you reach the West Brookfield Community Church. Park here. Map: available from Slab City Bike & Sports.

Don't know any locals who will show you Vermont's secret trails or farmers who will let you ride on their land? Fret not. Head to Randolph and its environs for the best selection of public trails Vermont has to offer. Slab City Bike & Sports offers more than 10 maps with in-depth directions for the serious fat-wheeler. Bike treks include the outrageous 44.9-mile double-track Circus Ride (it can be considerably extended), used in the late 1800s to bring the circus into town, as well as the 9.8-mile Maple Ridge Sheep Farm Loop. Once you've parked your car at the church, veer left around the building and then bear right to ride next to the river. Disregard the BRIDGE CLOSED sign and head to the right of the bridge to cross the river. Veer left at the Y intersection and continue on the double tracks, crossing the river a second time. When you come to a three-way intersection, go straight on the dirt road until you reach a four-way intersection. A left turn will bring you out of the woods past several run-down buses at the bottom of the hill. When you hit a road, continue straight, veering left at the next three-way intersection. You'll cruise up and down the hills, eventually passing the Maple Ridge Sheep Farm and an old red schoolhouse on the left. Turn left just past the schoolhouse and start climbing on the single tracks before coasting downhill to a T-intersection. Veer left toward the white house called Davis Acres. Once in West Brookfield, take a sharp right turn to reach the church again. (If you understood these directions, your navigational skills are better than Captain Cook's. Get the map from Slab City!)

Union Village Dam Recreation Area

Allow 1 hr. Easy; mostly level ride. Access: From Exit 13 off I-91, take Rte. 113 west for 1.8 miles. Just before you reach Thetford Center on a downhill, look for a small white sign on the left side of the road that reads RECREATION CENTER. Turn left into the park and there's a parking lot on the left.

Like rail trails, this easy 5-miler (out and back) is a casual ride for the beginning mountain biker. You pedal south through the park alongside the Ompompanoosuc River and scenic gorge. At the end of the trail is the Union Village Dam, which you can ride across. Standing 170 feet high and spanning 1,100 feet, the dam offers excellent views of the countryside.

Lecister Hollow Trail

Allow 1 hr. Moderate; rolling dirt road. Access: From Rutland, take Rte. 7 north to Brandon and change to Rte. 73 west. 3.5 miles later, just past the Churchill House B&B, turn off onto a dirt road and into a small parking area.

This 4-mile beauty is one of the few mountain biking trails in the Green Mountain National Forest. It consists mostly of fire roads with a surface of hard-packed dirt, but there are some obstacles like roots and rocks. It's pretty much a straight shot to Silver Lake, a great place to take a break for lunch or a dip.

Outfitters

Escape Routes Adventure Tours (☎ 802/746-8943; www.escaperoutesoutdoors.com) offers guided and self-guided mountain biking tours around central Vermont. They operate out of the Pittsfield Inn.

POWERBOATING

Rent boats on Lake Dunmore from **Lake Dunmore Kamperville (☎ 802/352-4501)**. For a complete listing of all motorboat, sailboat, and canoe rentals, contact the **Vermont Department of Travel,** 134 State St., Montpelier, VT 05602 (**☎ 800/VERMONT**), for the "Vermont Boating, Rentals & Marinas" publication.

ROAD BIKING

Lake Champlain

Allow 3 hr. Easy to moderate; relatively flat farmland. Access: From Burlington, take U.S. 7 South to State Rte. 22A South. Park around the town square in Vergennes. Map: Any good state road map will do.

South of Burlington, rich farmlands and desolate country roads replace the strip malls and steady flow of traffic on U.S. 7. Lake Champlain's 12-mile girth narrows to bring into view a dramatic backdrop of the Adirondacks and the New York shore. This 27-mile ride takes you on relatively flat roads along the waters of this immense and historic lake, on a route where silos and cows outnumber cars. Start your ride from the town square in Vergennes and go south on State Route 22A. A half mile later, turn right onto Panton Road for a steady downhill run. The Adirondacks appear directly in front of you while carpets of green blanket both sides of the road. A right turn onto Basin Harbor Road will bring you past numerous dairy farms along the shores of Otter Creek. Continue biking on this road as it curves right to Basin Harbor. You'll pass the Lake Champlain Maritime Museum and its large collection of wooden watercraft built around the shores of the lake in the past 150 years. Veer left by the boats anchored in Basin Harbor for your first views of the lake. Basin Harbor Club's main house and golf course are located a few hundred yards farther on the right.

Backtrack less than a mile on Basin Harbor Road to Button Bay Road. Turn right on this unmarked street, following the signs for Button Bay State Park to see one of the most majestic sights in all of Vermont. Lake Champlain and the Adirondacks are to your right; cornfields and dairy farms lead up to the Green Mountains on your left. The wedge of rock above, aptly named Camel's Hump, is seen in the distance. Turn right on

Arnold's Bay Road, which soon turns to gravel. Watch out for large bumps and potholes as you ride through the dense woods. A mile later, the road becomes paved again as Arnold's Bay comes into view. Here, in October 1776, Benedict Arnold and his small band of boats successfully thwarted the attempts of the British flotilla to sail south toward Fort Ticonderoga. Arnold's fleet was decimated but won nonetheless. Before the British could return south, the lake was frozen over.

Veer right at the stop sign onto Pease Road as you continue to hug the shores of the lake. Apple orchards appear on both sides of the hilly road. Soon you'll see the Yankee Kingdom Country Store and Orchards. This is a good place to stop, have lunch, go apple-picking, taste home-made cider moments after it's made, or simply pet the rabbits in the small petting zoo. This is also the spot where I usually turn around and retrace my tread marks to Vergennes (excluding the Basin Harbor detour). However, if you're a loop lover, continue on Pease Road (now called Lake Road) and turn left on State Route 17. This will bring you to State Route 22A North back to Vergennes. Be forewarned: State Route 22A is hilly and can be congested since it's a main thoroughfare. The loop is a little over 30 miles long.

Woodstock

A 25-mile loop. Allow 3 hr. Moderate to strenuous; two tough uphills worth a 7-mile downhill run. Access: The tour starts at the intersection of Rte. 4 and 12 in Woodstock. Park anywhere in town.

"What comes up must come down" is an apropos old saw for this ride. Once you've purchased your maple syrup and other Vermont curios like a 19th-century apple peeler at Gillingham's, a general store at 16 Elm Street in operation since 1886, head out to the countryside. Pedal out of town on Elm Street (Route 12 North). You'll quickly pass over the Ottauquechee River and ride by the Southdown sheep and Jersey cows of Billings Farm and Museum (to your right) and the old-growth forest of spruces and pines at Marsh-Billings National Historic Park (to your left). After 1.1 miles, take a right turn at the sign toward South Pomfret and the Suicide Six ski area. For the next 2 miles the road is level as you ride parallel to Barnard Brook past several picturesque barns. At Teago General Store in South Pomfret, bear right for the hardest part of the ride. The road climbs some 700 feet over 3 miles as you make your way into Pomfret. You'll pedal alongside a cascading brook, past the Appalachian Trail and a slew of farms and pasture that seem lost in the countryside. Once you reach the white town hall of Pomfret, get ready for a thrilling 7-mile downhill run through the towns of North Pomfret and West Hartford.

When I took this ride several times last summer, I went in the early morning when the dew on the surrounding pasture glistened in the rising sun. Indeed, I was ecstatic as the freshly paved road swept downhill through the mountainside. Be careful not to bear left in Hewlett's Corner toward Sharon. Continue straight and you'll pass several horse farms as the White River widens to your left. At the West Hartford bridge, turn right onto Quechee–West Hartford Road for another climb above the majestic White River Valley. Your legs will start to feel like jelly at this point, but you'll be happy to know that there's another wonderful downhill cruise up ahead. Be on the lookout for an inverted Y sign. Just 0.1 mile later, you'll take a sharp right turn onto River Road for a relatively level 5.5-mile run along the Ottauquechee River. This is one of the most popular biking roads in the state. On your left, just past the Quechee Club, the river never leaves your side. On your right, you cruise past cornfields, horse pastures, wonderful farm estates, and undeveloped forest. At the Taftsville covered bridge, turn right on unpaved River Road, keeping the river to your left. Even though this is a dirt road, the gravel is packed hard and easy for hybrids. Be on the lookout for herons, ibis, and wood ducks on this stretch of the river. Soon you will reach the Billings Farm and Museum on your left. Turn left on Route 12 to return to the center of Woodstock.

Upper Connecticut River

Allow 3 hr. Moderate; rolling hills with one steep climb. Access: Fairlee is located off Exit 15 on I-91. Take U.S. 5 North to the junction of State Rte. 5 and 25A. Park at Cumberland Farms. Map: Any good state road map will do.

New England's longest river, the Connecticut, is perhaps most scenic at the Vermont–New Hampshire border, north of White River Junction and Hanover. Here, the river snakes through the rural landscape, looking like it has for the past hundred years. This 28.4-mile loop brings you to both states as you ride through small historic villages that sit above the winding waters. Start your trip in Fairlee at the junction of State Route 25A and U.S. 5, continuing on Route 25A East across the river into another state and another era. You have entered Orford, New Hampshire, a small village listed in the National Register of Historic Places. Bear left on State Route 10 North to view the seven Federal-style buildings, known as the Orford Ridge houses, constructed between 1773 and 1840. Continuing on the rising and falling road, you will see the Connecticut River on your left, hemmed in by farmland on either side. Patches of pumpkins, zucchini, and butternut squash line the route prior to entering the handsome village of Haverhill and its double Commons. Historic 18th- and 19th-century houses are gathered about the Village Green. Just past the town, the Indian Corn Mill is a great place to stop for apple cider and doughnuts.

Take the next left, crossing the river once again into Vermont, and veer left onto U.S. 5 South. Fields of corn soon vanish, replaced by Bradford's stores. Eight miles from the junction of U.S. 5 and the bridge, veer right onto unmarked Maurice Robert Memorial Highway. The road goes slightly upward, under two bridges, before heading up and down a steep hill. Another right on Lake Morey West Road brings you to a lake. The lake is named after native Samuel Morey, an inventor who some locals credit with designing and operating the world's first steamboat. Ten years before Robert Fulton launched the ***Clermont,*** Samuel Morey was supposedly seen cruising down the Connecticut on a homemade boat that housed a steam boiler. Ride around the perimeter of the lake, which is bordered by numerous summer camps. The road swings by a golf course and under I-91, before veering left onto U.S. 5 North back to the starting point.

Silver Maple Lodge in Fairlee offers bikes to its guests for the Upper Connecticut River ride (see "Campgrounds & Other Accommodations," below).

Randolph

Allow 3–4 hr. Easy to moderate; relatively flat terrain. Access: Park at Slab City Bike & Sports, at the junction of State Rte. 12 and 12A in Randolph.

In an area of Vermont renowned for its road and off-road biking, this 36.5-mile loop is easily one of the best in the state. From the Slab City parking lot, turn left onto State Route 12A North through Randolph and the outskirts of Braintree. Civilization soon fades away as the ride becomes a mix of green meadows, cornfields, and farms nestled at the foothills of the Green Mountains. Come late September, the trees' leaves display their various hues—burnt red, bright orange, and egg-yolk yellow. The road is soon hidden by hills on both sides as you ride along a railroad bed and small stream. You'll pass Roxbury, with its requisite white steeple, and Northfield Country Club, whose putting greens are camouflaged by the surrounding hillsides. At 20.6 miles, prior to entering the town of Northfield, turn right on State Route 12 South to pedal by apple orchards, a small pond, and more farmland. Gradually, you go uphill on Route 12's only ascent, before zipping downhill on a serpentine road past a flash of forest color. Don't blink or you might miss the small town of East Braintree.

The final 6 miles are a special treat—acre upon acre of uninterrupted land so rich and green you'll consider quitting your job and becoming the next Johnny Appleseed. Riding through this fertile farmland on a rolling country road with just a trace of traffic, you'll find it easy to understand why Vermont is rated one of the best places to bike in the country. At the junction of State Routes 12 and 12A, bear left and then make an immediate right to return to your car.

Waitsfield-Warren Loop

Allow 2 hr. Easy to moderate; one short hill. Access: Park at the junction of State Rte. 100 and State Rte. 17 between Waitsfield and Warren.

The Waitsfield-Warren area is home to Sugarbush and Mad River, two of the best-loved ski resorts in the Northeast. This short, 15-mile loop skirts the mountains and enters these two small villages via covered bridges. Start your ride at the junction of Route 100 and Route 17, turning right on Route 100 South. Considering the high peaks of Lincoln, Ellen, and Abraham to your right, the road is remarkably flat. When I took this ride in early autumn, the maples on the hillside to my left were as red as a newly painted barn. At 5.4 miles, take a sharp left onto Covered Bridge Road. Constructed in 1880, the wooden bridge spans the Mad River. Turn left and ride through the village of Warren, making a point to stop at the Warren Store for lunch. Dagwoodesque sandwiches on thick French bread can be savored at the picnic tables overlooking Mad River. Try to save room for the homemade peanut butter, oatmeal raisin, and chocolate chip cookies. You'll easily burn off the calories when you take your next right onto Brook Road and climb into Lincoln Valley. Dairy farms, green meadows, and fields of corn, typical of Vermont's bucolic scenery, stand at the side of the now East Warren Road. The slopes of Sugarbush appear to your left, and a rare round barn can be seen to your right. Built in 1910, the barn is now part of the Inn of the Round Barn. From here, you cruise downhill all the way to the covered bridge in Waitsfield, built in 1833. Pedal through town and turn left onto State Route 100 South, being cautious of traffic.

Rentals

In Montpelier, check out **Onion River Sports** (☎ **802/229-9409**).

Outfitters

John Friedin, author of ***25 Bicycle Tours in Vermont*** (Countryman Press, 1996) and founder of **Vermont Bicycle Touring (VBT),** P.O. Box 711, Monkton Rd., Bristol, VT 05443 (☎ **802/453-4811** or 800/245-3868; www.vbt.com), knows every country road in the state. His knowledge shows in his catalog and in the success of his company. VBT now runs bike tours through 14 states in nearly every region of the country, and it has teamed up with Travent International to guide Americans abroad in places like New Zealand, Switzerland, and Italy. In the central part of the Green Mountain State, he takes bikers on 6-day inn-to-inn trips to the Champlain Valley and the Mad River Valley.

Bike Vermont, P.O. Box 207, Woodstock, VT 05091 (☎ **800/257-2226;** www.bikevermont.com), features 2- to 6-day guided tours around the Mad River and Champlain Valleys.

POMG (Peace of Mind Guaranteed) **Bike Tours of Vermont** (☎ **888/635-BIKE;** www.pomgbike.com) features 2- to 5-day tours in the Mad River Valley. Also check out its family camping tours to Silver Lake and Lake Dunmore, starting as low as $249.

ROCK CLIMBING

Vermont's rock-climbing scene isn't what you might think it would be judging from all those mountains and cliffs. Problem is, the flaky metamorphic schist that is the most common foundation of the Green Mountains is about the worst climbing rock imaginable. Yet, there are some small crags, 50 to 300 feet in height that are ideal for a quick climb.

There are a few moderate-sized walls of good rock around the state that have kept the locals happy. Most of these walls are still relatively undiscovered. Probably the best walls in the middle part of the state are at **Deer Leap Mountain,** off U.S. 4 at Shelburne Pass, right behind the Long Trail Inn (a half-dozen climbs on good rock, in the 5.8 to 5.10 range, upper cliff is mostly for beginners); and the rock at **Lake Dunmore** just across from the entrance to Branbury State Park (looks like about eight climbs, 5.5 to 5.6 or so, developed climbs).

The one-stop-shopping source for equipment and all sorts of information about Vermont rock climbing is **Climb High,** 2438 Shelburne Rd., Shelburne, VT 05482 (☎ **802/985-5056** or 802/985-9141; www.climbhigh.com).

The **Green Mountain Rock Climbing Center** (☎ **802/773-3343;** www.bestclimb.com) in Rutland has guided rock climbing and ice climbing trips around the state. They also have clinics and an indoor climbing wall.

SAILING

Sailboats can be rented on Lake Dunmore from **Lake Dunmore Kamperville** (☎ **802/352-4501**). For a complete listing of all sailboats, motorboats, and canoe rentals, contact the **Vermont Department of Travel,** 134 State St., Montpelier, VT 05602 (☎ **800/VERMONT**), for its "Vermont Boating, Rentals & Marinas" publication.

SNOWMOBILING

There are literally thousands of miles of unparalleled snowmobile trails all over Vermont. Contact the **Vermont Association of Snow Travelers,** P.O. Box 839, Montpelier, VT 05601 (☎ **802/ 229-0005;** www.vtvast.org), for information and maps.

SNOWSHOEING

With such great hiking available in central Vermont, it should come as no surprise that there's top-notch snowshoeing. When there's snow on the ground in Ripton, walkers head to the **Robert Frost Interpretive Trail** (see "Walks and Rambles," below). In Woodstock, snowshoe up 1,240-foot Mount Tom for views of the town and nearby Killington. The 1.6-mile (one-way) **Faulkner Trail** is a yellow-blazed series of switchbacks that gradually make their way to the peak. The trail originates in Faulkner Park on Mountain Avenue in Woodstock.

The 1.5-mile **Cooke's Crest Trail** at Brookfield's Green Trails Inn winds through pristine forest. Take I-89 to Exit 4 and follow Route 66 East for 7 miles to Brookfield. A moderate climb is the 2-mile Echo Mountain climb in Fairlee. The trail has great views of Lake Morey. Take Exit 15 off I-91 and head west on Lake Morey Road. Go up Brushwood Road and look for the trail on the left.

In Quechee, Marty Banak, owner of **Wilderness Trails** (☎ **802/295-7620**), takes snowshoers on guided walks to nearby Quechee Gorge.

SWIMMING

No, they're not mirages; they're authentic Vermont swimming holes:

- **Quechee Gorge,** U.S. 4, Quechee. An easy trail from the highway leads down to this genuine geological phenomenon; at its north end is an excellent swimming hole. At the south end, near the souvenir stand on

Route 4, is a trail that leads down to **Dewey's Mills Pond.** Just beyond the dam, this is a perfect place to slip away from the masses, roam among the tall wildflowers, and swim in the gentle waters.

- **North Hartland Lake,** good swimming beach at the base of a dam, but there's very little shade. Also a great canoeing spot during fall foliage. Contact **Wilderness Trails,** Clubhouse Rd., Quechee (☎ **802/295-7620;** www.scenesofvermont.com/wildernesstrails/), for a canoe and shuttle.
- **Silver Lake State Park,** State Route 12, Barnard. A scenic lake with paddleboat, canoe, and tube rentals, large grass beach, snack bar, and swings. A good place to take the kids.
- **White River,** off State Route 14 in the South Royalton–Sharon area. The joining of the four branches of this river just upstream creates big enough water for some great swimming holes. Keep your eyes peeled for cars parked at pullovers.
- **White River,** near the intersection of State Routes 100 and 73, Rochester.
- **The Floating Bridge,** State Route 65, Brookfield. Where all the locals go—a genuine scene.
- **Osgood Brook Culvert,** Tunbridge Road, East Randolph. The real thing—an icy, crystal-clear swimming hole known to only a few—and so small you couldn't fit more than two or three people in it—about a half mile up this dirt road that heads east off State Route 14.
- **Mad River,** off State Route 100 immediately after Lincoln Gap Road; park at the gravel pit.
- **Mad River,** off State Route 100 between Moretown and Waitsfield; look for the parking lot and picnic area on the riverbank. Large, very popular, and graced with more skipping-stones than any 12-year-old boy could throw.
- **Beaver ponds, Winooski feeder streams, Winooski River,** in the North Calais–Kents Corner area, off U.S. 2 east of Montpelier. Boundless swimmin' options in a little area that seriously contends to be Vermont's prettiest.
- On the west side of the Green Mountains, check out **Bartlett's Falls** in Lincoln 2 miles east of Bristol and the **Middlebury Gorge** off State Route 125 in East Middlebury.

WALKS & RAMBLES

Robert Frost Interpretive Trail

Allow 1 hr. Access: From Ripton, take State Rte. 125 East (Robert Frost Memorial Hwy.) for 2 miles. A sign for the small parking area is located on the right side of the road. Map: available at the trailhead.

In 1920, 44-year-old Robert Frost moved from New Hampshire to Vermont. For the next 39 years, he would summer in a scanty log cabin standing on the crest of a hillside in Ripton, Vermont. The state adopted Frost as its native son, designating him the official poet laureate in 1961, and in 1983 bestowing the name "Robert Frost Country" to this section of the Green Mountain National Forest. Robert Frost Country includes the farm where he lived, the Robert Frost Wayside Picnic Area, the Robert Frost Memorial Drive, Middlebury's Bread Loaf School of English (which Frost cofounded), and the Robert Frost Interpretive Trail.

This mile-long level dirt path weaves through a forest setting where seven Frost poems are posted at regular intervals. I took the trail in late winter, an ideal time since many of the mounted poems are set in this season, like "Stopping by Woods on a Snowy Evening" and "A Winter

Eden." I crossed over Beaver Pond into a forest of birches, beeches, and spruce. Frost's words, like his 1946 poem "A Young Birch," perfectly complement the scenery:

> *It will stand forth, entirely white in bark,*
> *And nothing but the top a leafy green—*
> *The only native tree that dares to lean,*
> *Relying on its beauty, to the air.*
> *(Less brave perhaps than trusting are the fair.)*

The trail seems far too short, leaving the forest and entering a field of blueberries and huckleberries before arriving back at the parking lot. To continue the Frost tour, I drove to the dirt road just east of the Robert Frost Wayside Picnic Area. In typical Vermont fashion, the road is unmarked. I followed the dirt road for approximately a half mile and parked near a white house. A hundred-yard walk past this house brought me to a clearing on my left. The rustic cabin where Frost lived for 2 months every summer was situated here. Middlebury College now owns the grounds and keeps the door to the interior of the cabin locked.

Chittenden Brook

2.5 miles. Allow two hr. The diversity of terrain on this stroll includes tumbling streams, meadows, thick forest, and beaver ponds. Access: From the junction of Rte. 53 and 73 in Forest Dale, head east on Rte. 73 for 9 miles. Turn right on Forest Rd. 45 to Chittenden Brook Campground. Park at the sign for the Campground Loop Trail.

Climb along a wide grassy path lined with sugar maples and yellow birches. At 0.75 mile, the trail turns sharply to the right and meets up with Chittenden Brook. Follow the brook downstream through the forest. At 1.5 miles, continue on to the beaver ponds where, if you're here late in the afternoon, you might see one of these furry creatures working diligently in the water. When you're ready, head back to the Campground Loop Trail, which will lead you back to the car.

Button Bay State Park

1.5 miles round-trip. Allow 1 hr. A pleasant walk on the Champlain shoreline. Access: From Vergennes, head south on Rte. 22A to Panton Rd. Turn right and continue 2 miles to Basin Harbor Rd. Turn right again and proceed 4.5 miles to Button Bay State Park. The trailhead for the Champlain Trail is located at the end of the park road.

Much of Lake Champlain's shoreline is privately owned, so it's a treat to take a walk along the water. This short trail weaves through the cedars of Button Bay State Park along a crescent-shaped bay. Afterward, visit the park's nature center.

Marsh-Billings National Historic Park

2 miles. Allow 1 hr. Access: Located north of Woodstock on Rte. 12, across from Billings Farm & Museum. Park at the farm.

"Every middle-aged man who revisits his birthplace after a few years of absence, looks upon another landscape than that which formed the theater of his youthful toils and pleasures." So said George Perkins Marsh in 1847 in a speech at the Agricultural Society of Rutland County, Vermont. Growing up in Woodstock, Vermont, Marsh had seen three-quarters of Vermont's forest cover destroyed for potash, lumber, crops, and pasture. Seventeen years later, Marsh would delve further into these egregious practices in his epic book on the American environment, ***Man and Nature.*** Reflecting on what he had seen, Marsh wrote about a concept of sound husbandry where humankind could mend nature.

A generation younger, Frederick Billings was deeply touched by Marsh's writings and, in 1869, purchased Marsh's childhood home in order to make the estate a model of progressive farming and forestry. Beginning in the 1870s, Billings designed a forest with numerous tree plantations and constructed a 20-mile network of carriage roads to showcase his work. On the lowlands, Billings developed a state-of-the-art dairy. In 1982, Billings' granddaughter Mary French Rockefeller and her husband, the conservationist Laurance Rockefeller, established the farmland as the Billings Farm & Museum. In June 1998, the Marsh-Billings-Rockefeller Mansion and the surrounding forest became the Marsh-Billings National Historical Park.

Marsh-Billings National Historical Park is the first unit of the National Park System to focus on the theme of conservation history and stewardship, the main concern of Marsh and Billings. With their emphasis on the careful cooperation of humankind and nature, they had the utmost desire to pass land on undiminished, even enhanced, to the next generation and generations to come. The Park Service will continue a program of forest management on the site, offering workshops on how to use the forest most efficiently.

Tour the exhibits in the Carriage Barn and, of course, in the mansion, which has a wonderful collection of 19th-century American landscape paintings by the likes of Albert Bierstadt, Thomas Cole, John Frederick Kensett, and Asher Durand. Then hit the carriage path trails through Billings's dream 550-acre forest. Eleven of his original plantings remain, including groves of Norwegian spruce and Scottish Pine from the 1880s, mixed in with an indigenous Vermont forest of white pine, red pine, and maples. The longest carriage-path trail circles around The Pogue, a pond where swimming and fishing are prohibited. Then simply loop back to the mansion.

Ourfitters & Inn-to-Inn Trips

Wonder Walks (☎ **802/453-4169;** www.wonderwalks.com) are owner-led walking tours through the Green Mountain National Forest and the Champlain Valley. Trips of 3 to 5 nights, inn-to-inn, are available.

Campgrounds & Other Accommodations

CAMPING

There are 94 campsites scattered across the **Green Mountain National Forest,** available on a first-come, first-served basis for a small fee. Free camping is also permitted anywhere on national forest land. For more information, contact the Green Mountain National Forest, 231 N. Main St., Rutland, VT 05701 (☎ **802/747-6700**).

Vermont State Parks (103 S. Main St., Waterbury, VT 05671; ☎ **802/241-3655;** www.vtstateparks.com) maintains 39 campgrounds in the state. Contact them for a brochure.

Button Bay State Park

On Panton Rd., just south of Basin Harbor. ☎ **802/475-2377.** 72 sites, no hookups, public phone, wheelchair-accessible rest rooms, showers, sewage disposal, tables, fire rings, wood, snack bar, playground.

Located on the southern shores of Lake Champlain, all of Button Bay's sites have exceptional views of the Adirondacks across the lake. The site's history and geography, plus its nature center and resident naturalist, only add to the allure.

D.A.R. State Park

Off Rte. 17, 7 miles southwest of Addison. ☎ **802/759-2345.** 71 sites, no hookups, public phone, wheelchair-accessible rest rooms, showers, sewage disposal, tables, fire rings, wood, and playground.

A good alternative to Button Bay, D.A.R.'s sites also sit on the shore of Lake Champlain. A great place to swim and fish.

Bomoseen State Park
Follow U.S. 4 west of Rutland and take Exit 3. The park is located 5 miles north on West Shore Rd. ☎ **802/265-4242.** 66 sites, no hookups, public phone, wheelchair-accessible rest rooms, limited grocery store, picnic tables, fireplaces, wood, snack bar, and playground.

Large Lake Bomoseen is popular with powerboaters, especially anglers searching for rainbows, brownies, brook and lake trout, pickerel, pike, and perch. The campsites are set slightly back from the shores of the lake in a wooded refuge.

Half Moon State Park
On West Shore Rd. past Bomoseen State Park. ☎ **802/273-2848.** 69 sites, no hookups, showers, flush toilets, picnic tables, fireplaces, playground, and boat rentals.

More secluded than Lake Bomoseen, Half Moon has campsites set near the shore of the pond. A good place to swim, canoe, and fish for bass, pike, and trout.

Chittenden Brook Recreation Area
From Brandon, travel east on Rte. 73 for 12 miles. Turn right on Rte. 45 and drive 2 miles to the campground. ☎ **802/767-4261.** 17 sites, no hookups, fire grates, outhouses.

The sites are set in the secluded forest along Chittenden Brook. To get even deeper into the woods, take the Campground Loop (see "Walks & Rambles," above).

Allis State Park
From Randolph, travel 12 miles north on Rte. 12 to Rte. 65. Turn right; go 1.5 miles to the park entrance on the right side of the road. A park road leads to the summit of Bear Mountain. ☎ **802/276-3175.** 27 sites, no hookups, stone or brick fireplaces, showers, flush toilets, and playground.

For a campground with a view, head to the summit of 2,020-foot Bear Mountain. The small quiet campground is set off in the woods near the fire tower. At the base of the mountain are several lakes, good for swimming and boating.

Silver Lake State Park
From Barnard, head 0.25 mile north on Town Rd. ☎ **802/234-9451.** 47 sites, no hookups, public phone, wheelchair-accessible rest rooms, showers, fireplaces, wood, snack bar, playground, and boat rentals.

Just north of Woodstock, Silver Lake is open to nonmotorized boating only. Thus, this gem of a lake is the perfect place to swim, canoe, or catch sunfish or perch from the shores. Campsites are in the woods, close to the lake.

Quechee Gorge State Park
From I-89, take Exit 1 and head west on Rte. 4 for 3 miles to the park entrance on the left side of the road. ☎ **802/295-2990.** 54 sites, no hookups, showers, flush toilets, picnic tables, fireplaces, firewood, and playground.

Located next to Quechee Gorge on the Ottauquechee River, these scenic sites are set back in the forest. A small loop trail provides good views of the gorge, or head to the north end to take a dip in a swimming hole.

INNS & RESORTS

Woodstock Inn & Resort
Fourteen the Green, Woodstock, VT 05091. ☎ **802/457-1100** or 800/448-7900. Double room rates start at $159.

Locals at Richardson Tavern never discussed synthetic fibers when the bar opened in 1793. Yet, more than two centuries later, the small village of Woodstock features some of the most stylish polar fleece boutiques in the East, and the Richardson Tavern, now the Woodstock Inn, caters to families who yearn to put these latest fashions to use.

From the steps of this grand, Colonial-style resort, it's only a 45-minute climb to the state's newest National Historic Park, atop Mount Tom. After a picnic on this small summit, you can continue your walk on more than 30 miles of pine-laden trails or head back to the inn on a route that leads to a covered bridge over the Ottauquechee River. The river is stocked with rainbow trout, so grab a couple of fishing poles at the resort and try your luck. The inn also rents bikes to ride on Vermont's lightly traveled backcountry roads. Travel north on Route 12 and you'll pass green meadows and small villages.

Back at the Woodstock Inn, kids can tinker on the putting green at the golf course designed by Robert Trent Jones, Sr. Guests also enjoy 10 outdoor tennis courts and a large indoor sports center where parents can soak their tired bodies in Jacuzzis.

Silver Maple Lodge

R.R. 1, Box 8, Fairlee, VT 05045. ☎ **802/333-4326** or 800/666-1946; www.silvermaplelodge.com. Double rooms start at a remarkably low $56 for double occupancy, including breakfast.

In addition to its hot-air balloon package (see "Ballooning," above), the Silver Maple Lodge arranges self-guided biking, canoeing, and walking inn-to-inn tours. The inn is located near the banks of the Connecticut River, north of Hanover, New Hampshire. First opened to guests in the 1920s, the lodge's antique farmhouse dates from the late 1700s.

Three Stallion Inn

Randolph, VT 05060. ☎ **802/728-5575** or 800/424-5575; www.3stallioninn.com. Rates start at $137 for double occupancy.

Set on 1,300 acres of pasture, this former farm caters to outdoor enthusiasts. The affordable inn features 50 kilometers (31.25 miles) of groomed cross-country skiing trails, two tennis courts, an adjoining golf course, and, of course, mountain biking at the Green Mountain Stock Farm.

The Inn at the Round Barn Farm

R.R. 1, P.O. Box 247, E. Warren Rd., Waitsfield, VT 05673. ☎ **802/496-2276;** www.innattheroundbarn.com. The 11 rooms start at $135 and include a gluttonous breakfast.

There's always some special event happening at the Round Barn. When I was there last, they were hosting two weddings in the same week. People were more sociable than relatives at a family reunion. The inn gets its name from the adjacent round barn built in 1910, one of the few round barns that remain in Vermont. The barn's lower level now has a 60-foot lap pool. Snaking through the outlying farmland and forests are 23 kilometers (14.38 miles) of groomed cross-country trails. If you feel like going downhill skiing, you're close to Sugarbush and Mad River. East Warren Road is part of a good biking loop (see "Road Biking," above).

The Pitcher Inn

Warren, Vermont 05674; **888/TO-PITCH;** www.pitcherinn.com. Rooms start at $300 per night.

Skiers who've traveled from Killington to Stowe already know that Vermont's Route 100 is one of the finest stretches of country road in America. Now, with the addition of the Pitcher Inn to the small village of Warren, visitors can finally stop and savor this beauty while being pampered at an upscale retreat. Opened in December 1998, the 11-room inn sits just down the road from Sugarbush and Mad River Glen ski areas.

The inn is the brainchild of local architect David Sellers, best known for his design of the south transept in Manhattan's Cathedral of St. John the Divine. Outside, the white columns and stately porch are a welcome addition to Warren. Inside, each room has a distinctive Vermont feel. The large Mallard Room evokes the image of duck hunting. Decoys line the wooden trim of the bed, and wainscoting resembles the look of a marsh. In the Trout Room, birch trees were used to create the bed frame, a fly-fishing desk is fully stocked, and a semi-circular verandah overlooks a rambling stream. In less-talented hands, the result might be cloying, but Sellers used more than 40 local craftspeople to give the rooms a classic agrarian appeal. This Vermont pride stems to the restaurant where many of the entrees include cheeses, vegetables, and other native produce.

Blueberry Hill
Goshen, VT 05733. ☎ **802/247-6735;** www.blueberryhillinn.com. Rates per person start at $100 and include breakfast and dinner.

Blueberry Hill is one of those secluded, intimate inns that you would never know about unless you read about it in a guidebook like this. The eight-room inn is nestled in the foothills of the Green Mountain National Forest. Guests eat dinner together family-style at long tables, but you might not have any appetite after sneaking homemade chocolate chip cookies all day. The inn's cross-country ski center is one of the best and oldest in Vermont; 50 to 75 kilometers (31.25 to 46.88 miles) of trails weave in and out of the forest. British-born owner Tony Clark is an avid traveler who knows from his own experience how to treat guests royally.

4

Lake Champlain, the Northern Green Mountains & the Northeast Kingdom

It's not for nothing that the hub of northern Vermont, Burlington, is Vermont's biggest city. Straddling the line between friendly, medium-size town and burgeoning metropolis, Burlington has an attractive waterfront and the vigorous cultural life that comes with playing host to five colleges. The Champlain Valley also has a milder climate than most of Vermont—if the difference between –10° and –25° on a January morning means something more to you than "head south."

But the lure of Burlington for its young, active population is the diversity of outdoor playgrounds within shooting range. Sailing and deep-water fishing on Lake Champlain; the mix of open water, freshwater marsh, and farmland that is visible from almost any vantage on the roads of Grand Isle County; miles upon miles of quiet two-lane roads through the rolling, wide-open farmland of the Champlain Valley; Vermont's highest peaks and best ski areas in the northern Green Mountains; and the rugged and remote reaches of the Northeast Kingdom—all of these are within a short drive of Burlington. People who live in central Vermont or the Northeast Kingdom—and especially Montpelier, Burlington's chief rival as a sort of center of the intelligentsia—like to disdainfully portray Burlington as the kind of overdeveloped landscape you find almost anywhere else in the country. But if you want to live within reach of the best skiing, birding, canoeing, road and mountain biking, sailing—really, any outdoor pursuit you can think of—and be able to eat in a good restaurant and catch a first-run movie of your choice, there's no place in the state like the "Queen City."

The outdoor playgrounds of northern Vermont, most of them a whopping 7-hour drive or so from New York, are more for the locals than they are for tourists. Towns up here (with the notable exception of Stowe) don't have the manicured charm of places like Manchester and Woodstock to the south. Yet they're just as beautiful—take a look at the perfect little villages of Craftsbury and Cabot and see what you think. The Northeast Kingdom is unabashed cow country, still characterized by working family farms and small-time timbering operations. What does all this mean for the sportsperson who ventures this far north? You're entering the ***real*** Vermont with ***real*** people. The rolling green farmland and high peaks are here, perhaps even more spectacular than farther south; but the majority of people do not have jobs that cater to tourists, and the majority of farms have not been refurbished as country inns.

This is especially true of the Northeast Kingdom, the large chunk of land bordering Quebec and New Hampshire in the northeast corner of the state. Ride a bike on one of the country roads here and you'll find hills and farms branching out in every direction. Come winter, the Nordic and Alpine ski areas have much more snow than in the south and there are far fewer people on the trails.

Located south of the Northeast Kingdom, Stowe began as a resort after the Civil War, when travelers would take the train to Waterbury, ride the trolley to Stowe, and then hire a horse-drawn carriage to bring them to the Mount Mansfield House. Atop the barren summit of Vermont's highest peak, urbanites could enjoy the views and fill their lungs with the crisp mountain air. Over a century later, the trails are still filled with hikers who yearn for the same pleasures. Then there's Lake Champlain and its many tributaries. Canoeists head toward the lake via Vermont's three great canoe-camping rivers, the Winooski, the Lamoille, and the Missisquoi, while sailors, anglers, kayakers, and scuba divers stake out their spots on Champlain itself. Head to this part of the state and you'll soon understand why it's worth the extra 1- to 2-hour drive.

The Lay of the Land

North of **Bolton Gorge**—a notch cut by the Winooski River through the ridge of the **Green Mountains**—the summits climb to 4,393-foot Mount Mansfield, the state's highest point. From here, the Greens pass the baton to the **Cold Hollow Mountains,** which extend close to the Canadian border. The range includes Belvidere Mountain and Jay Peak. Paralleling the main ridge 10 to 20 miles to the east is the **Worcester Range,** which boasts peaks such as Mount Hunger, near Stowe.

To the east of Jay Peak is the **Northeast Kingdom,** a sparsely populated, very hilly land of farms and lakes. A fine example of glacial scouring is evident at Lake Willoughby, north of St. Johnsbury. The indigenous granite has been carved into a deep trough lined by dramatic cliffs on either side of the water.

West of the mountains is 120-mile-long **Lake Champlain** and the outlying land known as the Champlain Valley. The massive lake was formed when an ice cap retreated to the St. Lawrence Seaway and the ocean. Close to 1,500 feet lower than the mountains, the lake's islands and outlying valley contain prodigious amounts of marble. Isle La Motte, an island in Lake Champlain, was once home to a black marble quarry.

Fall foliage usually peaks in late September in northern Vermont. The Department of Travel maintains a foliage hotline, updating the conditions of the leaves (**☎ 800/VERMONT**). The rest of the year, summer days are usually in the high 70s, but cooler at night. In the Northeast Kingdom, it is not uncommon to find frost on your window in early September. January temperatures are below freezing most of the time (especially near the Canadian border), with snowfall averaging 55 inches in the valleys to over 120 inches on high elevations. For current weather conditions in northern Vermont, call ☎ **802/862-2475** or 802/476-4101.

The chances of finding moose in the northern fringes of Vermont are becoming better and better. Last summer, a local told me she spotted a moose every time she took the trail up to the summit of Mount Hor on Lake Willoughby. Sightings of black bears and otters are far less common. Beavers, gray foxes, and white-tailed deer are frequently observed on the shores and waters of Vermont's northern lakes. (Speaking of deer, the Northeast Kingdom is definitely the kind of place where hunting is such an obsession that high schools have closed down for deer season, at least until fairly recently.) The state's numerous wildlife management areas and preserves are prime birding territory. Wood ducks, herons, mallards, and green-winged teals are prevalent.

Orientation

This chapter covers Burlington, the region of Lake Champlain north of Burlington, the entirety of the Green Mountain chain above Waterbury (I-89), and all of the Northeast Kingdom above the Barre-Montpelier area and U.S. 302. (This is a broader definition than most people give the Kingdom, but this whole area really is of a piece, and it works for my purposes.)

Interstate 89 connects Montpelier, Waterbury, and the Mount Mansfield area with Burlington. North of Burlington, **U.S. 2** takes you to the Lake Champlain Islands. When you get within a half hour or so of Burlington, **State Route 15** becomes one of the ugliest and most congested routes in the state.

North of Waterbury, **State Route 100**—the Ski Country corridor all the way up and down the state—continues to Stowe and Jay Peak. The village of **Stowe** and the roads within 5 miles of town are really the only clearly touristy area in northern Vermont; nevertheless, this is definitely one of Vermont's most beautiful places, well deserving of all the attention. **State Route 108** through Smuggler's Notch is one of the most majestic drives in New England.

The **Northeast Kingdom** got its name when Sen. George Aiken, speaking to a small group of his constituents in Lyndonville in 1949, noted that "this is such beautiful country up here. It ought to be called the Northeast Kingdom of Vermont." The Northeast Kingdom now consists of Essex, Orleans, and Caledonia Counties, a large tract of land wedged between the Quebec and New Hampshire borders. To get to the gems of the Northeast Kingdom—**Craftsbury, Greensboro,** and **Lake Willoughby**—you have to earn the pleasure. A combination of smaller byways like State Routes 14, 16, and 5A will eventually guide you there. There are numerous scenic drives to and through the Kingdom: **State Route 5A,** skirting the shores of Lake Willoughby; **State Route 58** from Montgomery Center to Lowell through Hazen's Notch; **State Route 14** from Irasburg to Craftsbury Common; and—my favorite—**State Route 12** from Montpelier to Morrisville.

Even Vermonters speak of the Kingdom as the Boonies, or the Sticks. Wave after wave of unspoiled hillside forms a vast sea of green. No slick resorts, just a few inconspicuous inns and lots of Holsteins. **St. Johnsbury** and **Lyndonville** are its business centers, workmanlike towns with nary a fancy carved-wood roadside sign between them. Around them for many miles are spread small villages and farms, a few high mountains, and a lot of abruptly hilly countryside. Some of these villages, like Craftsbury and Greensboro, are iconic in their appeal. You haven't seen a New England village green until you've visited Craftsbury Common. Founded in 1789, Craftsbury Common is an incredibly peaceful village where white clapboard houses embrace the

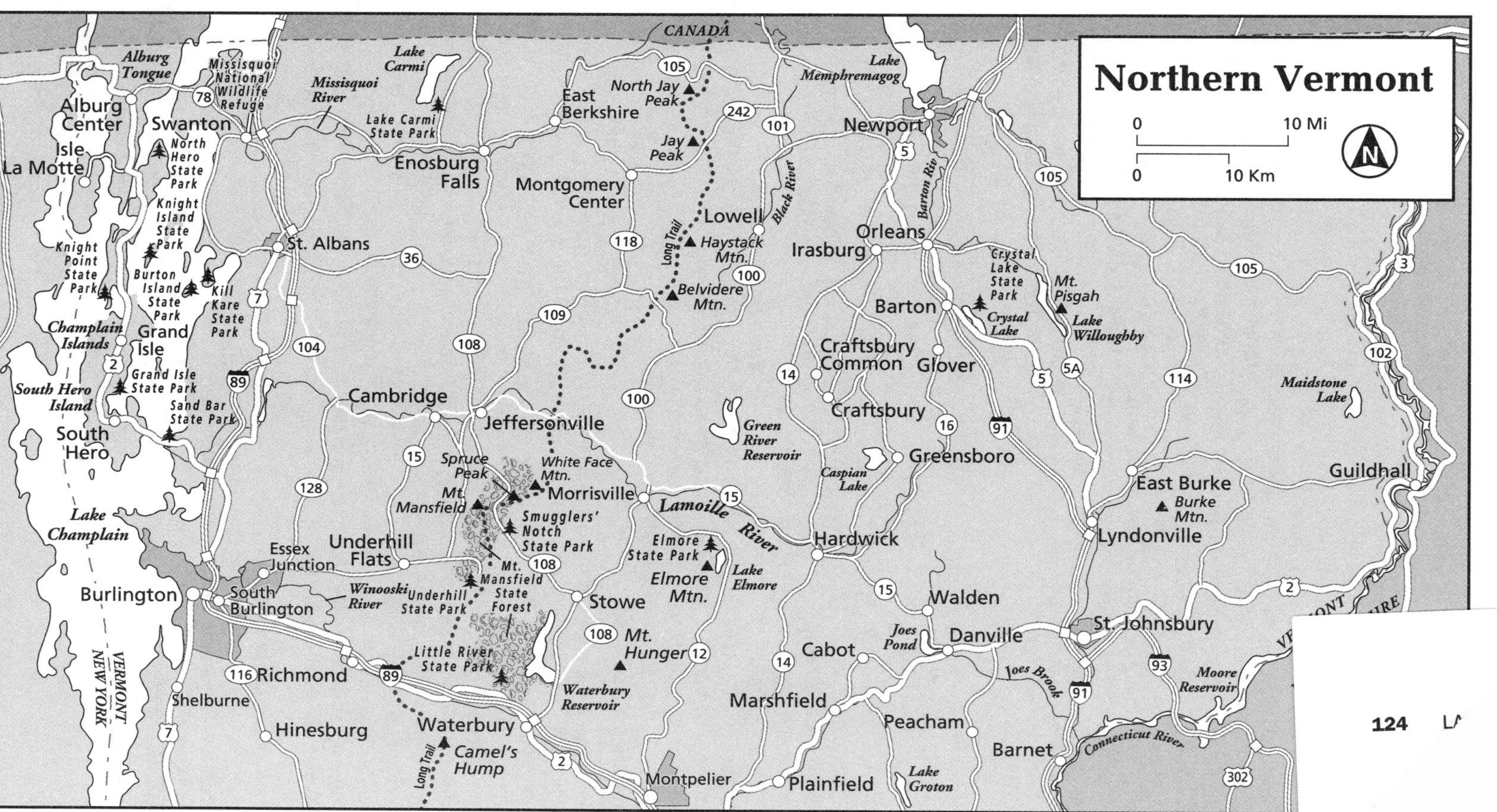

Northern Vermont
0
10 Mi
0
10 Km
N
CANADA
Alburg Tongue
Missisquoi National Wildlife Refuge
Missisquoi River
Lake Carmi
Lake Carmi State Park
East Berkshire
North Jay Peak
Jay Peak
Lake Memphremagog
Newport
Alburg Center
Swanton
Isle La Motte
North Hero State Park
Knight Island State Park
Enosburg Falls
Montgomery Center
Lowell
Black River
Barton Riv
Orleans
Irasburg
St. Albans
Haystack Mtn.
Long Trail
Knight Point State Park
Burton Island State Park
Kill Kare State Park
Belvidere Mtn.
Crystal Lake State Park
Mt. Pisgah
Barton
Crystal Lake
Lake Willoughby
Champlain Islands
Grand Isle
Craftsbury Common
Glover
Grand Isle State Park
South Hero Island
Sand Bar State Park
Cambridge
Jeffersonville
Craftsbury
Maidstone Lake
South Hero
Green River Reservoir
Greensboro
Spruce Peak
White Face Mtn.
Caspian Lake
Guildhall
Mt. Mansfield
Morrisville
Lamoille River
East Burke
Burke Mtn.
Lake Champlain
Smugglers' Notch State Park
Hardwick
Lyndonville
Essex Junction
Underhill Flats
Elmore State Park
Mt. Mansfield State Forest
Lake Elmore
Elmore Mtn.
Burlington
South Burlington
Winooski River
Underhill State Park
Stowe
Walden
St. Johnsbury
Mt. Hunger
Joes Pond
Danville
Cabot
Little River State Park
Richmond
Joes Brook
Moore Reservoir
Waterbury Reservoir
Marshfield
Shelburne
VERMONT
NEW YORK
Hinesburg
Waterbury
Peacham
Camel's Hump
Barnet
Connecticut River
Montpelier
Plainfield
Lake Groton
105
78
242
101
5
118
36
100
7
109
104
108
14
5A
114
102
3
2
89
15
16
91
128
12
116
93
302

perimeter of the town square. And the small community of Greensboro, located on the shores of Caspian Lake, is vintage Vermont. Sitting in the center of the village is Willey's, one of Vermont's largest country stores, selling everything from apple cider to rubber barn boots. Other villages up here are plagued by an all-too-apparent rural poverty. For more information, contact the **Northeast Kingdom Chamber of Commerce,** 30 Western Ave., St. Johnsbury, VT 05819 (☎ **802/748-3678;** www.travelthekingdom.com).

Parks & Other Hot Spots

Lake Champlain

Accessible from the east off State Rte. 22A, U.S. 7, and U.S. 2; from New York, off State Rte. 22, U.S. 9, and I-87. For information, contact the **Vermont Department of Travel,** 134 State St., Montpelier, VT 05602 (☎ **800/VERMONT**). Boating, kayaking, water skiing.

Forming the western boundary of Vermont with New York, this 120-mile-long lake swells with boaters in the summer. Sailboats jibe along the shore, powerboats cruise through the center of the lake with water skiers in tow, and kayakers head north to the islands. Burlington, the largest city in Vermont with close to 125,000 people, sits on the eastern shores of the lake overlooking New York's Adirondack Mountains.

Lake Champlain Islands

Accessible via U.S. 2. For information, contact the **Champlain Islands Chamber of Commerce,** South Hero, VT 05486 (☎ **802/372-5683;** www.champlainislands.com). Biking.

With the Green Mountains to the east and the Adirondacks to the west, the islands of Lake Champlain have the perfect vantage point. The three islands, Grand Isle, North Hero, and Isle La Motte, are located at the northern end of the lake, just south of the Quebec border. State Route 129 and Isle La Motte are popular bike routes.

Mount Mansfield

Accessible via State Rte. 108 from Stowe or Jeffersonville in the summertime. State Rte. 108 is closed from Jeffersonville in the winter. For information, contact the **Stowe Area Association,** P.O. Box 1320, Stowe, VT 05672 (☎ **800/24-STOWE** or 802/253-7321; www.gostowe.com). Cross-country and downhill skiing, hiking.

Vermont's tallest mountain is the most popular hiking destination in the state and the premier cross-country skiing area in New England. Home to Stowe, it could arguably be the state's finest downhill ski area as well. Needless to say, it's the cornerstone for outdoor sports in Vermont and well worth the extra effort to get here.

Smuggler's Notch

Accessible via State Rte. 108 in summer only. Driving.

Who said New Hampshire has all the notches in New England? This is one of the most spectacular passes in the Northeast, one that I would definitely go out of my way to drive through. Large slabs of rock force State Route 108 to twist and turn as it narrowly coasts through the mountainous gap. Not surprisingly, the road is closed to cars in the winter (but open to snowshoers).

Jay Peak

Accessible via State Rte. 105. Skiing.

The 3,861-foot peak, known for its abundance of snow and long skiing season, is the northernmost skiing destination in the state.

Lake Willoughby

Accessible via State Rte. 5A. Canoeing, fishing, rowing, swimming.

One of the most striking sights in New England, the 5-mile-long Willoughby is sandwiched between the cliffs of Mount Pisgah and Mount Hor.

Northern Lakes
Accessible via I-91 or State Rte. 114. Boating, fishing.

Some of the best fishing and boating spots in the state are north of Lake Willoughby. They include Seymour Lake, the Averills, Norton Pond, and 32-mile-long Lake Memphremagog.

Burke Mountain
Accessible via State Rte. 114. Skiing.

Virtually unknown to most skiers outside the state, Burke has uncrowded yet challenging trails. The mountain towers over the small village of East Burke.

Lamoille, Winooski, and Missisquoi Rivers
Canoeing.

These three tributaries of Lake Champlain are the finest long-distance canoeing routes in Vermont. For more detailed information, see "Canoeing," below.

Connecticut River
Accessible via I-91. Fishing.

North of White River Junction, New England's longest river looks more like its old self—an unspoiled and undeveloped waterway fringed by farmland. This is especially true of the Connecticut Lakes region at the Quebec border and the section of the river just north of Fairlee. Blue-ribbon trout are found in the waterway between the Connecticut Lakes and Bloomfield.

What to Do & Where to Do It

BALLOONING

Stoweflake Resort (☎ 802/253-7355; www.stoweflake.com) is the site of the annual Hot Air Balloon Festival. Happening in early July, more than 30 balloons are launched over 2 days. There's also live music and a Kids Korner with arts and crafts.

BIRD WATCHING

The northern part of Vermont offers exceptional birding, with far more opportunities than you would find in southern and central Vermont. This is largely due to the presence of an immense number of wetland areas, from the huge bird sanctuary of Lake Champlain's open waters and freshwater marshes to the myriad fens, marshy ponds, and kettlehole bogs of the Northeast Kingdom.

I'm going to concentrate on wetlands birding here, although of course there's also plenty of hardwood and boreal-forest birding in the piedmont and mountains of northern Vermont, just as there is in the state's southern reaches. Expect to find **broad-winged hawks, grouse, barred owls, kingfishers, woodpeckers,** and many other birds; see "Bird Watching," in chapter 2 for more information on the kinds of uplands birding habitat and species you find in the New England woods.

Lake Champlain and the **Champlain Valley** are a crucial rest stop for migratory birds traveling the Atlantic Flyway. Out on the open water of the lake, you may see **buffleheads, ring-necked ducks, canvasbacks, ruddy ducks,** and **mergansers,** along with the occasional sea duck, such as a **scoter** or **eider.** The huge freshwater marshes on the Vermont side of the lake are even richer. Waterfowl and shorebirds like the **pied-billed grebes, Canada geese, black-crowned night herons,** and **green herons** top the long list of native birds.

In the spring and fall, thousands of migratory **snow geese** can be found at **Missisquoi National Wildlife Refuge (☎ 802/868-4781;** www.fws.gov/r5lcfwro/Miss.html), in Swanton near the Canadian border. Elsewhere in northern Vermont, the **South Bay Wildlife Management**

Area on the southern end of Lake Memphremagog is good for the same kind of birding.

The Northeast Kingdom has a number of large kettlehole bogs; amid the pitcher plants, sundews, orchids, and sphagnum moss of the bog environment are a lot of birds—songbirds, primarily, such as **olive-sided flycatchers; black-backed woodpeckers;** and **Nashville, black-throated blue,** and **blackburnian warblers.** Three such bogs are: **Victory Bog** in the 4,970-acre Victory Basin Wildlife Management Area, just east of St. Johnsbury; **Moose Bog** in the Wenlock Wildlife Management Area, 9.7 miles east of Island Pond off State Route 105; and **Yellow Bog.** This last bog is about 5 miles east of Island Pond on State Route 105. The second real road you'll see to the left of Route 105 after Island Pond is Lewis Pond Road, where you turn left; follow the road for a few miles, then veer right at the fork. You'll find yourself in this huge bog; you can backtrack out of it or follow a counterclockwise loop through the bog area that will eventually bring you back to State Route 105.

Watch yourself in a bog—there may be quicksand-like areas from which you'll have trouble extricating yourself if you're alone. Furthermore, it's easy to get lost. Bring a good map; the USGS 7.5-minute quadrangles for the above areas are: the Concord map for Victory Bog; the Bloomfield map for Moose Bog; and the Spectacle Pond map for Yellow Bog. On the plus side, these northern bogs are also moose country—you have a decent chance of seeing one of these huge, ungainly animals here. Just keep your distance.

Peregrine falcons are back and can be seen at 12 nesting sites, including the cliffs of **Mount Pisgah** and **Smuggler's Notch.** Also, many nesting loons can be found on the quiet waters of northern Vermont.

BOARDSAILING

After becoming a member at **The International Sailing School and Club,** 253 Lakeshore Drive, Colchester, north of Burlington (☎ **802/864-9065;** www.vermontsailingschool.com), you are entitled to unlimited use of the sailboards.

CANOEING

Most of the longer river journeys in the state are located in the north. The **Winooski, Lamoille,** and **Missisquoi Rivers** are all tributaries of Lake Champlain. For the Winooski, canoeists usually put in at Montpelier and head west to the lake. The Lamoille is popular from Johnson to the lake, and the Missisquoi is canoeable from Richford to the lake. Be prepared to see your share of blue herons, black terns, and cormorants. If you plan on canoeing the Winooski, the **Winooski Valley Park District,** Ethan Allen Homestead, Burlington, VT 05401 (☎ **802/863-5744**), publishes the ***Winooski River Canoe Guide,*** a 33-page book with maps that costs $4.

In addition to these three rivers, there's also the Upper Connecticut River, which runs with mild riffles and flat water through an endless succession of dairy farms. The 24.5-mile stretch between Canaan and Bloomfield, about as far as you can go for a little recreation in Vermont, is a scenic (but not wilderness), nicely paced paddle. About 2 miles before you reach Bloomfield are the remains of an old dam, which should be portaged by all but the experts, and scouted by anyone.

Green River Reservoir

Northeast of Morrisville. Access: From the junction of State Rte. 15 and State Rte. 15A, head east on State Rte. 15 for several hundred yards and turn left onto paved Garfield Rd.; 3.1 miles from State Rte. 15, turn right at the T-intersection in Garfield and then immediately left up a hill. 1.3 miles later, bear left on the gravel road and head downhill for 0.2 mile to a large parking lot. The road is in poor condition, so be careful. Map: USGS 7.5-min. Morrisville, Eden.

It was early morning when I reached the Green River Reservoir, and a hazy mist skimmed over the waters as if something were brewing under the surface. Within moments, the mist vanished and the sun took its rightful place atop the cloudless skies. The blue-green waters of Green River Reservoir shone as if they had just been washed with Windex.

I slid my canoe into the water and paddled to the right around a large island that sat in the center of the reservoir. It was early autumn and the red maples, yellow birches, and beeches were slowly starting to put on their coats of vibrant colors. Thankfully, the absence of farmland and all other forms of real estate have left these shores undeveloped and heavily forested. I paddled around a bend where two mating loons called to one another between dunks in the water. The Green River Reservoir is one of the few places in Vermont where nesting loons are found. Friends have spotted otters, beavers, moose, and bears in the northern reaches of the lake, where it turns into a narrow stream. However, I was content with the loons and the cedar waxwings. By the end of the morning I was convinced that the only way to truly enjoy the splendors of fall foliage was not from behind the glass windows of an automobile, but inside the wooden frame of a canoe.

Morrisville has seen fit to allow camping along the shores of this reservoir, and this place is thus one of the treasured secrets of Vermont's canoeists. Even when there are a lot of cars in the lot, you should still be able to find a peaceful site a long way away from anyone else and to spend the night with no company but the loons.

Lamoille River

The Lamoille River runs from Horse Pond north of Greensboro down to Hardwick, following State Route 15 to Lake Champlain. Below Johnson, it is mostly quick water and flat water, navigable at most water levels. Put-ins are at Johnson Bridge, Fairfax Falls, and Milton; portages at the ledge under State Route 15 bridge and Ithiel Falls (a few miles below Johnson), dam at Fairfax Falls, two dams in Milton, and Peterson Dam 1.75 miles beyond I-89. Above Johnson, you'll find a number of portages and Class II and III rapids, navigable at high and medium water.

It was while I was canoeing the Lamoille River, paddling through the sylvan splendor of this rural state, that it finally dawned on me how incredibly tranquil and private this sport really is. Biking inevitably shares the road with car traffic, and the best hiking trails are popular. Mountain biking and backcountry skiing give you the same sense of solitude but are far more strenuous. Canoeing is a sport in which the workout is small and the rewards are great. Paddling down a river where no motorboats are allowed ultimately leaves me in a state of solace.

This was certainly the case with the Lamoille. Smuggler's Notch Canoe Touring, run by the Mannsview Inn, helped transfer my car to the take-out and shuttled me to the put-in, just off Hogback Road between Jeffersonville and Johnson. They offer two trips on the Lamoille, either 6 or 9 miles. I chose the former because of time constraints, and off I went down the narrow curving river. For the next 2 hours, I did not see or hear another human being. Instead, I saw numerous cows grazing at the river's edge and large families of ducks. The cows tended to pick up their heads and stare at me in bewilderment, perhaps astonished at my presence. Tall fields of corn fringed the river, surrounded by the foothills of the Green Mountains. Everywhere was farmland; the smell of manure permeating the air served as a remembrance just in case I dropped my head to look at my stroke. Mount Mansfield, shrouded in clouds, came into view at the end of the trip. The trip went far too quickly. I tied my canoe to a tree and drove my car back to the Mannsview Inn, feeling relaxed, almost catatonic.

Peacham Pond

South of Marshfield. Access: From Rte. 2 East, turn onto Rte. 232 South for 3 miles. When Rte. 232 curves to the right, take the road to the left and you'll see a sign for Peacham Pond. Take the right fork and you'll reach the parking lot and boat launch.

West of St. Johnsbury, dabs of blue paint the Vermont map. Arguably, the finest of these small ponds to canoe is Peacham Pond, set on the northern edge of Groton State Forest. Motorboats are allowed on this 331-acre pond; but if you paddle up to the shallow northern section of Peacham, you'll escape the hum of engines and glide through the marsh. This is a favorite nesting spot for loons, so be prepared to hear the echo of their high-pitched call bounce off the trees. There's no camping on the pond, but nearby Groton State Forest, off Route 232, has plenty of options.

May Pond

East of Barton. Access: Take Rte. 16 north from Barton for 1.6 miles and turn right onto Pond Rd. After 1.4 miles, when the road forks, stay to the right. Another 0.7 mile and you'll turn left into the state fishing access. The pond is 0.25 mile down the road.

If you've made it this far northeast, you deserve to paddle in tranquility. Part of the Vermont Nature Conservancy, this pristine gem is a wonderful paddle in the early morning hours when you're bound to spot otter, beaver, loons, or ospreys. There are several cabins on the western shores, but, besides that, the 116-acre waterway has a remote and wild feel. Sedges and cattails line the marshy shores; farther back, maples, birch, balsam firs, spruce, and hemlocks form the forest. Afterward, sit down at the counter and treat yourself to a milkshake at Barton's Pierce Pharmacy. This malt shop hasn't changed much since the 1950s.

Outfitters

Smuggler's Notch Canoe Touring and Mannsview Inn are located on State Route 108 just south of Jeffersonville (☎ **800/937-6266;** mannsview.com/canoe.htm). Canoe rentals, including shuttle, are $50, and tours leave at 9:30am, 11:30am, and 1:30pm. Mannsview Inn also offers a 2-night, 2-day canoe package for $199 double occupancy.

Umiak Outdoor Outfitters, 849 S. Main St., Stowe, VT 05672 (☎ **802/253-2317;** www.umiak.com), offer rentals and guided trips on the Lamoille, Winooski, White, and Mad Rivers. They also provide private guides and instruction.

Clearwater Sports, State Route 100, Waitsfield, VT 05673 (☎ **802/496-2708;** www.clearwatersports.com), offers day and overnight trips on the Winooski, Mad, and White Rivers.

Raven Ridge, in Richford, Vermont (☎ **802/933-4616;** www.together.net/~ravenrdg/), offers guided and self-guided canoe trips on the Missisquoi River.

Dartmouth's **Ledyard Canoe Club** (☎ **603/643-6709;** www.dartmouth.edu/~doc/clubs/ledyardcanoeclub.html) in Hanover, New Hampshire, rents canoes on the Connecticut but no longer operates a shuttle service.

Waterfront Boat Rentals (☎ **802/864-4858**) in Burlington rents canoes and sea kayaks on Lake Champlain.

CROSS-COUNTRY SKIING

In the Backcountry

With more than 400 kilometers (250 miles) of interconnected ski trails, the area around Mount Mansfield is the premier cross-country skiing destination in the Northeast. Five of the top ski touring centers in New England, including the oldest in the nation, connect via some of the most challenging backcountry ski runs available. These backcountry trails are not simple loops around ponds but are grueling uphill and exhilarating downhill runs for skilled skiers only. They include the **Bruce** and **Teardrop Trails,** two of the earliest downhill trails in the country, cut by the Civilian Conservation Corps in the 1930s. Maintained cooperatively by the Mount Mansfield and Trapp Family Ski Touring Centers, the Bruce Trail drops 2,600 feet as it plummets down the slopes of Mount Mansfield. The trail starts from the Octagon, reached by Stowe's Forerunner Quad chairlift, and ends 6 kilometers (3.75 miles) later at the Mount Mansfield Touring Center ski shop. Also starting at the Octagon, but even steeper, is the Teardrop Trail. The 1.2-mile trail starts south of Mansfield's Nose and swoops down the backside of the mountain for 1,700 feet.

Much easier backcountry trails are the **Nebraska Notch** and the **Sky Top.** The Nebraska Notch Trail starts from the Underhill side of Mount Mansfield and gently climbs close to 600 feet to Nebraska Notch. The round-trip is 6 kilometers (3.75 miles), and you can add an extra 2 kilometers (1.25 miles) to reach Taylor Lodge, a spacious wooden shelter built by the Green Mountain Club. Known for its impressive views of Mansfield, the Sky Top Trail is one of Vermont's most popular backcountry routes. Reached from Topnotch, Trapp Family, or Mount Mansfield Ski Touring centers, the 4.5-kilometer (2.8-mile) trail ascends the Burt Trail to Dewey Saddle, before descending eastward along Sky Top Ridge toward Rob George Saddle.

If you want to ski one of the nicest parts of the 280-mile-long Catamount Trail (see below), try the **Bolton-Trapp Trail.** Created in 1972, the 20-kilometer (12.5-mile) route connects the Bolton Valley Ski Touring Center with Trapp Family Ski Lodge. Starting in Bolton, the path ascends through the hardwoods on the east slope of Bolton Mountain, plunging almost 2,000 feet to Nebraska Valley before heading on to Trapp's. A side trail from Nebraska Valley Road is the Lake Mansfield Trail, which skirts the lake as it climbs steadily to Taylor Lodge.

Besides these routes, two other CCC trails have been restored—the Steeple and the Dewey. The Steeple is a very fast and steep 1.1-mile run for experts. Dewey is a downhill run from the Underhill Trail to Ranch Camp Trail.

If you're serious about backcountry skiing in the Mount Mansfield area, consider purchasing two indispensable guides. One is the book ***Classic Backcountry Skiing***, by David Goodman (Appalachian Mountain Club, 1989). Goodman, who lives in nearby Waterbury, Vermont, details the most challenging yet thrilling backcountry and telemark skiing in the Northeast, including the treacherous trails listed above. The second important purchase is the "Adventure Skiing" map, published by Map Adventures. The map depicts all the backcountry trails and ski-touring centers around Mount Mansfield. The map can be purchased from the Mountain Wanderer Map & Book Store (☎ **800/745-2707;** www.mountainwanderer.com).

For additional information, get a copy of the "Winter Recreation" map from the **Green Mountain National Forest,** 231 N. Main St., Rutland, VT 05701 (☎ **802/747-6700**). There is also a cross-country ski report recorded every Thursday (☎ **802/828-3239**). Contact the Cata-mount Trail Association, P.O. Box 1235, Burlington, VT 05402 (☎**802/864-5794;**www.catamounttrail.together.com), for a map of the 200-mile **Catamount Trail,** the cross-country trail that runs the length of the state.

Champlain Valley Nordic Ski Centers

Located in a small family farm outside of Burlington, **Catamount Family Center,** 421 Governor Chittendon Rd., Williston, VT 05495 (☎ **802/879-6001;** www.catamountoutdoor.com), offers 40 kilometers (25 miles) of trails over gently rolling fields and woods. There are good views of Mount Mansfield and Camel's Hump to the east.

Mansfield/Stowe Area Nordic Ski Centers

Thanks to the **Trapp Family Lodge,** Stowe, VT 05672 (☎ **802/253-8511;** www.trappfamily.com), ski touring in northern Vermont is legendary. The lodge, made famous by Maria von Trapp, whose flight from the Nazis was immortalized in *The Sound of Music,* is one of the oldest ski-touring centers in the nation. It's also one of the finest. The ski touring center is one of the few places in the East that take backcountry skiing as seriously as track-set skiing; 60 kilometers (37.5 miles) of groomed trails, 95 kilometers (59.4 miles) total, weave through the 1,700 acres of forest and open fields. Elevations range from 1,100 to 3,000 feet.

Located on Mountain Road 6 miles from the center of Stowe, the **Mount Mansfield Cross Country Ski Center,** also known as the Stowe Mountain Resort Touring Center, Mountain Rd., Stowe, VT 05672 (☎ **802/253-7311;** www.stowe.com), is neatly tucked in between the slopes of Mount Mansfield and Sky Top Ridge. Its 50 kilometers (31.25 miles) of trails, 30 kilometers (18.75 miles) groomed (over 100 kilometers, 62.5 miles, more if you consider the backcountry connections to other ski touring centers), line the slopes of RanchValley. Intermediates love the 9-kilometer (5.6-mile) Timber Lane/Bear Run/Burt Trail loop, and beginners enjoy the Peavey Trail.

When Trapp and Mansfield are packed on winter weekends, **Edson Hill Nordic Center,** Edson Hill Rd., Stowe, VT 05672 (☎ **802/253-7371;** www.stowevt.com), gets remarkably little traffic. Skiers don't realize that the 25 kilometers (15.6 miles) here are just as much fun as at the other two centers. Intermediates enjoy the West Hill Trail; beginners are content with the 1-mile Center Loop.

Just down the road from Mount Mansfield, the 25 kilometers (15.6 miles) of trails at **Topnotch Touring Center,** Mountain Rd., Stowe, VT 05672 (☎ **802/253-8585;** www.topnotch-resort.com), cater to intermediates and beginners. Try the 3.5-kilometer (2.2-mile) Deer Run Loop or the Lower Meadow Loop. Topnotch is also linked with the other ski touring centers.

Northeast Kingdom Nordic Ski Centers

It was late March 1995 and, surprisingly, there was no snow anywhere in Vermont. I had just left the Trapp Family Lodge in Stowe because the trails were open only to walkers that day. Desperate to ski, I called one last place, the **Craftsbury Outdoor Center,** Craftsbury Common (☎ **802/586-7767;** www.craftsbury.com). "Yeah, come on up," the voice on the other end said, "we just had a race this morning." Needless to say, the season at Craftsbury lasts far longer than it does in the rest of Vermont. The 130 kilometers (81.25 miles) of trails, 80 kilometers (50 miles) groomed, are impressive. They rise and dip over meadows and through a forest of maples and firs, ideal for all levels. The ski center is located on a hill overlooking the picturesque Northeast Kingdom.

Just down the road, **Highland Lodge,** Caspian Lake, Greensboro (☎ **802/533-2647;** www.thehighlandlodge.com), has 65 kilometers (40.6 miles) of trails that connect to Craftsbury. Many of the trails weave through this Currier and Ives setting—a mix of old maple-tree-lined lanes, barns, serene forests, and open farm fields—down to the shores of Caspian Lake. The lodge itself is one of the most comfortable places to stay in the Northeast Kingdom (see "Campgrounds & Other Accommodations," later in this chapter).

The well-groomed trails at **Burke Mountain Cross-Country,** East Burke, 1.5 miles from the Alpine ski area (☎ **802/626-8338**) start at 1,300 feet and snake through a rolling tapestry of maple, dark pine, and spruce forests. Not only is there less traffic than the better-known touring centers in the state, but Burke offers stunning views on many of its 80 kilometers (50 miles) of trails. On the Northview Trail, you have a vista of Mount Hor and Mount Pisgah (see "Hiking," below) with majestic Lake Willoughby sandwiched in the middle. North Pasture goes along an 1850s sheep driving road, and the MacDonald Trail climbs up to 2,400 feet.

You're bound to find snow at **Hazen's Notch Ski Touring Center,** State Route 58, Montgomery Center (☎ **802/326-4708;** www.scenesofvermont.com/hazens). Connected with the Catamount Trail, 45 kilometers (28.1 miles) of narrow trails sweep through this old sugarbush wood to clearings that offer good views of Jay Peak.

Outfitters, Rentals & Information

Umiak Outdoor Outfitters, 849 S. Main St., Stowe, VT 05672 (☎ **802/253-2317;** www.umiak.com), offers guided cross-country ski tours and rentals.

In the Northeast Kingdom, Bruce Aschenbach owns **Kingdom Tele Boys** (☎ **802/472-6128**). He takes backcountry and telemark skiers on 3- to 6-hour tours to Woodbury Mountain, Stannard, Mount Mansfield, and Mount Hunger. He also offers full-moon skiing.

The Catamount Trail

If you have not yet heard of the 280-mile cross-country ski trail known as the Catamount, you soon will. Ben Rose and Steve Bushey's dream to build a state-long trail is almost on the verge of completion. Rose and Bushey conceived of the idea during the summer of 1981 on a bike ride from British Columbia to Vermont. Joined by a third skier, Paul Jarris, the threesome started mapping the Catamount in March 1984. They stayed as close to the central corridor of the state as possible, running along the ridge of the Green Mountains. At the completion of their expedition, they were determined to make their dream a reality. They founded the Catamount Trail Association (CTA) and solicited memberships. Today, the CTA has over 1,000 members and, more importantly, the trail is almost 92% completed.

Starting in Readsboro, just north of the Massachusetts border, you ski down from town along an old railroad bed to the border and then retrace your tracks north to the town of Wilmington. The trail follows a brook, skirts the Harriman Reservoir, and then enters the trail system of the White House Ski Touring Center. From here you follow the black pawprint signs, the symbol of the Catamount, on remote wilderness trails, groomed ski center tracks, and old logging roads. You pass by Stratton Pond and Stratton Mountain, go through Killington to Waitsfield to Camel's Hump, Mount Mansfield, Craftsbury, and Jay, all the way to North Troy on the Canadian border. Along the way, you ski through the top ski touring centers in the state, like Mountain Top, Mountain Meadows, the Village Inn, Blueberry Hill, Camel's Hump, Bolton Valley, Trapp Family, Craftsbury, and Hazen's Notch. You also ski on some of the finest backcountry trails in New England, like the Bolton-Trapp Trail in Mount Mansfield and the route from Waitsfield to Camel's Hump. And with average elevations above 1,500 feet, you are almost guaranteed to have white fluffy stuff on the ground from late December to late March.

Over 280 miles of the trail are now in use. The Catamount Trail Association publishes a guidebook with up-to-date maps and route descriptions. For more information, contact the **Catamount Trail Association,** P.O. Box 1235, Burlington, VT 05402 (☎ **802/864-5794;** www.catamounttrail.together.com).

DOWNHILL SKIING

Stowe

5781 Mountain Rd., Stowe, VT 05672. ☎ **802/253-3000;** www.stowe.com. Snow report: ☎ 802/253-2222. 47 trails

(16% beginner, 59% intermediate, 25% expert), 11 lifts including an 8-passenger gondola, 1 quad, 1 triple, and 6 doubles; 2,360-ft. vertical drop. Full-day tickets $54 all week.

Every year I see them. Cocky adolescents who run roughshod over my skis as they cruise down the black diamonds of Stratton, Mount Snow, or Okemo. Down at the bottom, I smile, stoke their ego, and tell them that they're pretty good. "Have you skied Stowe yet . . . the Front Four. Oh no. Well, I think you guys would love that." Then I walk away and giggle maliciously at the thought of these young hotdoggers hurling themselves down the face of 4,393-foot Mount Mansfield. The Front Four teaches the brazen the meaning of respect. There's Starr, with a 37° pitch, the Lift Line, Goat, and National. The latter two separate the men from the boys and the women from the girls. Goat is a narrow serpentine trail that weaves down Mansfield. National is a little bit wider than Goat, but it's still one of those trails where you stand at the edge and look way down. Don't worry. Many people before you have stood there, whimpering statements like, "I don't know. I think I'm gonna try to take another trail." Smart idea.

One of the oldest ski resorts in New England, Stowe deserves its reputation as one of the best. And don't worry if not all of your group are experienced skiers. The variety of terrain at Stowe is unparalleled in the East. Beginners can chute through the scenic 3.7-mile Toll Road or venture to Spruce Peak; middle-of-the-roadies can glide down Tyro or Lullaby Lane; while the hard-core tackle the Front Four or more-coveted spots like the Chin or the Birthday Bowls off Big Spruce.

The last time I visited Stowe, the skies opened up and dumped close to a foot of snow on the ground. Needless to say, it was probably the most popular day of the season. My brother and I decided to sidestep the crowds and ski the adjoining part of Stowe known as Spruce Peak. At the farthest reaches of the mountain, we found a trail named Sterling that was simply sterling. This corkscrew run was steep enough to challenge but slow enough to enjoy the serene landscape. The branches on the balsams and birches were laden with snow, creating a white winter wonderland. Sterling was so enchanting that we spent most of the day cruising down it with few other skiers.

Smuggler's Notch

State Rte. 108, Smuggler's Notch, VT 05464. ☎ **802/644-1156;** www.smuggs.com. Snow report: ☎ 802/644-8851. 67 trails (22% beginner, 53% intermediate, 25% expert), 5 double chairlifts; 2,610-ft. vertical drop. Full-day tickets $39 weekends, $36 weekdays.

"A family that skies together stays together" should be the motto for Smuggler's Notch Resort, situated just outside of Stowe. Their fully equipped condos cater exclusively to families, and their lineup of activities for children is longer than a kid's wish list for Santa. Kids have three trails of their own Green Mountains to ski on, including a magic learning trail where young children ski up to exhibit panels and learn about winter animals. Families can also enjoy horse-drawn sleigh rides; indoor pools; outdoor skating rinks; a lighted tube-sliding hill; 23 kilometers (14.38 miles) of cross-country trails; and nightly family entertainment. Junior won't get bored here, nor will his parents.

The three-mountain ski area caters to all levels. Morse is gentle, Sterling's trails are good for intermediates, and Madonna Mountain is for experts only. (Madonna's always had a complex personality.) The view of Mount Mansfield atop Madonna is staggering.

Experts take note: A good deep dump of snow brings Smuggler's right to the top of the heap, especially midweek when there are no lift lines. Narrow Robin's

Run, Upper Lift Line, and F.I.S. soften up their bad attitude just enough with a fresh coat of powder to make them as good as any steeps in Vermont.

Bolton Valley

Bolton Access Rd., Bolton Valley, VT 05477. ☎ **802/434-3444;** www.boltonvalleyvt.com. Snow report: ☎ 802/434-7669. 51 trails (27% beginner, 47% intermediate, 26% expert); 6 lifts including 1 quad, 4 double chairlifts; 1,625-ft. vertical drop. Night skiing top to bottom on 12 trails. Full-day tickets $39 weekends, $32 weekdays.

Bolton Valley is also family oriented. It was completely refurbished in 1999, adding more than $2 million in renovations and a new 325-foot-long half pipe. Most of the trails are on moderate terrain, some with views of Lake Champlain. Because the base is so high (2,150 feet), snow doesn't seem to be a problem here. The mountain averages between 250 and 270 inches of snow a year. If you're with someone who's a cross-country fanatic, Bolton's also got an excellent network of Nordic and backcountry trails.

Jay Peak

State Rte. 242, Jay, VT 05859. ☎ **802/988-2611;** www.jaypeakresort.com. Snow report: ☎ 800/451-4449. 66 trails (20% beginner, 55% intermediate, 25% expert); 7 lifts including a 60-passenger tram, 1 quad, 1 triple, and 2 doubles; 2,153-ft. vertical drop. Full-day tickets $49 all week.

When it's balmy in Boston in winter, you can still expect a blizzard at Vermont's northernmost ski resort, Jay Peak. If only it weren't so far away from most of us. Whenever Killington, Sugarbush, or Stowe gets 3 inches of snow, Jay Peak

Northern Vermont Ski & Winter Sports Shops

City	Shop	Location	Telephone	Additional Services
Burlington	Alpine Shop	1184 Williston Rd., S. Burlington	802/862-2714	repairs; alpine ski, cross-country ski, snowboard, snow shoe rentals
	The Downhill Edge	65 Main St.	802/862-2282	repairs
Stowe	Action Outfitters	2160 Mountain Rd.	802/253-7975	repairs; alpine ski, cross-country ski, telemark, snow shoe, bike, canoe rentals; alpine-ski and boot demos
	AJ's	300 Mountain Rd.	802/253-4593	repairs; alpine ski, cross-country ski, snowboard, snow shoe, ice skate, ski rack, and bibs/parkas rentals; alpine-ski and boot demos
	Boots & Boards	430 Mountain Rd.	802/253-4225	repairs; alpine ski, cross-country ski, snowboard rentals
	Pinnacle Ski & Sports	Upper Mountain Rd.	800/458-9996	repairs; alpine ski, snowboard rentals; alpine-ski and boot demos

gets 8. In fact, Jay supposedly gets more snow than any other mountain in New England. Close to the Quebec border, the ski area also has a distinctly French flavor. If you come in March and April, you'll enjoy great snow with few crowds. Black diamond lovers will enjoy the steeper tree runs off the tram, whereas neophytes will find the trails in Bonaventure Basin to their liking. Add the natural "off-piste" terrain and you have some of the most-challenging backcountry snowboarding and skiing runs in America. In the 1990s, the ski area shrewdly started clearing the glades. Some of the best lines are on the east face of Big Jay, through spruce and birch studded with cliffs.

Burke

P.O. Box 247, East Burke, VT 05832. ☎ **802/626-3305;** www.burkemountain.com. Snow report: ☎ 800/SKI-BURKE. 33 trails (25% beginner, 50% intermediate, 25% expert); 4 lifts including 1 quad and 1 double; 2,000-ft. vertical drop. Full-day tickets $42 weekends, $25 weekdays (a steal).

Considering that some of Burke Mountain's trails were cut in the 1930s, it's surprising that this Northeast Kingdom ski area is still relatively unknown. Unknown, that is, outside of Vermont. Locals love the challenging trails and the lack of lift lines.

FISHING

An abundance of **trout** and **landlocked salmon** are found in the deep cold-water lakes and long streams in the Northeast Kingdom. Most notable are **Willoughby, Caspian, Seymour, Memphremagog** (good for lake trout), and **Big Averill lakes.** Stream fishing for **trout** is prevalent on both branches of the **Passumpsic River** and on the **Black, Barton, Willoughby,** and **Clyde Rivers.** Runs of spawning **rainbow trout** occur around opening day in April on the Willoughby. The Black features runs of spawning **browns** during the fall. Indeed, the fish feed ferociously this time of year. Use wet flies on the rivers and you'll catch your fair share of browns, rainbows, and brookies. Newark and Island Ponds are spawning grounds for brookies in October, so you'll have good luck throwing your line in these waters as well. **Brown** and **rainbow trout** are caught in the upper Connecticut River.

Heading west, you get to fish the state's longest rivers—**Winooski, Lamoille,** and **Missisquoi.** Winooski is known for its trout and occasional salmon, but it also offers a variety of warm-water species like smallmouth and largemouth bass, northern pike, walleye, and chain pickerel. The heaviest fishing is between Montpelier and Burlington. Salmon Hole is a great place for casting from shore or a canoe. Near Waterbury, not far from the cool waters of the Waterbury Reservoir, is one of the best brown trout sections of the river. Closer to Champlain, you'll find salmon.

North of Winooski, the Lamoille travels over 60 miles from the heart of the Green Mountains to Lake Champlain. The stretch near Hardwick Lake is a good bet for trout like brownies. Missisquoi is the northernmost of the three rivers. Try between Richford and Enosborg Falls for brown trout, or East Berkshire, where the Missisquoi meets the aptly named Trout River flowing from the southeast.

Lake Champlain has a wealth of fish, including lake trout, landlocked salmon, steelhead, smelt, sauger, walleye, large- and smallmouth bass, northern pike, pickerel, yellow perch, and channel catfish.

If you're looking for more information, contact the **Vermont Fish and Wildlife Department,** 103 S. Main St., Waterbury, VT 05671-0501 (☎ **802/241-3700;** www.anr.state.vt.us/fw/fwhome), and ask for a "Vermont Fishing Kit." The kit includes the new "Fish Vermont Map & Guide" as well as fishing rules and a license application. Nonresident fishing licenses good for the entire year cost $38 for adults, $15 for anglers 15 to 17 years old. Anyone under 15 does not need a license. Temporary licenses are $11 for 1 day, $18 for 3 days, and $25 for 7 days.

DeLorme Mapping Company, P.O. Box 298, 2 DeLorme Drive, Yarmouth, ME 04096 (☎ **800/452-5931** or 207/846-7000; www.delorme.com), publishes the *Vermont Atlas & Gazetteer,* which has a profusion of detail on fishing, in both text and maps. Also, the guides and bait-and-tackle stores listed below will provide the most up-to-date handle on stream and river conditions and what the fish are hitting.

Instruction, Guides & Bait-and-Tackle Shops

The Lake Champlain International Fishing Derby (☎ **802/862-7777;** www.lciderby.com) is the largest and oldest freshwater derby in the nation. Held in mid-June in Burlington, it awards cash and prizes.

Fly Fish Vermont, 954 S. Main St., Stowe (☎ **802/253-3964;** www.flyfishvt.com), offers half-day and full-day outfitted tours on some of northern Vermont's local tributaries—the Dog River, Winooski, and the Lamoille. Learn to perfect the roll cast, false cast, and the double haul and try your luck hooking the brookie. Experienced anglers can head to the upper Connecticut to test their abilities in the riffles, runs, and deep pool flats with undercut banks hiding big brown and rainbow trout.

On Lake Champlain, **Sure Strike Charters** offers half- and full-day tours from Perkins Pier, 218 River Rd., Essex Junction (☎ **802/878-5074;** www.fishvermont.com). **Nomad Fishing Charters** (☎ **802/878-2080;** pages.prodigy.net/artjud/) is located at Rivers End Marina at the mouth of the Winooski River in Burlington. The 25-foot Baja Cruiser brings guests out on Champlain in search of lake trout and Atlantic salmon. A good retail shop is **Schirmer's Fly Shop,** 34 Mills Ave., South Burlington (☎ **802/863-6105**).

Charlie North is the fishing guru in the islands. He can be found at **Charlie's Northland Lodge** in North Hero (☎ **802/372-8822**). Charlie rents boats and operates a retail store.

In the Northeast Kingdom, the Village Sport Shop in Lyndonville (☎ **802/626-8448**) will answer all your nagging fishing questions and is a good place to stock up on bait and tackle.

Quimby County, Averill, VT 05901 (☎ **802/822-5533** or 717/733-2234), offers a 19th-century lodge and 20 cabins spread out on the shores of 70-acre Forest Lake. If the fish aren't biting at Forest, the lodge is close to Little and Big Averill Lakes.

GOLF

Until the summer of 1998, golfing in northern Vermont was not nearly as good as in the southern half of the state, **Stowe**'s (☎ **802/253-4893**) hilly, par-72 course and the **Country Club of Barre** (☎ **802/476-7658**) being the notable exceptions. Then along came the **Country Club of Vermont** (☎ **802/244-1800;** www.countryclubvt.com) off Route 100 in Waterbury. Designed by Graham Cooke, the layout utilizes the finer points of Vermont's landscape—some holes set upon gentle farmland, others nestled within the hardwood forest, while the stunning vista of nearby Camel's Hump follows you around the whole course. Standout holes include the par-four seventh, with its triple-tier green, and the short par-four tenth featuring a chasm to the left and a pond to the right. Afterward, treat yourself to an ice cream cone at the Ben & Jerry's world headquarters across the street.

Another newcomer to the ranks is the Jack Nicklaus–designed **Vermont National Country Club** (☎ **802/864-7770;** www.vnccgolf.com) in South Burlington. The front nine of the par-72 course is gentle and rolling, with the holes winding through the meadows. The back nine is far more rugged, with dramatic rock outcroppings. The view of

Camel's Hump from the 10th hole gets the perfect-picture award of the day, though the view of the Adirondacks on the 18th is not too shabby either.

HIKING & BACKPACKING

North of I-89, the 265-mile **Long Trail** heads straight over 4,393-foot Mount Mansfield, through breathtaking Smuggler's Notch to the top of Jay Peak, and finally reaches the Canadian border. Unlike the ridge walks of, say, the Lincoln Gap area, this part of the Long Trail is rarely flat. It's up and down all the way, but your rewards are vast—stunning vistas atop barren summits overlook miles of undeveloped landscape. This is especially true of the last 29 miles from State Route 118 to the summit of Belvidere Mountain, through Hazen's Notch to the top of Jay Peak, and ending at the Canadian border. If you don't have time to do the whole trail, these last 29 miles are a good 3- to 4-day run.

For more information regarding time, access, shelters, useful guides, and the history of the nation's oldest long-distance trail, see "The Long Trail," in chapter 2. The **Green Mountain Club,** which maintains the Long Trail, can be reached at 4711 Waterbury-Stowe Rd., Waterbury Center, Waterbury, VT 05677 (**☎ 802/244-7037;** www.greenmountainclub.org).

Northern Vermont's best hiking is centered around Mount Mansfield and the Long Trail. As in the southern part of the state, the trails tend to be steady uphill climbs. In the eastern part of the state, I found one incredible trail:

Mount Pisgah

3.4 miles (round-trip). Allow 3 hr. Moderate to strenuous; a short steep ascent with extraordinary views of Lake Willoughby. Access: From West Burke, take State Rte. 5A North for 6 miles to a parking area on the left side, just south of Lake Willoughby. The South Trail begins across the highway. Map: USGS 7.5-min. Sutton.

Nothing prepared me for the striking beauty of Lake Willoughby, not even the earnest recommendation from my sister-in-law, a University of Vermont graduate. As I approached the lake from the north, the dark blue waters came into view, dwarfed by faces of rock that stand directly across from each other—Mount Hor and Mount Pisgah. Cliffs plummet over 1,000 feet to the glacial waters below, creating, in essence, a landlocked fjord. The scenery became even more enchanting as I made my way up to the 2,751-foot summit of Mount Pisgah.

Several bridges crossed ponds inundated with twisted white pines, the result of forceful gales or hard-working beavers. The trail started gradually on switchbacks but soon took a much more precipitous course. More than halfway up the peak, the trail leveled off as I walked along a ridge. Before the path curved to the right and began its rigorous uphill climb once again, a small detour to the left brought me to aptly named Pulpit Rock. This small, semi-oval rock juts out of Mount Pisgah's sheer cliff like a box seat at a Broadway play. Looking down at Lake Willoughby in its entirety and across at Mount Hor, a mountain that's been sliced in half, I felt as if I were trespassing on sacred ground. This small platform should be reserved for the likes of Virgil, Lincoln, Churchill, and other noted orators who could engage the masses below.

The strenuous trail continues upward, proceeding in a spiral fashion as it climbs to the summit. Just prior to reaching the peak, I had excellent views to the east—the ski slopes of Burke Mountain, the Connecticut River, and the White Mountains forming a ridge line in the horizon. Since the peak was not above the tree line, I had to continue down a side trail to a level rock that provided vistas to the west. Now I could see beyond Mount Hor to Mount Hunger, Mansfield, Camel's Hump, and all the other mountains that stood in between.

Mount Mansfield, via Laura Cowles and Sunset Ridge Trails

6.5 miles (round-trip). Allow 4–5 hr. Moderate to strenuous.. Access: From Jeffersonville, take Upper Valley Rd. toward Underhill Center for approximately 7 miles, until you see a sign for Underhill State Park. Turn left for 3 miles on the dirt road and park in the lot. Map: available from the Park Ranger Station. The GMC's Long Trail guide also includes a map of all the Mansfield side trails.

There are numerous approaches up Mount Mansfield. The Long Trail meanders southwest from State Route 108 to Taft Lodge and the summit. A toll road leaves you at the Nose of the mountain (4,062 feet) where you can then take a 1.4-mile walk on the Long Trail heading east to the Chin or summit (4,393 feet). A gondola ride leaves you even closer to the summit on the same stretch of the Long Trail. You can also take the Haselton–Nose Dive Trail from Smuggler's Notch State Park Campground to the Nose and continue onward to the Chin. However, my favorite hike up the mountain is from the south, up the Laura Cowles Trail and down the Sunset Ridge Trail.

The hike starts at the Underhill State Park Ranger Station, where you pay a small fee and continue walking uphill on the gravel road for about a mile to the trailhead; 0.1 mile later, the Sunset Ridge and the Laura Cowles Trails split. Veer to the right on the Laura Cowles Trail for a steep 1.7-mile ascent. (For a more-moderate hike, continue on the Sunset Ridge Trail.) The trail climbs on rocks along trickling water in the beginning, before sharply rising halfway up. Several times you have to walk in the shallow water as you grab tree roots and rocky grips to pull yourself upward. Close to the summit, views of Lake Champlain open up to the west. When you reach the Long Trail, veer left to reach the Chin. The path on the right called Profanity leads to Taft Lodge. Be prepared for strong winds as you make your final ascent. From atop the summit, Lake Champlain can be seen in its entirety, as well as the northern islands, Burlington, and the Adirondacks on the far shores. Look to the north to see Jay Peak and Canada, to the east to see the White Mountains. Everywhere you turn your head, you see more hills and mountains. I hate to inform you bikers, but Vermont ain't flat.

To reach the Sunset Ridge Trail and the descent, backtrack past the Laura Cowles Trail and continue right along the ridge. Sweeping views of Lake Champlain and points west are seen as you walk along the open ridge for the next mile. A little more than halfway down, where hardwood forests have replaced bare rocks, veer right for a 0.1-mile detour to Cantilever Rock. This axe-like rock juts precariously out of the ridge like a guillotine ready to sever the head of anyone who dares to look up. The trail becomes more gradual as you continue to the trailhead and the dirt road back to the State Park.

Mount Hunger, via Waterbury Trail

3.8 miles. Allow 4 hr. Moderate; an off-the-beaten-track climb that's one of my top 5 trails in Vermont. Access: From Waterbury, follow State Rte. 100 North to Waterbury Center. Turn right on Barnes Hill Rd., left onto Maple St., and right onto Loomis Hill Rd. Bear left atop the hill as the road turns to dirt. Park 3.7 miles from the junction of Maple St. on the right side of the road. Map: USGS 7.5-min. Stowe.

Judging from the three cars parked at the trailhead, all with Vermont license plates, the climb up Mount Hunger is a trail treasured by locals only. After my brother, Jim, and I made it to the 3,538-foot peak, we easily understood why. From the barren summit, we could see every mountain that forms the backbone of the Greens, from Killington to Camel's Hump to Mount Mansfield. First we had to hike up the Waterbury Trail. Like most of Vermont's trails, the climb started at the first step, a steady uphill walk that became steep at some stretches. Since this was Jim's first ascent up a mountain in over a decade, we took numerous stops along the way so he could catch his breath, the first clean air my citified brother had inhaled in a long time. Eventually the beeches, yellow birches, and maples gave way to white birches, spruces, and balsam firs. Then, 0.2 mile from the top, the trail meandered over large boulders bordered by scrub brush. The bare rocks atop the summit offer commanding views of the entire state. Burke and Bald mountains are seen guarding the entranceway to the Northeast Kingdom; Mount Mansfield's chin, nose, and other facial features are visible to the east, with the Camel's Hump Trails close behind. Waterbury Reservoir sits in the valley below, fringed by White Rock, Hunger's next door neighbor. Unlike Camel's Hump, Mount Mansfield, and the other popular peaks of the Green Mountains, here atop Hunger you can relish the view in relative solitude before making the descent back down.

Sterling Pond

2.6 miles (round-trip). Allow 2 hr. Moderate; a fun hike for families. Access: Park at Smuggler's Notch, situated on State Rte. 108, 10 miles north of Stowe and 8 miles south of Jeffersonville. Map: USGS 7.5-min. Mount Mansfield, or Long Trail guidebook.

The 1.3-mile hike on the Long Trail to the Sterling Pond Shelter starts from Smuggler's Notch, one of the most majestic sights in all of New England. From the mountainous cliffs above, sheer walls of quartzite and mica drop down to the large boulders resting on the floor below. The result is a mountainous pass, or notch, formed by a glacial retreat over 10,000 years ago. The notch's name comes from the Vermont smugglers who ventured north to illegally trade with Canada after Thomas Jefferson declared an embargo in 1807. The route was also used by fugitive slaves to find freedom in Canada, and by Vermonters in the 1920s to sneak liquor into America during Prohibition.

Cross State Route 108 and continue on the rock steps up the side of the ridge. The views of the notch and surrounding Green Mountains get better with every steep step. At the top of the slope sits Sterling Pond, which was engulfed in a cloud during my last ascent. The water could barely be seen under a layer of white mist, providing an ominous setting ideal for a Stephen King novel. Veer left around the pond to reach one of the Smuggler's Notch ski trails, offering impressive views to the north and west. Follow the white blazes to reach the Sterling Pond Shelter, a small lean-to at the edge of the pond maintained by the Green Mountain Club for backpackers. From here, you can continue on the Long Trail for another mile to reach Madonna Peak, skirt the pond to find the Elephant's Head Trail, or backtrack to your car. The Elephant's Head Trail leads to a massive ledge approximately 1,000 feet above the notch.

Prospect Rock (Johnson)

Allow 1–1.5 hr. Easy to moderate. Access: From Johnson, drive west on State Rte. 15 for 1.5 miles and turn right before the bridge onto Hogback Rd. You can park on the right across from Ithiel Camp 2.3 miles later, or on the left in a small parking lot at 2.2 miles. The hike starts from the driveway on the right. Map: USGS 7.5-min. Johnson or Long Trail guidebook.

Prospect Rock is an ideal picnic spot, so don't forget to bring lunch. The climb is one of the easiest hikes on the Long Trail. Believe it or not, this part of the trail actually has switchbacks instead of the typical Vermont hike—straight up a mountain. Start on the driveway and then veer left following the white blazes up the soft, spongy trail. The hike becomes more strenuous as you approach the switchbacks. In less than 45 minutes, you'll be on top of Prospect Rock staring across at Vermont's Whiteface Mountain and down at the Lamoille River as it snakes through the sylvan landscape. To extend the hike, continue north on the Long Trail for as long as your legs desire.

Devil's Gulch

5 miles (round-trip). Allow 3 hr. Moderate; complete with glacial cirque and glacial erratics. Access: From Eden, take State Rte. 118 4.9 miles. Park on the right side of the road in the small parking area. Map: USGS 15-min. Hyde Park.

Climbing just over 1,000 feet, this section of the Long Trail brings you to the boulder field known as Devil's Gulch and the deep-in-the-forest Ritterbush Pond. Follow the Long Trail south in a pasture before ascending through the hardwood forest on an old logging road. At 1.5 miles into the trail, you'll get an overlook of Ritterbush Pond, a glacial cirque. The pond is part of the Babcock Nature Reserve, a prime birding locale in northern Vermont as well as an occasional overnight for moose. The trail then heads downhill past Ritterbush Camp, veering left to arrive at Devil's Gulch. Ferns cover many of the boulders to give it a lush, almost tropical feel. Return on the same trail.

Belvidere Mountain

5.6 miles (round-trip). Allow 4–5 hr. Moderate to strenuous; you'll be rewarded by exceptional views atop the fire tower. Access: From Eden, take Rte. 118 4.9 miles. Park on the right side of the road in the small parking area. (Note: For a long day in the woods, you can combine Belvidere with the above Devil's Gulch hike. Simply cross State Rte. 118.) Map: USGS 15-min. Hyde Park.

Heading north on the white-blazed Long Trail, climb gradually on an old road that is parallel to a brook. The trail begins to climb steeply along a ridge before leveling off on a series of switchbacks. At the 2.6-mile mark, the Long Trail veers left. You'll take the right-hand trail to the 3,360-foot summit. The 70-foot public lookout tower atop Belvidere rewards you with some of the finest views in the state. The panorama includes Jay Peak to the north; New Hampshire's White Mountains to the east; Camel's Hump, Mount Hunger, and Mount Mansfield to the south; and New York's Adirondack Mountains to the east. It will be hard to tear yourself away from this vista, but once you manage, head back down on the same trail.

Jay Peak

3.4 miles (round-trip). Allow 2.5–3 hr. Moderate; good climb to top off your stay in Vermont. Access: From Montgomery Center, drive 6.8 miles on State Rte. 242 North and park in the lot on the right. The trailhead is across the street. If you want to take the gondola down the mountain, park a second car at Jay Peak, 1.4 miles north on Rte. 242. Map: USGS 15-min. Jay Peak or Long Trail guidebook.

One of the most picturesque stretches of the Long Trail is from State Route 242 up to the summit of Jay Peak. Starting at an elevation of over 2,000 feet, the trail climbs steadily through a forest of birches and spruces until you reach one of Jay Peak's ski trails. Continue straight, following the white blazes over the rocky bare ledges to the 3,861-foot peak. The summit is legendary for its blustery winds, where twisted branches creak with each successive gale. The mountain is also known for its snowfall: It has the most accumulation of any ski area in the Northeast. If you can somehow stand in the unmerciful winds, you can spot Mount Washington to the east, Lake Memphremagog to the northeast, Montreal to the northwest, Mount Mansfield to the south, and all the small farms and rural communities that exist in between. Less-ambitious hikers can park one car at State Route 242 and one car at the bottom of Jay Peak and simply take the tram down. You also have the option of walking down one of the ski trails.

Outfitters & Gear

New England Hiking Holidays, P.O. Box 1648, North Conway, NH 03860 (☎ **800/869-0949;** www.nehikingholidays.com), has a 5-day tour to the Northeast Kingdom that includes stops at Trapp Family Lodge in Stowe and Highland Lodge in the heart of the region.

Backroads, 1516 Fifth St., Berkeley, CA 94710-1740 (☎ **800/GO-ACTIVE;** www.backroads.com), has an excellent 6-day tour through northern Vermont that also includes Trapp, Highland Lodge, and a night at the Inn on the Common in Craftsbury Common.

Wild Earth Adventures, P.O. Box 655, Pomona, NY 10970 (☎ **914/354-3717**), offers an 8-day guided backpacking trip through Mount Mansfield and the other Green Mountains.

Umiak Outdoor Outfitters, 849 S. Main St., Stowe, VT (☎ **802/253-2317;** www.umiak.com), offers guided tours for groups and maps for self-guided hikes.

Country Inns Along the Trail, 834 Van Cortland Rd., Brandon, VT 05773 (☎ **802/247-3300;** www.inntoinn.com), custom designs self-guided hiking trips in which you can walk inn-to-inn.

HORSEBACK RIDING

Numerous stables scattered across the northern part of the state offer trail riding and lessons. They include **Topnotch Stables** in Stowe (☎ **802/253-8585;** www.topnotch-resort.com) and **Mountain Ridge Ranch,** just south of Island Pond on State Route 114 (☎ **802/723-6153**).

In addition to guided trail rides, **Cambridge Stables** (☎ **802/644-5568**) and **Vermont Horse Park** (☎ **802/644-5347**), just north of Smuggler's Notch, feature overnight trips.

Greenhope Farm (**802/533-7772;** www.greenhopefarm.com) in the Northeast Kingdom has been offering horseback riding since 1982. You can take hourly rides on their 10 horses or go on a women-only retreat for a week.

ICE CLIMBING

Some consider **Mount Pisgah's** cliffs to be the best ice face in the world—a 500-foot cliff, smeared with fat ice floes and pillars on an exposed mountainside. Consult ***An Ice Climber's Guide to Northern New England,*** by Rick Wilcox, International Mountain Equipment Inc., for more information. **Smuggler's Notch,** with Elephant's Head and Blue Room, is also a popular ice climbing destination.

Contact the good people at **Climb High,** 2438 Shelburne Rd., Shelburne, VT (☎ **802/985-5056** or 802/985-9141; www.climbhigh.com), for equipment and all sorts of information about ice climbing in the state.

ICE FISHING

Considering ice fishing's brief, 2-month season, you might find it surprising that almost three-quarters of the state's trophy fish are caught during this time. Larger fish spend most of the year cruising the deep waters. But when the ice starts to form, these prize winners head to shallow waters, closer to the schools of smaller fish . . . and your lines. So start drilling.

Lake trout are caught in the Northeast Kingdom, at **Caspian, Willoughby, Echo, Crystal, Maidstone, Seymour,** and **Averill Lakes.** Northern pike can be found in **Lake Champlain.** Try Keeler Bay, Dillenbeck Bay, Kelly Bay, Missisquoi Bay, and Willow Bay, where 10-pound fish are common and pike over 20 pounds are iced-over every year. Go with a 10- to 12-inch sucker rigged with a treble hook. Anglers have also been known to hook smelt and perch at Lake Champlain, **Lake Memphremagog, Fairlee,** and Echo Lakes.

For maps and additional information, contact the **Vermont Fish and Wildlife Department,** 103 S. Main St., Waterbury, VT 05671 (☎ **802/241-3700;** www.anr.state.vt.us/fw/fwhome).

LLAMA TREKKING

If you want to go llama trekking but can't afford that $1,000 to $2,000 flight to the Andes Mountains in South America, head to northern Vermont. **Northern Vermont Llama Treks** in Waterville (☎ **802/644-2257**) guides hikers into the Mount Mansfield State Forest.

MOUNTAIN BIKING

For the mountain biker who yearns to have the hillside to himself or herself, there is no better time to visit Vermont. The Green Mountain State has always been cherished by a few inveterate bikers for its incredible network of trails. Yet, for decades, this expansive web was open only to locals who had befriended the farmer next-door. Every other sorry sap was forced to bike at crowded downhill and cross-country ski centers with the rest of the *flatlanders*. This brings up the philosophical mountain-biking question of fate versus predestination. I tend to agree with that well-known mountain biker Immanuel Kant, who firmly believes that bikers can only experience the ecstatic feeling of freedom when routes lead to nowhere in particular (fate). When trails are numbered or proceed in a circular fashion back to the starting point (predestined), as is the case at ski areas, mountain-biking bliss is considerably lessened.

Fortunately, freedom now reigns supreme in northern Vermont, thanks to a handful of generous Vermonters like John Worth.

East Burke

Allow 2–3 hr. Moderate to strenuous; rolling single tracks. Access: East Burke Sports is located in the village of East Burke, on Rte. 114. Map: available from East Burke Sports (☎ **802/626-3215; www.kingdomtrails.org**).

In the summer of 1998, John Worth, co-owner of a outdoor store called East Burke Sports, and several other dedicated locals like Jeff Hale linked together more than 150 miles of single tracks and dirt roads into a network they call the Kingdom Trails. Many of these routes were created from logging roads and former cross-country skiing trails that were abandoned 50 to 70 years ago.

One fall day, I had the pleasure of riding with seasoned Vermont trail hound Jeff Hale. His golden retriever, Quincy, led the way as we pedaled uphill from the center of East Burke to Darling Hill's Mountain View Creamery. Here, immense red barns from the turn of the last century stand intact, forming a stark contrast with the green pastures. Add the kaleidoscopic blur of fall foliage that tints the hillside in early October and you'll feel as if you're riding into a Jackson Pollack drip painting. A short downhill cruise past the barns leads you into the neighboring woods and a trail called Coronary. Don't be put off by the name. This is not rugged western riding, like Moab, where you often walk your bike just as much as you ride. No, this is the best of eastern riding, a soft forest single track, dusted with pine needles. We cycled up and down this roller-coaster route, banking hard around corners, all within an arm's length of fragrant spruces and firs. Small, dilapidated sugar shacks seemed lost in the countryside.

Several white-tailed deer sprinted by, giving the dog (and us) a thrill, before we crossed Darling Hill Road and entered an area of woods known as the Darion Ridge. Technical single-track trails like Pines and Widow Maker are root-studded, rock-littered gems that snake their way through the dense forest. As we cruised closer to the east branch of the Passumpsic River, maples and birches replaced the evergreens, and piles of leaves covered the trail. This created the interesting dilemma of not having the slightest idea what type of trail hid under the heavy covering. We managed to hop over roots, but suddenly found ourselves stuck in a mud bog, like moths in a spider's web. An excited Quincy ripped a branch off a tree and started barking. He thought we had stopped to play fetch. Sludge up to our calves, we pulled our bikes out of the pit and threw Quincy's drool-slickened stick into the woods about 20 times. Then we coasted downhill back into town.

Burke Mountain

Allow 1–2 hr. Moderate to strenuous; every type of terrain imaginable. Access: From the village of East Burke, bear right at the sign for Burke Mountain and right again at the Sherburne Base Lodge. Map: available from East Burke Sports (☎ **802/626-3215**).

I was fortunate that the people of East Burke were setting up a professional mountain-biking course during the few days I stayed at Burke Mountain. The race was scheduled for the following Sunday, but I had the 6-mile loop to myself the weekday I rode it. All the arrows showing direction were in place and, according to the guys at East Burke Sports, will remain in place for the mountain-biking season. East Burke Sports can also suggest trails at the mountain's cross-country ski center, which is free to the public.

The ride begins to the left of Sherburne Base Lodge, where I cruised up the grassy double tracks to a dirt road. To my left, Mount Pisgah and Mount Hor stood like bookends on opposite sides of Lake Willoughby. I continued up the dirt road, venturing on grass across a paved road to reach the mid-Burke section of the mountain. The ski slopes stood straight ahead. Narrow single tracks soon appeared as I veered left on the grassy double tracks for the last time. A grueling hill stood before me, but once I made it up, the single tracks swept down through the forest, soon becoming level again. Eventually, the course turns into a dirt road that goes right down the ski slopes of the mountain. Another left turn and I was pedaling up and down the mountain on single tracks, double tracks, dirt roads, and grassy ski slopes as the ride became an exhilarating blur. I thought I was finally down at the bottom when the course took one more uphill turn and then cruised downhill on technical single tracks back to the lodge.

Craftsbury Common

Allow 1.5–2 hr. Easy to moderate, on hilly dirt road. Access: From Craftsbury Common, follow the white signs to Craftsbury Center. You can park in their parking lot.

I'm still not sure whether riding on a dirt road is mountain biking or road biking with fat tires. Regardless of category, biking through the Northeast Kingdom is like biking through the Vermont of your imagination, a bucolic landscape replete with grazing horses and cows, bright white steeples, decrepit barns, and mile after mile of mountainous hillside. This secluded 11-mile loop on a hard-packed dirt road is a good warm-up for more-technical riding at Craftsbury Center. However, here you'll have the trails to yourself, give or take a couple cows. From the parking lot, cruise up and down the short hills. At 2.3 miles, take a sharp right turn past a balsam tree farm and the stubby headstones of an old cemetery. A little more than a mile later, after biking uphill, you'll get exquisite views of Vermont's countryside. I was momentarily delayed by a dairy farmer who was herding his cows from the meadows back to the barn. At 7.7 miles, take another sharp right and continue straight on TH 28 (do not make a right turn 0.4 mile later onto TH 32). Views of Great Hosmer Pond soon appear. Bear right around this blue-green body of water to return to Craftsbury Center.

Rail Trails

Colchester Causeway or Trail on the Lake

3 miles one-way. Easy; hard-packed gravel. Access: Take Rte. 127 north from Burlington past the Ethan Allen homestead. Cross the Winooski River into Colchester. Take a left on Porters Point Rd. and a left at Colchester Point Rd. to

Airport Park. The trail goes through the Causeway Bog and reaches the causeway in less than a mile.

One day soon, a ferry might take bikers from Burlington across the 200-foot-wide Winooski River to the Colchester Causeway. But for now, bikers will have to drive to the start of this unique rail trail. Back in 1900, the Lake Champlain Islands were linked by railroad causeways built on massive marble boulders and chips. So far, the Colchester Causeway is the only former bed that has been converted to a rail trail, but the day may soon come when these causeways could arguably be the longest water crossing of any recreational path in the world. The 3-mile causeway, no more than 7-feet wide, juts out into Lake Champlain toward South Hero Island. In summer, you can pedal over the water, smelling the wildflower and herbs that grow along the narrow banks. The trail ends where a drawbridge used to open for boats sailing into Malletts Bay.

Alburg Recreational Rail Trail

3.5 miles; Easy; hard-packed cinder and gravel. Access: Take I-89 to Exit 21 in Swanton. Follow Rte. 78 West to Rte. 2 North into Alburg. Park anywhere in town. The trail starts across the street from the Volunteer Fire Station located at the rear of the Industrial Park.

Who says you can't go mountain biking and bird watching at the same time? Certainly not the folks who run the Mud Creek Waterfowl Area. An easy rail trail skirts a wetland that's teeming with incredible bird life. Look for great blue herons as they hide within the millions of cattails. At 1.5 miles, you cross a small wooden bridge. The trail starts to narrow as the woods move in. At 2.4 miles, you cross Blue Rock Road (a quick right turn onto this paved road rewards you with great views of Lake Champlain), and soon the trail abruptly ends at Route 78. If you still haven't had your fill of bird life, you can cross Lake Champlain on Route 78 and reach the Missisquoi National Wildlife Refuge in another mile. This 6,000-acre wetlands is a haven for waterfowl (see "Bird Watching," above, and "Walks & Rambles," below).

Montpelier and Wells River Trail

14.5 miles; Easy; sand and hard-packed gravel. Access: Take I-91 to Exit 17 and follow Rte. 302 west for approximately 8 miles. Turn right onto Rte. 232 north and go 1.6 miles to a parking lot on the right side of the road near Ricker Pond. The trail heads north through Ricker Campground.

You're never far from water on this rail trail that snakes through Groton State Forest. Start at Ricker Pond and within 2 miles, you'll start to see views of Lake Groton to your right. Continue with your gradual ascent until you reach a paved road that leads to Big Deer and Stillwater Campgrounds. If you turn right on this paved road, you'll reach Boulder Beach on the shores of Lake Groton 2 miles later. This is a great picnic spot. Back on the trail, ride under evergreens until the forest opens up around mile 6. You'll soon be treated to excellent views of the sheer granite cliffs of Owl's Head Mountain on the right. At the 8-mile mark, Marshfield Pond appears to your right, surrounded by a mountainous panorama. The trail ends at the Winooski River in Plainfield.

Rentals & Outfitters

East Burke Sports is located on State Route 114 in the center of East Burke Village (☎ **802/626-3215**). They rent bikes for $25 daily.

In Craftsbury you can rent bikes at the **Craftsbury Outdoor Center,** Craftsbury Common (☎ **802/586-7767**).

POWERBOATING

Fishing boats and motorboats can be rented at **McKibben Sailing Vacations,** 176 Battery St., Burlington (☎ **800/522-0028** or 802/864-7733); **Charlie's**

Polo, Anyone?

The sport of polo brings to mind images of Prince Charles working up a sweat on a manicured field as he battles it out with other well-groomed men on horseback. Indeed, polo has always been a sport reserved for the affluent or royalty, to be played in places like Monaco, Dubai, or West Palm Beach. No one ever expected that the sport would be played in Burlington, Vermont, by (gasp) the middle and lower rungs of the socioeconomic ladder. But that's exactly what's happening in small public parks across the country now that the mountain bike has replaced the quarter horse as the mode of travel.

Teams of about four or five bikers line up on either side of a soccer field. Equipped with heavy mallets in their right hands, players dribble a wiffle ball downfield or pass the ball in front, behind, or between the bike wheels. The team that smacks the ball into the 5-foot-wide goal scores. Rules require players to keep both feet off the ground at all times and to respect a player's right of way if they approach the ball. This helps keep accidents to a minimum, but let's be realistic. This is no genteel day on a horse. It's a 3-hour game that often leaves broken wheels and derailleurs littering the playing field.

"Crashes are bound to happen in a friendly yet competitive game," says Burlington's David Bradbury who's been playing in a league every Sunday (when the ground's not covered with ice and snow) for the past 7 years.

The sport supposedly originated in India over a century ago, when homesick British troops used bicycles to hone their equestrian polo skills. On any given week in Vermont, the game attracts between 10 and 20 players from all walks of life–doctors, students, outdoor reps. All love to ride, and many of the younger riders can turn their bikes on a dime. When winded, which happens frequently in this stop-and-start game, players can lean on their mallets to nurse their water bottles.

Eventually, Bradbury hopes to compete with other leagues around the country for a national title. In the meantime, he's content playing polo on two wheels instead of four legs. Says Bradbury: "Who knows? Maybe one day I'll even go on a mountain-bike hunt with hounds."

For more about the sport, check out www.bikepolo.com/index.html.

Northland Lodge in North Hero (☎ **802/372-8822**); and **Newport Marina** in the northern lakes area (☎ **802/334-5911**).

For a complete listing of all motorboats, sailboats, and canoe rentals, contact the **Vermont Department of Travel** for their "Vermont Boating, Rentals & Marinas" publication, at 134 State St., Montpelier, VT 05602 (☎ **800/VERMONT**).

ROAD BIKING

The same rolling terrain and small villages that entice bikers in the south can be found in the north. However, some of the pavement turns to gravel for brief stints, so it might be wise to ride with hybrid tires.

Burlington Bike Path

7.5 miles (one-way). Easy; level, paved bike bath. Access: Take I-189 to Shelburne Rd. (State Rte. 7). Turn left onto Flynn Ave. and proceed 0.8 mile to Oakledge Park. There's ample parking.

All 7 miles of the Burlington Bike Path lie within the limits of the state's largest city, but let's be real. This is no metropolis ride. We're talking about Vermont, land of cows, rolling mountains, and far too much fertile farmland. This gem of a route hugs the shores of Lake Champlain with the Adirondack Mountains peering down from the New York State side. The Central Vermont Railroad built the line, and the first train arrived in Burlington in December 1849. Within 20 years,

Burlington would be the third-largest lumber port behind Chicago and Albany. Although the business went into a steady decline leading up to the early 1900s, the railroad continued to thrive throughout much of the 20th century.

Oakledge Park, the starting point on the southeastern side, is one of many spots along the trail where you'll find small beaches and picnic areas. Heading north, at Roundhouse Point, you'll start to see the first of numerous sailboats tacking across the large lake. North Beach, at the trail's midpoint mark, is a good place to picnic along the rocky shores. One of the best features of the Burlington Bike Path is that you're always a block or two away from a good deli if you need to reenergize on water and food. The next mile is a quiet ride through a wooded forest of maples, oaks, willows, and sumacs. Leddy Park is another fine place to stop, before the trail tails off into a residential neighborhood. Less than a mile later, Champlain reappears for the remainder of the trip. More sailboats, mountains, and a whole lotta lake.

Isle La Motte

Allow 1–2 hr. Easy; relatively flat terrain. Access: From Burlington, take I-89 North to U.S. 2 North, bearing left at State Rte. 129. Follow the signs to Isle La Motte and cross over the bridge. Park your car on the left side of the road at the small monument. Map: Any good state road map will do.

Venture off U.S. 2 in the Lake Champlain Islands and the sound of cars fades away, replaced by the quietude of backcountry roads and the seemingly endless expanse of water. This 12.6-mile loop around Isle La Motte is the finest ride in the region. I parked my car just across the bridge at the small monument. Happily riding on two wheels, I noticed a great blue heron and a family of ducks lounging on Blanchard Bay. A half mile later, I turned right toward St. Anne's Shrine, passing small stone houses rich with history, dilapidated barns, and rolled hay on large tracts of the greenest grass I've ever laid eyes on. St. Anne's Shrine is an open-sided Victorian chapel that marks the site of Vermont's first French settlement, founded in 1666. Today, more than 50 boats dock in the harbor each Sunday so boaters can attend mass in the church. Across the road there's a statue of Samuel de Champlain, created for Montreal's Expo '67.

I continued along the shores of the lake, passing long barns that would seem more at home in the hills of Provence than Vermont. A right turn at the sign for Terry Lodge brought me to a vast wilderness—sweeping vistas of rolling forests to my left and broad views of the lake to my right. Halfway into the ride, I spotted a deer grazing in the meadows on the outskirts of the forest. The road then became hard gravel, switching back to pavement a mile and a half later. Apple orchards and another stone house, home of the Isle La Motte Historical Society, came into view. A right-hand turn here brought me to the Ruthcliffe Lodge, irrefutably the best restaurant in the Lake Champlain island region. After making reservations for that evening, I backtracked to the main road, veered right, and turned right again at the 9-mile mark. A stone Methodist church built in 1893 appeared on the left, followed by more farmlands and the bright yellow patch of a mustard field. At 10.7 miles, I turned left, avoiding the dead-end road, and pedaled uphill. A right-turn on State Route 129 brought me back to the monument and my car.

Note: You can easily extend this route by crossing the bridge and veering left, following the road along the water, and then taking any number of right-hand turns into the countryside.

Jeffersonville Loop

Allow 1–2 hr. Moderate; hilly terrain. Access: From Stowe or Smuggler's Notch, take State Rte. 108 North to Jeffersonville. Park anywhere on the main street. Map: Any good state road map will do.

This spectacular 14.6-mile jaunt through the backroads of Smuggler's Notch and Jeffersonville was a tip from a local, Barbara Thompke. Once you've taken this route, you'll feel indebted to her as well. Some of the roads are hard-packed gravel, so a hybrid or mountain bike will survive better than a road bike. Park the car in Jeffersonville, veering right onto State Route 108 North and making a quick left onto Upper Valley Road near the Smuggler's Notch Inn. The road gradually goes uphill, bordered by mountain ridges on your right. Just when your legs start to burn from the steady uphill run, the road veers left, sweeping downhill as Vermont's highest peak appears directly in front of you. The sight of massive Mount Mansfield towering over you is breathtaking. At 3.7 miles, continue straight on Westman Road. A little more than a mile later, turn left onto Andrews Road and then left again onto Iron Gate Road. These are country roads that only locals who have lived here for years know about. Iron Gate goes up a short hill and then rolls down a narrow road past apple orchards, sheep farms, and a dark, deep forest. The road can be somewhat bumpy, so use caution. Turn right on Stebbins Road for views of Smuggler's Notch Ski Area. At the stop sign, turn left for 0.1 mile and then veer right onto paved State Route 108 South.

Here's where this route gets a little tricky. You need to turn left onto Edwards Road, but skip the ***first*** Edwards Road sign, turning left over a mile later at the ***second*** Edwards Road sign. The paved road goes steadily uphill before cruising down through fields of wildflowers and tall, tasseled corn. The peaks of Vermont's mountains stand before you, as compact as skyscrapers on the Manhattan skyline. Turn right at Junction Hill Road, rolling up and down with the farmland; 1.8 miles later, veer left past an old barn onto Canyon Road. This road sweeps downhill through a narrow canyon and a dark-ribbed covered bridge, before bearing right on State Route 108 North back to Jeffersonville.

Montpelier Ride

17.2 miles. Allow 2 hr. Moderate; hilly terrain. Access: Park anywhere in the town of Montpelier. The ride starts on Main St. heading north.

With a population of less than 9,000 people, Montpelier is the smallest state capital in the United States. Just minutes outside of town, you can be on backcountry roads eyeing centuries-old stone walls, barns, farmsteads, and of course, rolling pasture. Climb steadily out of the city on Upper Main Street, which becomes County Road after a sharp left bend. At 3.9 miles, turn right on unpaved Barnes Road and, shortly thereafter, make a left onto Center Road. You'll be riding through East Montpelier past the Old Meeting House, built around 1823. Continue pedaling on the hard-packed dirt of Center Road, which appears in state records as early as 1793. The farmsteads and sugar maples that line the road look just as old. At 6.6 miles, turn right on Sibley Road and then a left fork onto Foster Road. The road climbs uphill through pasture and then woods. When it ends, turn right on Chickering Road and 1 mile later you will come to a T. Turn right onto Guyette Road. One more mile, it's another T. This time, turn left onto Snow Hill Road. The view from atop the road is quintessential Vermont—a mixture of farms, fields, mountains, and woods. Snow Hill Road turns into Dodge Hill Road back into the hamlet of East Montpelier. Turn left on Center Road and views of the state capital can be seen. Another left onto County Road will bring you back to Upper Main Street and Montpelier.

Greensboro-Craftsbury Common Loop

32.6 miles. Allow 4 hr. Strenuous; hilly terrain. Access: Start on N. Main St. in Hardwick, near the Memorial Building.

This up-and-down run takes you to two of my favorite villages in Vermont—Greensboro, on the pristine shores of Caspian Lake, and Craftsbury with its mid-1850s village green of Craftsbury Common. Start on North Main Street in Hardwick and turn right on Church Street, which soon becomes Center Road. The next 2 miles are a quad burner—a strenuous climb before descending for a mile. Near the 6.5-mile mark, you'll reach Willey's General Store in Greensboro, which not only sells food for a picnic, but has an eclectic mix of antiques, paintings, and furniture. Bear left at the fork onto East Craftsbury Road and you'll soon be riding near the shores of Caspian Lake. The road becomes very steep as you near the end, close to 14 miles into the ride. At the stop sign, turn right and a mile later you'll be at Craftsbury Common. The immaculate village green, shaded by sugar maples and surrounded by white clapboard buildings, is the perfect place to stop and picnic. Continue straight through town for another 2.5 miles, keeping the common on the left. At the stop sign, turn left onto Route 14 south, which brings you all the way back into Hardwick.

Lake Willoughby Loop

31.6 miles. Allow 4 hs. Moderate; hilly terrain. Access: From Barton, take Rte. 16 north and follow signs to Crystal Lake State Park. You can park in the lot.

One of the most picturesque lakes in New England, Lake Willoughby is a glacial-carved body of water sandwiched between the cliffs of Mount Pisgah and Mount Hor. It's especially majestic when viewed while biking around its shores. From Crystal Lake State Park, continue on Route 16 through the rolling farmland. There's a couple of steep climbs in the early going, but you'll be rewarded later. At the 6-mile mark, sweep downhill with the shores of Lake Willoughby in sight. Turn right on 5A south, following signs for Westmore. For the next 5 or so miles, you'll be hugging the shores of Willoughby, peering at the waterfalls to your left, Mount Hor's cliffs across the water to your right. The road remains fairly level as you continue on Route 5A all the way to the small town of West Burke. Bear right onto Route 5 heading north and 12 miles later you'll be at the Route 16 intersection again, turning right to Crystal Lake State Park. The cool waters will look pretty inviting at this point.

Rentals & Outfitters

Both the **Thomas Mott Homestead** and **Ruthcliffe Lodge** furnish bikes and maps to their guests for the Isle La Motte Loop (see "Campgrounds & Other Accommodations," later in this chapter).

Foot of the Notch Bicycles, State Rte. 108, Church St., Jeffersonville, VT 05464 (☎ **802/644-8182**), rents bikes for the Jeffersonville ride.

In the northern part of the state, **Vermont Bicycle Touring,** P.O. Box 711, Bristol, VT 05443 (☎ **800/245-3868** or 802/453-4811; www.vbt.com), takes bikers on 5-day inn-to-inn trips to the Mount Mansfield Region and the Northeast Kingdom.

Bike Vermont, P.O. Box 207, Woodstock, VT 05091 (☎ **800/257-2226;** www.bikevermont.com), features 5- and 6-day guided tours to the Northeast Kingdom and the upper Connecticut River Valley.

Backroads, 1516 Fifth St., Berkeley, CA 94710-1740 (☎ **800/GO-ACTIVE;** www.backroads.com), offers a 5-day inn-to-inn tour through Craftsbury Common, Greensboro, Stowe, and Montpelier.

ROCK CLIMBING

The **Bolton Valley Walls,** north off U.S. 2, not far west of the Bolton Valley Ski Area access road is rumored to be as good as it gets in the Green Mountains, but it's difficult to find. **Smuggler's Notch State Park** is home to Elephant's Head, a large buttress on the north side of the Notch. Park at the caretaker's hut on Route 108, top of the notch.

The one-stop-shopping source for equipment and all sorts of information about Vermont rock climbing is **Climb High,** 2438 Shelburne Rd., Shelburne, VT 05482 (☎ **802/985-5056** or 802/985-9141; www.climbhigh.com).

The **Green Mountain Rock Climbing Center** in Rutland (☎ **802/773-3343;** www.bestclimb.com) has guided rock climbing and ice climbing trips around the state. They also have clinics and an indoor climbing wall.

RUNNING

Craftsbury Running Camp, Craftsbury Common, VT

It's not every day that I bike 20 miles, climb a 2,000-foot peak, and then run 6 miles along the shores of a lake, but I was in the midst of Craftsbury Running Camp's midweek Endurathon. Now in its 24th year, the running school set in the hills of Vermont attracts runners from all over the country. I visited the camp during Marathon Week when experienced marathoners who had previously run 26-mile marathon races in Chicago, Nashville, Cape Cod, San Diego, or Orlando descended on Vermont to perfect their running technique. Many had aspirations of bettering their times to qualify for the prestigious Boston Marathon.

Led by Greg Wenneborg and Randy Accetta, they were in good hands. Wenneborg had just come in 20th in the U.S. Olympics Marathon trials, and his personal best was 2:19:24. Accetta's personal best was a second slower at 2:19:25. Premier runners do not necessarily make premier teachers. This is especially true of most marathoners, who are not exactly known for being gregarious. But Wenneborg and Accetta break the mold, joking with the students and, more important, going over every minute detail of a marathon run, from training months beforehand to marathon day to getting back in the groove after the race. Away from the classroom, they review your technique in the finer settings of the Northeast Kingdom—along the shores of majestic Lake Willoughby, through the dairy farms of Craftsbury Common, from the village of Stowe to the base of Vermont's tallest peak, Mount Mansfield.

Marathon Week is the most extreme week. Other sessions are devoted to getting the runner ready for his or her first marathon (Marathon 101); or for Road Race Week, which focuses on shorter distances like the 5K; or for Master's Week for the over-40 runner. For more information, contact the **Craftsbury Outdoor Center** at ☎ **800/729-7751.**

SAILING

Lake Champlain

Access: Winds of Ireland is located at Burlington's Community Boathouse on Lower College St.

Approximately 120 miles long and 12 miles wide, Lake Champlain is the largest freshwater lake in the country after the Great Lakes. Consistently good wind, sheltered bays, hundreds of islands, and scenic anchorages combine to make this immense body of water one of the top cruising grounds in the Northeast. One overcast day in midsummer, my family decided to charter a Hunter 35 from Winds of Ireland, located at the edge of Burlington Bay. When we heard the forecast for the day on my father's weather radio (a new toy that my dad couldn't bear to turn off even after we had heard the weather report for the umpteenth time), we decided to hire a captain. "Lake Champlain, 25- to 35-knot winds with 3-foot swells. A wind advisory is in effect," said the monotone voice over and over again.

Winds of Ireland provided us with Captain Mikey, who during the summer lives on the bay in a 30-foot Yankee built in 1938. We were surprised that anyone would take us out in these ominous conditions. Whitecaps were thrashing against the breakwater, and the haunting sky was steel gray; but Mikey was as cool as a chunk of chocolate in a pint of Ben & Jerry's New York Super Fudge Chunk. He loaded us into the spacious boat and off we went into the wild blue yonder. Outside the bay, we turned off the motor and put up the jib, and already we were sailing across the lake at 6 or 7 knots. There was no need to put up the mainsail. Even in this wild weather, the Hunter was as smooth as the bark on a birch tree. We each took turns at the helm (no tiller on this big boy), guiding the boat along the eastern shores of the lake. Black cormorants flew over our heads as we cruised by a privately owned island called Juniper, the luxury homes of South Cove, and Shelbourne Point Peninsula, and on into sheltered Shelbourne Bay. Hundreds of sailboats were wisely docked at the Lake Champlain Yacht Club, their bare masts bobbing from side to side. Indeed, we were the only boat on the lake, except for the ferry going back and forth to the New York side. However, the sun was starting to peek through the layers of clouds, and we felt confident in Mikey's sailing ability.

Views of Shelbourne Farm and other fertile fields appeared on the eastern shores before we left the bay and ventured toward the Adirondack Mountains on the other side of the lake. Once in the open water, we asked Mikey if he's ever seen "Champ," Lake Champlain's version of the Loch Ness Monster. Fortunately, he hasn't, but some of his friends have sworn they've seen this sea monster lurking in the depths. We headed for Four Brothers, four small islands that were not very inviting. Stunted and gnarled trees stood atop rocky cliffs, wet with the continuous bombardment of waves. A more appropriate name would have been the Four Ex-cons. From here we returned to Burlington and the dock, knowing that we'd be back on this lake for a longer sail on sunnier days.

Outfitters, Rentals & Instruction

Winds of Ireland, P.O. Box 2286, South Burlington, VT 05407 (☎ **802/863-5090;** www.windsofireland.com), charters five Hunters, from 30 to 40 feet, on a day or weekly rate. Prices start at $145 per day. A captain costs extra. Winds of Ireland also offers 2-hour daysails and sunset sails.

McKibben Sailing Vacations, 176 Battery St., Burlington, VT 05407 (☎ **800/522-0028** or 802/864-7733), also offers bareboat and crewed charters on the lake.

The **Burlington Community Boathouse,** at the foot of College Street (☎ **802/865-3377**), offers daily Rhodes and Laser rentals and lessons.

The **International Sailing School and Club,** 253 Lakeshore Drive, Colchester, VT 05446 (☎ **802/864-9065;** www.vermontsailingschool.com), charges a membership fee that entitles you to sailing workshops, clinics, and unlimited use of their sailboats and sailboards.

Tudhope Sailing Center and Marina, at the foot of the Grand Isle Bridge in the Lake Champlain Islands (☎ **802/372-5320**), provides instruction and charters.

In the northern lakes region of the Northeast Kingdom, sailboats can be rented at the **Newport Marina** (☎ **802/334-5911**).

SCUBA DIVING

Who needs the Caymans when you have Champlain!

Lake Champlain

Access: Waterfront Diving Center is located on 214 Battery St. in Burlington, right next to the lake. Divers must be certified.

Lake Champlain has always been a major thoroughfare from the St. Lawrence Seaway to Champlain Canal and the Hudson River. Numerous historic battles were fought on the lake during the French and Indian Wars, the Revolutionary War, and the War of 1812 to control this navigational stronghold. In the mid- to late 19th century, commercial vessels replaced gunboats. Many of the military and merchant ships never made it out of the water, sinking to the deep, dark bottom from the power of the cannonball or the temperamental weather. These vessels' misfortunes are good luck to the scuba diver.

Indeed, the cool waters of the lake contain one of the finest collections of wooden shipwrecks in North America. Two hundred wrecks have already been discovered, and that number could rise dramatically in the next decade when a complete and accurate inventory will be made over the entire lake. So far, the list includes the 54-foot Revolutionary War boat ***Philadelphia,*** pulled from the waters in 1935 to sit in the Smithsonian Institute; the ***Eagle, Allen,*** and ***Linnet,*** three naval craft that participated in the War of 1812; and the remains of a Revolutionary War gunboat that was once under the command of Benedict Arnold, found in June 1997 by Arthur Cohn, historian and director of the Lake Champlain Maritime Museum.

"We're still developing a management plan to decide whether to leave the boat in the water or salvage the remains," says Cohn. Unfortunately, many of these earlier wrecks are far too deep for scuba divers, but six of the commercial vessels that lie on the lake's floor are preserved by the state of Vermont as underwater historical sites.

Jonathan Eddy, owner of the Waterfront Diving Center in Burlington, brought me to see the ***General Butler.*** Located near the southern end of the Burlington Breakwater, this 88-foot commercial vessel is one of the preserved boats. On December 9, 1876, this schooner-rigged ship set sail for Burlington from Isle La Motte with a cargo of marble blocks. The boat was almost in the bay when a powerful gale broke the steering mechanism. The captain put a chain around the tiller to try to steer the boat, but to no avail. The ***General Butler*** continued to thrash about on the rocks of the breakwater, before sinking 40 feet below, where she now rests. Fortunately, the five people aboard the ship were saved.

Jonathan tied up to one of the large yellow buoys provided by the state, and we soon made our descent. The water was a frigid 65° on the surface, and 10° lower by the wreck. Needless to say, we wore wet suits from the top of our heads to the bottoms of our feet. Several minutes later, we were staring at the long length of the wooden boat. Visibility, normally 15 feet, was lower than average. Nevertheless, we could still see everything on the boat, including the jury-rigged chain still wrapped around the tiller, the cargo of marble blocks, and the cleats used for lowering and raising the anchors. Unfortunately, her masts are no longer there. We swam around the boat several times, followed by rock and smallmouth bass. Small, snail-like zebra mussels had attached themselves all over the wood. These mussels are causing an alarming epidemic in the northern lakes. They clog boat engines and can cause irreversible damage to these historic ships. "They're extremely bad news," says Cohn. "The stability of this collection of shipwrecks and their archaeological potential are in danger." Since there is no remedy in sight, Cohn advises seeing the wrecks before they're all coated in green slime.

The ***General Butler*** is an easy dive, accessible to all levels. There are no special permit fees, but all divers must register with the **Vermont Division for Historic Preservation** (☎ **802/828-3051**). What you get in return is a nifty little book that details all six wrecks. You can register at any dive shop in the state.

Since the ***General Butler*** is located about 300 yards from the Burlington Harbor, you'll need to charter a boat to get there. **Waterfront Diving Center,** 214 Battery St., Burlington (☎ **802/865-2771**), offers rental, charters, and instruction. You can rent boats at Perkins

Pier, Burlington's Municipal Marina, situated across the street from the Waterfront Diving Center.

SCULLING

Craftsbury Sculling Center is located in Craftsbury Common, Vermont (☎ **800/729-7751**).

Sandwiched between the hills of the remote Northeast Kingdom, Hosmer Pond is the idyllic setting for the Craftsbury Outdoor Center's sculling school. Now in its 25th year, the school is run by Steve Wagner, Head Crew Coach at Rutgers University. His large staff includes a slew of other college coaches and Olympians like Marlene Royle and Carlie Geer. If you ever wanted to learn the sport of sculling or if you already scull and want to perfect your stroke, Craftsbury is arguably the best place in the country to do just that.

I tried sculling for the first time last summer at Craftsbury, and my class included other novices like me, former crew members from Columbia and Yale, even a silver medalist on the eight-man crew team from the 1972 Munich Olympics. The week-long course goes over all aspects of rowing and, depending on expertise, splits up groups on the lake with instructors. Balancing the boat proved to be the hardest part for my group of beginners, many of whom spent the better part of the first day swimming. Both oars have to be together at all times or the boat quickly tips to the left or right. Coach Ben Foster told me to think of the oars as a bike chain and to move in that oval-like fashion. Legs are thrust up against a board to push off and scoot your behind back as you propel the oars forward. Indeed, many of the coaches had immense quad muscles, proving that legs are more important than arms in the stroke.

After getting the feel of the boat, I spent the better part of the day paddling up and down the placid waters. We novices often got tangled up, because it's one of the few sports I can think of where you go backward, turning your head often to see where you are. But once you get in a flow, all is forgotten as you quickly skim across the water. Folks who use a rowing machine at their local gym know what a great workout sculling is for the whole body. But it's a far superior one when you're cruising along a lake in the Vermont woods.

SEA KAYAKING

Across the country, the trendy new adventure last summer was inn-to-inn sea kayaking. During the day, clientele kayak 7 to 8 miles along the vast shores of oceans and large lakes, paddling close to uninhabited land that's accessible only by small watercraft. In the evening, you dine at some of the region's finest restaurants and then plop down in a nearby bed.

Solace at sea and pampered evenings seem to be a winning combination as inn-to-inn sea kayaking jaunts are proliferating across North America, challenging the better-known overnight biking trips. Olaf Malver, Director of Development at Mountain Travel-Sobek, a large adventure outfitter that offers inn-to-inn sea kayaking trips along the Maine coast, says that biking and sea kayaking trips are very similar. "Both sports are accessible to everyone—women, men, children, families. And both incorporate the concept of being part of a larger group but going at your own pace so you have some degree of independence," says the Danish-born Malver, an avid kayaker who's guided more than 100 trips on all seven continents. "However," he adds, "the major difference is that bikers have a destination in mind while sea kayakers simply paddle to explore places that can't be seen any other way." This is the reason, Malver notes, why sea kayaking is now the second-fastest-growing sport in America after snowboarding.

Kayak Vermont (☎ **888/525-3644;** www.vermontkayak.com) features trips through the Lake Champlain Islands where you sea-kayak a relaxed 3 to 8 miles by day and stay in the historic North Hero House (built in 1891) by night. You'll kayak to Knight Island, a rugged state park that's good for hiking. The following day you might visit Missisquoi National Wildlife Refuge, known for its bird watching. Price for the 3-day tour including meals, lodging, and guides is $595 per person.

SNOWMOBILING

The **Vermont Association of Snow Travelers** (VAST), P.O. Box 839, Montpelier, VT 05602 (☎ **802/229-0005;** www.vtvast.org), is a group of more than 200 local snowmobile clubs that maintain over 3,000 miles of groomed trails. The trails extend from the Massachusetts border to Canada, from the Connecticut River to Lake Champlain. Eighty-five percent of the land is located on private property; without the work of volunteers, the use of this land would not be possible. Contact the association for detailed maps, route suggestions, and information about guided tours. A "Winter Recreation" map is also available from the **Green Mountain National Forest,** 231 N. Main St., Rutland, VT 05701 (☎ **802/747-6700**).

In Stowe, **Nichols Snowmobile Rentals** offers daily rentals (☎ **802/253-7239**). In the northern lakes region, **Seymour Lake Lodge,** State Route 11, Morgan, VT 05853 (☎ **802/895-2752**), is a good base for snowmobilers.

For a complete list of snowmobile tours and rentals in the state, get a copy of the "Vermont Winter Guide" from the **Vermont Department of Travel,** 134 State St., Montpelier, VT 05602 (☎ **800/VERMONT**).

SNOWSHOEING

A 1998 study by American Sports Data (ASD) reported that there were 1.2 million snowshoers, an 80% increase from the 1997 study. It's easy to see why snowshoeing has become one of the trendiest winter activities over the past several years. First and foremost, snowshoeing is about as easy as walking. There's no balancing issue as there is in skiing; and no matter what the surface, you're always in control. Thus, you go from beginner to intermediate in about 4 minutes and you're an expert in, oh, 7 minutes. As with walking or hiking trails, you don't have to travel far to find a local trail system or neighborhood park that offers winter serenity in a quiet, uncrowded environment. The whole family can venture out together, and they all get a great workout, burning up some 1,000 calories an hour.

Most important, the shoe is lightweight, durable, and maintenance free. For years, snowshoes looked as big as wooden tennis racquets and as awkward as walking on stilts. But about a decade ago, the snowshoe company Tubbs, based in Stowe, Vermont, created a new lightweight aluminum shoe. With fabric stretched over the frame and a pivoting crampon toepiece (metal teeth that bite into the snow and ice and swivel with the movement), the snowshoer now has the maneuverability necessary to attack any trail or mountain slope. **Tubbs** (☎ **800/882-2748;** www.tubbssnowshoes.com) now offers a variety of shoes—for women, children, runners, casual use, or backpackers. All it takes is a modest investment of $80 to $250 and you're off and running in the woods, near streams, or up mountains.

One of the best places to snowshoe in northern Vermont is the **Kingdom Trails Network** (www.kingdomtrails.org) in East Burke (see "Mountain Biking," above). These trails roll over the countryside past hundred-year-old farms, sugar shacks, and into deep forests of fir and spruce. Several of these trails are marked pink. Avoid walking on the groomed cross-country ski trails in the area. Nearby, experienced snowshoers can try the Mount Pisgah Trail (see "Hiking," above). If you think Lake Willoughby is a gem in the warm-weather months, you should see this glacial-carved lake during winter. Parts of the trail can be rocky, so use caution and don't step too far out on Pulpit Rock.

If you're up in the Lake Memphremagog area, try the 5-mile jaunt around Newport's bike trail. The large lake is always by your side. Another good snowshoe run on a bike trail is the Burlington Bikeway on the shores of Lake Champlain (see "Road Biking," above). The Moss Glen Falls Trail, 3 miles north of the village of Stowe and then right on Randolph Road, is a wonderful hour-long jaunt along a brook that leads to an iced-over waterfall. A more strenuous hike in the Stowe area is the 3-mile walk on the Long Trail to Taylor Lodge in the Nebraska Valley. From the lodge, you get excellent views of the Greens under a blanket of white. South of Stowe, turn onto Moscow Road and take it to the end. Park at the Lake Mansfield Trout Club.

Trapp Family Lodge offers snowshoe clinics taught by outdoor experts, along with a good selection of rentals and guided tours to deep-in-the-woods destinations like the Slayton Pasture Cabin. Here, hearty lunches, soup, and hot cocoa are served. If you prefer snowshoeing to cross-country skiing at Greensboro's Highland Lodge, try the 1.4-mile Rabbit Trail, a scenic nature trail that offers views of Caspian Lake.

Snowshoeing expeditions can be arranged through **Umiak Outdoor Outfitters,** 849 S. Main St., Stowe, VT 05672 (☎ **802/253-2317;** www.umiak.com). They offer rentals, lessons, and guided snowshoeing tours through Smuggler's Notch on unplowed State Route 108.

SWIMMING

With **Lake Champlain** to the west, the **Connecticut River** to the east, and hundreds of lakes, rivers, and ponds in between, choices of swimming holes in northern Vermont are virtually unlimited. **North Beach Park** is a crowded beach on Lake Champlain. Just outside of Burlington, **Bristol Falls** in Richmond attracts the University of Vermont (UVM) crowd. In Stowe, check out **Sterling Falls** and the other small ponds in Ranch Valley. **Brewster River Gorge** is located north of Smuggler's Notch outside of Jeffersonville.

In the Northeast Kingdom, swimming options increase exponentially. There's **Shadow Lake Beach** in Glover, **Lake Groton** just outside of Rickers Mills, **Harvey's Lake** in West Barnet, **Miles Pond** in Concord, **Crystal Lake State Beach** in Barton, and **Prouty Beach** in Newport.

WALKS & RAMBLES

Ethan Allen Homestead

2-mile loop. Allow 1 hr. Enjoy the wetlands behind the former home of Ethan Allen. Access: From Burlington and Rte. 127, take the North Avenue Beaches exit. Follow the Ethan Allen Homestead access road to the visitors center.

It was May 1775 when Ethan Allen and his Green Mountain Boys seized Fort Ticonderoga from the British. Captured ammunition and other supplies were shipped to Boston where they would be used by the Colonists to drive away the redcoats. After the war, Vermont's most famous son retired to a farm on the outskirts of Burlington, where he would live until his death in 1789. Tucked into a sylvan meadow on the bend of the Winooski River, the home is now administered by the Winooski Valley Park District. Stroll from Allen's home and gardens down to the river, where the Peninsula Trail snakes along the water. The Wetlands Nature Trail explores the marshlands along the river.

Burton Island State Park

2 miles round-trip. Allow 1 hr. A wonderful trail on an island in Lake Champlain that prohibits cars. Access: From St. Albans, head west on Rte. 36 for 5 miles and turn left, following signs for Kill Kare State

Park. A ferry will take you from Kill Kare to Burton Island State Park. Walk through the camping area where you'll see the sign for the North Shore Trail.

Surrounded by Lake Champlain, Burton Island is a welcome refuge from the woes of modernism. No cars are allowed on this 250-acre island, replaced instead by the songs of birds as they scamper across beaches, meadows, and woodlands. On the North Shore Trail, the waters of this great lake are never far from your side, but occasionally you slip into a forest of white pines, spruce, and speckled alder. You return through the woods on the Eagle Bay Trail.

Missisquoi National Wildlife Refuge

2–3 miles (round-trip). Allow 1–2 hr. Easy; don't forget your binocs on this bird-watcher's delight. Access: From Swanton, drive 2.4 miles west on Rte. 78. The National Wildlife Refuge headquarters and parking are located on the left side of the road. Map: USGS 7.5-min. East Alburg.

Missisquoi is the Abnaki word for "much waterfowl." So it should come as no surprise that this refuge is one of the largest stopovers for migrating waterfowl. During the peak months of September and October, there might be more than 20,000 ducks calling the refuge home. Herons, egrets, ospreys, great horned owls, and the occasional bald eagle can also be found in this flyway. There are a variety of trails to choose from in the refuge, including the Black Creek and Maquam Creek Trails. Both trails snake alongside the blackened water of the creeks. Add a thick marsh and you'll feel as if you were walking around the Louisiana bayou, not northern Vermont.

Stowe Recreation Path

5.5 miles one-way. Spend as much time as you want.

The 8-foot-wide paved trail starts behind the Stowe Community Church on Main Street and weaves back and forth over the Little River to the foothills of Mount Mansfield. Gradually, the trail becomes more rural, venturing over rolling pasture where cows graze. Never far from the restaurants on Mountain Road, you can have lunch and then make your way back to town.

Darling Hill

5 miles round-trip. Allow 2 hr. A fine walk along a country road. Access: Take Rte. 114 north from Lyndonville, turning left on Darling Hill Rd. toward the Wildlflower Inn. Park at the inn.

One of my favorite strolls in the Northeast Kingdom is simply along Darling Hill Road from the Wildflower Inn to Burke Green Cemetery and back. Offering superb views of Burke Mountain, the Willoughby Gap, and the fertile valley below, the walk passes Elmore Darling's former farm, now known as the Mountain View Creamery (see "Campgrounds & Other Accommodations," below).

Moose Bog

1 mile round-trip. Allow 30 min. Chances are good that you'll spot wildlife here in the early morning or evening hours. Access: From the junction of Rte. 114 and 105 in Island Pond, head east on 105 for 8.5 miles.

Deep in the heart of the Northeast Kingdom, this quick walk will take you to a bog nestled in a forest of spruce and fir. Part of the 2,000-acre Wenlock Wildlife Management Area, Moose Bog is reportedly Vermont's largest deer wintering area and, as the name implies, a pit stop for moose as well. The trail ascends to a huge boulder and then drops down to the soft moss-covered shores of the bog.

Outfitters

Backroads, 1516 Fifth St., Berkeley, CA 94710-1740 (☎ **800/GO-ACTIVE;** www.backroads.com), features a 6-day inn-to-inn walking tour through majestic Stowe, Greensboro, and Craftsbury Common.

Campgrounds & Other Accommodations

CAMPING

The **Department of Forests, Parks, and Recreation,** 103 S. Main Street, Waterbury, VT 05676 (☎ **802/241-3655;** www.state.vt.us/anr/fpr/), maintains 35 campgrounds in the state. Contact them for a brochure. If you find yourself without something like, oh, a tent, proceed to Montpelier's **Onion River Sports** (☎ **802/229-9409**), which stocks excellent camping gear.

North Hero State Park

From North Hero, go 4 miles north on Rte. 2, then 4 miles northeast on Town Rd. ☎ **802/372-8727.** 117 sites, no hookups, handicapped rest room, flush toilets, hot showers, public phone, tables, fire rings, and wood.

The sites are located in three loops in a lowland forest, with access to a beach on Lake Champlain.

Knight Island State Park

Accessible only by boat. Larry Tudholpe offers a Knight Islander Taxi service from North Hero. ☎ **802/372-8389** or 802/524-6353 for reservations. 7 sites, no hookups, fire rings, and wood.

Located on Lake Champlain 2 miles east of North Hero, these seven sites are strictly reserved for those who yearn for privacy.

Burton Island State Park

Accessible only by boat or day ferry. From St. Albans Bay, travel southwest on Rte. 36 and then Point Rd. to Kill Kare State Park. Parking spaces and a boat ramp are provided. ☎ **802/524-6353.** 17 tent sites, 26 lean-to sites, 15 boat moorings, and a 100-slip marina. Fireplaces, wood for sale, metered hot showers, and rest rooms.

Set apart from the busy boat marina, these campsites are located on the north shores of this 250-acre island in Lake Champlain. Not only is Burton Island an excellent place for strolling (see "Walks & Rambles," above), but the island has a resident naturalist who hosts interpretive programs.

Smuggler's Notch State Park

Located on State Rte. 108, 10 miles west of Stowe. ☎ **802/253-4014.** 38 sites, no hookups, handicapped rest rooms, flush toilets, hot showers, public phone, tables, fire rings, and wood.

Located at the north end of the notch. this area can be extremely windy at times. It's a good jumping off point for numerous hikes in the Green Mountains.

Underhill State Park

From Underhill Center, off State Rte. 15, go 4 miles east on paved Town Rd. and then head 4 miles east on gravel Town Rd. ☎ **802/899-3022.** 25 sites, no hookups, handicapped rest rooms, flush toilets, hot showers, public phone, tables, fire rings, and wood.

The campground is scattered around the base of 4,393-foot Mount Mansfield, near the Laura Cowles and Sunset Ridge trailheads. The limited sites are extremely popular during the summer months.

Little River State Park

From the junction of State Rte. 100 and U.S. 2, go 1.5 miles west on U.S. 2 and 3.5 miles north on Little River Rd. ☎ **802/244-7103.** 101 sites, no hookups, handicapped rest rooms, flush toilets, hot showers, public phone, tables, fire rings, and wood.

Located on Waterbury Reservoir, some of the northern sites are on remote stretches of shoreline while the remainder hide in the hilly forest. Part of the Mount

Mansfield National Forest, the park is close to the Mount Hunger and Mount Mansfield day hikes (see "Hiking," above).

Brighton State Park

From Island Pond, go 2 miles east on State Rte. 105 and then 0.75 mile south on local road. ☎ **802/723-4360.** 63 sites, no hookups, handicapped rest rooms, flush toilets, hot showers, public phone, tables, fire rings, and wood.

The sites are on the shores of Spectacle Pond, a well-known fishing hole near Lake Willoughby. Nature trails, a small beach, canoeing, and fishing are the benefits of this wilderness retreat.

Stillwater Campground

From Groton, head 2 miles west on State Rte. 302, 6 miles north on State Rte. 232, and then 0.5 mile east on Boulder Beach Rd. ☎ **802/584-3822.** 79 sites, no hookups, flush toilets, hot showers, public phone, tables, fire rings, and wood.

Stillwater Campground is located on the northwest side of Lake Groton, a favorite swimming and canoeing spot. Sites are set on or near the lake, next to a sandy beach.

Ricker Pond Campground

From Groton, go 2 miles west on State Rte. 84 and then 2.5 miles north on State Rte. 232. ☎ **802/584-3821.** 55 sites, no hookups, flush toilets, hot showers, public phone, tables, fire rings, and wood.

The campground is located on the south side of Ricker Pond, near larger Lake Groton.

INNS & RESORTS

Thomas Mott Homestead

R.R. 3, P.O. Box 149B, Alburg, VT 05440-9629. ☎ **802/796-3736;** www.thomas-mott-bb.com. Rooms from $79 a night, including breakfast.

The year 1987 was a busy one for Pat Schallert. He retired from the wine-exporting business, moved from Los Angeles to Alburg, Vermont, and completely refurbished an 1838 farmhouse into one of the nicest inns on the Lake Champlain Islands. Years of selecting the finest wines in the world seems to be the perfect training ground for becoming a competent innkeeper. Pat has an impeccable eye for detail that makes guests feel right at home. Little touches, like keeping a freezer full of free Ben & Jerry's ice cream, showing visitors where the ripe raspberries are on the property, and selecting the finest restaurants in the region for his guests are the reasons why people return year after year. The inn is located on the northern shores of Lake Champlain. Pat also provides canoes and bicycles.

Ruthcliffe Lodge

P.O. Box 32, Isle La Motte, VT 05463. ☎ **802/928-3200.** Double rooms from $81, including breakfast.

Situated on Isle La Motte, my favorite Lake Champlain island, the Ruthcliffe Lodge has been a summer hideaway since 1951. Seven of the nine guest rooms are on the lake, and canoes are available. Owner Mark Infante is a talented chef—the reason many locals consider Ruthcliffe's restaurant to be the best on the islands.

Burlington Radisson

Battery St., Burlington, VT 05401. ☎ **800/333-3333** or 802/658-6500; www.radisson.com. Double rooms from $109.

If you plan on spending several days in Burlington, you can't go wrong with the Radisson. Ask for a room overlooking the lake and the Adirondack Mountains. The hotel is conveniently located across from the 8.2-mile Burlington Bike Path and down the road from sailboat rentals and scuba-diving charters.

Smuggler's Notch Resort

State Rte. 108, Smuggler's Notch, VT 05464-9599. ☎ **800/451-8752;** www.smugglersnotch.com. Write or call regarding package deals.

Smuggler's Notch's reputation as one of the finest family-oriented resorts in the state is well-deserved. The resort is located at the foothills of Morse, Sterling, and Madonna mountains, just north of the notch. Families can cross-country or downhill-ski the mountains in the winter, and mountain-bike and hike on the trails in the summer. Climbing to the peak of Mansfield, canoeing on the Lamoille River, and good road-biking are all in close proximity. The hodgepodge of accommodations ranges from studios with fireplaces to fully equipped five-bedroom condos.

Trapp Family Lodge

Stowe, VT 05672. ☎ **800/826-7000** or 802/253-8511; www.trappfamily.com. Doubles start at $150 per room.

"The hills are alive with the sound of . . . cross-country skiers swooshing through snow" (I'd like to see Julie Andrews sing that line). Maria von Trapp, the woman who inspired *The Sound of Music,* is no longer with us and the original building burned down in 1980, but the Trapp Family Lodge endures. Set on a crest overlooking the Green Mountains, the new Austrian-style lodge has the same stunning view. Members of the Trapp family are often found dining with guests and leading sing-alongs in the living room. The cross-country ski-touring facility offers some of the finest groomed and backcountry skiing in the country.

The Inn at Turner Mill

Mountain Rd., Stowe. ☎ **802/253-2062;** www.turnermill.com. Rooms start at $75 and apartments go up to $210 (2 bedrooms, 2 private bathrooms, with full kitchen and fireplace).

Hidden in the woods near cascading Notch Brook, a mere mile from Stowe's lifts, the Inn at Turner Mill offers an assortment of rooms and apartments in a rambling wood building. Ask owner Greg Speer, an avid outdoorsman, about his special winter adventure weekends (called Expeditions Stowe) that include snowshoeing, cross-country skiing, and ice climbing. In the summer, Greg creates furniture that you might want to purchase after you see it in the rooms. Also bring home a bag of wife Mitzy's granola.

Inn at Trout River

Main St., Montgomery Center, VT 05471. ☎ **800/338-7049** or 802/326-4391; www.troutinn.com. Double rooms with breakfast start at $86.

Built by a lumber baron over a century ago, the Inn at Trout River now features ten guest rooms, one suite, and a top-notch restaurant. The inn is located just down the road from Jay Peak and Hazen's Notch Ski Touring Center, in Montgomery Center. Along with her usual steak, chicken, and lamb dishes, owner and chef Lee Forman offers a "Wholesome Choices" menu featuring low-calorie, low-cholesterol dishes. Try her zucchini and squash, some of the freshest vegetables I've ever tasted.

Inn on the Common

Craftsbury Common, VT 05827. ☎ **800/521-2233** or 802/586-9619; www.innonthecommon.com. Double rooms with breakfast and dinner start at $250.

Driving into Craftsbury Common is like entering another century. I always expect the car radio to shut off, only to turn on again with Rod Serling's voice. "You are entering another time, another place. It's the mid-1800s and you've just arrived in Craftsbury Common, a town of gleaming white clapboard houses on a village green. A town where peace and quiet not only are attainable, but could be alarming to some. You are entering the Twilight Zone." To call Craftsbury Common sleepy is an understatement. This town has been slumbering longer than Rip Van Winkle.

The Inn on the Common, three stately houses just off the square, fits right into the scheme of things. Owners Michael and Penny Schmitt come from a time and a place where service and comfort are of the utmost importance. The five-course dinner and breakfast are served in a luxurious setting overlooking the manicured English-style gardens. The inn is located near the cross-country and mountain-biking trails of Craftsbury Center.

Highland Lodge

Greensboro, VT 05841. ☎ **802/533-2647;** www.highlandlodge.com. Double rooms start at $99.50 per person, including breakfast and dinner.

Located in Greensboro, one of my favorite Northeast Kingdom towns, the Highland Lodge sits on a hill overlooking Caspian Lake. There are 11 rooms in the main inn and 10 cottages scattered about the grounds. The lodge is known for its extensive network of cross-country skiing trails in the winter. During the warm-weather months, guests can fish and canoe on the lake or play tennis on the shores.

The Inn at Mountain View Creamery

P.O. Box 355, East Burke, VT 05832. ☎ **802/626-9924;** www.innmtnview.com. Double rooms with breakfast start at $125.

When I first laid eyes on the Mountain View Creamery, my jaw dropped. It was like walking onto the grounds of the Shelburne Museum outside of Burlington. Set on a hill overlooking 440 acres of Northeast Kingdom scenery, the red-brick creamery is surrounded by four immense barns. The barns and the creamery were built in 1883 by Elmer Darling, owner of the elegant Fifth Avenue Hotel in New York. They were once used to house hundreds of cows, pigs, sheep, and Morgan horses. Today, the creamery functions as a 10-room B&B and the grounds are yours to stroll upon. The inn is a 5-minute drive from Burke Mountain and a 15-minute drive from Mount Pisgah and Lake Willoughby.

5

Southern New Hampshire & the Lake District

The towering granite notches of the White Mountains might get most of the acclaim, but southern New Hampshire has its own distinct charm. The timeless appeal of this area stems largely from its long history. Portsmouth was founded in 1630 as an attractive harbor with an easily accessible entry into the Piscataqua River from the Atlantic. New Hampshire borders the Atlantic Ocean for an 18-mile stretch from the Massachusetts to the Maine border. During the Revolutionary War, this colonial seaport was an entry point for ammunitions, clothing, and other supplies sent from France. By the 19th century, Portsmouth was a major East Coast center for shipbuilding and commerce. Inland, textile mills and factories producing leather goods sprouted up along the Kennebec and Merrimack Rivers. Large deposits of granite were quarried around the western part of the state near Lake Sunapee, and the pastoral Connecticut River Valley was a haven for farming.

Today, most of the textile mills have given way to high-tech firms, many of them migrating from the Boston area and its high tax rates. Indeed, the I-93 corridor up through Manchester and Concord can seem like a congested offshoot of that metropolis to the south. Yet, east or west of this major thoroughfare, in places like Durham (home to the University of New Hampshire) or Francestown, you'll still find 200-year-old Federal-style buildings lining the village green. Much to the road biker's delight, backcountry routes lead from small town to small town through covered bridges and past state forests and dairy farms.

Sounds like Vermont, right? Well, much of southern New Hampshire has that same rural appeal, but don't tell that to a New Hampshirite. This bastion of conservatism wants nothing to do with its liberal neighbor to the west. Inhabitants of the two states even fight about which state can claim Robert Frost as one of its own. He lived in both states, but he did mention that each of his poems "has something in it of New Hampshire." Perhaps even more telling is that ***Our Town,*** the classic small-town play, was based on the time that author Thorton Wilder spent in Peterborough, New Hampshire.

The lure of the outdoors has been keen in these parts since Henry David Thoreau climbed Mount Monadnock in 1858. Yet, even Thoreau couldn't believe how many hikers came before him and inscribed their initials on the peak's large boulders. Thoreau's vista from the summit of Monadnock was a web of waterways—from the Connecticut River to the west, to the Atlantic to the east—interspersed with small blue dots that suddenly become massive at places like Lake Sunapee and Lake Winnipesaukee. If the wilderness of the Whites is the green part of the state, then blue is the predominant color of southern New Hampshire. Sure, it has its share of large state parks like Pisgah and Bear Brook, but the waters in this part of the state are the main attraction. Thousands of sun worshippers flock to Hampton Beach on the Atlantic coast during summer weekends. Anglers find that hidden anchorage from which to fish on Winnipesaukee. Canoers find hundreds of lesser-known ponds, dotted across the landscape like a pointillist painting, in which to seek solitude. Even bikers head to the waters of the Connecticut River to pedal by its shores. Just don't cross the bridge into that other state. You might turn into of those yoga-lovin', granola-crunchin' liberals.

The Lay of the Land

South of the White Mountains, New Hampshire starts to soften. Sharp-edged granite is replaced by blue waters the color of cobalt or slate; 273 lakes and ponds are found in the Lakes Region, an area that begins at the Maine border and spreads west, covering much of central New Hampshire. The largest and most popular body of water is Lake Winnipesaukee, bordered by more pristine Squam Lake. Lake Sunapee, a hidden gem, lies to the west. The larger lakes sit in broad, shallow basins that were scooped out by the overwhelming force of an ice sheet.

Farther south and west, the state is quintessential New England, with undulating mountains of green, small towns, and covered bridges still standing from the mid-19th century. To the southeast are the ocean and the shoreline that connects Massachusetts to Maine.

Contrary to popular notion, fall foliage is not restricted to Vermont's borders. Leaf peeping in southern New Hampshire is just as spectacular. Color starts to appear in higher elevations during mid-September and gradually spreads south. Its peak is usually from late September through mid-October. I'd avoid Columbus Day Weekend since the traffic can be heavy and rooms are booked well in advance. The state maintains a **Fall Foliage Hotline** (☎ **800/258-3608**) that provides updated conditions.

Orientation

This chapter covers all of southern New Hampshire, from the Lakes Region southwest to the area around Mount Monadnock and southeast to the Atlantic coast. The major routes to reach the region from the south are I-95, I-93, I-89, and I-91. Interstate 95 cruises from Boston along the New Hampshire coast north to Maine, and I-93 heads from Boston north to Manchester and Concord, before skirting the western part of the Lakes Region. Take Exit 20 off I-93 and follow Route 3 to reach Weirs Beach on Lake Winnipesaukee and Holderness on Squam Lake. In Concord, I-89 veers northwest toward Lebanon and White River Junction, Vermont. This is the best way to reach the Lake Sunapee region from Boston. New Yorkers will want to cruise north on I-91 before heading east on one of the smaller routes, like Routes 4 and 104, to reach the Lakes Region.

Lake Winnipesaukee is the largest and best-known lake in the Lakes Region. Route 109 borders the eastern half of Winnipesaukee from Melvin Village to Wolfeboro. On the eastern shore of Lake Winnipesaukee, the town of **Wolfeboro** claims to be the oldest summer resort in the country. Pointed church steeples and quaint inns line the streets of this picture-postcard village. Wolfeboro's alter ego, **Weirs Beach,** is located on the western side of Winnipesaukee at the junction of Routes 3 and 11B. This is a raucous summer playland, where boardwalks and tacky amusements like go-carts, water slides, bumper cars, a large arcade, and miniature golf courses, attract families.

Smaller than Winnipesaukee is **Squam Lake** to the north and **Lake Sunapee** to the southwest. The town of Holderness is the gateway to Squam, perhaps best known as the locale for the filming of *On Golden Pond.* On Lake Sunapee, near the base of 2,743-foot Mount Sunapee, Newbury attracts a good mix of boaters and anglers. This part of the state, which is easily accessible off I-89 from Concord to Lebanon, is far less congested than the roads near Winnipesaukee.

South of Lake Sunapee are narrow roads lined with historic towns, dairy farms, and undeveloped forest. Add mountain vistas and rambling rivers and you have quintessential New England. Called the **Monadnock Region,** after the most climbed peak in New England, this rural region in the southwestern part of the state is similar to its neighbor to the west, Vermont. It has an equal amount of agrarian space and historic novelties like covered bridges and hundred-year-old white steeples. For the outdoorsperson, it's the region to head to for the best road biking and canoeing in the state.

Only 18 miles long, **New Hampshire's oceanfront,** accessible from U.S. 1 or I-95, is rarely seen by travelers heading north to the sprawling Maine coast. What drivers miss is the historical seaside city of **Portsmouth** and lively **Hampton Beach.** Settled in 1630, Portsmouth was the colonial capital and an important seaport for more than 200 years. Today, Portsmouth's maritime heritage is present in the city's architecture, from the waterfront to its historical houses and inns. At the opposite end of the spectrum and seacoast is Hampton Beach, a popular hangout for New England families during the summer. The beach is covered with suntanners on hot weekend days; and the restaurants, arcades, and shops are packed during summer nights.

Parks & Other Hot Spots

Pisgah State Park

Chesterfield, Hinsdale, Winchester. Off Rte. 63, 119, and 10. ☎ **603/239-8153.** Fishing, mountain biking.

This huge chunk of land in southwestern New Hampshire—a mere 13,500 acres—attracts outdoorsmen and -women who like their parks primitive. Expect good fishing and miles of trails for the mountain biker.

Pillsbury State Park

Washington. On Rte. 31, 3.5 miles north of Washington. ☎ **603/863-2860.** Camping, canoeing, fishing.

The string of ponds in Pillsbury State Park is a Mecca for canoers and anglers. Campers can choose from more than 30 primitive camping sites on the shores of May Pond, with additional sites accessible only by canoe. Thus, this park is one of the better places in southern New Hampshire to spend a night.

Fox State Forest

Center Rd., Hillsborough. ☎ **603/464-3453.** Biking, hiking.

A coveted treat for local bikers and walkers, these 1,793 acres of woodland feature some 20 miles of trail. There's also an environmental center and forestry museum on this former working farm.

Mount Monadnock

Off Rte. 124, 4 miles north of Jaffrey. Monadnock State Park, Jaffrey Center, NH 03454. ☎ **603/532-8862.** Hiking.

Only 3,165 feet high, Monadnock recently surpassed Mount Fuji as the most popular ascent in the world. Why is it so fashionable? Perhaps it's Monadnock's proximity to Boston (1.5 hours away) or its long history (hundreds of people from as far back as the early 1800s have inscribed their names in the boulders, prompting Thoreau, Emerson, and other writers to make the ascent). I think Monadnock's popularity has more to do with the geography of the mountain. The mountain is a *monadnock,* an isolated mountain on a plain; it offers expansive vistas of southern New Hampshire and northern Massachusetts.

Bear Brook State Park

Allenstown. Off Rte. 28, 5 miles northeast of Hooksett. ☎ **603/485-9874.** Canoeing, cross-country skiing, hiking, mountain biking, snowshoeing, swimming, wildlife watching

Close to Concord and Manchester, this 9,600-acre state park is a heavily forested playground for urbanites. There's a nature center, good hiking and mountain-biking trails, canoeing, and swimming. Come winter, many people use these woods to snowshoe and cross-country ski.

Pawtuckaway State Park

Nottingham, Raymond. 3.5 miles north of the junction of Rte. 101 and 156. ☎ **603/895-3031.** Cross-country skiing, hiking, mountain biking, swimming.

A little bit farther away than Bear Brook State Park for people in Concord and Manchester, Pawtuckaway has the same appeal. There's a 700-foot beach for swimmers and decent trails for mountain biking, hiking, and cross-country skiing.

Great Bay National Estuarine Research Reserve

Concord Rd., Durham. ☎ **603/868-1095.** Bird and wildlife watching.

With some 4,500 acres of tidal waters and wetlands and 800 surrounding upland acres, Great Bay has been designated a part of the national estuarine research system. Some 23 rare or endangered species, including the wintering bald eagle, depend on this Atlantic flyway as a refuge. It's also known for its winter smelt fishing, oystering, and waterfowl. For birdwatchers, Adams Point has several good strolls. Across the bay is the new Great Bay National Wildlife Refuge, part of the deactivated Pease Air Force Base.

Odiorne Point State Park

On 1A, south of Portsmouth. ☎ **603/436-7406.** Walking.

The only spit of undeveloped coastline in New Hampshire has quite a storied past. Scottish fishermen landed here in 1623 and created the first European settlement in the state. During World War II, Fort Dearborn, a U.S. Army base, was built on this site to protect Portsmouth Harbor from possible attack. Today, there are 300 acres of protected coastline, ideal for walkers. Interpretive panels are located throughout the park, and there is a small visitors center.

The Lakes Region

Bordering the White Mountains, the hundreds of placid waterways that make up the Lakes Region are the perfect antidote to its rough-and-tumble neighbor to the north. The centerpiece is **Lake Winnipesaukee,** 28 miles long and 13 miles wide. The lake is known for its

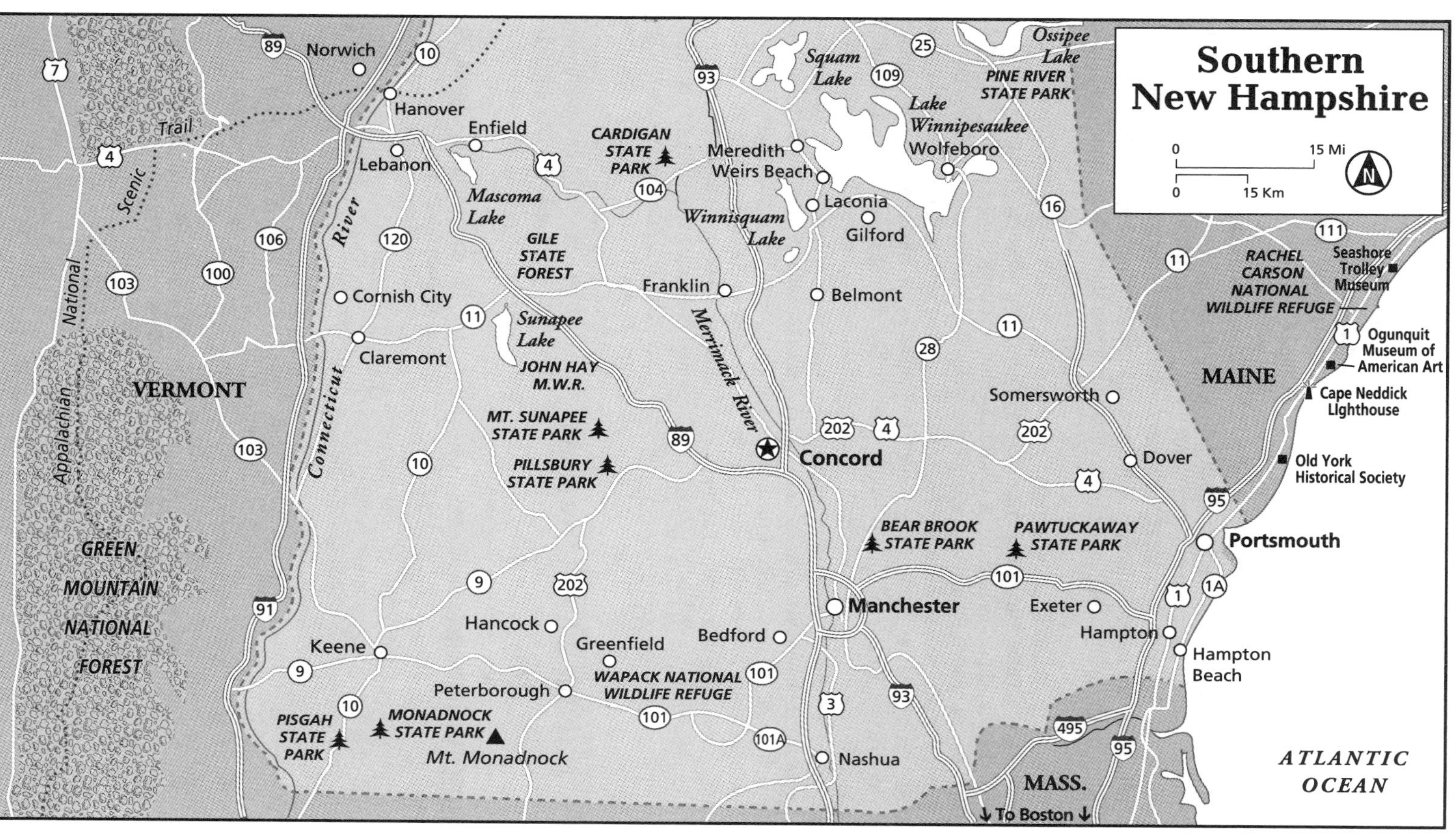

Southern New Hampshire
0 15 Mi
0 15 Km
N
Norwich
Hanover
Enfield
Lebanon
Mascoma Lake
Connecticut River
Cornish City
Claremont
VERMONT
Appalachian National Scenic Trail
GREEN MOUNTAIN NATIONAL FOREST
CARDIGAN STATE PARK
GILE STATE FOREST
Sunapee Lake
JOHN HAY M.W.R.
MT. SUNAPEE STATE PARK
PILLSBURY STATE PARK
Keene
PISGAH STATE PARK
MONADNOCK STATE PARK
Mt. Monadnock
Hancock
Peterborough
Greenfield
WAPACK NATIONAL WILDLIFE REFUGE
Bedford
Meredith
Weirs Beach
Squam Lake
Lake Winnipesaukee
Wolfeboro
Laconia
Gilford
Winnisquam Lake
Franklin
Belmont
Merrimack River
Concord
Ossipee Lake
PINE RIVER STATE PARK
Somersworth
Dover
BEAR BROOK STATE PARK
PAWTUCKAWAY STATE PARK
Manchester
Exeter
Hampton
Hampton Beach
Nashua
MASS.
To Boston
Portsmouth
MAINE
RACHEL CARSON NATIONAL WILDLIFE REFUGE
Seashore Trolley Museum
Ogunquit Museum of American Art
Cape Neddick Lighthouse
Old York Historical Society
ATLANTIC OCEAN

landlocked salmon and smallmouth bass, but anglers have to contend with pleasure boats for space and quiet.

People in search of a bit more peace head to **Squam Lake,** New Hampshire's second-largest lake, measuring about 5 by 7 miles. Much of the filming of ***On Golden Pond,*** the Academy Award–winning Fonda-Hepburn movie, took place here in 1981. Unfortunately, the lake has limited public access.

One of the best kept secrets of New Hampshire is **Lake Sunapee.** Remarkably clear, the lake is still a source of drinking water for the locals. You can swim at the beach at **Lake Sunapee State Park** (off State Route 103, 3 miles west of Newbury), launch a boat onto the sparkling clean waters, or climb Mount Sunapee for the best views of the lake. Contact the Division of Parks and Recreation, P.O. Box 1856, Concord, NH 03302 (☎ **603/271-3556;** www.nhparks.state.nh.us/), for more information.

What to Do & Where to Do It

BIRD WATCHING

On the coast, State Route 1A from Seabrook to Portsmouth is home to many tidal estuaries and saltwater marshes and, thus, migratory shorebirds. **Seabrook Harbor** is a good locale for year-round birding. In July and August, Roseate, Forster's, and common terns can be seen. In September, look for plovers, killdeer, whimbrels, ruddy turnstones, sanderlings, and several kinds of sandpipers. Migrating waterfowl include common loons, common goldeneyes, buffleheads, and common and red-breasted mergansers.

The rocky shore of **Odiorne Point State Park** in Portsmouth is a good place to see ring-billed and black-backed gulls feeding. Watch for double-crested cormorants on the rocks, drying their wings. In the wintertime, see rafts of eiders, scoters, and other sea ducks. During spring and fall migrations, observe shorebirds, warblers, and songbirds.

The 5,280-acre **Great Bay Estuary** is a complex embankment on the New Hampshire–Maine border composed of the Piscataqua River, Little Bay, and Great Bay. Ocean tides and river runoff mix 15 miles inland from the Atlantic Ocean in Durham, making Great Bay one of the most recessed estuaries in the nation. The Reserve's estuarine salt marshes, estuarine waters, and uplands are utilized by 281 species of birds. Among the more common are ospreys, American black ducks, double-crested cormorants, and great blue herons. Winter migration includes the Canada goose, bufflehead, common goldeneye, American black duck, mallard, red-breasted merganser, and bald eagle. Seabirds (such as cormorants and gulls) are common year-round within Great Bay. The common tern can be found in Great Bay in the spring and summer. Waterfowl are most abundant in the estuary during the fall and winter months. The refuge is also an excellent place to see and hear wild turkeys throughout the year.

The 82-acre **Adams Point Wildlife Management Area** in Durham is arguably the finest spot on Great Bay from which to view bald eagles in the winter. Use the platform near the parking area. Adams Point also provides great vantage points from which to observe a variety of waterfowl and shorebirds. In summer, you may see snowy egrets, great blue herons, glossy ibises, and greater yellowlegs. The marsh and field areas provide nesting and forage for many songbirds, including song sparrows, bobolinks, and a variety of warblers. From autumn through spring, watch for greater scaup, Canada geese, common goldeneyes, mallards, American black ducks, buffleheads, and red-breasted mergansers.

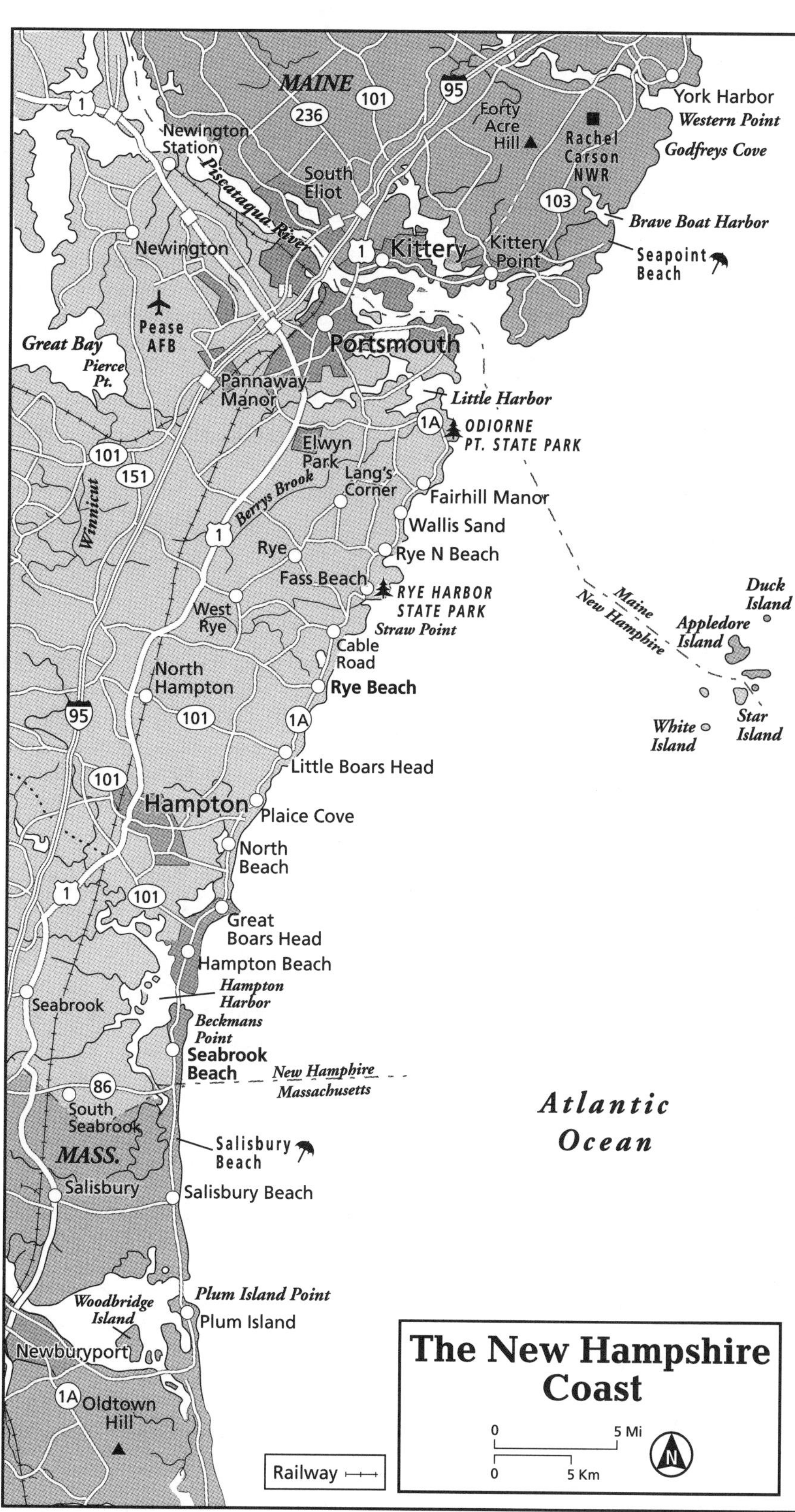
MAINE
York Harbor
Western Point
Godfreys Cove
Forty Acre Hill
Rachel Carson NWR
Brave Boat Harbor
Seapoint Beach
Newington Station
Piscataqua River
South Eliot
Kittery
Kittery Point
Newington
Pease AFB
Great Bay
Pierce Pt.
Portsmouth
Pannaway Manor
Little Harbor
ODIORNE PT. STATE PARK
Elwyn Park
Berrys Brook
Lang's Corner
Fairhill Manor
Wallis Sand
Winnicut
Rye
Rye N Beach
Fass Beach
RYE HARBOR STATE PARK
West Rye
Straw Point
Cable Road
Maine
New Hampshire
Duck Island
Appledore Island
White Island
Star Island
North Hampton
Rye Beach
Little Boars Head
Hampton
Plaice Cove
North Beach
Great Boars Head
Hampton Beach
Hampton Harbor
Seabrook
Beckmans Point
Seabrook Beach
New Hampshire
Massachusetts
South Seabrook
MASS.
Salisbury Beach
Salisbury
Salisbury Beach
Atlantic Ocean
Woodbridge Island
Plum Island Point
Plum Island
Newburyport
Oldtown Hill
Railway
The New Hampshire Coast
0
5 Mi
0
5 Km
N

Nearby, the 400-acre **Bellamy Wildlife Management Area** in Dover is a significant feeding and resting area for migrating waterfowl in fall and winter. Species seen include the black duck, mallard, and Canada goose. Watch for bald eagles in the winter. The agricultural land provides habitat for many field-dependent songbirds such as bobolinks, indigo buntings, and field sparrows. Summer brings red-tailed hawks and ospreys.

Six miles offshore, double-crested cormorants, common eiders, great black-backed gulls, and black guillemots nest on the **Isles of Shoals.** Visitors to the Shoals can also look for seabirds such as Manx shearwaters, Wilson's storm-petrels, black-legged kittiwakes, dovekies, thick-billed murres, and razorbills. During fall and spring migration, you are likely to see a variety of warblers such as Wilson's, hooded, orange-crowned, mourning, and Cape May. You can arrange boat trips to the islands with the **Isles of Shoals Steamship Company,** Market St., Portsmouth, NH 03801 (☎ **603/431-5500,** or 800/441-4620 outside New Hampshire, 800/894-5509 inside the state).

At the **Ponemoh Bay Wildlife Sanctuary,** near Milford, a 3-acre pond is surrounded by oak and pitch-pine woods. Bird life in the sanctuary includes rufous-sided towhees, blue jays, tree swallows, common yellowthroats, mourning and Canada warblers, and song sparrows. Watch for green herons and other waterfowl, woodpeckers, and belted kingfishers.

Amherst is home to the 21-acre natural wetland **Minot J. Ross Bird Sanctuary.** Heading west, the **John Hay National Wildlife Refuge** is a 1-mile stretch of shoreline on Lake Sunapee, north of the town of Newbury. This former estate of John Hay, ambassador to Great Britain and personal secretary of Abraham Lincoln, and the immediate grounds, known as "The Fells," are ideal for migratory birds. The John Hay II Forest Ecology Trail offers a self-guided walk through mature mixed hardwood conifer forest and along the shore of Lake Sunapee.

Cedar waxwings, bobolinks, and American goldfinches are some of the species found in the **Lakes Region.** For more information, contact the **Audubon Society of New Hampshire** (☎ **603/224-9909;** www.nhaudubon.org).

BOARDSAILING

Winni Sailboarder's School & Outlet, 687 Union Ave., Laconia (☎ **603/528-4110**), offer lessons and rentals on Lake Opechee. **Mount Sunapee State Park,** Rte. 103, Newbury (☎ **603/763-2356**), gives instruction on the lake.

CANOEING

With so many lakes and ponds to choose from in southern New Hampshire, you should have no problem finding a great paddling spot within 30 minutes of your home base. Here are several of my favorites:

Hubbard Pond

North of Rindge. Access: From the junction of Rte. 119 and 202, head east on Rte. 119 for 1.2 miles and turn left onto Cathedral Rd. At 2.4 miles later, turn right into Annett State Forest to reach the northern shores of Hubbard Pond. Park by a small dam.

In the summer months, a Boy Scout Camp on this 250-acre pond wreaks havoc on the quietude of this hidden waterway. Come fall, however, the kiddies are gone, the maples are rich in color, and there's a splendid view of Mount Monadnock to the northwest. With many inlets and islands, you can easily spend a day paddling around the pond. You'll be sharing the waters with herons, ducks, turtles, and beaver who like to hang in the thick marsh. Except for the Boy Scout Camp, the lake is undeveloped, adding to its primitive appeal. There's no camping on the pond.

LOONY OVER LOONS

Long a hallmark of New Hampshire's lakes, loons soared to national prominence in the 1980s when they essentially starred with Henry Fonda and Katherine Hepburn in the movie *On Golden Pond,* which was filmed on Squam Lake. The echoes of the loon were heard and seen on a good portion of the movie's footage. The Audubon Society of New Hampshire estimates that there are now some 500 loons in the state. That's more than double the population of the bird over the last 30 years, but the Loon Preservation Committee still feels that the loon is in great danger. Over the last several years, many of the birds have perished from swallowing lead sinkers that anglers have left in the water. Loons survive by swallowing fish whole. They then scour lake bottoms for pebbles, which they use to grind up the fish in their stomachs. But apparently loons are mistaking the sinkers for pebbles, grinding those up along with the fish. Once in the bloodstream, the lead attacks the bird's nervous system. The loon becomes uncoordinated and weak, unable to feed itself and fly, eventually starving to death. If you love to hear that crazed laugh of the loon echoing across an empty lake, a sound cherished by most outdoorsmen and -women, then throw away your lead. A new law that took effect on January 1, 2000, bans the use of lead sinkers and jigs in New Hampshire's freshwater lakes and ponds.

Willard Pond

North of Hancock. Access: From the intersection of Rte. 123 and 137 in Hancock, head northwest on Rte. 123 for about 3 miles. Turn right on an unmarked road and you'll reach the southern end of the pond in 1.5 miles.

Part of a wildlife preserve owned by the Audubon Society of New Hampshire, the 100-acre Willard Pond is the perfect place to while away a couple of hours in early morning or late afternoon. Gasoline-powered boats are prohibited, and the body of water is fly-fishing only; so if there's more than you and the birds here, I'll be shocked. Bring your binoculars and you might spot a pair of nesting loons, warblers, or a slew of songbirds. The heavily forested shores are laced with birch, beech, white pine, red oak, and red maple; and the water is as clear as gin, helping to create one of the most pristine spots in southern New Hampshire.

Pillsbury State Park

North of Washington. Access: Take Rte. 31 north for 2 miles and you'll see the entrance to Pillsbury State Park on your right. Park near Butterfield Pond.

Pillsbury State Park and its string of four ponds provide one of the best overnight canoe jaunts in southern New Hampshire. Start your paddle on the southern end of Butterfield Pond, near a dam, and proceed west through a narrow, rocky inlet into May Pond. Over 30 primitive campsites on May Pond are ideally set on the forested shores of the water. Contact Pillsbury State Park (☎ **603/863-2860**) for reservations. You can continue on your journey by portage to the smaller Mill Pond and another short carry to the most remote of the waterways, North Pond. Cranberry bushes and other heaths line the shoreline, attracting a large variety of birdlife.

Grafton Pond

East of Enfield Center. Access: Take Rte. 4A 2.2 miles south of Enfield Center and veer left onto Bluejay Rd. Drive 0.8 mile and turn right onto Grafton Pond Rd. Drive another 0.8 mile and turn right to reach the dam in 0.2 mile. A boat ramp and small parking lot are here.

Bring your fishing pole to this 235-acre jewel of a pond and you're bound to catch your share of pickerel, smallmouth bass, and perch. While waiting for a tug on the line, enjoy the views of this remote outpost. The shores are lined with firs, white pine, and hemlocks; and the rocky islands have grassy picnic sites for your lunch. Bird lovers might find nesting loons, wood ducks, ospreys, and great blue herons.

White Oak Pond

East of Holderness. Access: From Holderness, take Rte. 3 west for 1.8 miles and turn right onto College Rd. You'll spot a small boat ramp and parking area.

Squam Lake might have seemed enchanting in the movie ***On Golden Pond,*** but there's a good deal of development on the shoreline and motorboat traffic in summer can be fairly heavy. Thus, my choice for placid retreat in the highly developed Lakes Region goes to White Oak Pond, due south of Squam Lake. The 291-acre waterway prohibits motorboats larger than 7.5 horsepower, and the dozen or so houses on the pond have canoe racks, not powerboats. Paddle to the mostly undeveloped eastern shores of the lake through the cattails and thick marsh habitat, which is lined on the wooded shores with maple, oak, and pine. Don't be surprised to find loons, warblers, and marsh wrens lounging in the lake.

White Lake

North of West Ossipee. Access: From West Ossipee, take Rte. 16 north for 1.5 miles and you'll see signs for White Lake State Park.

White Lake State Park is an ideal spot for young families in midsummer. There's a white sandy beach and plenty of shallow water for toddlers. More than 180 campsites (some of which sit on the water) are available, and the 120-acre round lake is fun to paddle on. There's also a trail that goes around the perimeter of the lake where blueberries are in season come August. The trail leads to a large stand of pitch pines on the northwestern part of the lake. Canoeing is fairly easy with the forested shores blocking the wind and the lake being shallow.

CROSS-COUNTRY SKIING

In the Backcountry

All the relatively flat rail trails (see "Mountain Biking," below) are excellent cross-country skiing runs in the winter. Here are several other good backcountry trails in southern New Hampshire:

Bear Brook State Park

Allow 2 hr. Easy; a web of cross-country trails through this large state park. Access: Take Exit 13 off I-93 and continue on Rte. 3 south and Rte. 28 north to Allenstown. Travel 3 miles to the entrance of the park, where you turn right and drive 3.2 miles to Podunk Rd. A right on Podunk Rd. and you'll be at the skier parking area in 0.3 mile.

Situated just outside of Concord, 9,600-acre Bear Brook State Park offers a heavily forested retreat when there's snow on the ground. The circular blue signs and arrows will direct you on a variety of trails that make up a 5-mile loop. Weave through a forest of pine, birch, beech, and red oak as you skirt Archery Pond. The trails are a bit hilly at the end, but it's a good go for novice to intermediate skiers.

Heald Pond Trail

Allow 1 hr. Easy; 2-mile loop near the shores of a pond. Access: From Peterborough, take Rte. 101 east to Rte. 31 south. Turn right and after 2.5 miles turn right onto King Brook Rd. Travel 0.9 mile and turn left on Kimball Rd. and then a quick right onto Heald Rd. Continue for 0.3 mile and park just after you see the sign for the Heald Tract. The Pond Trail is across the road from the parking area.

A worthy introduction to nature in southern New Hampshire in winter, the yellow-blazed Pond Trail has 25 markers that point out bushes and trees like white pine, red maple, hemlock, red oak, and mountain laurel. The trail skirts Heald Pond before heading into an open field and returning back to the woods.

Pisgah State Park

Allow as much time as you need. Moderate to strenuous; choose from a variety of trails in this large state park. Access: From Exit 3 off I-91 in Vermont, take Rte. 9 east for 6 miles and turn right on Rte. 63. Travel about 4.5 miles to the Kilburn Rd. trailhead into the park.

With more than 13,500 acres, Pisgah is the largest state park in New Hampshire. What this means for the cross-country skier and mountain biker is a seemingly countless number of trails that will leave you lost in the woods. That includes the 6-mile Kilburn Loop around Kilburn Pond. For more experienced skiers, this rolling narrow trail is an up and down jaunt that snakes through a dark forest of evergreens. If you do the loop in a clockwise fashion, the end of the trail will be a fairly level ski along the shores of the pond.

Nordic Skiing Centers

Gunstock Cross-Country Center, P.O. Box 1307, Laconia, NH 03247 (☎ **603/293-4341;** www.gunstock.com); and **Nordic Skier,** 79 N. Main St., Wolfeboro, NH 03894 (☎ **603/569-3151;** www.wolfeboroxc.org/ski); offer 42 kilometers (26.25 miles) and 25 kilometers (15.6 miles), respectively, of groomed trails close to the shores of Lake Winnipesaukee.

The Lake Sunapee Country Club becomes the **Norsk Cross-Country Ski Center,** New London, NH (☎ **603/526-4685;** www.skinorsk.com), in the winter. The center features some 70 kilometers (43.75 miles) of groomed trails, the majority appropriate for the intermediate skier. As the name implies, the Cascade Brook Trail parallels a cascading stream on its way to a warming hut some 3 miles from the center.

For more information on New Hampshire's cross-country ski centers, contact **Ski New Hampshire** (☎ **800/887-5464;** www.skinh.com).

DOWNHILL SKIING

For years now, Bostonians have been taking I-89 through southern New Hampshire to get to such ski resorts as Stratton and Mount Snow in southeastern Vermont. That all changed in the summer of 1998 when Tim and Diane Mueller, owners of Okemo Mountain Resort in Ludlow, Vermont, acquired a 40-year lease on southern New Hampshire's only big-league ski mountain, Mount Sunapee.

Mount Sunapee

Rte. 103, Newbury, NH 03255. ☎ **603/763-2356;** www.mountsunapee.com. 50 trails (13 novice, 24 intermediate, 13 expert); 9 lifts including 2 quads and 2 triples; 1,510- ft. vertical drop. Full-day adult tickets are $44 weekend, $39 weekday.

The Sunapee region was once a major summer resort. Trains from Boston connected with steamboats on the lake to bring guests to a half-dozen big hotels. Now it looks like the area is going to be popular year-round. Over the past 2 years, the Muellers have invested over $6 million to add three new quad lifts, new skiing terrain, and increased snowmaking capacity. Tackle the Sun Bowl in the morning on the Goose Bumps or Flying Goose Trail and then take the Sunbowl Quad to the summit. Only 2,743 feet high, Sunapee is still the highest mountain in this part of New Hampshire. Atop the peak, you can make out the ski trails to the southeast at Ascutney, Okemo, Stratton, even Killington on a clear day. Directly below, Lake Sunapee stretches to the north punctuated by the peaks of Mount Cardigan and Mount Kearsarge.

Novices can take the 2-mile Ridge Trail off the summit; intermediates and experts can try the new glade skiing at the Summit Glades. Another good cruising trail is the new Lynx off the North Peak Triple.

Ragged Mountain
Danbury, NH. ☎ **603/768-3600;** www.ragged-mt.com. 40 trails (12 novice, 16 intermediate, 12 expert); 5 lifts including 2 triples and 3 doubles; 1,250-ft. vertical drop. Full-day tickets $38 weekends, $23 weekdays.

With an old New England–style base lodge—white clapboard building with dormers, multipaned windows, and shutters—Ragged retains the feel of yesteryear. But don't expect slow-moving lifts and little terrain. Brothers Al and Walter Endriunas have poured more than $6 million into the ski area, expanding the terrain to include adjacent Spear Mountain and modernizing the lifts. With the majority of the runs in the middle-of-the-road range, the ski resort, less than a 2-hour drive from Boston, is a great place to challenge the family. The appeal is decidedly low-key.

Gunstock
Rte. 11A, Gilford, NH 03247. ☎ **800/GUNSTOCK;** www.gunstock.com. 45 trails (6 novice, 28 intermediate, 11 expert); 7 lifts including 1 quad and 2 triples; 1,400-ft. vertical drop. Full-day tickets $42 weekends, $30 Tues–Fri, $20 Mon.

Owned by Belknap County, Gunstock's affordability has made it one of the most popular ski areas in New Hampshire. The view doesn't hurt either. Atop the summit, Gunstock treats you to a panorama of Lake Winnipesaukee. If you're intimidated by the crags of northern neighbors Cannon and Wildcat, you'll like the wide cruisers at Gunstock. Trails like Recoil and Gunsmoke have woodsy and wide layouts that are ideal for the whole family. The other side of the mountain features Tiger's blue-black steeps and two faster cruisers, Stonebar and Redhat. Look at the other skiers and you'll realize that anything goes. You'll find hotdoggers, telemarkers, snowboarders, ski jumpers—plenty of opportunity for cross-training. No wonder it's been a local favorite for, oh, some 63 years.

Pat's Peak
Henniker, NH 03247. ☎ **603/428-3245;** www.patspeak.com. 20 trails (8 novice, 6 intermediate, 6 expert); 7 lifts including 1 quad and 2 triples; 710-ft. vertical drop. Full-day tickets $39 weekends, $25 weekdays.

Located less than 30 minutes from Concord and 45 minutes from Manchester, Pat's Peak is one of the state's most accessible learn-to-ski-and-snowboard mountains. Three separate beginner areas introduce kids to the sport, and a new chairlift takes you to the 1,402-foot summit in under 4.5 minutes. To challenge more-experienced skiers and snowboarders, two new glade trails were cut last summer between the Hurricane and Tornado Trails.

For more information on any of the ski resorts in New Hampshire, contact **Ski New Hampshire** (☎ **800/887-5463;** www.skinh.com). They provide a ski map and help with trip planning.

FISHING

With so many lakes and ponds, the freshwater fishing in southern New Hampshire is superlative. In **Lake Sunapee** a large quantity of trout and salmon find a home in a scattering of basins more than 125 feet deep. Troll between Blodgett Landing and Georges Mills along the northeast shore, near Herrick Cove, and you're bound to get lucky. This is especially true in late May and early June before the water gets too hot. Nearby, Pleasant Lake is known for its abundance of lake trout, brook trout, and smallmouth bass.

Southwest of Sunapee, the **Sugar River** flows for 35 miles, dumping into the Connecticut in Ascutney, Vermont. This is top-notch trout water as are the tributaries Grandy Brook, Redwater Brook, and Quabbinnight Brook. The upper half of the river from Sunapee to Newport is fast water with native brook trout. Popular spots are along Routes 11 and 103. The southern portion of the river, near Claremont, is well-stocked with brookies, rainbows, and browns.

Winnipesaukee is the big kahuna of all fishing spots in New Hampshire. The lake produces large numbers of legal-sized salmon. The public docks on the lake (Glendale, Alton, Meredith, Wolfeboro, and Weirs Beach) are all excellent early-season locales for rainbow trout. Look for spawning white perch near the Long Island Bridge. If you want to go crazy catching smallies in late May, head to the Wolfeboro section of the lake.

Dwarfed by Winnipesaukee, its large neighbor to the north, **Merrymeeting Lake** in New Durham also has good deep water. Anglers can catch togue, perch, and salmon here. Bass anglers head farther south to the 900-acre Pawtuckaway Pond in Pawtuckaway State Park, which has good camping facilities.

The **Merrimack River** from Bristol to Concord is fly-fishing-only territory for Atlantic salmon broodstocks that range upward of 10 pounds. Daily-catch limit is one fish of at least 15 inches, with a five-per-season limit. East of Concord in East Barrington, the **Islinglass River** stocks some large brownies along the stretch of water that runs from Bow Lake through East Barrington to the Cocheco River.

Surf-cast on the coast from May through the fall for stripers while bluefish peak in August. If you have a boat, head up the Piscataqua River on the border between New Hampshire and Maine, where the rip is big, deep, and hard flowing. For charters, contact the **Atlantic Fleet,** Rye Harbor Marina, State Rte. 1A, Rye, NH 03870 (**☎ 603-964-5220;** www.atlanticwhalewatch.com), to cast for salt-water fish. Anglers on their 70-foot party boat reel in cod, pollocks, and haddock. In Hampton Beach, **Smith & Gilmore** (**☎ 603/926-3503;** www.smithandgilmore.com) offer a variety of deep-sea fishing trips off the coast of New Hampshire and into the Gulf of Maine. They fish for cod, haddock, pollock, striped bass, and bluefish.

For an information packet and nonresident license application for fishing in New Hampshire, contact the **New Hampshire Fish and Game Department,** 2 Hazen Drive, Concord, NH 03301 (**☎ 603/272-3421;** www.wildlife.state.nh.us).

GOLF

Consistently rated one of the top golf courses in the state by *Golf Digest* and other golfing publications, the **Shattuck Inn Golf Club** (**☎ 603/532-4443**) is situated on the mountainous slopes of Monadnock in the town of Jaffrey. All golfers, regardless of level, will find the par-71 course extremely challenging. Two more golf courses in the southern part of the state that are worth playing are nearby **Ragged Mountain Ski & Golf Resort** (**☎ 603/768-3600**) in Danbury, where the eighth hole offers great views of Mount Washington and the Presidential Range, and the oceanside **Portsmouth Country Club** (**☎ 603/436-9719**) in Greenland. The **Country Club of New Hampshire** (**☎ 603/927-4246**), a rarely crowded gem in North Sutton in western part of the state, is also a good choice.

HANG GLIDING

Located on Route 12 in western New Hampshire, **Morningside Flight Park,** P.O. Box 109, Claremont, NH 03743 (**☎ 603/542-4416;** www.flymorningside.com), is the best place to learn how to hang glide in the Northeast. The 250-foot hill gently slopes to a big bull's-eye painted in the landing area, used for students to practice their spot landings. The hill is wide enough to accommodate 20 gliders side by side. Certified instruction is available by reservation only. Prices start at $100 for a 4-hour bunny slope lesson.

HIKING

Obviously, the Whites to the north reign supreme, but southern New Hampshire can boast a handful of great hikes. It'll even throw in some history.

Mount Monadnock

4 miles round-trip. Allow 3 hr. Easy to moderate. Access: Follow State Rte. 124 West through Jaffrey Center and look for the signs for the Monadnock State Park headquarters. The trailhead is located in front of the visitors center. Map: Ask one of the rangers when you drive in to the state park.

Mount Monadnock has been a popular ascent since the early 1800s. Indeed, Monadnock has recently surpassed Japan's Mount Fuji as the most-hiked mountain in the world. The rocky summit can be as crowded as Hampton Beach on a clear day. Yet, standing only 3,165 feet high, Monadnock is the perfect introduction to mountain climbing—high enough to give you a sense of accomplishment, short enough to inspire you to bag another New Hampshire peak.

The well-trodden **White Dot Path** rises above the tree line less than 45 minutes after leaving the State Park visitors center. Southern New Hampshire and northern Massachusetts are a bed of green, accentuated by the sporadic hill or small pond. This view sharply differs from Thoreau's vista of endless pasture and little hardwoods when he made the ascent in 1858 and 1860. Leave the dusty trail behind and start to meander up Monadnock's rocky slope to the bald peak. The view from the summit is a spectacular panorama of New Hampshire's far less precipitous lower half. Thousands of names are inscribed in the summit rocks from as far back as 1801, representing one of the earliest examples of American graffiti. This abuse greatly annoyed Thoreau. "Several [visitors] were busy engraving their names on the rocks with cold chisels, whose incessant click you heard, and they had but little leisure to look off." However, this didn't stop Thoreau from writing in large letters atop a massive rock, "H.D.T. ate gorp here, 1860." Just kidding. You can return on the same trail or try the steeper **White Cross Trail** to complete the loop.

Belknap Mountain

1.5 miles round-trip. Allow 2 hr. Easy. Access: At Guilford, turn right off Rte. 11A and head south through the village. The road curves all the way around to the base of Belknap. If the gate is closed at the bottom, park just outside and start hiking on the red blazes (this makes the trail almost twice as long). If the gate is open, continue upward to a level parking lot.

With a vertical rise of only 740 feet, Belknap was the first summit my 4-year-old Jake ever bagged. The red-blazed trail left the road, snaking into a forest of pines. We had our first view of the Lakes Region as we started to ascend some large boulders. Jake gripped the large rocks and pulled himself upward but grew tired quickly, so I had to carry him a bit. At last, we were on the peak, eating our apples and looking at Lake Winnipesaukee in its entirety. "Wow!" Jake exclaimed, "we're higher than the clouds." Not quite, but for such a short hike, Belknap whets a preschooler's appetite to climb more mountains.

Red Hill

3.5 miles (round-trip). Allow 2 hr. Easy. Access: From Center Harbor on the northern shores of Lake Winnipesaukee, take Bean Rd. for 1.5 miles to the sign for Red Hill Forest. Turn right and drive 1.25 miles to the parking area and trailhead. Map: USGS 7.5-min. Center Harbor.

The trail up Red Hill is rather plain and uninteresting. A former wagon trail, the dry, wide path is a steady uphill climb, slowly curving as you begin to reach the top. The surrounding red oaks are charred and leafless near the summit, a result of forest fires, the most recent in 1990. Thus, nothing prepares you for the sight you'll see 1.75 miles and less than an hour later when you pass the fire warden's cabin sitting atop the peak. The western shores of Lake Winnipesaukee gleam under the slopes of Mount Major and Belknap Mountain. Climb the four flights of stairs to the top of the fire tower, for, arguably, the most spectacular view of the Lakes Region. Winnipesaukee can be seen in its entirety. To your right, smaller Squam Lake sits below Rattlesnake Mountain. Behind you is the village of Sandwich and the Sandwich Range, the southernmost tip of the White Mountains. On your left are the mountains of the Ossipee Range. Everywhere you turn, each view of mountains and lakes seems more stunning than the last. Who would have thought that such a dull, short ascent would reward you with one of the most incredible views in New Hampshire?

Blue Job Mountain

1 mile round-trip. Allow 1 hr. Easy. Access: From Rochester, take Rte. 202A west and continue on Crown Point Rd. as Rte. 202A bears left to Center Strafford. Drive for 0.5 mile to Strafford Corner and continue another 5 miles when you start to see Blue Job topped by the tower on your right. Across from a farmhouse on the left, park before a locked gate leading into a blueberry field. There are no trail signs, but you'll follow the service lines into Blue Job's forest.

For young hikers who want to relish the rewards of climbing a mountain without working too hard, we bring you Blue Job Mountain. The drive to the trailhead leaves you at an elevation around 1,000 feet, so it's just another 356 feet of hiking before reaching Blue Job's summit and fire tower. Enter into a forest of oak and bear right (the trail to the left leads to blueberry bushes), following the gradual path. Circle around the knob of a mountain through spruce and pine. Soon you'll arrive at the warden's cabin and the fire tower. Climb the tower; on a clear day, the views are magnificent. Because of Blue Job's remoteness, you have unobstructed vistas to Mount Washington to the north and the Atlantic Ocean to the east. Your children will thank you.

Mount Kearsarge

2 miles round-trip. Allow 1–2 hr. Easy to moderate. Access: Take Exit 10 off I-89 and turn right onto Warner Rd. About 3 miles later, you'll see signs for the Winslow State Park picnic area, where the trail starts.

Not to be confused with the 3,268-foot Kearsarge North Mountain between Conway and Jackson, Mount Kearsarge is a 2,931-foot peak east of Lake Sunapee. The Northside Trail takes you through a forest of spruces and white birches before ascending rocky ledges up to the summit. Climb the tower for views of Lake Sunapee and Mount Cardigan. The peak is also a favorite of hang gliders who jump off and land down at the picnic area.

Lake Solitude

4–7 miles round-trip. Allow 3 hr. Easy. Access: From Newbury and the southern end of Lake Sunapee, follow Rte. 103 South for 1 mile to Mountain Rd. Turn right for 1.2 miles; there's a small parking area and trail sign on the right. Map: USGS 7.5 × 15-min. Newport.

Lake Solitude is an apt name for the lonely lake that sits on the slopes of Mount Sunapee, isolated by a thick forest from the rest of the world. There are no crowded beaches here—just the occasional frog jumping from lily pad to lily pad. To reach the lake, you need to climb 2 miles on the soft, gradual **Andrew Brook Trail.** Beeches and birches soon give way to the fragrant smell of spruces and firs. Sun starts to seep through as the forest opens up onto the shores of this quiet lake. You can continue around the lake and up the White Ledges on the orange-blazed trail to the peak of Sunapee. Add 3 miles and 2 more hours for this round-trip. Since the aerial tram brings throngs of tourists to the summit, I prefer to stop at Solitude, cool off in the icy waters, and return on the same trail.

The sound of one person swimming in a large lake is as peaceful as the sound of one hand clapping.

Mount Cardigan

3.5 miles round-trip. Allow 3 hr. Easy to moderate. Access: From the intersection of Rte. 4 and 118 in Canaan, head north on Rte. 118 and soon take a right onto a road to Orange. Keep to the right at the fork onto Grafton Rd. for 0.8 mile until you reach another fork. Turn left at the entrance to Cardigan State Park and continue 0.5 mile to the parking area and picnic tables.

The wind whipping around Cardigan's bare rock dome is a good indication of what's to come farther north in the Whites when you tackle the Presidential Range. Hikers have been climbing up Cardigan for almost as long as they've been hiking up Monadnock. Take the West Ridge Trail across two springs as you delve deeper into the woods. About 0.75 miles up, you'll pass the **South Ridge Trail,** which you'll be descending. Continue on the **West Ridge Trail** as it starts to climb over the rocky ledges. Soon you'll reach the solid rock summit with views north to the Franconia Notch and east to Lake Winnipesaukee. Pass the small cabin atop the peak to take the South Ridge Trail down, which offers great views to the south. The trail meets up with the West Ridge Trail and back to the parking lot.

HORSEBACK RIDING

Gunstock Mountain in Gilford (☎ **800/GUNSTOCK**) offers 1- to 2-hour rides on cross-country ski trails from its Cobble Mountain Stables. Nearby, **Castle Springs,** Route 171, Moultonborough (☎ **800/729-2468**), features horseback rides in the hills over Lake Winnipesaukee. Closer to Concord, **Hardscrabble Farm** in Belmont (☎ **603/267-7065**) and **24 Carrot Horse Farm** in Raymond (☎ **207/698-9989**) both offer rides.

ICE FISHING

Come early February in Meredith, more than 7,000 anglers head out on iced-over Lake Winnipesaukee to take part in the Great Rotary Fishing Derby (☎ **603/279-7200**). Drill your hole in the 22-inch-thick ice, put up your bobhouse, and start jigging. Catch the largest speckled lake trout, fat-bellied yellow perch, toothy green pickerel, white perch, or cusp, and you might be headed home with your new 90-horsepower fishing boat. Some $50,000 in prizes are awarded.

Besides Winnipesaukee, the other big lakes popular for ice fishing are Winnisquam, Squam, and Sunapee. For additional information, contact the **New Hampshire Fish and Game Department,** 2 Hazen Drive, Concord, NH 03301 (☎ **603/272-3421;** www.wildlife.state.nh.us).

MOUNTAIN BIKING

Open up a southern New Hampshire map and you'll notice the numerous green circles across the state, indicating state forests and parks. A web of trails weaves through more than 50,000 acres of unspoiled hardwood forest. Add the numerous rail trails, all branches of the Boston & Maine Railroad, and you have trails for every level of mountain biker.

Pawtuckaway State Park

10–15 miles. Allow 2 hr. Easy to moderate. Access: Take Exit 5 off Rte. 101 and head north on Rte. 156 for 1.5 miles. Turn left on Mountain Rd., and 1 mile later you'll see the entrance to the park on the left.

Because of its proximity to Concord and Manchester, Pawtuckaway is one of the most popular places in the state to ride. With very little elevation change and a network of dirt roads, it's also a great place for novice riders to get lost in the 5,500-acre woods. From the ranger station, turn right and follow the paved road for a mile, before bearing left on the

Fundy Trail. This relatively easy dirt road crosses a wooden bridge past a wetland. Turn left at the T onto Shaw Trail for a bit more of a challenge. This double track is a series of steep ups and downs obstructed by rocks and the occasional high water. Follow it to the more moderate Mountain Trail to loop back home.

Bear Brook State Park

Up to 40 miles of trails. Allow as much time as necessary. Easy to strenuous. Access: From Concord, take Rte. 3 south and turn left in Suncook on Rte. 28. Follow it for 3 miles into Allenstown. Turn right on Deerfield Rd. Follow the signs to the park entrance.

Only a few miles from Concord, 9,600-acre Bear Brook State Park is another fat-wheelin' hot spot. The park features more than 40 miles of trails from the easy 4-mile Podunk Road to the more strenuous Hall Mountain Trail, which ascends the tree-covered peak of Hall Mountain. In the western part of the park, the Catamount Trail is a rock-littered single track with tight corners that will challenge any decent mountain biker.

Rockingham Recreational Trail

25 miles (one-way). Allow 5–6 hr. Easy. Access: Take Exit 7 off I-93 onto Rte. 101 East. Take Exit 1 off Rte. 101 and head south on Rte. 28. Proceed around a rotary (traffic circle) and turn left into a parking lot at Lake Massabesic.

Just outside Manchester's city limits is the longest rail trail in the state, the 25-mile Rockingham Recreational Path. Once part of the Boston & Maine Railroad, the trail runs east of Manchester to within a couple miles of the Atlantic Ocean. Note that motorized traffic like ATVs are allowed on the trail, so the best time to avoid the hum is on a weekday. Starting from the west, the trail follows the shoreline of Lake Massabesic. At the 5-mile mark, you venture through the first of three short tunnels, becoming more secluded as you make your way to Onway Lake. Pass through a narrow granite corridor and then another tunnel before arriving at Raymond, the halfway point. This is a good place to have a snack before continuing onward. On the second half of the ride, you cross a large old railroad bridge and are soon pedaling along the Lamprey River. You cross several rural highways before arriving in the town of Epping. The last 2 miles of the trail through Newfields are a peaceful jaunt through meadows and woods before ending at an abandoned railroad depot.

Mason Railroad Trail

7 miles (one-way). Allow 2 hr. Easy. Access: From Massachusetts, take I-495 to Rte. 119 northwest to Townsend. Continue west toward West Townsend, veering right at a sign that points to Mason, NH. In 1.5 miles, veer right at the fork and head 1 mile to the Massachusetts–New Hampshire border. A gravel parking lot is located on the left side of the road. From the parking area, head uphill 0.3 mile on Morse Rd. You will see an orange gate on the left.

The 7-mile Mason Trail was once a branch of the Boston & Maine Railroad until the line was abandoned in the late 1970s. Local lore has it that Henry David Thoreau took the railroad on his way to climb Mount Monadnock. Now you can take this route on two wheels on the way to Pratt Pond. The trail starts in a forest of pine, oak, maple, and birch before traveling slightly uphill. The trail gets wider as you continue uphill past large granite slabs, remnants of a granite industry that once flourished in these parts. After passing Sand Pit Road at the 4-mile mark, the road gets sandy and narrows. Two miles later, you reach the rocky shores of Pratt Pond, shaded by thickets of white pine. The trail ends in the state forest a mile later.

Pisgah State Park

At least 20 miles of trails. Allow as much time as necessary. Easy to strenuous. From Rte. 9, turn south on Rte. 63 and go for 1 mile to Chesterfield. Turn left onto

Old Chesterfield Rd. and 0.25 mile later turn right onto Horseshoe Rd. This will lead you to the parking area.

Pisgah State Park's 13,000 acres constitute one of New Hampshire's largest public spaces. What does that mean to us mountain bikers? A vast network of old four-wheel-drive roads and narrower double tracks to get lost on. From the parking lot on Horseshoe Road, take the double tracks downhill and bear left at the fork. Cruise some 2.5 miles past Fullam Pond, where you can veer left on Fullam Pond Trail or pedal straight ahead to Old Chesterfield Road. There are more than 20 miles of trail, so make your own loop and bike to your adventurous soul's delight.

Fox State Forest

Up to 20 miles of trail. Allow as much time as you need. Easy to moderate. Access: From Hillsborough, turn north onto Rte. 140 toward Hillsborough Center. 2 miles later, turn right at the sign for Fox State Forest.

The well-marked double tracks in 1,445-acre Fox Forest were once used by old wagons to connect the farms and fields that stood here over a century ago. Now shaded by deep woods, hikers and bikers utilize the more than 20 miles of rutted trails. A series of old roads—Valley Road, Concord End Road, Old Gould Road, Mud Pond Road, Whitney Road, and Center Road—connect to form a loop, but be sure to pick up a trail map at forest headquarters to design your own route.

Sunapee Railroad Bed

7.2 miles. Allow 1–2 hr. Easy. Access: From the Rosewood Inn, turn right and drive for 0.9 mile on Pleasant View Rd. to South Rd. Turn right and drive 1.3 miles, just past a group of boulders on the right. Park on the left just past the double tracks.

This ride follows a former railroad bed carved out of the hills of the Lake Sunapee region. Park your car and look for a grassy double track that leads straight through a forest of birches, beeches, oaks, and maples. You'll cross over several wooden bridges and fallen logs before continuing across a dirt road on the same trail. At the 1.5-mile mark, veer left onto a dirt road for another 1.1 miles. Blackberries were ripe for picking when I rode through here in August. You can still see walls of rock and cement pylons, remnants of the railroad that last traveled through here in 1961. Cross over paved Mountain Road and continue on double tracks for the best part of the ride—a short cruise through a granite chasm of rock. Silver mica flickers in the darkness, guiding your way through the narrow tunnel. When the pass was blasted out with nitroglycerin in the 1870s, it took almost a year to finish. Continue for another half mile past the lumberyard to reach the Lake Sunapee Trading Post and the southern shores of Lake Sunapee. Picnic tables overlooking the lake are a good place to indulge in the Trading Post's own brand of root beer and their specialty, Uncle Buck's Hickory Smoked Teriyaki Venison Jerky (low in fat). A couple strips of this and you'll be ready to return by the same route back through the narrow chasm to your car.

Sugar River Trail

10 miles (one-way). Allow 3 hr. Easy. Access: Take Exit 9 off I-89 and head west on Rte. 103. In Newport, head north on Rte. 103 0.75 mile past the village green and turn left on Belknap Ave. A parking lot is located on the right side of the road.

Sugar River Trail is an apt name for this sweet trail that hugs the shores of a river. Formerly part of the Boston & Maine Railroad, this rail trail crosses more than a dozen bridges, including two large covered bridges. Two miles from the eastern terminus, Newport, the Sugar River widens and the landscape becomes a wooden mix of pine, hemlock, and hardwoods. In another 0.5 mile, you reach your first river crossing, an iron truss bridge. You won't reach the first covered bridge until the 6-mile mark. Spend time looking at the latticework, an incredible engineering feat when you realize it had to carry the weight of a 100-ton train. These covered railroad bridges are two of only a handful of their kind left in America. The second bridge will appear a mile later. The trail ends in Claremont, which is a good place for lunch before you head back.

Gunstock Recreational Area

Up to 20 miles of trails. Allow as much time as you need. Easy to strenuous. Access: Gunstock is located on Rte. 11A, 3 miles east of Gilford.

High above the shores of Lake Winnipesaukee, Gunstock offers a fun network of cross-country skiing trails in the winter. Come summer, these trails are taken advantage of by bikers. The trails vary from the relatively level Cobble Mountain Trail, a 2-mile cruise around Cobble Mountain, to the 1.7-mile Flintlock Trail, a quad-burning 1,300-foot climb to the peak of Gunstock Mountain. If you want a good loop, combine the Cobble Mountain Trail with the Birch and Maple Trails.

POWERBOATING

Wet Wolfe Rentals, Bay Street, Wolfeboro (☎ **603/569-1503**); **Anchor Marine,** Winnipesaukee Pier, Weir's Beach (☎ **603/366-4311**); and **Meredith Marina,** Bay Shore Drive, Meredith Bay, Meredith (☎ **603/279-7921**); all rent motorboats on Lake Winnipesaukee.

ROAD BIKING

Cyclists in Lake Winnipesaukee will often wake up at 6am and ride 31 miles around the lake to Weir's Beach. Here, they'll catch the M/S Mount Washington ferry back to Wolfeboro. Contact **Nordic Skier Sport,** Main Street, Wolfeboro (☎ **603/569-3151**), for all your road and mountain-biking information in the Lakes Region. If you're venturing to the western part of the state, near Hanover, try the Upper Connecticut River ride (see "Road Biking," in chapter 3).

Covered Bridge Loop

Allow 2 hr. Easy; relatively flat terrain. Access: From Keene, take State Rte. 12 South to State Rte. 32 South to Swanzey. At the junction of State Rte. 32 and Sawyers Crossing Rd., park at either Mount Caesar School or the Monadnock Regional High School.

The southwest corner of New Hampshire is a relatively flat section of woods, farmland, college towns, and, most notably, covered bridges. These wooden relics of yesteryear still stand as testament to simpler times. This 18-mile loop rides through four of the covered bridges on quiet country roads. Head south on State Route 32 for 1.5 miles till you reach Carlton Road. Turn left and you'll soon pass through covered bridge numero uno. First built in 1869, the Carlton Road Bridge uses a lattice of X-shaped wooden crosses to hold the ceiling in place. After traveling 1.1 miles from the junction of State Route 32 and Carlton Road, turn right at the T-junction onto Webber Hill Road. You'll swing downhill past the East Swanzey Post Office, where you'll meet up with State Route 32 again. Veer right for 0.1 mile to Swanzey Lake Road where you turn left. This 3.9-mile ride brings you past Swanzey Lake. For views of the water, turn right onto West Shore Drive; otherwise, continue straight between the houses, farms, and small towns to Westport Road. Turn left and ride 0.8 mile to a stop sign on Main Street. Another left will bring you to the junction of Route 10. Veer left for a mere 0.3 mile to reach Coombs Road, where you turn right for covered bridge number two. Built in 1837, the 118-foot Coombs Bridge spans the Ashuelot River.

Retrace your trail back to Main Street and turn right. Go 0.7 mile, bearing right again on Westport Road for an additional 2.4 miles. This brings you to a three-way stop at the intersection of Christian Hill Road. Turn left through the quaint village of West Swanzey to reach my favorite bridge on the trip, the Thompson Bridge. One of the two sidewalks still remains from the original construction (1832). To reach the final bridge, turn right on Winchester Road immediately after the Thompson Bridge. At the junction of Route 10, turn right for 0.6 mile and be cautious of the traffic. A right turn on Sawyer's Crossing Road will eventually bring you to Sawyer's Crossing Bridge, the longest of the four bridges. Continue straight to a stop sign and turn left on Eaton Road. This will bring you back to the two high schools.

Alstead-Marlow

27 miles. Allow 3–4 hr. Moderate to strenuous. Access: Park anywhere in Alstead on Main St. (Rte. 12A/123).

Close to the Vermont border, the loop from Alstead to Marlow is a quintessential Vermont ride. Cascading brooks and undeveloped forest are by your side, replacing the congestion and suburbia found in the southwestern part of the state. But you earn this bit of pastoral scenery. More than 6 miles of the route involves a climb, often steep, but then the rest of the ride is either level or an exciting downhill run. The route is easy to follow. Start on Main Street in Alstead (Routes 12A/123) and ride east to the intersection with Route 123A. Turn right at the fork and continue on Routes 12A/123. When the road forks again, stay left on Route 123. This 9-mile stretch takes you through the small communities of Mill Hollow and East Alstead before you do that long 6.5-mile climb into Marlow. Turn left in town onto Route 10 north. You can stop and rest around the lily pond, or continue 4.4 miles to the junction of Route 123A. Turn left and pedal 10.2 miles downhill through South Acworth back to the junction of Routes 12A/123. A small rocky stream will be by your side for most of this run. To head back to Main Street in Alstead and the start of the loop, simply turn right at the Routes 12A/123 intersection.

Hillsborough Loop

16 miles. Allow 2 hr. Easy to moderate. Access: Park at the Franklin Pierce Homestead near the junction of Rte. 9 and 31.

Starting at the home of Franklin Pierce, the 14th president of the United States, this ride takes you through the historic village of Hillsborough and into the neighboring countryside. The lightly traveled roads will guide you past dairy farms, open fields, lakes, and state forest. After touring President Pierce's humble beginnings, bike north on Route 31 for 1.9 miles. Bear right at the fork toward East Washington and continue on this road past the Holsteins and pastures for 3.3 miles. At a T, turn right toward Hillsborough Center and pedal for 4 miles as you ride on a narrow backcountry road into the old town. Continue on the road for another 3 miles, passing Fox State Forest (a good place to walk and mountain-bike; see those respective sections in this chapter) until you reach Hillsborough. This is the best spot for lunch before turning right on Route 9 and biking 1.7 miles. When you see a power station at the base of a large hill, turn left onto this unmarked paved road and follow it 1.4 miles to the junction of Routes 9 and 31. Continue on Route 31 back to the Franklin Pierce Homestead.

Francestown-Bennington

22.5 miles. Allow 3 hr. Moderate. Access: Park at the Francestown Village Store on Rte. 47.

With its large Federal-style homes lining the streets, including Francestown Academy, the former school of President Franklin Pierce, Francestown makes an ideal start to any bike tour. Add a covered bridge, a state park, and a mountain to skirt, and you have one of the finest loops in the state. Take Route 47 south out of Francestown village and almost immediately turn right onto Route 136 west toward Greenfield. At a fork 0.7 mile past Greenfield, veer right toward Hancock. You'll soon pass the entrance to the Greenfield State Park on the right; several miles later, go through a covered bridge over the Contoocock River. Cross Route 202 and at the upcoming fork veer left. A mile from Route 202, you continue straight onto Route 123 north. At 0.5 mile farther, bear left at the stop sign in Hancock and then take a sharp right onto Route 137 north. Crotched Mountain will soon come into view. Continue for 2 miles on Route 137 until you reach a stop sign. Turn left onto Route 202 East, and a large pond will appear on your right. A little more than a mile later, turn right onto Route 47 south. This will take you past the town of Bennington all the way back to Francestown.

Lake Sunapee Loop

23 miles. Allow 3 hr. Moderate to strenuous. Access: Park at Mount Sunapee Ski Area, off Rte. 103 in Newbury.

This challenging up-and-down route takes you around the shores of scenic Lake Sunapee. It's a great ride to take in the spring and fall, because traffic on this route in summer can be a bit heavy. Start at Mount Sunapee Ski Area, where the 2,743-foot peak rises above the southwestern shores. Cruise down to Route 103 and turn left, heading west. Ride for 4 miles and then turn right onto Route 11 East. This 7.7-mile stretch has its fair share of hills. There's a small store in Georges Mills at which to reenergize before turning right onto Route 103A and heading south for 7.9 miles. There are some short steep hills here, but they reward you with good views of the lake. Turn right on Route 103 west in Newbury and ride 2.5 miles to the rotary. Turn left and it's a 0.7-mile climb back to Mount Sunapee Ski Area.

Tamworth–North Sandwich

23 miles. Allow 3 hr. Moderate. Access: Park in the center of Tamworth near the intersection of Rte. 113 and 113A.

Sandwich is an apt name for the town in this ride that's sandwiched between the White Mountain National Forest to the north and Lake Winnipesaukee to the south. This rolling 23-mile loop takes you on two routes that are remarkably free of the congestion that plagues bikers in both the White Mountains and the Lakes Region. The ride starts in Tamworth, heading west on Route 113A toward the town of Wonalancet. The beginning of Route 113A has sharp dips and climbs before leveling off with the Swift and Wonalancet Rivers through the shaded trees of Hemenway State Forest. Pass Wonalancet and ride for another 6.8 miles into North Sandwich. A little more than the halfway point, this is a decent place to grab a sandwich before rolling on. At the T junction, turn left onto Route 113 and ride along the Bearcamp River past the small communities of South Tamworth and Whittier. The latter is named after the poet John Greenleaf Whittier, who spent his summers in this area. Less than 3 miles later, you'll be back in Tamworth at the intersection of Routes 113 and 113A.

SAILING

The **Lake Winnipesaukee Sailing Association** (☎ **603-279-8553;** www.lwsa.org) operates a youth sailing school in Gilford. They also promote racing on the lake. Their learn-to-sail fleet consists of four types of craft: 8-foot Optimist Prams; 14-foot Lasers; J22 keelboats; and, new last year, double-handed Daysailers, on loan from one of their members.

Windsurfers can rent sailboards and get lessons at **Winni Sailboard School** in Laconia (☎ **603/528-4410**).

SCUBA DIVING

Dive Winnipesaukee, Main Street, Wolfeboro (☎ **603/569-8080;** www.worldpath.net/~divewinn/) offers daily two-tank dives around the lake. Unusual rock formations and wrecks are found 30 to 40 feet below the surface. One of the wrecks, ***Lady of the Lake,*** is a 125-foot steamboat that sank in 1894. Remarkably, the cold waters of the lake have even preserved the paint.

If you have your own gear and want to dive the New Hampshire coast, check out the University of New Hampshire's sport-diving Web site (nemo.unh.edu/aqualung/nhdive_home.htm). The site shows you exactly where to go on the coast and what you'll find.

SEA KAYAKING

Portsmouth Kayak Adventures (☎ **603/559-1000;** www.portsmouthkayak.com) leads paddlers on a variety of tours—from an inland jaunt to Great Bay to an ocean kayak around the Isle of Shoals. Great Bay is a vast estuary where salt- and freshwater meet, creating a rich habitat for birds and fish (see "Bird Watching," above). For the 5-hour Isle of Shoals tour, begin in Portsmouth Harbor where you load up the boat and travel to Gosport Harbor, 7 miles offshore. The Isle of Shoals comprises nine islands once home to famous writers, poets, painters, and pirates. You'll paddle along rocky shoreline around Smuttynose Island while learning about the chronicles of each island. A true ocean experience for advanced paddlers only.

SNOWMOBILING

More than 6,000 miles of snowmobile trails snake through the state, all connected by a web of networks maintained by local snowmobiling clubs. To obtain more information on snowmobiling in the state, contact the **New Hampshire Snowmobile Association,** 722 Rte. 3A, Bow, NH 03304 (☎ **603/224-8906;** www.nhsa.com).

SNOWSHOEING

For perfect views in the winter of Squam Lake and, in the distance, Lake Winnipesaukee, make the climb up **West Rattlesnake** Mountain. The 1.8-mile round-trip snowshoe leads to the 1,260-foot summit in an hour's work. In Holderness take Route 113 east and at 5.6 miles turn left into the parking area.

There's no more intriguing mixture than snow and the salt of the sea. At **Odiorne Point State Park** in Rye, you can take the 2-mile Battery Seamen Loop as the waves crash along the rocky shores. From Portsmouth, take Route 1 to the Elwyn Road lights (Route 1A) and turn left. Follow Route 1A to the park entrance.

SURFING

The Wall at North Hampton Beach is the place to surf. For the daily surfing report on the New Hampshire coast, call **Cinnamon Rainbows** (☎ **603/926-WAVE;** www.cinnamonrainbows.com) or check out their surfboard store at 931 Ocean Blvd., North Beach, Hampton. They have the best selection of boards in the state.

SWIMMING

Yes, New Hampshire is not all mountains, lakes, and rivers. It boasts 18 miles of Atlantic coast shoreline, complete with large stretches of beach, dunes, and saltwater marshes. The ocean can be a wee bit on the chilly side (60° seems about the norm), but the sun will make your body toasty in the summer months, so any body of water will do nicely, thank you. **Hampton Beach State Park** is still the place to go for families, college kids, and everybody else who relishes a boisterous crowd. On summer weekends, come early to find a spot for your beach towels amidst the thousands of other sun-and-fun seekers. The center of activity still focuses around the almost 100-year-old Casino, featuring restaurants, penny arcades, shops, and a nightclub. To the south, **Seabrook Beach** is a heavily developed residential area with little public access to the ocean, since parking is limited. **North Hampton Beach** is a good place to stroll past the old fish houses, which are now summer cottages. A sidewalk follows the coast for some 2 miles to the Rye Beach

Club. **Jenness Beach** and **Wallis Sands Beach** in Rye, north of Hampton Beach, are far more accessible, with a wide crescent of sand and ample parking. They tend to be a little more laid-back than Hampton, but with so little shoreline in the state, all the beaches are on-the-beaten-track. For the only undeveloped strip of coastline, head to **Odiorne Point State Park** in Portsmouth (see "Walks & Rambles," below).

If you're yearning for freshwater sand, try **Ellacoya State Beach,** the only state beach in Winnipesaukee (Route 11, Gilford); **Sunapee State Park Beach** on the shores of the lake (Route 103, 3 miles west of Newbury); and **Wadleigh State Beach** on Kezar Lake in Sutton (just off Route 114). For something smaller, try **Profile Falls,** a small natural pool under a 40-foot waterfall (U.S. 3A, 2.5 miles south of Bristol); **Contoocock Lake** in Jaffrey; and the **Greenfield State Park** beach in Greenfield.

WALKS & RAMBLES

Odiorne Point State Park

2-mile loop. Allow 1 hr. An ocean walk along Portsmouth Harbor. Access: From Portsmouth, take Rte. 1 to the Elwyn Rd. lights (Rte. 1A) and turn left. Follow Rte. 1A to the park entrance.

Located at the tip of Portsmouth Harbor, Odiorne Point became a state park in 1972. A 2-mile loop around the shores is popular with bird watchers, walkers, and joggers. Bring your binoculars and out in the marsh you might find red-winged blackbirds, swallows, and snowy egrets. The walk takes you along the shores of Pebble Beach before you head inland around marsh and low-lying shrubs like winterberry. If you brought lunch, you can picnic on the shores in relative quietude compared to New Hampshire's other more-developed beachfront.

Great Bay National Wildlife Refuge

2 miles round-trip. Allow 1 hr. Access: From the Spaulding Turnpike, 3 miles west of Portsmouth, take the Pease International Tradeport exit. Continue on Merrimac Rd. to McIntyre Rd.; you'll see a sign to enter the Great Bay National Wildlife Refuge.

Once part of the Pease Air Force Base, Great Bay is now New Hampshire's largest refuge, protecting more than 6 miles of bay shore. The massive bay has more than 48 miles of shoreline overall as it makes its way 10 miles inland from the Atlantic. This long shoreline attracts birds that migrate along the Atlantic Flyway, including ospreys, marsh hawks, and terns (see "Bird Watching," above). The 2-mile Ferry Way Trail enters the woods, where you might also spot wild turkey and ruffed grouse, before snaking past small beaver ponds and an old apple orchard and heading down to the shores of Great Bay. The loop then brings you back to the parking area.

Fox State Forest

From 1 to 20 miles. Allow as much time as you need. Access: From Hillsborough, turn north onto Rte. 140 toward Hillsborough Center. 2 miles later, turn right at the sign for Fox State Forest.

In 1922, Mrs. Charles Fox bequeathed her 348-acre farm with house and barn to the state of New Hampshire. The state has since added more land, totaling 1,445 acres; built an environmental center and forestry museum; and created more than 20 miles of well-marked trails through the woods. This includes the 4.5-mile Ridge Trail, which winds through a forest of maples, pines, hemlocks, and birch before arriving at Mud Pond. Most of the abandoned farmland Mrs. Fox left to the state is now forest, perfect for strolling.

WHALE WATCHING

It was a perfect day for whale watching the day I boarded the ***M/V Atlantic Queen II*** out of Rye Harbor, New Hampshire. The sky was blue and the sea was as flat and reflective as a mirror. Less than 90 minutes into our ride, someone shouted on the starboard side of the boat. Everyone ran over to find a huge shadow rising from the water only 15 feet away. A small geyser shot from the whale's backside as the sounds of clicking cameras reverberated around the deck. Several minutes later, the whale's tail fin, or fluke, surfaced.

According to naturalist Josh Miller from the Center for Oceanic Research and Education, we had just spotted a humpback whale. On the ride over to Stellwagen Bank, Josh had given us an extensive introduction to the whales of the Northeast. Stellwagen, located about 7 miles north of Provincetown, 25 miles east of Boston, and 25 miles southeast of Rye, is an 18-mile-long crescent-shaped underwater mesa. The bank ranges from 80 to 500 feet below the surface. Currents slam into the bank, bringing nutrient-rich cold water to the surface. This attracts fish, which in turn attract numerous species of whales from April to November—humpbacks with their larger fins, and smaller minkes. One gulp from a hungry humpback whale can take in a ton of fish.

We followed the humpback for a good hour and watched him playing with a buddy, and then we returned to Rye Harbor. The whole trip took about 4 hours. The boats of **Atlantic Whale Watch,** Rye Harbor State Marina (☎ **800/WHALE-NH;** www.atlanticwhalewatch.com), leave daily in the morning during the summer and several times a week in the off-season. The cost is $23.

Campgrounds & Other Accommodations

CAMPING

Gunstock Campground

From the northern edge of town in Gilford, travel east on Rte. 11A for 3.5 miles to the campground. ☎ **800/GUNSTOCK,** ext. 191. 300 sites for tents and RVs, 113 with water and electric hookups, rest rooms, full showers, picnic tables, fire rings, grills, pool, playground, ice and wood at grocery store.

Close to the southern shores of Lake Winnipesaukee, these sites are at the base of Gunstock Mountain. It's a four-season resort, great for hiking, mountain biking, and downhill and cross-country skiing.

Pillsbury State Park

The park is located 3.5 miles north of Washington on U.S. 31. ☎ **603/863-2860.** 38 sites, no hookups, pit toilets, piped water, tables, fire rings, and wood.

These primitive sites are located on the shores of May Pond, with three of the sites accessible by canoe only. The park is just south of Mount Sunapee State Park and its slew of activities including biking, hiking, and boating.

Surry Mountain Camping Area

From the junction of Rte. 12 and 12A in Keene, head north on Rte. 12A for 4 miles. Turn right on the entrance road and you'll reach the campground in 0.25 mile. ☎ **603/352-9880.** 43 sites for tents and RVs, 38 with water and electrical hookups. Flush toilets, hot showers, picnic tables, fire rings, grill, ice and firewood sold on-site.

These private and spacious sites are near the shores of 265-acre Surry Mountain Lake. Good warm-water fishing for largemouth bass, pickerel, and yellow perch. There's also a maintained beach and picnic area.

Monadnock State Park

From the junction of Rte. 124 and 202 in Jaffrey, travel 4 miles west on Rte. 124 to Slade Rd. Turn right and follow signs to the state park and campground. ☎ **603/532-8862.** 21 sites, no hookups, flush toilets, piped water, picnic tables, fire rings, ice and firewood for sale.

Set in the woods at the base of the mountain, simply hike to the peak and spend the night.

INNS & RESORTS

Three Chimneys Inn

17 Newmarket, Durham, NH 03824. ☎ **888/399-9777;** www.threechimneysinn.com. 23 rooms. Rates range from $119 to $209.

If you want to go whale watching from Rye Harbor or sea kayaking from Portsmouth, or perhaps you simply want to stroll around Odiorne Point State Park, but you don't want to stay on the congested coast, you can while away your nighttime hours at Durham's Three Chimneys Inn. A 10-minute drive from Portsmouth, Three Chimneys Inn is a newly restored mansion from 1649 and adjacent carriage house from 1795. Most of the 23 rooms have fireplaces, and the inn features a restaurant and cozy tavern.

The Inn at East Hill Farm

460 Monadnock St., Troy, NH 03465. ☎ **603/242-6495;** www.east-hill-farm.com. Summer rates are $74 per adult, $54 for children 5 and over, $27 for children 2–4. Rates include all meals daily, complete children's program, and use of all facilities—farm animals, boats, tennis, indoor and outdoor pools, fishing on the pond, weekly hayride, water-skiing, and pony rides.

"Where Kids are Kings" is the motto of this working farm that's set against the backdrop of Mount Monadnock. The inn is popular with young Boston families who want to play outdoors in southwestern New Hampshire. The inn features two outdoor pools, one indoor pool, two whirlpools, a wading pool for the younger children, sauna, tennis court, shuffleboard, recreation rooms, horseback riding, boats on the pond, fishing, square-dancing, and mountain climbing. At the inn's Silver Lake cottage 2 miles away, there is swimming, water-skiing, motorboat rides, fishing, and boating, and a weekly cookout for the whole family during the summer. Another highlight for children at the 150-acre resort is petting the barnyard animals, milking a cow or goat, or feeding the sheep.

Rosewood Country Inn

67 Pleasant View Rd., Bradford, NH 03221. ☎ **603/938-5253;** www.rosewoodcountryinn.com. 11 rooms. Rates $95–$175.

Who says the Granite State doesn't have a soft, tender side? This hidden gem, formerly known as the Pleasant View Farm, near the slopes of Mount Sunapee in the Lakes Region is one of the most romantic inns in New England. The roster of names on the guest list from the early 1900s includes Gloria Swanson, Mary Pickford, Douglas Fairbanks, Charlie Chaplin, and Lillian Gish. Wake up to a breakfast of Belgian waffles topped with peaches, homemade maple syrup, and a hint of Grand Marnier. Then try to get your bloated body to go cross-country skiing on trails located across the street, or mountain-bike down the Sunapee Railroad Bed (see "Mountain Biking," above). At night, the skies are so clear that you can see the Milky Way.

Home Hill Inn

River Rd., Plainfield, NH 03781. ☎ **603/675-6165;** www.homehillinn.com. 7 rooms and 2 suites. Rates start at $150.

Situated 10 miles north of Hanover, on the Connecticut River, it's no wonder Home Hill offers a cycling package in these serene settings (see the Upper Connecticut road-biking ride in chapter 3). Included in the package are two bikes, a gourmet picnic lunch, and detailed self-guided routes. The real treat happens when you return to the inn to feast on a four-course Provençal dinner at the Home Hill Restaurant. Co-owner and chef Victoria du Roure trained at the renowned Ritz-Escoffier Culinary School in Paris. The inn is nestled on 25 acres in a restored 1818 mansion and carriage house.

6

The White Mountains & Northern New Hampshire

When the Republican Party picked New Hampshire as the site for its first presidential primary, they didn't just throw darts at a map of America. New Hampshire has had Herbert Hoover's old slogan, "Pick yourself up by your bootstraps," written all over it from its earliest days. The locals are strongly independent, rugged individualists who at times can seem as hardened as the Old Man of the Mountain—the famous rock jutting out of Franconia Notch that resembles a stern male countenance. Other times, New Hampshirites are as gentle and inviting as the cerulean blue waters of the Lakes Region.

The state's diverse landscape definitely has an impact on the complex personality of its natives. The rolling green hills of the south give way to large lakes in the center of New Hampshire. It is the peaks of the impressive White Mountains in the north, however, that shape our image of this New England state and her people. Stunted trees border steel gray granite that has been carved by glaciers and ice beds into fantastic formations—nature's foray into abstract sculpture. At lower elevations, forests of firs and spruce hide ponds, streams, and hundreds of waterfalls. Mountains tower at over 6,000 feet high, including Mount Washington, the highest peak in the Northeast, known for its fierce winds and weather that change faster than Clark Kent turning into Superman.

Aside from Robert Frost who once said, "The only fault I find with New Hampshire is that her mountains aren't quite high enough," most people walk away from the Whites awed and inspired. Tourists have been visiting the region since the early 1800s, when the Crawford family built inns and constructed bridle paths and hiking trails into the mountains. One of the trails, the Crawford Path, is the oldest hiking trail in the country. Most of these 30- to 40-room accommodations were simple, straightforward wooden structures built near a body of water. Visitors would go on guided hikes or horseback rides, usually around Mount Washington, and then return to the hotel for a copious meal.

In the 1850s, the Whites were home to the state's first art colony. Thomas Cole, Albert Bierstadt, and George Innes were just a few of the American landscape painters who devoted themselves to this enchanting scenery. By the latter half of the 19th century, two very different types of traveler had emerged: the pampered urbanite and the able-bodied outdoors enthusiast.

Great rambling resorts like the Glen House, Crawford House, and Kearsage House were built in the 1870s and 1880s to provide sybaritic pleasures to those visitors seeking the solace of nature within a luxurious environment. They came on sleeper trains from Boston and New York; dined on gourmet food; took carefully organized excursions to the Old Man of the Mountain, the Flume, and other notable places of interest; and then returned to the hotel for tea in the manicured gardens. These comfortable resorts, like their counterparts in Europe, were created as salubrious retreats to revive the spirit. After 1869, when the Cog Railway was constructed to bring guests up to the peak of Mount Washington, fashionably dressed travelers could go on 3-day excursions from the Eastern cities at a cost of $17 per person. The journey included a train ride to one of the sumptuous hotels, a ride on the Cog Railway, a night in the summit hotel, and transfer by carriage down the eastern side of the mountain to the railroad line back home.

Another group from Boston was seeking to provide a much different type of shelter—small mountain huts that would lodge hikers, or "trampers" as they were called in their day. In 1888, this small contingent of outdoor lovers built the Madison Spring stone cabin in the Presidential Range. The price for a roof over your head was half a dollar; and you were responsible for your own sustenance, blankets, and other basic needs.

Now, more than a century later, the exquisite Balsams in Dixville Notch is regrettably the only grand resort that still stands from the late 1800s in northern New Hampshire. The good news is that this small group of outdoors crusaders, who had the vision and willpower to provide shelter for America's early hikers, is now the Appalachian Mountain Club (AMC), with more than 87,000 members nationwide and eight mountain huts. Best of all, the Whites continue to entice and challenge every imaginable type of sports person, from rock climber to hiker to canoeist to biker.

The Lay of the Land

The glacier that retreated 10,000-plus years ago to form the White Mountains seems to have left in a hurry, without first smoothing the edges of the rocky detritus that remained. Narrow and steep mountainous passes, called notches, were sharply cut through walls of granite that refused to budge. Gorges now plummet to the forest floor, cliffs protrude from bare summits over 6,000 feet high, circular domes remain not fully hewn, and massive boulders are found in the most absurd spots.

One-third of New Hampshire rock is granite, thus the state's nickname of the Granite State. The granite is the result of intense igneous activity—huge masses of molten rock that welled up into layered rocks, where they solidified to form granite. Visitors from the West, who are used to viewing mountains twice this size, will inevitably find these unusual configurations dramatic. Unlike the Green Mountains to the west, which are smooth and form a narrow range running from

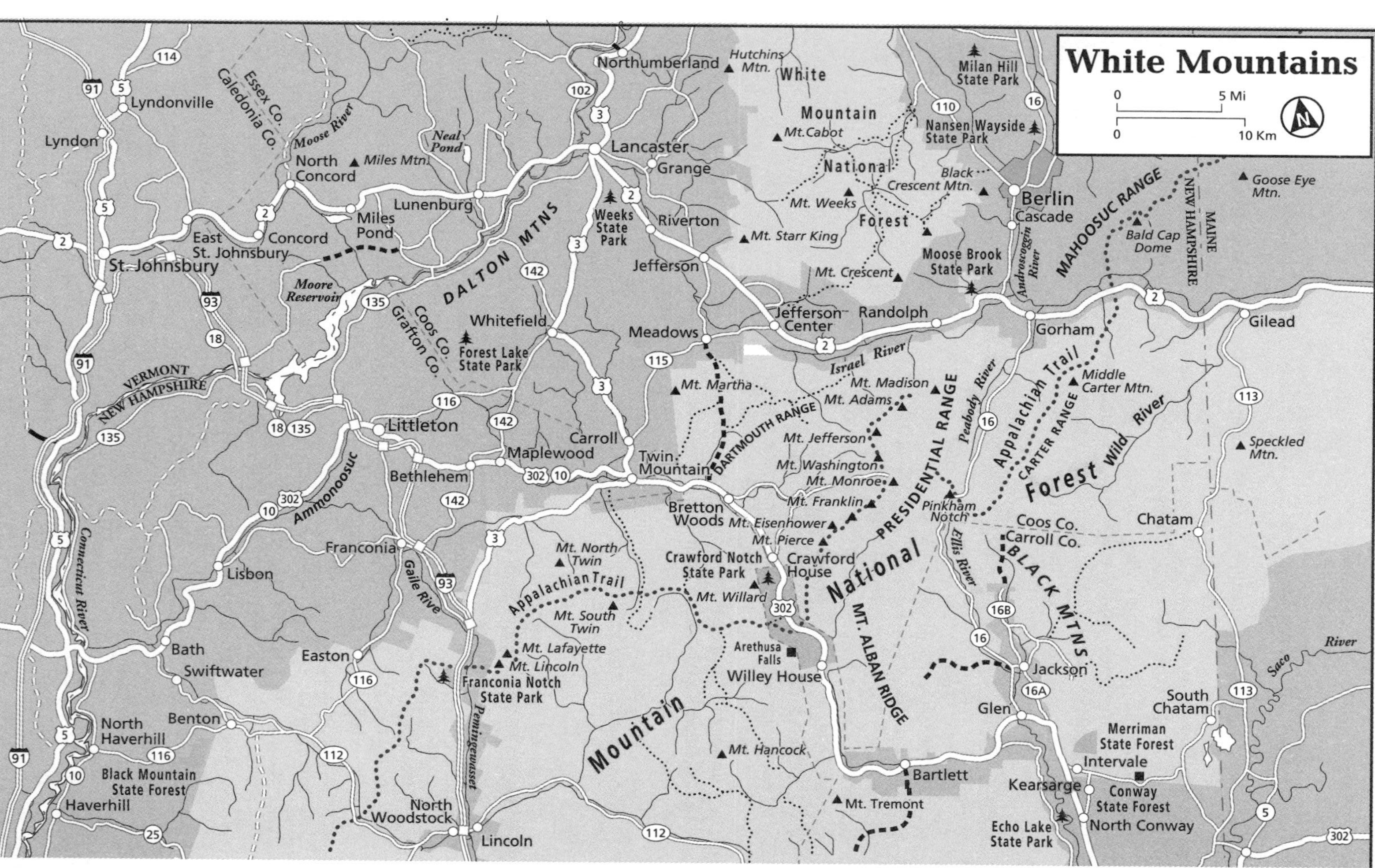
White Mountains
0
5 Mi
0
10 Km
N
Lyndonville
Lyndon
St. Johnsbury
East St. Johnsbury
Concord
North Concord
Miles Mtn.
Miles Pond
Lunenburg
Neal Pond
Moose River
Essex Co.
Caledonia Co.
Moore Reservoir
VERMONT
NEW HAMPSHIRE
Connecticut River
DALTON MTNS
Coos Co.
Grafton Co.
Whitefield
Forest Lake State Park
Littleton
Bethlehem
Maplewood
Carroll
Lancaster
Grange
Northumberland
Weeks State Park
Riverton
Jefferson
Meadows
Jefferson Center
Randolph
Twin Mountain
Hutchins Mtn.
White
Mountain
National
Forest
Mt. Cabot
Mt. Weeks
Mt. Starr King
Mt. Crescent
Black Crescent Mtn.
Milan Hill State Park
Nansen Wayside State Park
Moose Brook State Park
Berlin
Cascade
Androscoggin River
MAHOOSUC RANGE
Bald Cap Dome
Goose Eye Mtn.
MAINE
NEW HAMPSHIRE
Gorham
Gilead
Israel River
Mt. Martha
DARTMOUTH RANGE
Mt. Madison
Mt. Adams
Mt. Jefferson
Mt. Washington
Mt. Monroe
Mt. Franklin
Mt. Eisenhower
Mt. Pierce
PRESIDENTIAL RANGE
Peabody River
Appalachian Trail
CARTER RANGE
Middle Carter Mtn.
Wild River
Forest
Speckled Mtn.
Pinkham Notch
Coos Co.
Carroll Co.
Chatam
BLACK MTNS
Ellis River
Bretton Woods
Crawford Notch State Park
Crawford House
National
MT. ALBAN RIDGE
Mt. Willard
Arethusa Falls
Willey House
Mt. North Twin
Mt. South Twin
Appalachian Trail
Mt. Lafayette
Mt. Lincoln
Franconia Notch State Park
Franconia
Gaile Rive
Ammonoosuc
Lisbon
Bath
Swiftwater
Easton
Benton
North Haverhill
Black Mountain State Forest
Haverhill
Pemingewasset
North Woodstock
Lincoln
Mountain
Mt. Hancock
Bartlett
Mt. Tremont
Jackson
Glen
Kearsarge
Echo Lake State Park
Intervale
Merriman State Forest
Conway State Forest
North Conway
South Chatam
Saco River
91
5
114
2
93
18
135
142
3
102
116
302
10
115
110
16
16B
16A
113
112
25

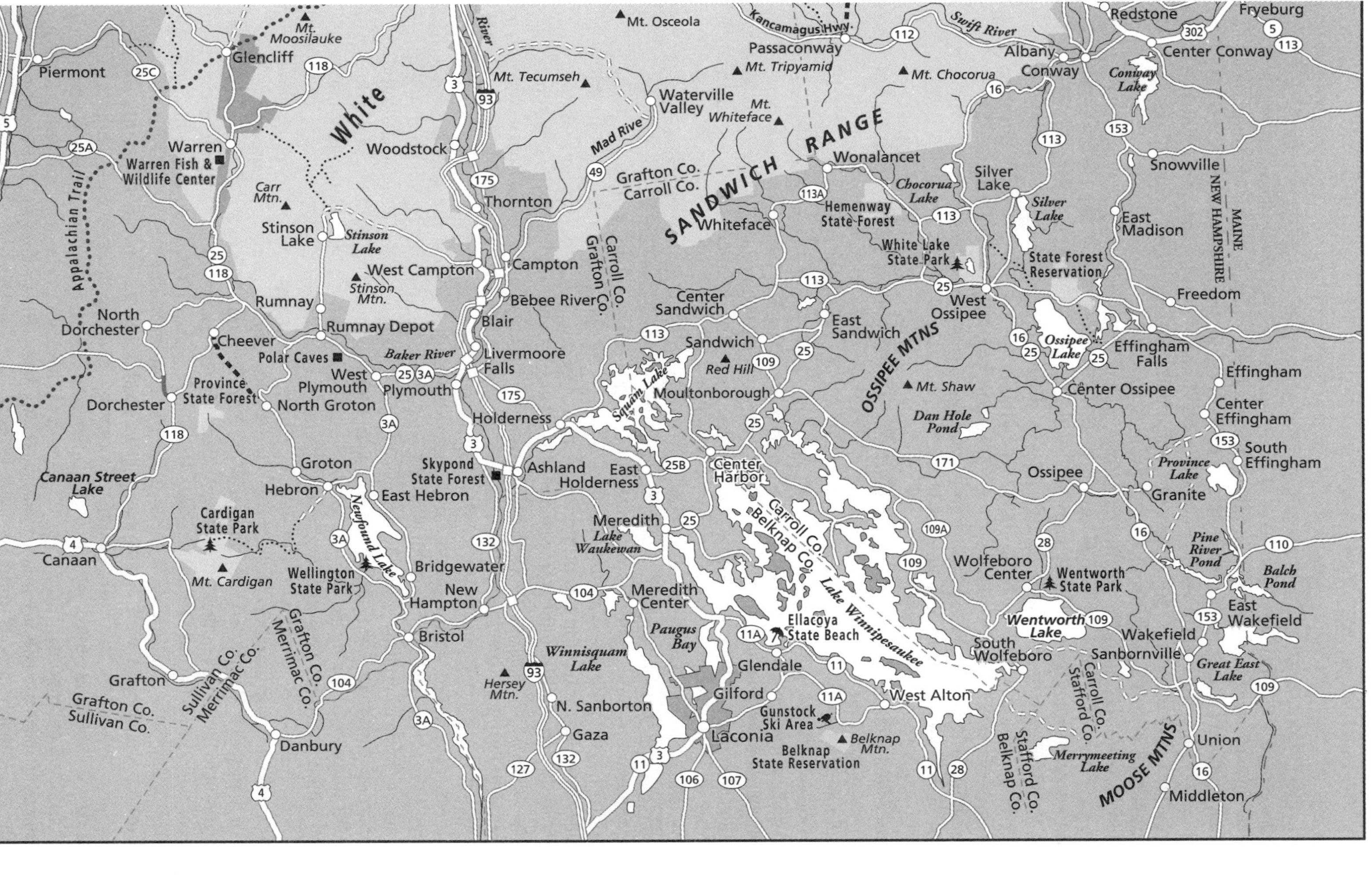
White
SANDWICH RANGE
OSSIPEE MTNS
MOOSE MTNS
MAINE
NEW HAMPSHIRE
Appalachian Trail
Kancamagus Hwy.
Swift River
Mad River
Baker River
River
Mt. Moosilauke
Mt. Osceola
Mt. Tecumseh
Mt. Tripyamid
Mt. Whiteface
Mt. Chocorua
Mt. Shaw
Red Hill
Carr Mtn.
Stinson Mtn.
Mt. Cardigan
Hersey Mtn.
Belknap Mtn.
Piermont
Glencliff
Warren
Warren Fish & Wildlife Center
Woodstock
Thornton
Waterville Valley
Passaconway
Redstone
Fryeburg
Center Conway
Albany
Conway
Conway Lake
Snowville
Wonalancet
Silver Lake
Silver Lake
Chocorua Lake
Hemenway State Forest
White Lake State Park
State Forest Reservation
East Madison
Freedom
Whiteface
Grafton Co.
Carroll Co.
Stinson Lake
Stinson Lake
West Campton
Campton
Bebee River
Rumnay
Rumnay Depot
Blair
Center Sandwich
East Sandwich
West Ossipee
North Dorchester
Cheever
Polar Caves
Livermoore Falls
Sandwich
Ossipee Lake
Effingham Falls
Effingham
Province State Forest
West Plymouth
Plymouth
Dorchester
North Groton
Moultonborough
Squam Lake
Center Ossipee
Center Effingham
Holderness
Dan Hole Pond
South Effingham
Groton
Skypond State Forest
Ashland
East Holderness
Center Harbor
Province Lake
Ossipee
Canaan Street Lake
Hebron
East Hebron
Granite
Cardigan State Park
Newfound Lake
Meredith
Lake Waukewan
Pine River Pond
Balch Pond
Canaan
Wellington State Park
Bridgewater
Wolfeboro Center
Wentworth State Park
New Hampton
Meredith Center
East Wakefield
Wentworth Lake
Lake Winnipesaukee
Ellacoya State Beach
Paugus Bay
Wakefield
Bristol
South Wolfeboro
Sanbornville
Great East Lake
Winnisquam Lake
Glendale
Grafton
Gilford
West Alton
Sullivan Co.
Merrimac Co.
Grafton Co.
Merrimac Co.
Grafton Co.
Sullivan Co.
Carroll Co.
Belknap Co.
Carroll Co.
Stafford Co.
Stafford Co.
Belknap Co.
N. Sanborton
Gunstock Ski Area
Union
Danbury
Laconia
Gaza
Belknap State Reservation
Merrymeeting Lake
Middleton
5
91
25C
25A
118
25
3
93
175
49
112
302
113
16
153
113A
109
25B
171
109A
28
110
3A
132
104
4
11
11A
106
107
127

north to south, the White Mountains are a chaotic group centered in the north-central portion of the state and straggling off in every direction. They venture into Maine and come within 10 miles of Vermont and 50 miles of Quebec.

Climate is not taken lightly in this part of the country. The highest winds ever recorded, 231 miles per hour, occurred atop Mount Washington on April 12, 1934. Every year, because of the vast difference in weather between the bottom and the summit, several people perish and hundreds more are saved by search-and-rescue squads in the Whites. Mark Twain's famous line about New England, "I have counted one hundred and thirty-six different kinds of weather inside of four-and-twenty hours," easily applies to the Whites. When taking hikes in the height of summer or in the depths of winter, it's imperative that you know the weather atop the mountains.

The climate in the Northeast is becoming increasingly hard to predict. Summer temperatures in New Hampshire range from 70° to 80°F, winters from the teens to the 30s (unless you're on top of Mount Washington where the temperature can dip as low as 40° below 0). If there's snow on the ground, late November and mid-March are my favorite times to ski. Far fewer people are on the slopes and the weather is reasonably warmer than in the other winter months. Late August, when the humidity and bugs have vacated the countryside, is the perfect time to hike and bike. Leaf peeping is at its peak from late September through mid-October. Color starts to appear in higher elevations during mid-September and gradually spreads south to the other parts of the state. I'd avoid Columbus Day Weekend, since the traffic can be heavy and rooms are booked well in advance. The state maintains a **Fall Foliage Hotline (☎ 800/258-3608)**, which provides updated conditions.

More and more moose are relinquishing their Canadian passports and traveling south into New Hampshire. Two of the best places to spot these large mammals are north of Berlin on Route 16, along the Androscoggin River, and Route 26, east of Errol. Other New Hampshire wildlife inhabitants include deer, beavers, porcupines, raccoons, woodchucks, skunks, otters, muskrats, and the occasional black bear and bobcat. There are close to 200 types of birds in the Whites, ranging from ruby-throated hummingbirds to eastern kingbirds to yellow-bellied flycatchers. The bird-watching highlight is the pair of nesting eagles on Umbagog Lake.

Orientation

From the Canadian to the Massachusetts border, New Hampshire is almost 200 miles long. The northern tip is less than 20 miles wide; the girth at the base close to 100 miles. This chapter contains information on the White Mountains and the area north of the Whites called the North Country. All other information on the Lakes Region, the area around Mount Monadnock, and the Atlantic coastline can be found in chapter 5, "Southern New Hampshire & the Lake District."

Travelers from Boston and other points east cruise up **I-93** past the state capital, Concord, to Franconia Notch and the Whites. Visitors from the west and south take **I-91,** following the Connecticut River along the borders of New Hampshire and Vermont.

There are many scenic routes within the Whites, perhaps the most scenic being the **Kancamagus Highway,** or "Kanc." A veritable corkscrew of a road, the 34.5-mile Kanc rises to 3,000 feet as it runs by rivers, waterfalls, mountains, and forests. The road starts in Lincoln and ends in Conway, heading west to east. Many of the easier hiking and cross-country routes in the Whites start from the highway.

U.S. 302, from Bartlett to Bretton Woods, is a spectacular drive through Crawford Notch. Mount Washington and

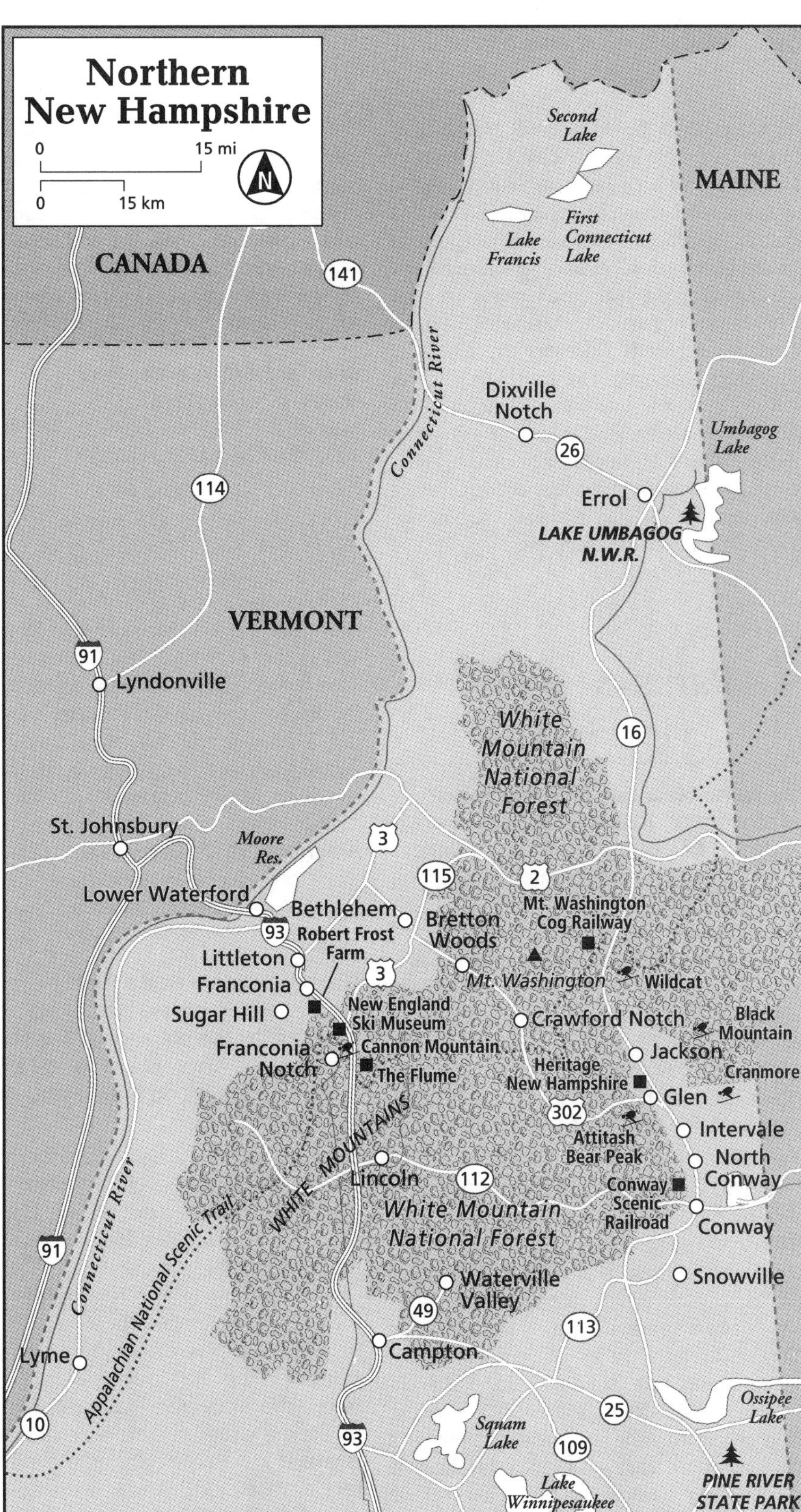

Northern New Hampshire
0
15 mi
0
15 km
N
CANADA
MAINE
VERMONT
Second Lake
First Connecticut Lake
Lake Francis
141
Connecticut River
Dixville Notch
26
Umbagog Lake
Errol
LAKE UMBAGOG N.W.R.
114
91
Lyndonville
16
White Mountain National Forest
St. Johnsbury
Moore Res.
3
115
2
Lower Waterford
Bethlehem
Bretton Woods
93
Robert Frost Farm
Mt. Washington Cog Railway
Littleton
Franconia
3
Mt. Washington
Wildcat
Sugar Hill
New England Ski Museum
Crawford Notch
Black Mountain
Franconia Notch
Cannon Mountain
The Flume
Jackson
Heritage New Hampshire
Cranmore
Glen
302
Attitash Bear Peak
Intervale
North Conway
WHITE MOUNTAINS
Lincoln
112
Conway Scenic Railroad
Conway
White Mountain National Forest
Appalachian National Scenic Trail
Connecticut River
91
Snowville
Waterville Valley
49
113
Lyme
Campton
25
Ossipee Lake
10
Squam Lake
93
109
Lake Winnipesaukee
PINE RIVER STATE PARK

the other high peaks of the Presidential Range are best seen from U.S. 302 or **Route 16** north of Jackson. There is also an auto road that climbs to the peak of Mount Washington, but we expect you to do the climb on foot, skis, or crampons.

Depending on your entry point into the Whites, the towns of **Lincoln, Woodstock,** and **North Conway** are the best places to stock up on food and water before you hit the trails. Lincoln and Woodstock are located in the western part of the White Mountain National Forest. North Conway, known for its long list of outlet stores, is the gateway to Mount Washington and Pinkham Notch.

Parks & Other Hot Spots

The White Mountain National Forest

Headquarters: 719 Main St., Laconia, NH 03247. ☎ **603/528-8721.** Ranger Districts (RD): Ammonoosuc RD, Trudeau Rd., Bethlehem. ☎ 603/869-2626. Pemigewasset RD, Rte. 175, Plymouth. ☎ 603/536-1310. Androscoggin RD, Rte. 16, Gorham. ☎ 603/466-2856. Saco RD, Kancamagus Hwy., Conway. ☎ 603/ 447-5448. Pinkham Notch Camp, Rte. 16, Pinkham Notch. ☎ 603/ 466-2725. Evans Notch RD, Bridge St., Bethel, Maine. ☎ 207/824-2134. Cross-country and downhill skiing, fishing, mountain biking, rock climbing.

Occupying 11% of New Hampshire, the White Mountain National Forest composes the highest percentage of federal land in any eastern state. More than 3 million visitors annually come to test their muscle on 1,167 miles of grueling talus-covered and soft, stream-laced paths; as well as to ski down some of the oldest trails in North America; cross-country ski through more than a hundred miles of backcountry woods; or hook a trout or bass in the numerous ponds and streams. The 798,305-acre forest is also attracting a new breed of hard-core adventurers. Mountain bikers are pedaling up and cruising down single-track ridge trails, and rock climbers face the daunting task of ascending a sheer wall of rock. The region is so vast and complex that it's best to break it up into specific features.

Crawford Notch State Park

North of Bartlett on U.S. 302. Headquarters: Star Rte., Bartlett, NH 03812. ☎ **603/374-2272.** Hiking.

Crawford Notch State Park is one of two spectacular state parks surrounded by the National Forest. A highly popular route since stagecoach days, this sinuous 6-mile mountainous pass goes through some of the most rugged terrain in the Northeast. When the Crawford family began taking travelers to the Notch and advertising in the Boston papers, the tourism industry in the White Mountains blossomed. Ethan Allan Crawford, who operated the first inn here, is the namesake of the oldest continuously maintained hiking trail in America. First blazed in 1819, the Crawford Path begins near the old Crawford House and climbs above the tree line to Mount Washington.

Franconia Notch State Park

South of Franconia on I-93. Headquarters: by the entrance to the Flume in Franconia, NH. ☎ **603/823-8800.** Camping, cross-country skiing, hiking, mountain biking.

Located on I-93, a half-hour drive to the west of Crawford Notch, this state park is extremely crowded during the high season. The stunning 8-mile-long pass sits on the eastern side of the Whites between Cannon Mountain and the high peaks of the Franconia Range. The notch offers an incredible display of unique scenery. The **Flume** is an 800-foot-long gorge with steep, moss-covered walls as high as 90 feet and a width as narrow as 12 feet. The **Basin** is a deep glacial pothole almost 30 feet in diameter that sits at the base of a waterfall. The **Old Man of the Mountain** is a 40-foot-high rock formation that looks like the chiseled face of a proud man. It was immortalized in the story "The Great Stone Face" by Nathaniel Hawthorne, who wrote, "It seemed as if an enormous giant, or Titan, had sculpted his own likeness there upon the precipice."

Mount Washington and the Presidential Range

Rte. 16 at Pinkham Notch. ☎ **603/466-3347.** Backpacking and hiking.

Standing 6,288 feet tall, Mount Washington is the highest peak in the Northeast. The mountain is broad with three major ridges; numerous valleys; and two immense glacial cirques, the renowned Tuckerman Ravine and the Great Gulf. Similar to Crawford Notch, the mountain has attracted visitors for almost a century and a half. The Summit House was built in 1852, the toll road completed in 1861, the Cog Railway constructed in 1869, and the first weather observatory created in 1870. Pinkham Notch, one of the wider New Hampshire notches, and the headquarters of the Appalachian Mountain Club are both located to the east of the mountain on Route 16. The surrounding mountains in the Presidential Range include six mountains over 5,000 feet high, all offering sweeping views of the region.

Androscoggin River

Rte. 16. Contact the Northern White Mountains Chamber of Commerce, 164 Main St., Berlin, 03570. ☎ **800/992-7480** or 603/752-6060. Canoeing, fishing.

Measuring 35 miles long in New Hampshire, the Androscoggin River enters the state from Maine at Wentworth's Location and flows south, through Errol, Milan, and Berlin, before turning sharply east and going back into Maine. Once used to float logs down to the paper mills, the river is now one of the state's finest recreational locales. Fly-fishing anglers try their luck with the numerous trout, and canoeists come to paddle down Class II and III rapids. The Thirteen Mile Woods Scenic Area, just south of Errol, is the most splendid area of the waterway.

Umbagog Lake National Wildlife Refuge

5.5 miles north of Errol on Rte. 16. ☎ **603/482-3415.** Bird watching, canoeing, fishing, wildlife watching.

Umbagog Lake, best known for its pair of nesting bald eagles, is largely undeveloped, with roughly 60 miles of shoreline. It's home to a diverse array of wildlife: Loons, ospreys, even raptors share the skies with the eagles. Moose are spotted regularly while bears are seen infrequently. Situated on the Maine–New Hampshire border, the lake's canoeing and fishing are first-class. Anglers have been known to hook salmon, brook trout, brown trout, pickerel, and yellow perch.

Dixville Notch State Park

Rte. 26. Contact the Northern White Mountains Chamber of Commerce, 164 Main St., Berlin. ☎ **800/992-7480** or 603/752-6060. Hiking.

Dixville Notch, the narrowest notch in New Hampshire, lies in the north across from the famous Balsams resort. Carved between Sanguinary Mountain and Mount Gloriette, the rocky cleft barely allows the two-lane Route 26 to squeeze through. The notch, once owned by Daniel Webster, is now part of a state park, replete with waterfalls, flume, and hiking trails. The short, steep walk up to Table Rock leads to an exposed ledge that juts out over a cliff (see "Hiking," below).

Connecticut River

New England's longest river, the Connecticut, forms most of the border between New Hampshire and Vermont. As a general rule, the closer you get to the Canadian border, the more pristine and tranquil the Connecticut becomes. This is especially true of the Connecticut Lakes region at the Quebec border and the section of the river just north of Hanover. Blue-ribbon trout are found in the waterway between the Connecticut Lakes and North Stratford. Farther south, the river is known for its warm-water bass fishing.

What to Do & Where to Do It

BIRD WATCHING

Although approximately 38 species of birds can be found in the **White Mountain National Forest** year-round, including chickadees, ravens, nuthatches, and downy woodpeckers, their ranks swell to 110 or more during the summer months when migratory birds arrive to breed—the ovenbird, wood thrush, red-eyed vireo, and black-throated blue warbler, to name a few. Another 35 species pass through the forest as migrants or winter visitors. In some years, you're apt to find northern hawk owl and great gray owl from the far north, as well as bohemian waxwings, red and white crossbills, pine grosbeaks, and common redpolls.

Remarkably, the wood thrush, which include the American redstart and black-throated blue warbler, spend the winter months in the subtropical regions of Central America before flying north thousands of miles to North America to breed. Many of them spend summers in the White Mountains, filling the woods with beautiful songs and raising their young before once again returning south.

Concern over the apparent decline of neotropical birds has led to efforts aimed at guaranteeing their continued survival. The White Mountain National Forest has joined forces with several universities, research centers, the New Hampshire Fish and Game Department, and the Audubon Society of New Hampshire to monitor bird population and nesting sites to ensure that forest management enhances these birds' ability to survive.

Late spring and early summer are the best times for enjoying the greatest number and variety of birds. Since many birds prefer one habitat or another and are most active at different times, you'll see more species if you plan on visiting different habitats throughout the course of the day.

Also in the Whites, the **Zealand Trail** (see "Hiking," below) is a good place to spot warblers and other colorful birds in August on their way south for the winter. The Appalachian Mountain Club usually takes birders on a weekend tour of Zealand Valley during this time. Cost is $135 including instruction, lodging, and meals. Call ☎ **603/466-2727** for dates.

Further north, canoeing **Umbagog Lake** to view the only pair of nesting bald eagles in New Hampshire is a spectacle not to miss (see "Canoeing," below). Herons, loons, and ospreys can also be found in the northern lakes.

CANOEING

After all, the Whites aren't solely for hikers.

Quiet Water

Saco River

From a 1-hr. paddle to a 3-day trip. Class III to IV white water in reaches above Bartlett; mostly Class I to II white water from Bartlett to North Conway; quick water below North Conway, quieting to placid, smooth current as the river crosses into Maine. Put in at Saco Bound Outfitters for easy quick water run: From North Conway, take State Rte. 16 south to where U.S. 302 veers off to the east. River access is located 2 miles east of Center Conway on U.S. 302 (at old covered-bridge site, or Saco Bound Outfitters). Map: USGS Carroll County.

When your legs are weary from days of arduous hiking in the Whites, let your arms take over and canoe down the Saco River. This narrow waterway weaves from Crawford Notch in the heart of the White Mountains all the way through southeastern Maine, before emptying into the

Atlantic at the city of Saco, south of Portland. The river rapidly changes character as it descends from Crawford Notch. It falls steeply at first—the Upper Saco is one of New England's more renowned white-water runs. But by the time the river reaches North Conway, most of its fury has been dissipated. In the Conway area and east into Maine, you'll find any number of access points and canoeing options along the Saco, from 3- and 6-mile day trips to a 3-day, 40-mile canoe-camping journey to Hiram, Maine. There are a host of camping sites in the spruce forests that line the river.

One extremely hot summer afternoon, I rented a canoe from Saco Bound Outfitters and paddled for 3 hours and 6.4 miles to the put-out at Pigs Farm. Saco Bound's parking lot was packed, but I soon learned that the long stretch of river helps to keep you from playing bumper boats with other canoeists. Most boaters I passed were already entrenched in the sand, either having a picnic on the shore or keeping cool in the water. Shortly after starting off with my canoe, I passed a large flock of Canada geese playing "follow the leader" by order of size: The little babies were struggling to keep up at the back of the line as they floated across the border into Maine. At the 3-mile mark, I passed under Weston's Bridge to find a town beach blanketed with sunbathers. Views of the mighty Whites opened up to the west. I soon passed a girls' camp on the right, where instructions, amplified through the public address system, echoed in the surrounding forest. Far too quickly, I arrived at Pigs Farm, where the Saco Bound bus was waiting to pick people up. The river kept my hot skin wet for 3 cool hours—the small jaunt whet my appetite for a longer journey.

Saco Bound Outfitters, P.O. Box 119, Center Conway, NH 03813 (☎ **603/447-2177;** www.sacobound.com), rents canoes at their put-in, 2 miles east of Center Conway. The list of canoeing options they offer includes 3-, 6.4-, and 10.2-mile day trips; a 22-mile overnight jaunt to Lovewell Pond; and a 3-day, 40-mile journey to Hiram. Saco Bound will pick up you and the canoe at a designated time. Cost for rental is $25.50 per day, including shuttle and parking.

Long Pond

South of Benton. Access: From Exit 32 off I-93, head 11 miles west on Rte. 112 to the intersection of Rte. 116. Follow both roads. for 1 mile; after the split, follow Rte. 116 south for another 1.6 miles. Turn left onto unpaved North South Rd. After 2.4 miles, turn right, following the sign for Long Pond. You will reach a small parking and picnic area in 0.6 mile.

Tucked away in the White Mountain National Forest, the 124-acre Long Pond is truly a gem in the rough. Entirely uninhabited and surrounded by the White Mountains, the shoreline is a mix of tall fir and spruce, white birch, and red maple. Come here in the early morning, when the rising mist adds to the primitive allure, and you're bound to find some otter or beaver. Maybe even moose. The parking lot and picnic area leaves you at the northern tier of the pond, where you can paddle around a dozen islands or head south where the shoreline is more marshy and better for bird watching.

Umbagog Lake

Allow 4–5 hr. Easy paddling, though this is a large lake—be watchful of the weather, as winds and waves can make for dangerous conditions. Access: public boating access at southern end of lake, off State Rte. 26; at Umbagog Lake Campground, east of public boat access; at Androscoggin River (Errol) at northern end of lake; and at Magalloway River, off State Rte. 16 near the Maine border. Map: USGS 7.5-min. Umbagog Lake South, Umbagog Lake North.

Wildlife is abundant in the vast forests of northern New Hampshire and Maine—moose, white-tailed deer, red fox, beaver, and coyote are common sightings. However, my wife, Lisa, and I weren't prepared for the extraordinary pair of birds we found nesting on a dead oak tree on Umbagog Lake. Loons were lounging on the glass waters, their call (the sound of laughter) echoed atop the spruce and fir trees. Many of the trees tilted toward the river, the result of hard-working beavers and the blustery winds of winter. We glided along the calm waters, following a great blue heron into a small channel that led into Umbagog. This vast 7,850-acre lake, whose shores lie half in New Hampshire and half in Maine, is a National Wildlife Area, known for its exemplary landlocked-salmon and trout fish-ing. Several islands dotted the western shores of the lake, one of which has the distinct honor of housing the only pair of nesting bald eagles in New Hampshire. We slowly paddled to our right, where we saw a large nest perched atop the highest branch of a leafless, dead tree. We drew closer to find the mother guarding her home, her pointed beak sticking out through the maze of twigs. The sight of her mate standing on the branch below was mesmerizing. His white head was cocked in a regal pose, his eyes aware of everything around him, hence the nickname "eagle eye." We skirted the island for a long time, fascinated by the awesome sight, before continuing on our 8.5-mile jaunt. Four immature eagles (in age, not attitude) learning how to fly hovered above as we turned right down the Errol River to the Errol Dam.

For those who want to get out for a longer wilderness experience on Lake Umbagog, there are established campsites scattered all around the lake run by **Umbagog Lake Campground,** P.O. Box 181, Errol, NH 03579 (☎ **603/482-7795**). Contact them for information about rates and for maps of the site locations.

Second Connecticut Lake, East Inlet

Northeast of Pittsburg. Access: There are several places to put in along Rte. 3 for Second Connecticut Lake. Drive north on Rte. 3 and you'll see a sign for the well-marked access roads to the lake. Perhaps the best spot for put-in is 0.6 mile south of Deer Mountain Campground on Rte. 3, where you turn right onto a gravel road. Drive 0.4 mile and you'll reach a small timber bridge where you can launch the canoe. To reach East Inlet, follow the same road across the timber bridge and bear right at the fork. 1.6 miles later, you'll reach the dam at East Inlet whee you can put in.

If you've traveled this far north into the New Hampshire wilderness, you deserve to paddle with moose. Second Connecticut Lake is where the Connecticut River, barely a trickle at this point, finally runs out of water in the north. The 1,286-acre lake has more than 11 miles of mostly undeveloped shoreline where moose love to hide knee-deep in the marsh, putting their large snouts in the water to search for food. At the northern end of the lake, near the timber bridge, Scott Creek is a sinuous river curving through grass marshes and a deep green forest of spruce and fir. Not only will you find moose, but you could also spot otters, beavers, loons, and great blue herons. About a mile into the paddle, Scott Creek widens into the main lake. Hopefully, the winds won't be too bad, or the paddling can get rough as you head south around two large islands.

The entirety of East Inlet is like that first mile on Scott Creek—paddling through a dark forest of tall spruce and fir, the rhythm of your stroke interrupted only by the sound of a slurping moose. Add brackish water and large ferns lining the marshy shores and you truly have a wild setting, one that you would expect in these parts.

White-Water Canoeing or Kayaking

Northern Waters Canoe and Kayak Company, Errol, NH (☎ **603-447-2177;** www.sacobound/kayak.html), offers white-water canoe trips and instruction on Androscoggin River's Class II and III rapids. Enter the Androscoggin at either

Umbagog Lake or the ramp by Errol Dam. Class II and III rapids follow the dam, with a large pool at the mouth of Clear Stream that makes it easy to pull out your canoe or kayak and head back up to run the rapids again. The river has good eddies and Class II rapids all the way to Pontook Dam in Milan.

CROSS-COUNTRY SKIING

In the Backcountry

The granite that cuts through the Whites puts on its frosty face come winter, looking even less inviting than it does in the warm weather months. Don't worry: It's bark is bigger than its bite. Many of the backcountry routes are on level logging roads that head deep into the firs and spruces of the White Mountain National Forest. Other backcountry routes, like the freewheeling Wildcat Trail, is a great telemark run into the Jackson Ski Touring Center, arguably the finest touring center in the East.

The Appalachian Mountain Club (AMC) leaves two huts open in the winter. The huts are self-serve and can be downright chilly in the wintertime, so dress appropriately. The **Zealand Trail** (see "Hiking," below) is a relatively easy trail that leads to one of those huts. Since most of Zealand Road is unplowed in the winter months, the 6.8-mile ski trail is much longer than the hike. You must first take the 4.1-mile-long **Spruce Goose Ski Trail** to reach the Zealand Trail. Skiers staying overnight can ski back the next day or continue on the **Ethan Pond Trail** through narrow Zealand Notch to Shoal Pond or Thoreau Falls. The Carter Notch Hut is the only other AMC lodge open in the winter months. The **Nineteen-Mile Brook Trail** (also in "Hiking," below) to the hut is far more strenuous than the Zealand Trail, attracting hordes of snowshoers.

Hayes Copp Ski Trail

Allow 2–4 hr. Easy to moderate; logging road with gradual ascent. Access: From Gorham, travel south on Rte. 16 for 5 miles and turn left onto Pinkam B Rd. After several hundred yards, turn left into the Dolly Copp Campground.

Bordering the Great Gulf Wilderness, much of the Hayes Copp Ski Trail is on logging roads, so it's ideal for the beginner who wants to get lost in the woods of the White Mountains. From the Dolly Copp Campground, the trail climbs gently until you veer right onto the Great Gulf Trail. Cruising along the banks of the Peabody River, more-experienced skiers can turn right on the Leavitt's Link Trail for excellent views of the Carter Range. Novices can simply turn around and head back to Dolly Copp. The Leavitt's Link Trail is somewhat hilly, but soon the Hayes Copp Trail returns from the left to take you back to the campground.

Tuckerman Ravine, Mount Washington

Allow at least 3 hr. for the climb. Experts only! This is a steep, mountainous wall. Access: trailhead behind the Appalachian Mountain Club Pinkham Notch Lodge, off State Rte. 16, between Jackson and Gorham.

Skiing Tuckerman Ravine is one of the most thrilling backcountry winter experiences in the Northeast. This large glacial cirque, or bowl, is on the southeast shoulder of Mount Washington. During the winter months, the ravine fills up with snow transported by intense winds from the mountain's summit. So, by springtime, this natural amphitheater is ready for you to cut your line down some of the steepest pitches in the country. Late March to mid-May is the best time to ski Tuckerman, but, some years, people have skied here until the Fourth of July!

"Tuck" should be attempted only by expert downhill and telemark skiers! I can't emphasize this enough. Every year someone dies on its slopes. A week before I arrived, a skier slid down a patch of ice on one of the runs, Hillman Highway, and slammed into the rocks. He simply became another statistic. That said, people have been skiing "the bowl" since 1926, when legendary Appalachian

Mountain Club guru Joe Dodge and several of his cronies bushwhacked up the mountain and made their way down. During the 1930s, the place became so popular that races were held from the top of the headwall all the way back to Pinkham Notch Lodge. That's a 4,200-foot drop in 4 miles.

In 1932, the U.S. Forest Service constructed a fire trail, which is still the only way to get to Tuckerman today. Now called the Tuckerman Ravine Trail, it is an unrelenting, 2.4-mile, 2-hour climb to Hermit Lake Cabin, or HoJo's as the regulars call it. The trail is challenging enough without skis, but with full gear be prepared to sweat. From HoJo's, the trail climbs steeply another 0.7 mile to the base of the ravine. Throw on a fresh layer of polypropylene so you don't freeze to death up top. Then decide your destiny.

There are no tow ropes, T-bars, or super quads here—just your two feet to hike up to the trail of your choice. Left Gully climbs to the lip just left of the main headwall. From here it's an 800-foot drop over a quarter of a mile. Right Gully is slightly shorter with less of a pitch. The longest run is Hillman Highway, a little over 0.5 mile. Pitches range from 35° to 55°, depending on the trail you choose. It's wise to talk to other skiers to see which trail has the best snow and is the easiest to climb. When I went, I saw one fool take almost an hour and a half to climb Left Gully, only to have a horrible run on patches of ice afterward.

On a sunny spring day, hundreds of spectators and skiers congregate on the Lunch Rocks. These large boulders on the lower right side of the headwall are the place from which to cheer on other skiers. But watch out for falling ice, which sometimes drops from the top of the headwall.

Don't worry about hiking the 2.4 miles down. You can ski on the John Sherburne Trail, a sweeping downhill run that will have you back at the Pinkham Notch Lodge in less than 25 minutes.

Echo Lake Trail

Allow 1 hr. Easy loop around a lake. Access: From North Conway, travel on River Rd. for approximately 1 mile and turn right on West Side Rd. A half mile later, veer right onto Echo Lake Rd., following the signs to the park entrance.

If you happen to be in the North Conway region in the winter, this 1-mile loop around Echo Lake is a great lunchtime escape in the woods. It's also ideal for young children who want to have their first shot at cross-country skiing. Simply head around the lake through a forest of pine and oak and you'll be back at the starting point in no time. In the distance, you can see the cliffs of Whitehorse Ledge and might even spot several ice climbers dangling from a line.

Lower Nanamocomuck

Allow 2–4 hr. Moderate; along the scenic Swift River. Access: From Conway, travel 12 miles west on Rte. 112 (Kancamagus Hwy.) and turn right on Bear Notch Rd. Drive 1 mile and park in the plowed area.

Paralleling the Swift River for much of the jaunt and then weaving through the evergreens, this up-and-down trail rewards skiers with great vistas of Bear Mountain and the perfect picnic spot above Falls Pond. A good 4 miles into the run, Falls Pond is usually my turn-around spot, but if you want to continue onward another 3 miles you'll reach the Albany Covered Bridge (ca. 1858). It's possible to put a second car here by turning right at Passaconaway Road off Kancamagus Highway.

Lincoln Woods

Allow 2–4 hr. Easy to moderate; 8 miles of trail along the Pemigewasset River. Access: From Exit 32 off I-93, head east on the Kancamagus Hwy. (Rte. 112) for 5 miles. You'll see the signs for the Lincoln Woods Cross-Country Ski Trails on the left side of the road.

Lincoln Woods, one of the most accessible networks of backcountry trails in the White Mountain National Forest, is a popular hangout in winter when the fluffy white stuff starts to fall. The Lincoln Woods Trail cruises along the west side of the Pemigewasset River, crossing a 160-foot suspension bridge in the early goings. The trail meets up with the much longer Wilderness Trail, and for intermediate skiers it's possible to connect with the Pemi East Side Road Trail for a good 11-mile loop along the river. Novices can follow the Lincoln Woods Trail to the stone wall that abuts a bridge over the Franconia Brook.

If you want more, drive on the Kancamagus Highway 4.3 miles to the east and you can try the Greeley Pond Ski Trail (see "Mountain Biking," below).

Franconia Notch State Park Recreation Trail

Allow 1–2 hr. Easy to moderate; 9-mile bike trail is perfect for cross-country skiers in the winter. Access: Heading north on I-93, take the first exit off the Franconia Notch State Parkway to the parking area for the Flume. You can't miss the signs.

Although extremely crowded in the summer and fall, this 9-mile trail will be practically all yours in the winter. The trail starts at the Flume, a long gorge that is 800 feet long and no more than 20 feet wide, with steep, moss-covered walls. Next stop is the Basin, a granite pool 30 feet wide and 15 feet deep. A short uphill and you'll see the sign for the 2.5-mile Basin Cascade Trail, a relaxing snowshoe along a rolling brook. Or stay on the trail for a view of Profile Lake and the state's official symbol, the Old Man of the Mountain. The final stop is Echo Lake, whose iced-over waters stand at the base of Mount Lafayette and Cannon Mountain. If you want to get a closer look at Cannon, take the 5-minute tram ride to the 4,200-foot summit and go downhill-skiing.

Nordic Skiing Centers

Combine all the ski touring centers in New Hampshire and you have more than 1,000 kilometers (625 miles) of groomed trails. First and foremost is the **Jackson Ski Touring Foundation,** P.O. Box 216, Jackson, NH 03846 (☎ **603/383-9355;** www.jacksonxc.com), the largest cross-country skiing network in the Northeast. Over 157 kilometers (98 miles) of trail (91km, or 56.9 miles, groomed daily) escort skiers high up into the mountains, away from the country inns of the charming New England village of Jackson. Besides the challenging Wildcat Trail, try the Ellis River Trail, which hugs a small brook as it heads into the woods.

Situated in the western valley of Mount Washington, almost every trail in the **Bretton Woods Ski Touring Center,** Bretton Woods, New Hampshire 03575 (☎ **603/278-3322;** www.brettonwoods.com), offers breathtaking vistas of the Presidential Range. There are 60 miles of trails evenly split between beginner, intermediate, and expert. Most of the novice trails are on the wide, flat Ammonoosuc Trail System. The Deception System has more-challenging terrain, like a trail that climbs Mount Deception.

Great Glen Trails, Pinkham Notch, New Hampshire (☎ **603/466-2333;** www.greatglentrails.com), has 40 kilometers (25 miles) of trails at the base of the largest mountain in the Northeast, Mount Washington. The trails wind through the open meadows, then duck into the forest, always in the shadow of the Presidential Range. If you can manage to get to Dixville Notch in the winter, you'll rarely find crowds at the remote **Balsams,** Dixville Notch, New Hampshire 03576 (☎ **603/255-3400;** www.thebalsams.com), where 50 miles of secluded trails reward the skier who journeys this far north. Many of the trails, especially in the northern part of the system, cater to beginners and intermediates. The Canal Trail leaves you at a warming hut on the shores of Mud Pond. Another 2-mile loop skirts the pond.

Known for its Alpine skiing, **Waterville Valley,** in Waterville Valley, New Hampshire 03215 (☎ **603/236-4666;** www.waterville.com), also offers more than 100 kilometers (62.5 miles) of runs to cross-country skiers, including the Cascade Brook Trail. The White Mountain Criterion Trail is fun for skating. Intermediate skiers can choose the Sloppy Joe Trail, which rolls and turns on a short climb with good views of the valley.

For more information on New Hampshire's cross-country ski centers, contact **Ski New Hampshire (☎ 800/887-5464;** www.skinh.com).

DOWNHILL SKIING/ SNOWBOARDING

Looking for a nice cozy ski area where the sun shines daily and the snow is soft, cushioning every fall? Then beat it, buddy—head to Utah. Here, in the Granite State, skiing is all about being outdoors and facing the elements—20° temperatures with swirling 20- to 30-mile-per-hour winds are considered a warm day. Hard-packed powder can change to ice at any given moment, and stunted trees and submarine-gray skies provide little encouragement when you wipe out. This is the heart of New England, after all, the state that brought you Joe Dodge, where rugged individualism pervades every aspect of daily life, even the ski slopes. Flannel and wool sweaters still hold sway here as the clothing of choice over trendy Gore-Tex.

With so much of New Hampshire covered in rock, it's incredible that skiing exists at all. But you'll be surprised how good the trails are here, leaving you far more invigorated than battered. Let's start with the two granddaddies, Cannon and Wildcat—mountains that have been skied for over 60 years.

Cannon

Franconia Notch State Park, Franconia, NH 03580. **☎ 603/823-8800;** www.cannonmt.com. 39 trails (5 novice, 20 intermediate, 14 expert); 6 lifts including 2 quads and 3 triples, in addition to the tram; 2,146-ft. vertical drop (the longest in New Hampshire outside of Tuckerman Ravine). Full-day tickets $42 weekend, $30 weekday; Tues and Thurs 2 for 1.

Cannon is the home of the first ski trail in North America, the first ski school, and the first aerial tram, installed in 1938. The mountain is notorious for its tough trails, especially the ones facing the north, which tend to be icy. One of its signature trails, Hardscrabble, is a challenging ride down a winding, heavily moguled route. Zoomer is a classic New England ***bump run***—in other words, a trail that will beat you to a pulp most times, if only to make your good runs seem more luminous. The short, steep, and bumpy Avalanche is another expert trail. Peabody's slopes have great lower-intermediate terrain; and Upper Canyon, Tramway, and Vista Way are free-flowing cruisers.

Wildcat

Jackson, NH 03846. **☎ 800/255-6439;** www.skiwildcat.com. Snow report: ☎ 800/643-4521. 44 trails (25% novice, 45% intermediate, 30% expert); 5 lifts, which can handle 8,500 skiers per hour; 2,100-ft. vertical drop. Full-day tickets $49 weekends, $39 weekdays. Every Wed is 2 for 1, and every first Mon of the month is an unbeatable $19.

Another forbidding place to ski is Wildcat, first used in the mid-1930s when racers hiked up the mountain to compete on the original Wildcat Trail. Sitting on the wall of Pinkham Notch, the views of nearby Mount Washington and Tuckerman Ravine will take your visible breath away. Try to concentrate on your skiing, though—this is a big, rugged mountain that doesn't take well to cavalier attitudes among supplicants. Trails range from the slow-moving Polecat to the much steeper Lynx, a narrow route that falls through a succession of pitches and flats. Generally speaking, this is an expert's hill—there are more choices and flavors here for strong skiers than for newbies.

Black Mountain
Five Mile Circuit Rd., Jackson, NH 03846. ☎ **800/698-4490;** www.blackmt.com. 62 trails (18 novice, 22 intermediate, 22 expert). Full-day tickets $32 weekends, $20 weekdays.

Entering its 66th season, the oldest ski resort in New Hampshire is nestled among pastures and farmlands in the quaint village of Jackson, New Hampshire. At Black Mountain, beginners can relax and improve their skills on Sugarbush and Black Beauty, and experts can test their skills on the new supersteep Mr. Rew or the winding narrows of Upper Galloping Goose. An easier go than nearby Wildcat.

Waterville Valley
Town Sq., Waterville Valley, NH 03215. ☎ **800/468-2553;** www.waterville.com. Snow report: ☎ 603/236-4144. 52 trails (10 novice, 32 intermediate, 10 expert); 11 lifts including 2 high-speed detachable quads, 2 triples, and 3 doubles; 2,020-ft. vertical drop. Full-day tickets $49 weekends, $41 weekdays for adults.

Waterville Valley—like Loon, Attitash, and Cranmore—is one of the more modern White Mountain ski resorts. With sweeping runs like Upper Bobby's Run and Tippecanoe, Waterville Valley is known as a great family resort. It's a lot like Stratton and Mount Snow in southern Vermont: a mountain within easy range of the big city (primarily Boston) and blessed with a bumper crop of fast-skiing, ego-boosting, wide, cruising boulevards. Try the Tree Line/White Caps/Sel's Choice combo.

Loon
Kancamagus Hwy., Lincoln, NH 03251. ☎ **603/745-8111;** www.loonmtn.com. Snow report: ☎ 603/745-8100. 46 trails (10 novice, 27 intermediate, 9 expert); 8 lifts including a fast 4-passenger gondola, 2 triples, and 4 doubles; 2,100-ft. vertical drop. Full-day adult tickets $49 weekends, $41 weekdays.

Loon Mountain attracts more skiers per year than any other New Hampshire ski area. However, its limited ticket policy ensures that lift lines are kept to 15 minutes or less. Loon is even more of an intermediate skier's cup of tea, with huge snowmaking and grooming operations and a plethora of wide cruisers. Loon is a little more homogenous—there's not too much challenging skiing here.

Attitash Bear Peak
U.S. 302, Bartlett, NH 03812. ☎ **603/374-2368;** www.attitash.com. Snow report: ☎ 603/374-0946. 70 trails (14 novice, 33 intermediate, 23 expert); 12 lifts including 3 quads, 3 triples, and 3 doubles; 1,750- ft. vertical drop. Full-day adult tickets $49 weekends, $42 weekdays.

Attitash is known for having better weather and quieter winds than any other New Hampshire resort, but its low base elevation costs it the fluffier natural snow you find high in the Whites. It's the sort of rolling, unpredictably pitched ski mountain New England is famous for. Trails like Ptarmigan and Northwest Passage are moderately steep, if not quite long enough for my taste.

Mount Cranmore
North Conway, NH 03860. ☎ **603/356-5543;** www.cranmore.com. Snow report: ☎ 800/Sun-N-Ski. 39 trails (14 novice, 18 intermediate, 7 expert); 9 lifts including a triple and 4 doubles; 1,200-ft. vertical drop. Full-day tickets $29.

Another old-timer, Cranmore is mostly a novice-to-intermediate hill. But this is a great place to go to check out their other ski toys. Tubes, ski bikes, skifoxes, and snowscoots all head down the mountainside. ***Snowscoots*** are part scooter, part snowboard where you use the handlebars to turn and jump. ***Skifoxes*** are ergonomically shaped bench seats with a wooden support and shock absorber. ***Ski bikes*** are equipped with two shock absorbers and long comfortable seats, and riders wear two little skies to aid in balance and control.

Bretton Woods

U.S. 302, Twin Mountain, NH 03595. ☎ **603/278-3300;** www.brettonwoods.com. 66 trails (31% novice, 41% intermediate, 28% expert); 8 lifts including 3 quads, 1 triple, and 2 doubles; 1,500-ft. vertical drop. Full-day adult tickets $51 weekends, $42 weekdays. Pricing is is 2 for 1 on Wed.

In the 1999–2000 season, Bretton Woods expanded to West Mountain and opened 24 new trails and glades serviced by a new quad chair. Now the largest ski area in New Hampshire, Bretton Woods plans to keep on building, next developing Mount Stickney to the east in the 2002–03 season. This will create another 18 to 25 trails. Adding to the allure is the news that the Mount Washington Hotel, at the base of the mountain, is now open year-round. This sprawling mountain resort will turn 100 in 2002. Bretton Woods has always been known for its calm, wide-open style of skiing, but add West to the equation and the more-experienced skier now has some glades, chutes, and bowls to try. A bright yellow Mount Washington Cog Railway passenger car is the new summit warming hut after you disembark the quad on West.

The Balsams

Dixville Notch, NH 03576. ☎ **603/869-5506;** www.thebalsams.com. Snow report: ☎ 603/255-3400. 13 trails (4 novice, 6 intermediate, 3 expert); 4 lifts including 1 double; 1,000-ft. vertical drop. Full-day tickets $25 weekends, $22 weekdays.

If you're looking for a remote resort with rarely a line, head to one of the last grand resorts in the Whites, The Balsams in Dixville Notch. The skiing will strike not an ounce of fear into your heart, but that's not the point here. See "Resorts & Inns," below, for more information.

For more information on any of the ski resorts in New Hampshire, contact **Ski New Hampshire** (☎ **800/887-5464;** www.skinh.com). They provide a ski map and help with trip planning.

FISHING

In the northwestern part of the state, brown and rainbow trout are caught on the Connecticut River. Indeed, the Connecticut offers more than 70 miles of unparalleled trout fishing, beginning at the outlet of the Second Connecticut Lake in Pittsburg down to its confluence with the Upper Ammonoosuc in Groveton. The stretch below the 100-foot-high Murphy Dam in Pittsburg offers excellent trout habitat due to the constant release of cold water from Lake Francis. The Upper Connecticut can be accessed from Route 3 at several points north of Pittsburg.

The **White Mountain National Forest** offers a guide to the best trout fishing in the Whites. Their headquarters are located at 719 Main St., Laconia, NH 03246 (☎ **603/528-8721**). Other highlights include salmon fishing in Waterville Valley's Mad River and the East Branch of the Pemigewasset River near Lincoln, and trout fishing on the Saco and Swift Rivers close to Conway. **North Country Angler,** on Route 16, just north of North Conway (☎ **603/356-6000;** www.northcountryangler.com), offers trout and landlocked-salmon tackle and information.

Farther north, you're bound to see anglers fly-fishing or casting on the Androscoggin River, known for its abundance of trout, which is stocked at 1,000 trout per mile. June is the best month for fishing here, as well as at nearby Rapid River, which flows into the northeast part of Lake Umbagog. Lake Umbagog is good for brook trout and landlocked salmon. Also, the smallmouth-bass fishing here is some of the best in the state. With plenty of smallies weighing 1.5 to 2 pounds, the action can be fast and furious. Large fish in the 4- to 5-pound range are also being reported. Your fishing companions here will be ospreys, herons, kingfishers, and eagles (see "Canoeing," above).

Head to the Evans Notch area for brookies and rainbows. The accessibility of Wild River makes it a popular fishing area, especially since it is stocked. Stocking is also heavy in the ponds in areas near Patte Brook. Spruce and Blue Brook, which feed into the Wild River, are worthy of a hike-in. Other well-liked areas are Cold River, Basin Pond, Province Pond, and ponds in the Crocker Area.

For an information packet including a nonresident license application, contact the **New Hampshire Fish and Game Department,** 2 Hazen Drive, Concord, NH 03301 (☎ **603/272-3421;** www.wildlife.state.nh.us).

GOLF

Like most New Englanders, New Hampshirites play their golf fast and fair (a 2-hour round is the norm), think golf carts are for wimps, love to play in all types of weather, and don't give a hoot about golf fashion. Get those parkas and mittens on and head toward the tee. First stop is in the north at the **Balsams Golf Shop** (☎ **603/255-4961;** www.thebalsams.com) where, even in May, it's never too late to snow. Located on the majestic grounds of the Balsams in Dixville Notch, the course was designed by Donald Ross in 1912. Like most Ross designs, the fairways are lush and generous, and the greens are small, roundish, and slope toward ruin. At least, you'll have the scenery to savor. High on the western side of Keyser Mountain, the Balsams' aptly named Panorama Golf Course overlooks acres of pristine forest and meadowlands.

Voted one of the top 10 courses to play during fall foliage by ***Golf Magazine,*** the **Owl's Nest Golf Course** (☎ **603/726-3076;** www.owlsnestgolf.com) is easily accessible off I-93 in Campton. Situated just south of the White Mountain National Forest and along the Pemigewasset River, the course has one of the most scenic locales for golfing in the state.

HIKING

Time for a pop quiz. Don't worry; it's only one short SAT analogy question:

Hawaii: surfing

A) Maine: swimming

B) Vermont: whale watching

C) New Hampshire: hiking

D) Rhode Island: rock climbing

If you chose C, you're correct. Please collect your grade of 1600 and proceed to Harvard. Hawaii is one of America's premier surfing spots; New Hampshire is one of America's premier hiking locales. (For those of you who thought the correct answer was A, we recommend that you collect your diploma at the University of Maine in Orono. B is incorrect because "Champ" is not a whale. If you thought D was the answer, you have rocks in your head.)

Vermont has the rolling Green Mountains and the Long Trail, but no New England state can match the spectacular mountain scenery found in the White Mountains, nor can any other state offer the wide range of hikes available to all levels of expertise. From 5,000-foot-high ridge walks to quick mountain ascents to soft, springy paths that climb along a waterfall, New Hampshire has it all. So pull on those dirty mountain boots and get those thighs moving!

A good purchase for hikers is the "White Mountains Hiking Map" published by Map Adventures. The map depicts all the hiking trails in the Presidential Range, Franconia Notch, North Conway, and Mount Chocorua. The map can be purchased from the Mountain Wanderer Map & Book Store (☎ **800/745-2707;** www.mountainwanderer.com).

Day Hikes in the White Mountains

Welch-Dickey Mountain Trail

4.5 miles. Allow 3 hr. Moderate. Access: From I-93, take Exit 28 and go east on Rte. 49 toward Waterville Valley. Turn left approximately 6 miles later, crossing a bridge and following Upper Mad River Rd. for 0.7 mile. At Orris Rd., turn right and go 0.6 mile to the parking lot. Map: USGS 7.5-min. Waterville Valley. Available at the Pemigewasset Ranger District.

The short summits (relative to the rest of the White Mountains) of Welch and Dickey Mountains offer such majestic vistas that friends of mine got married atop this trail. That's not to say this 4.5-mile loop is easy. The bride decided to forego the traditional wedding gown for T-shirt, shorts, and hiking boots, and the groom wore a tuxedo jacket over his shorts. The trail leaves the parking area and enters a forest of beeches, maples, and oaks, before turning sharply to the right to reach the southern ridge of Welch Mountain. At 1.3 miles, you reach a broad exposed ledge that offers panoramic views of verdant Waterville Valley and the miniature cars weaving their way through the mountains on Route 49. However, this ledge is deceptive. The summit is 0.7 mile away, up a sheet of steep rock and over boulders where twisted jack pines and dwarf birches have been stunted by their exposure to the extreme climate. The 2,605-foot peak is a good place to stop, enjoy the view, and have lunch. Then proceed down into the col and steeply upward for 0.2 mile to the summit of Dickey Mountain (2,734 feet). Here, you can see the mountains that form the Franconia Ridge. The exquisite views continue for the next mile as you walk down the exposed ledge through patches of scrub spruce. Eventually you enter the woods again, where the trail becomes gradual. Don't be surprised to find a wedding reception back at the parking lot.

Mount Moosilauke

6 miles (round-trip). Allow 5–6 hr. Moderate. Access: From Warren, take Rte. 118 east for 6 miles and turn left onto an access road for 1.5 miles to the lodge.

Climbing 4,810-foot Mount Moosilauke is a rite of passage for most members of the Dartmouth Outing Club. On the western-most part of the White Mountain National Forest, Moosilauke has been a popular climb for Dartmouth students and alums since the 1920s when the university ran the Tip-Top House, a summit hotel that could accommodate up to 80 hikers. The Tip-Top House burned down in 1942, but the college continues to maintain the Ravine Lodge at the base of the peak. From the lodge, the Gorge Brook Trail rises steadily on an old logging road. Soon you begin to switchback along the east shoulder. As you walk through twisted evergreens (above the tree line, the winds are often fierce), the trail begins to rise steeply along the rocky ledges of East Peak. A final push to the bare summit and you can still see the foundation that once supported the Tip-Top House. The panorama from the top includes Mount Lafayette to the northeast, with Washington and other Presidentials standing mighty in the background. To the south is Mount Cardigan and to the east, the verdant Connecticut River Valley. Descend on Carriage Road, which brings you to Snapper Trail and home to the Ravine Lodge.

Falling Waters Trail/Franconia Ridge/ Old Bridle Path

8.7 miles. Allow 6–8 hr. Strenuous. Access: From Woodstock, take I-93 North to the Falling Waters/Bridle Path parking lot. Start the trail directly behind the parking lot. Map: available at the Ammonoosuc Ranger District.

Tumbling streams and waterfalls, steep ascents to three of the highest peaks in New England, a 1.7-mile ridge walk where the spruce-studded White Mountains stand below you in a dizzying display—this is the Falling Waters–Franconia Ridge–Old Bridle Path loop. When I say that this 8.7-mile trail is easily one of the most spectacular hikes in New England, I'm not using hyperbole. I'm also being sincere when I tell you that this loop is both popular and rigorous.

Turn into the woods from the parking lot and I-93's traffic is quickly replaced by the sounds of rushing water. Follow the Falling Waters Trail and the soothing waters will be your companion through the forest and over the stream for the next mile and a half. Within a mile, you'll reach the first of three picturesque waterfalls. The walk to the waterfalls makes a great hike in itself. When the path leaves the stream for good, the trail becomes steep and rocky, leading high up the mountainside to an Alpine forest of firs and spruces. As you approach the 4,760-foot summit of Little Haystack Mountain, views of Cannon Mountain and Lonesome Lake open up. The vistas only get better when you reach the top and start walking on the Franconia Ridge Trail to the peaks of Mount Lincoln and Mount Lafayette, 5,108 and 5,249 feet, respectively. Part of the Appalachian Trail, this above-tree-line path offers a stunning panorama of New England's highest summits, including Mount Washington.

Follow the Greenleaf Trail down the steep rocks for a little over a mile to reach the Greenleaf Hut. Run by the Appalachian Mountain Club, this is the only place on the loop to refill your water bottle and get lemonade for 25¢ a glass. Continue your descent on the section of the Old Bridle Path known as Agony Ridge. This is the steepest part of the trail, where you jump from boulder to boulder and slide down sheets of rock. It's astonishing to think that this was once a horse trail. I wonder how many dead horses surround the Greenleaf Hut? At the open ledges, savor your most recent accomplishment by looking up at the eastern flank of Mount Lafayette, Franconia Ridge, and Walker Ravine. After about a mile, the trail becomes less rocky and more gradual as you make your way back through the hardwood forest to the junction of the Falling Waters Trail. After such an arduous trek, plunging into the cool waters of the stream is the best way to end the day.

Basin-Cascades Trail

2.5 miles (round-trip). Allow 2 hr. Easy to moderate. Access: Take I-93 north of Woodstock and look for the signs to the Basin parking lot. Map: USGS 7.5-min. Franconia, available at the Ammonoosuc Ranger District.

One of the most meditative spots in New England is atop the Basin-Cascades Trail. Choose a rock in the middle of Cascade Brook and listen to the waters forcibly tumble, foam, and swirl down the mountainside. You reach this tranquil spot by walking along the rolling brook for a mile. Start down at the bottom with the crowds at the Basin. The Basin is a granite pool 30 feet wide and 15 feet deep. Called a pothole by geologists, this strange cavity was formed by a melting ice sheet 15,000 years ago. When Thoreau saw the Basin in 1839, he stated that "this pothole is perhaps the most remarkable curiosity of its kind in New England." Stroll uphill and you'll find the large sign for the Basin-Cascades Trail. A web of extended roots jutting out from hemlock, maple, beech, and yellow birch trees combines with the ubiquitous White Mountain rock to make maneuvering tricky at times. The trail meanders along the brook, passing Kinsman Falls, before crossing the rocks to reach the far side. Soon you'll reach Rocky Glen Falls and a chasm of rock that forms a chute up to the top of the trail. Here, the stress of the modern world is flushed away with the falling waters. You can make a 4- or 5-hour loop by turning right and venturing to Lonesome Lake, continuing on the

Lake Trail to Lafayette Campground, and turning right on the Pemi Trail back to the Basin.

Lonesome Lake

3.2 miles (round-trip). Allow 2 hr. Easy. Access: From Franconia Notch Hwy. (I-93), 1.5 miles south of the Old Man of the Mountains, take the Lafayette Campground exit. Park in the picnic area lot.

The Lonesome Lake Trail ain't very lonesome any more. Thousands of hikers climb some 900-feet and about a mile to reach the lake each year. There's a reason for the popularity. The lake is perfectly perched on the west side of Franconia Notch, looking up at the treeless peak of Mount Lafayette. President Ulysses S. Grant was one of the first visitors to see this striking vista in 1869, having traveled by horse and buggy from the nearby town of Bethlehem. Today, the Appalachian Mountain Club (AMC) maintains one of its most popular huts on the west shore facing the Franconia Range. The Lonesome Lake Hut serves meals from its octagonal-shaped dining room and accommodates up to 46 hikers overnight.

The Lonesome Lake Trail crosses the Pemigewasset River on a footbridge and passes through Lafayette Place Campground. Proceed into a forest of tall red spruce, fir, and abundant mosses, lifting upward, before descending to the shores of the lake. To reach the AMC hut, take the Cascade Brook Trail along the eastern shores of the lake. Continue on the Around the Lake Trail before taking the Lonesome Lake Trail back to your car.

Mount Chocorua

7.6 miles (round-trip). Allow 5 hr. Moderate. Access: From Conway, head west on the Kancamagus Hwy. (Rte. 112) for 11.5 miles and park at a large parking area on the left side of the highway.

Arguably the most photographed mountain in the Whites, Chocorua's distinctive spire stands tall over a fringe of cerulean lakes. Within 10 minutes of starting from the Kancamagus Highway, the Champney Falls Trail reaches Champney Brook. Gradually climb above the brook until you find the Champney Falls Bypass Trail. Turn left on the trail and you descend into a valley before reaching the base of the falls. The water cascades down the smooth boulders. Continue on the bypass trail back to the main trail, which now gets steep. A series of switchbacks creep up the slopes of Chocorua with the craggy peak in view. When the Champney Falls Trail ends at a ridge at the 3-mile mark, turn right onto the Piper Trail for a scramble over large stone slabs to the open summit. The natural rock tower has good views in every direction, including Mount Washington to the north and Squam Lake to the south. When you've had enough of lounging on the rocks, retrace your steps back to the Kancamagus Highway.

Moat Mountain Trail

9 miles one-way. Moderate. Allow 6–7 hr. Access: Drop off one car at the Diana's Baths parking lot on River Rd. in North Conway where the hike ends. To get there, turn west at the traffic lights at the junction of River Rd. and Rte. 16 in North Conway and go 2.5 miles. Turn left into the parking lot. After dropping off your vehicle, turn right out of the parking lot and drive 1.5 miles to West Side Rd. Turn right and drive for 5.5 miles, where you turn right onto Passaconaway Rd. (soon becomes Dugway Rd.). Travel for another 2.5 miles to the parking area on the right.

If you've had enough of the crowds and now want to hike with the folks from North Conway and environs, take the 9-mile one-way Moat Mountain Trail. The trail crosses all three Moat Peaks while providing unobstructed views of Mount Chocorua to the south, Mount Washington to the north, and Kearsarge North Mountain to the east. The trail starts in an open field before snaking through the forest and then heading steeply up 2,749-foot South Moat. Glimpses of Chocorua come into view as you make your way through the blueberry bushes. At the 2.3-mile mark, you make it to your first summit. Then it's a down-and-up stroll through the forest to reach 2,805-foot Middle Moat some 0.6 mile later. The hiking gets harder over the next 2 miles on your way to North Moat. You'll have to scramble up the large slabs of rock to reach the 3,201-foot peak. The last 4 miles are a coveted treat, descending into a forest of tall pines before walking along the banks of Lucy Brook. The final stop is Diana's Baths, an old mill site with waterfalls. From here, its about a half-mile walk to your second car.

Mount Willard

2.75 miles (round-trip). Allow 1–2 hr. Easy. Access: From North Conway, take Rte. 16 North to U.S. 302 West up through Crawford Notch. Park at the Crawford Notch Visitors Center just next to the Appalachian Mountain Club hut. Map: USGS 7.5-min. Crawford Notch.

Ideal for young children and inexperienced hikers, Mount Willard is one of the easiest climbs in the White Mountains. If the thought of mountain climbing makes you sweat long before leaving your car to start your ascent, wipe your brow and give Willard a try. In less than an hour, you'll make it to the peak where jaw-dropping views of Crawford Notch stand below you, a reward for your accomplishment.

The hike begins behind the Crawford Notch Visitors Center, which is the old Crawford railroad station used by tourists in the early part of the century. The trail starts off steep but becomes more gradual as you criss-cross through the forest of dense pines. Eventually, sunshine will seep into the woods and you'll reach a large opening, which is indeed "the light at the end of the tunnel." You have reached the 2,804-foot rocky summit where the vista of the surrounding mountainside will inevitably make you gasp. The old railroad line can be seen carved into the mountainside, superseded now by the onslaught of cars that make their way through the narrow pass on Route 302. The paved road slices the mountainside in two, with rocky ledges and verdant hills on either side. Mount Willard sits slightly off-center, offering expansive views of the whole panorama. After you pat yourself on the back for climbing one of the White Mountains, stroll back effortlessly to the Visitors Center.

Arethusa Falls and Frankenstein Cliff

4.5 miles round-trip. Allow 3–4 hr. Easy to moderate. Access: 3 miles south of the Willey House on Rte. 302. A large sign on the west side of the highway indicates the turnoff to Arethusa Falls. Take this access road uphill to a parking area.

Plunging over 200 feet, Arethusa Falls is the largest waterfall in New Hampshire. The 1.5-mile Arethusa Falls Trails is easy and very popular. The path snakes upward past a grove of white birches as you climb high above Bemis Brook. Gradually, the trail slants down to the brook, which you cross and soon see the falls. The frothy white water cascades down the rock terraces. Leave the crowds behind and continue on the Frankenstein Cliff Trail through the spruces. About a mile from the falls, the trail climbs steeply, soon arriving at Frankenstein Cliff. A clearing here provides sweeping views of Crawford Notch, Mount Chocorua's pointed peak, and Mount Passaconaway. Follow the trail to the cliff's edge back into a forest of maples and beeches. The trail steeply descends at points before becoming more gradual. Pass under the steel-framed railroad trestle and turn right to complete the loop.

Zealand Trail

5.4 miles (round-trip). 3 hr. Easy. Access: Zealand Recreation Area is located 2.3 miles east of Twin Mountain on U.S. 302. Turn right at the Zealand Campground and continue on the road for 3.6 miles to its end at the Zealand Trail parking lot. Map: available from the Ammonoosuc Ranger District.

THE APPALACHIAN MOUNTAIN CLUB

No book on New Hampshire outdoor recreation would be complete without including a worthy introduction to the Appalachian Mountain Club (AMC). In 1876, 39 outdoor enthusiasts met in Boston and formed an organization devoted to exploration of the White Mountains. Several of the members had visited Europe and knew firsthand about Alpine huts—mountain refuges that sheltered hikers. They wanted to build this same type of accommodation for the growing legions of avid "trampers." Twelve years later, dreams became reality when the Madison Spring cabin was opened in the col between Mount Adams and Mount Madison. The cost to stay in the stone cabin was 50 cents a night and you had to bring your own food. Lacking backpacks, hikers wrapped food and clothing in a blanket that was tied from shoulder to hip.

Three huts, replete with cooking facilities, were added to accommodate the steady stream of climbers who were coming to the White Mountains. New trails were eventually blazed, but it wasn't until the arrival of Joe Dodge in 1922 that the current AMC began to take shape. Hired as the Pinkham Notch Hutmaster, Dodge arrived in the White Mountains at a time when the huts weren't much more than a small and loosely joined foursome of rustic refuges. More than 30 years later, he left a unified chain of eight tightly run hostels that stretched over 50 miles of rugged wilderness. A tireless devotee of the mountains and the AMC, Dodge's gruff manner was cherished and respected by all who came in contact with him.

Three years after Joe Dodge retired in 1958, the AMC went through a third phase of development. In August of 1961, *National Geographic* published a 35-page article on "The Friendly Huts of the White Mountains." Authored by none other than Supreme Court Justice William O. Douglas, the publication reached 7 million readers—mass exposure that the AMC was not capable of handling. By the summer of 1962, far more people were coming to the Whites than the AMC could possibly accommodate. In addition to expanding facilities and maintaining trails, the AMC started to offer hiker information and education services, workshops in natural history, outdoor schools, research on endangered species and on the impact of hikers on the fragile ecosystem, and search-and-rescue missions for lost or injured climbers.

Today, the AMC has more than 87,000 members in the Northeast and is heavily involved in research, conservation, and education. The club keeps watch on the environment, testing mountain air for ground level ozone and visibility quality, and for levels of pollution and cloud water acidity. The AMC takes a leading role in conservation issues ranging from the White Mountain National Forest to the 26 million acres of Northern Forest in New England and New York. It also hosts hundreds of educational workshops in the White Mountains, the Acadia National Park, the Berkshires, and the Catskills. Courses range from mushroom identification and foraging to wilderness survival to mountain-biking clinics. It's incredible what 39 people accomplished in a small room in Boston!

If the numerous children under age 12 are any indication, the Zealand Trail is a great hike for young families. The easy 2.7-mile climb (one-way) starts at an elevation over 2,000 feet and rises gently over 700 feet to the AMC Zealand Hut at the trail's end. Leave from the parking lot through a hardwood forest of red maples, beeches, and white birches. Webs of extended roots cover a forest floor that was decimated at the end of the 19th century by logging and fires. The trail, lined with yellow and white wildflowers in the summer, weaves along a brook where families stop on the rocks to picnic and swim. After you pass several beaver ponds, the forest opens up to the expansive Zealand Valley and Notch. The vistas are much better after the arduous 0.2-mile climb up to the Zealand Hut. Whitewall, Carrigan, Lowell, and Anderson Mountains can be seen from the steps of the wooden hut, which was built by Joe

Dodge and company in 1931. Nearby, a waterfall drops down the mountainside, providing the perfect place to ruminate with a glass of lemonade. If you're fortunate, you've booked a bunk for an overnight in these idyllic surroundings. If not, you have to return via the same trail.

Mount Eisenhower

6.5 miles round-trip. Allow 5 hr. Moderate to strenuous. Access: In Fabyan, turn off Rte. 302 and head east on the Base Rd. for 5 miles. Turn right at the intersection onto Mount Clinton Rd. and drive 1.5 miles. The Edmands Path enters the woods on the left.

Far less arduous than the big boys just to the northeast, the gradual climb up 4,761-foot Eisenhower reaches a rounded summit with panoramic views of the Presidential Range. The Edmands Path climbs through beech and birch, then steepens as you snake through the higher-elevation woods of spruce and fir. Above the tree line, the Edmands Path continues around the north ridge of the mountain and soon meets up with the Crawford Path. Bear right on the Eisenhower Loop Trail for a slight descent down to Red Pond and then up the ledges to the open summit. The rounded peak rewards you with views in every direction of the Presidential Range, from Crawford Notch to Pinkham Notch and the peak of Mount Washington. Take the same trails on a gradual descent back to Mount Clinton Road.

The Presidentials: Southern Peaks

8.5 miles one-way. Allow 7–8 hr. Strenuous. Access: Drop off the first car on Rte. 302 at the northern end of Crawford Notch. Park at the Crawford Path parking area. Drive the second car a few yards past the Crawford Path parking area and turn right onto Mount Clinton Rd. Drive 4 miles to the Base Rd. and turn right, following the road to the parking area for the Ammonoosuc Ravine Trail. The trail enters from the right.

If you have an extra car to spare, this 8.5-mile one-way route is one of the finest day hikes in the Whites. You'll be bagging four of the southern Presidentials—Monroe, Franklin, Eisenhower, and Pierce—while above tree line for almost half of the trek. Take the Ammonoosuc Ravine Trail through a forest of spruce and fir as it snakes along a river of the same name. About an hour into the hike, you'll see a waterfall and cross a stream. As the evergreens get smaller, the trail becomes strenuous, with views of Mount Washington appearing to your left. Three miles into the journey, you'll reach the Appalachian Mountain Club's Lakes of the Clouds Hut. This is a good place to check the weather before heading south on the Crawford Path. If the weather report looks good, continue on the white blazes that make up the Appalachian Trail. As you approach Mount Monroe, turn right onto the Mount Monroe Loop to reach the 5,372-foot summit. You'll have a wonderful view downward at the Lakes of the Clouds. After enjoying the views, continue on the Mount Monroe Loop to rejoin the Crawford Path heading south. Next up is 5,001-foot Mount Franklin and Mount Eisenhower's round dome. The Eisenhower Loop Trail brings you to the summit. If bad weather starts to rear its ugly face, note that you can take the Edmands Path back down to Mount Clinton Road (see the Mount Eisenhower hike above).

Like the Mount Monroe Loop, the Eisenhower Loop catches up with the Crawford Path as it heads south. It's one more mile on the exquisite Crawford Path before reaching 4,312-foot Mount Pierce. Turn left on the Webster Cliff Trail and you'll reach the level summit shortly. Then it's back to the Crawford Path for a gradual 3.1-mile descent through the spruce and hardwoods to your second car.

Lowe's Bald Spot

4.2 miles. Allow 3 hr. Easy. Access: Park at the AMC Pinkham Notch Lodge on Rte. 16. The Tuckerman Ravine Trail starts from behind the lodge.

A good half-day trek from the Appalachian Mountain Club's Pinkham Notch Lodge takes you to this 3,000-foot opening on Mount Washington's eastern slopes. From the lodge, take the Tuckerman Ravine Trail 50 yards to the white blazes of the Appalachian Trail heading north. The trail climbs through a hardwood forest reaching the Auto Road in about 2 miles. Cross the road and continue following the Appalachian Trail (Madison Gulf Trail), and you'll reach Lowe's Bald Spot in another 10 minutes. Vistas from the opening look out onto the Great Gulf, Mount Adams, and Mount Madison. Return on the same route.

Mount Jefferson

6.5 miles. Allow 6 hr. Strenuous. Access: In Fabyan, turn off Rte. 302 and head east on the Base Rd. for 5 miles. Turn left at the intersection onto Jefferson Notch Rd. The gravel road takes you 3 miles up 3,000 feet to Jefferson Notch. Park on either side of the road. The Caps Ridge Trail enters on the left.

The climb to the third-largest mountain in New England, 5,715-foot Mount Jefferson, is on one of the most exhilarating loops in the Presidential Range. Almost half of the 6.5-mile hike is above tree line, offering stunning vistas of that large glacial cirque, the Great Gulf, and the backside of mighty Mount Washington. Think Thomas Jefferson and you have the image of a very intelligent, complex man who strove hard to achieve every goal he endeavored. The mountain is very much like the man. You start in Jefferson Notch on the Caps Ridge Trail, a complex series of ledges, and you strive hard to clamber straight up some 2,700 feet. Leave the evergreens behind as you climb steeply up the second jagged ledge or cap and you'll feel as if you're touching the sky. You are completely exposed to the elements from here on in, so be very sure there's no sign of rain or high winds. If there is, turn back. This is not your one shot at Everest, so don't be a fool.

Descend from the second cap, and climb the broad ridge along the mountainside. You'll soon pass the Cornice Trail and ascend three more crests before actually summiting. Atop the peak, pat yourself on the back for your Jeffersonian accomplishment and look around you at the Great Gulf sloping toward Mount Washington, with Mount Adams and Mount Madison to the northeast. To head down, turn north on the Castle Trail and follow the cairns along a series of ledges. You descend steeply over the rock slabs before turning left on the Link Trail. Now below tree line, walk through the evergreen forest back to the Jefferson Notch.

Mount Adams

9 miles (round-trip). Allow 8 hr. Strenuous. Access: Take Rte. 2 west from Gorham's traffic lights and drive 5.5 miles to Appalachia (on the left side of the road) and the sign TRAILS PARKING. Take the path at the right-hand corner of the parking area.

For sheer vertical rise, some 4500 feet, no climb in this book is more demanding than the trail to the summit of Mount Adams. It's more than 200 vertical feet higher than the Mount Washington climb from Pinkham Notch. And better yet, there is no auto road to the top, so weary hikers don't have to be accosted by cigar-smoking drivers who ask inane questions like "That must have been some hike, huh?" Thankfully, the 5,774-foot summit of Mount Adams, second in height in New England, is for hikers only.

The hike up Adams thrills with its narrow ridges, deep ravines, and craggy top. From Appalachia, take the Air Line Trail on the right through a forest of maples. The trail climbs steeply up Durand Ridge. Above tree line, you traverse the exposed Knife Edge that overlooks the expanse of King Ravine to your right. With Mount Madison in full view, Air Line joins the Gulfside Trail for a few yards before forking to the left for the final ascent to the summit. The view is simply astounding, looking over the abyss of the Great Gulf and the towering crags of Mount Washington sandwiched between the likes of Mount Jefferson and Mount Madison, and, to the east, large Umbagog Lake. For the descent, retrace your steps down the Air Line Trail to the Gulfside Trail, which steeply drops down to the Appalachian Mountain Club's Madison Hut. Flex your leg muscles with the other climbers who congregate here and then take the Valley Way Trail through the woods back to Appalachia.

Carter Notch

7.6 miles (round-trip). Allow 5–6 hr. Moderate to strenuous. Access: From North Conway, take State Rte. 16 North several miles past Pinkham Notch to a small parking lot on the right side of the road. If you reach the Great Gulf parking lot, you have gone too far. Map: USGS 7.5-min. Carter Dome.

The 19-Mile Brook Trail leads to Carter Notch, a col situated between the dramatic ridges of Carter Dome and Wildcat "A." Here, you can spend the night at the Appalachian Mountain Club's oldest standing hut, a stone building constructed in 1914, perched just above two glacial lakes. I headed in from Route 16 and started the uphill climb along the brook, soon reaching a small aqueduct a mile into the hike. Along the way, I found several types of indigenous flora, like the "Indian Pipe," a small white flower whose bulb has no chlorophyll; and the Clintonia, a green-leafed plant named after DeWitt, not Bill Clinton, which sports blue berries in the summertime.

The trail splits at the 1.8-mile mark, veering left to the top of Carter Dome or straight to Carter Notch. I crossed the bridge and continued my ascent to the notch, the trail becoming steeper at the higher altitudes. The northern hardwood forest was soon replaced by a boreal forest of sweet-smelling spruces and firs. The final 0.3 mile of the trail snakes down between the two ridges and the majestic glacial lakes to the old hut. Inside the cozy walls, several hikers who were walking the Appalachian Trail (AT) in its entirety were talking to each other in their own distinct language laced with hiker's nicknames.

"Have you seen Sam-I-Am, Trail-bunny, or Bushmaster?" said one of the through-hikers, referring to three other ATers.

"I passed them back at Pinkham," replied another long-bearded and strong-legged climber.

I had my sandwich and then went on a side trip to the Rampart. Large rocks sit precariously atop Carter Dome, waiting to fall down the ridge to add to the pile of glacial detritus, a mass of boulders ideal for hopping and easy rock climbing. Eventually, I had to walk back down to Route 16, wishing I could spend an extra day at the hut to take some more hikes through this vast wilderness. The ATers were certainly in no rush.

Mount Star King

5.5 miles (round-trip). Allow 4–5 hr. Moderate. Access: From the junction of Rte. 2 and 115 in Jefferson Highlands, head west for 3.6 miles and turn right at a Forest Service sign. The narrow gravel road leads to a parking lot.

North of Route 2, the White Mountain National Forest continues, but with far less foot traffic than that on the Presidential Range. You can climb such peaks as Mount Starr King and see Mount Washington, Jefferson, Adams, and Madison look grand as they pierce the clouds overhead, but you'll probably have this summit to yourself. The Starr King Trail climbs along an old logging road next to a brook on your left. After less than 0.5 mile, the trail bears to the right gradually up the slopes of spruce and fir. You pass several springs and pools of water on your left before a final push brings you to a clearing where the Presidentials stand tall in front of you. The awe-inspiring view continues as you reach the 3,913-foot peak. Enjoy the panorama before heading back on the same trail.

Table Rock

Under 2 miles (round-trip). Allow 2 hr. Steep, moderate-to-strenuous climb. Access: The steep 0.3-mile trailhead is located on Rte. 26, on the downhill portion of the Dixville Notch pass, just before reaching the Balsams from the east. The more-gradual trail to the rocks is also located on Rte. 26, a half mile down the road on the left, just past the Balsams. Map: USGS 7.5-min. Dixville Notch.

If you're fortunate enough to be staying at the Balsams, the two trails that lead up to Table Rock offer exquisite views of this historic resort, man-made Lake Gloriette, and the sharp ledges and hills that form craggy Dixville Notch. I usually take the 0.3-mile trail straight up the rocky slope and come down on the more gradual path that leaves me a half mile away from my car on Route 26. However, you should have good hiking boots since the trail up is an extremely steep, gravel-strewn path that tends to be slippery. You'll often have to grab onto tree roots to pull yourself up. Table Rock is a ledge that sits like a gangplank over the sheer walls of rock that form Dixville Notch. If you're not scared of heights, this is a good place to have lunch and peer over the cliffs to Route 26 below. To find the easy downhill path, simply go uphill a short way until you see a campfire site, turn right, and descend.

Overnight & Long Distance Hikes

Vermont has the Long Trail and Maine has its Hundred Mile Wilderness, but if I wanted to backpack for a week or less, I'd choose the Whites. The expansive forest offers a diverse network of soft, spongy, and root-studded trails. *Notches,* those sheer walls of granite that rise sharply from the forest floor, form narrow gaps that dwarf the backpacker. Domes, gorges, and bald ridges offer hikers spectacular above-tree-line views.

Between Crawford Notch and the Franconia Range, miles of trails slice through the high mountains and remote ponds of the Pemigewasset Wilderness. The region is popular for 3- to 5-day hikes. East of Gorham, the Appalachian Trail crosses the New Hampshire border into Maine, offering strenuous backpacking through the Mahoosuc Range.

If you want to do some serious hiking in the day, but don't want to rough it at night, consider hut-to-hut hiking. The Appalachian Mountain Club (AMC) operates eight mountain cabins—rustic accommodations with crews that offer two hot meals a day. All you need to bring in the summertime are sheets or a lightweight sleeping bag. The huts are strung along 56 miles of the Appalachian Trail, a day's hike apart. For more information, contact the **AMC,** P.O. Box 298, Gorham, NH 03581 (☎ **603/466-2727;** www.outdoors.org).

Outfitters

There's no better scenario than having owners of an outfitter run trips in their own hometown. That's exactly the situation with Clare and Kurt Grabher, owners of New England Hiking Holidays, who happen to live in the midst of the White Mountains in North Conway. Clare and Kurt know the trails of the White Mountains better than most park rangers. If you are planning to book an outfitter in the finest region for hiking in New England, then look no further than **New England Hiking Holidays,** P.O. Box 1648, North Conway, NH 03860 (☎ **800/869-0949** or 603/356-9696; www.nehikingholidays.com). The Grabhers also run a tennis school called Tennis Holidays.

HORSEBACK RIDING

In the White Mountains, the **Mount Washington Hotel,** U.S. 302, Bretton Woods (☎ **603/278-1000**); **Mittersill Riding Stable,** Route 18, Franconia (☎ **603/823-5511**); **Loon Mountain Park,** Kancamagus Highway, Lincoln (☎ **603/745-8111**); and **Waterville Valley Resort** (☎ **603/236-8311**) all offer guided rides and instruction.

ICE CLIMBING

Whether you want to climb steep, low-angle waterfall ice or do some winter mountaineering, the White Mountain National Forest has an abundance of excellent terrain well-suited to your needs. Novices and experts both can find the winter challenge they are looking for. The terrain here varies from short top-rope climbs near the parked car to multi-pitched ice and Alpine climbs high up in the Presidential Range.

First and foremost, there's Mount Washington. The hike to the summit in winter is a great introduction to winter mountaineering. At Tuckerman Ravine, you can climb low-angle ice as early as mid-November. When the Headwall and surrounding gullies fill up, "Tuck" is a good place to do some Alpine snow climbs. But note that these are technical with some 55° climbs. Huntington Ravine is arguably the most popular place to ice-climb in New England. It's only a 1.5-hour climb with crampons to get to the base of the ravine. The rest is up to you and your winter mountaineering skills. Pinnacle Gully, one of the White's most sought-after ice climbs is here, along with classic Alpine climbs like Central Gully, Yale Gully, Damnation Gully, and Odell's.

In Crawford Notch, Frankenstein Cliff has waterfall ice routes ranging from easy low-angle to very steep. The classic climbs at Frankenstein include Pegasus, Dracula, Chia, and the Standard Route. The short approach from a railroad track makes this one of the most accessible places to ice-climb in the Northeast. Then there's Willey's Slide, a big wide ice slope a short walk from Route 302. To get back down, you simply slide on your butt, or, as the French would say, ***glissade.*** Other routes in Crawford Notch lead to Mount Willard and the flank of Mount Webster.

Champney Falls (see "Hiking," above), off the Kancamagus Highway on the way to Mount Chocorua, is also a fun top-rope area. Located in a narrow gorge, you can try climbing steep ice here.

Rick Wilcox, owner of **International Mountain Equipment Climbing School** (**☎ 603/356-6316;** www.guides@ime-usa.com), operates the biggest ice-climbing and rock-climbing school in the eastern United States out of North Conway. Another good bet is **Chauvin Guides International** (**☎ 603/356-8919;** www.chauvinguides.com), also out of North Conway.

ICE FISHING

The big lakes are the best places to find lake trout, northern pike, even smelt and perch. Heading north, venture to Umbagog outside of Errol or the Connecticut Lakes near Pittsburg. Heading south, try Winnipesaukee, Winnisquam, Squam, or Sunapee.

For additional information, contact the **New Hampshire Fish and Game Department,** 2 Hazen Drive, Concord, NH 03301 (**☎ 603/272-3421;** www.wildlife.state.nh.us).

LLAMA TREKKING

If you want to hang with that big-eyed wooly llama for a hike, contact **Fairfield Llama Treks** (**☎ 603/539-2865**). They feature a handful of hikes in the 1- to 6-mile range in the southern Whites that include lunch. Best of all, the llamas carry your gear.

MOUNTAIN BIKING

Over the past 5 years, the phrase "mountain biking" has been used rather loosely. Any trail that is off-road, whether it is a wide dirt road or a double track in a flat state forest, is suddenly termed a trail for ***mountain*** biking. Sorry to bust your bubble, but the word "mountain" implies that you are riding on a large hill that surges upward from the depths of the forest. This is what makes riding in the White Mountains so invigorating. Whether you are riding on a fire road over streams or on a single track that skirts the ridge of a summit, the term is appropriate for the Whites. And believe it or not, riding in the hills can be much easier than riding through the notches on a road bike, especially with the lack of car traffic.

Bartlett Experimental Forest

Allow 2 hr. Moderate. Access: From North Conway, take Rte. 16 North to U.S. 302. Turn left onto Bear Notch Rd. and go uphill until you find two large boulders on the left side of the road. There's a small area here in which to park. Map: available at **Red Jersey Cyclery,** U.S. 302, Glen (☎ **603/383-4660**).

In a region where off-road riding excels, the trails that weave up and down the Bartlett Experimental Forest are the crème de la crème. The miles of trails created by snowmobilers in the wintertime are remarkably maintained by biking fairy godmothers come spring. Kevin Killourie, avid mountain biker and owner of Red Jersey Cyclery in Glen, recommended one particular trail he enjoys riding in these woods. I immediately understood why once I had parked my car at the boulders and cruised downhill across a shallow stream. Crossing the water with a bike is comparable to viewing a shark when scuba diving—leaving in its wake a thrilling feeling of freedom and an adrenaline high for the rest of the day. The springy single-track trail gradually made its way downhill through the dense blanket of pines, crossing another stream, and then veering right before the third stream. I followed the orange blazes for the reminder of the ride, an exhilarating run down the mountainside to Route 302. However, I now had to fight the laws of gravity and make my way back up. The going was slow but not as strenuous as expected. I eventually made it back to my car and, for a brief moment, contemplated cruising down the trail once again. That was a very brief moment.

Ridgepole Trail

Allow 2 hr. Strenuous. Access: From I-93, take Exit 25, veering left onto Rte. 175 North. About 5 miles later, you'll see a large bear in front of a gift shop. Turn right on Perch Pond Rd. and continue on the gravel road for 3.3 miles until you see a pond on the left. Park here. Map: USGS 7.5-min. Squaw Mountains, available at the Pemigewasset Ranger District.

Experienced fat-wheelers will savor the opportunity to ride the Ridgepole Trail. Nestled in the Sandwich Mountain Range, this single track offers some of the finest technical riding in the White Mountains. If you have never cruised down the side of a mountain with a relatively steep grade, I would not recommend this trail. Your lunch might consist of a dirt sandwich.

For the first 2.8 miles, I rode easily up and down Perch Pond's gravel road. At the bottom of a hill, I turned left onto Mountain Road for 0.2 mile. When the road veered right, I continued straight on the grassy double tracks for a grueling half-mile uphill run. At the top of the slope, I turned left at a yellow sign indicating the Crawford Ridgepole Trail. Almost immediately, this tough single track tested my skills, slicing up and down the mountain over rocks, roots, and mud. Hairpin turns made maneuvering that much harder. At the 5-mile mark, the yellow-blazed trail cruised along a ridge offering spectacular views of Squam Lake and the Red Hill fire tower in the distance. I got another sight of the lake a mile later, before the trail turned back to the Alpine forest, weaving in and out of the firs and balsams. After 1.1 miles (7.1 miles total), I veered left onto the blue-blazed Cascade Trail for one of the most thrilling and challenging downhill rides I've ever been on. I slid down sheets of rock, jumped extended roots that were impossible to avoid, and almost came to a complete stop in a mud basin as I was speeding down the mountain. Still in one piece, I reached a set of grassy double tracks that led back to Perch Pond Road and the pond itself. I turned right to reach my car and complete the 8.6-mile loop. Caked in sweat, mud, and dry dirt, I entered the waters of the pond for a therapeutic bath.

Boulder Path to Greeley Pond Trail

Allow 2 hr. Easy to moderate. Access: Start in Waterville Valley by the Base Camp. Map: available at the Pemigewasset Ranger District.

The trail to Greeley Pond was suggested by one of my mountain-biking buddies as being suitable for novice riders. I cruised around the tennis courts and veered left onto Greeley Hill Road. This brought me to Snow Mountain's ski trails. I rode on several trails across the mountainside, slid through mud down a hill, and was suddenly at the rushing waters of a stream. A well-trod hiking and biking trail along the water led me to an immense boulder in the middle of the stream. I learned later that I was on the "Boulder Path." I crossed the stream onto gravel Livermore Road, turned left, and soon found the sign for Greeley Trail. This rocky and level double-track trail goes straight for 3 or 4 miles to a pond popular with anglers. However, I soon grew bored with the trail's lack of incline and turned around. I made my way back to Waterville Valley the same way I came.

Bretton Woods Summer Park

Allow 45 min. Strenuous. Access: From North Conway, follow U.S. 302 North. The large sign for Bretton Woods is on the left side of the road. Map: available at the ski area.

The first time I tried lift-served mountain biking was five summers ago at Bretton Woods ski resort in the heart of the White Mountains. Going up on the lift with my bike, I glanced at the trail map and decided to check out Two Mile Run, an intermediate ski trail that seemed to gradually slope down the southeastern side of the mountain. I jumped off the chair, threw on my helmet, and pointed the bike downhill. Small bumps and large patches of mud kept me alert, and I was feeling comfortable, calmed by the serene view of neighboring Mount Washington. I veered left onto Two Mile Run and suddenly I'm flying down the side of the mountain, my knuckles turning the color of snow as they clutched the brakes. Every now and then I hit a gully and went airborne, praying that my Trek 950 would somehow manage to land upright and not leave me in a ditch. I had visions of my bike sliding down the mountain without me, like one of those old Westerns in which the horse returns to the lodge without the dead owner. I made it back to the base far quicker than the lift up, vowing never to try this foolhardy sport ever again.

Last summer, peer pressure prevailed over common sense, and there I was once again floating up the side of a New England peak with a bike. This time, however, I chose a beginner trail on the map and I also decided to rent one of the ski resort's bikes. If I returned with a twisted frame, I could return the bike, chuckle, and walk away (God willing). But to my surprise, the ride was so exhilarating that I spent the whole morning cruising over the slopes of Vermont's Jay Peak. Weaving through a dense blanket of pines, I crossed shallow streams and jumped over extended roots as I gradually made my way downhill on slick, muddy trails. By lunchtime, I was still in one piece, but I looked like the Swamp Thing. Thankfully, showers are included in the price of the lift ticket.

Lift-served mountain biking is proliferating across the country as more and more downhill-ski areas try to cash in on off-season recreation. The sport, while gaining momentum, is certainly not for everyone. By eliminating the need to bike up slopes, you don't realize how steep the terrain is until you're zipping downhill. More important, you lose your workout. The beads of sweat on your forehead are more from fear than exertion. What you gain in return is a Disneyesque type of amusement ride, an adrenaline-flowing thrill on two wheels where you control the course. And to create even more of a challenge, many ski areas are cutting single tracks through the woods, so your choices are not limited to wide-boulevard ski trails.

The most important piece of equipment besides a bike and a helmet is a trail map. You don't want to make the mistake of cruising down a double diamond your first time out. Most resorts also offer elbow and knee pads, which are advisable. If you wipe out on a ski trail in the winter, you eat snow. If you wipe out on a ski trail in the summer, you eat mud or, even tastier, rock.

Bretton Woods Ski Area, U.S. 302, Bretton Woods (☎ **603/278-3320;** www.brettonwoods.com) offers lift-served mountain biking.

Rob Brook Road

Allow 3 hr. Easy. Access: From Conway, take the Kancamagus Hwy. or Rte. 112 to your first right turn onto Bear Notch Rd. Start going uphill; just past the houses, you'll see a sign for biking and hiking on the left side of the road. This is Rob Brook Rd., or Fire Rd. 35. Park along Bear Notch Rd. Map: available at **Red Jersey Cyclery,** U.S. 302, Glen (☎ **603/383-4660**).

Mountain biking is a far better choice than road biking in the White Mountains, especially for families. Traffic is unrelenting during high-peak season, and many of the long uphill climbs through the mountainous passes are a challenge for even the most-experienced biker. The fire roads in the hills above the Kancamagus Highway offer children a chance to ride in the Whites. Rob Brook Road is a wide gravel road that rolls gently through the forest, eventually making its way to Swift River. Along the way, you'll have numerous opportunities to stop and take in the panoramic vistas of the verdant valley below.

Great Glen Trails in Gorham (☎ **603/466-2333;** www.greatglentrails.com) also offers easy-to-moderate mountain biking on its network of cross-country ski trails, which resemble carriage-path trails.

Hayes Copp Ski Trail

5.5 miles. Allow 1 hr. Moderate to strenuous. Access: From Gorham, travel south on Rte. 16 for 5 miles and turn left onto Pinkam B Rd. After several hundred yards, turn left into the Dolly Copp Campground.

Hayes Copp is not only a great backcountry ski run (see "Cross Country Skiing," above) but a challenging backcountry bike run, as well. Riding along the banks of the Peabody River, the loop has its fair share of boulders, roots, and chest-high weeds. You'll also have to hoist your bike on several of the elevated bridges. Besides that, experienced bikers will love this rolling, deep-in-the-woods run.

Cascade Falls

5 miles (one-way). Allow 1 hr. Easy. From Gorham, take Rte. 16 north until the road passes underneath a tall steel railroad trestle. Park in the area under the trestle on your right.

This easy 5-mile route will take you along the east banks of the Androscoggin River, downstream from the timber mills in Berlin. Walk your bike along the railroad trestle and turn right down a dirt road to a dam. Cross the dam by riding between the wooden sheds on the left and the brick powerhouse. When you hit the east shores of the river, turn left and follow the dirt road north along the water's edge. The farther north you head, the narrower the road gets. There are a couple of sharp hills. Turn around whenever you've had enough.

ROAD BIKING

The best road biking in New Hampshire is in the south near the Massachusetts border, or west near the Vermont border. The closer you get to the White Mountains, the more strenuous the riding becomes and the more congested the major routes. Steep 1,000- to 2,000-foot climbs are the norm, challenging the best-conditioned bikers. However, if you are still intent on riding in the mountains, I would suggest the following 36-mile ride.

Bear Notch Loop

36 miles. Strenuous, with a fairly abrupt 1,400-ft. rise in elevation. Access: Start on Main St. in North Conway, near Eastern Mountain Sports.

From Eastern Mountain Sports, turn left on River Road down to the Saco River. Just after you pass the river, River Road merges with West Side Road. Head north on this road for 5.6 miles, through Glen, to U.S. 302. Veer left (west) and ride for another 4.1 miles to the blinking light in Bartlett. Turn left at Bear Notch Road for your mountain climb. The road rises from 600 to 2,000 feet in approximately 5 miles before descending to the Kancamagus Highway, or "Kanc." At the T-junction, turn left onto the Kanc and ride 6 miles to the covered bridge at Blackberry Crossing. Turn left through the bridge and then right onto Dugway Road for 6.1 miles. At the junction of Allen Siding, turn left, cross the railroad tracks, and turn left again to meet up with West Side Road. Pedal 5.6 miles to River Road, veering right to return to North Conway.

Outer Conway Loop

Allow 2–3 hr. Moderate; hilly terrain. Access: From North Conway, take State Rte. 16 to the junction of State Rte. 153 in Conway. Turn left at Rte. 153 South and turn right almost immediately into the Pleasant St. Plaza parking lot. Park behind the bank.

As you approach the Maine border from Conway, rolling hills replace the towering heights of the Whites. Park your car and turn right onto Route 153 South, following a small brook to Crystal Lake, one of New Hampshire's many small lakes. Who would have known that a majestic swimming hole lies just minutes from the crowds of North Conway? Turn left at the beach on Brownfield Road, up through a forest of firs and spruces. You'll pass by several beaver ponds and Hart Brook Farm, whose picture-perfect barn stands alone amidst thousands of acres of crops. Entering Maine, turn left at the sign for North Conway, just past the white house with the red roof. Views of the White Mountains start to open up on the right as you approach the shores of Conway Lake on your left. Turn left on Route 302 to ride through the village of Center Conway. Continue west on Route 113 to the junction of Route 153 to complete this 23-mile ride.

ROCK CLIMBING

With an official nickname like the Granite State, you know that New Hampshire has to be a popular rock-climbing destination. The Whites' numerous granite outcroppings and sheer faces of rock have steadily earned respect as one of the top rock-climbing destinations in the country. Heights might not be as impressive as in the Western mountains, but the thrill of climbing a vertical ridge thousands of feet above the forest floor is just as exhilarating. Many of the climbs are only 5 or 10 minutes from the road, making the sport extremely accessible. **Cathedral Ledge, Whitehorse Ledge,** and **Cannon Cliffs** are known to challenge even the most adroit rock climber with their concentration of long multipitch routes.

Cathedral has many fine climbs ranging from face climbing to cracks and corners. Face-climbing routes include No Man's Land (5.6, 250 feet), Upper Refuse (5.5, 300 feet), and Thin Air (5.6, 450 feet). Moderate crack-and-corner climbs include Toe Crack (5.7, 200 feet) and Funhouse (5.7, 200 feet). Several of these routes can be combined together to create 5- to 6-pitch routes. A popular combo is Toe

Bullwinkle and Company

All along the routes of northern New Hampshire, you'll see signs for moose crossings and other signs that state "Please Brake for Moose, 193 Collisions." At sunrise or sunset, seeing a moose is a definite possibility, especially near the Androscoggin River from Berlin to Errol. Surprisingly, you'll also see bumper stickers on cars and trucks that read, "Don't brake for moose; fill your freezer." This statement is referring to a law in New Hampshire that says if you hit a moose or deer on the road and the animal is killed, you are entitled to bring home the animal. That's one way to deal with road kill.

Well, as one local recounted to me, the police were called to an unfortunate accident between driver and deer. The unharmed driver, seeing that the deer was killed, asked the officer if he could drive the deer back to his home. Since the man was driving a compact car, the officer inquired as to where he was going to put the deer. "In my back seat," the man responded as he started to drag the animal into the car. An hour later, another police officer responded to an accident and it was the same driver. The man had hit a tree and was knocked unconscious. The officer opened the rear door of the car and peered in at the back seat, only to find scratches all over the vehicle's interior and the deer barely breathing. The animal was not quite dead after all.

Moral of story: Hitting a wild animal can have *deer* consequences! Drive with a degree of caution—a collision with a moose is often fatal to the driver—and if you do have the misfortune of hitting a deer or moose, don't take the supposedly dead animal home unless you have a truck.

Crack to Thin Air. Whitehorse is known for its long exposed-slab climbs. Many routes exist between 5.6 and 5.8, including Sliding Board (5.7, 9 pitches) and Standard Route (5.7, 10 pitches). Because of the exposed slabs, Whitehorse is a great place to master the skill of multi-pitch rappels. The 1,000-foot Cannon Cliff is less accessible than Cathedral or Whitehorse but, with its mountainous setting, has more of an Alpine feel. Popular climbing routes include Whitney Gilman Range (5.8, 5 pitches) and Moby Grape (5.8, 9 pitches).

If you have never rock-climbed or would like to improve your level of competence, contact **Rick Wilcox** at **International Mountain Equipment Climbing School,** in North Conway (☎ **603/356-6316;** www.guides@ime-usa.com). Rick is legendary in these parts for his work on search-and-rescue squads and for accomplishing the mountain climber's ultimate goal, to reach the peak of Mount Everest. The school is the lar-gest of its kind in the eastern United States. Also highly recommended is North Conway's **Chauvin Guides Interna-tional** (☎ **603/356-8919;** www.chauvinguides.com).

SNOWMOBILING

Hundreds of miles of snowmobile trails criss-cross the White Mountains all the way to Maine, Vermont, and Quebec. Popular areas include **Mount Clinton Road** near Crawford Notch, **Twin Mountain,** and **Zealand Road** in Zealand Valley. Snowmobiling is a way of life in northern New Hampshire, especially in the towns of **Colebrook** and **Pittsburg.** Check with the **Trails Bureau,** New Hampshire Division of Parks and Recreation, P.O. Box 856, Concord, NH 03301 (☎ **603/271-3254**), and the **New Hampshire Snowmobile Association,** 722 Rte. 3A, Bow, NH 03304 (☎**603/224-8906;** www.nhsa.com).

SNOWSHOEING

The **Nineteen Mile Trail** to Carter Notch will give you a good snowshoeing workout in the winter. It leads to one of the Appalachian Mountain Club's huts that is open in the winter. Far less strenuous but just as rewarding is the hike up **Mount Willard** (see "Hiking," above).

The **Boulder Loop Trail** in Albany is a 3-mile snowshoe that rewards you with great views of the Whites. It's a 1,000-foot climb through spruce and fir on this yellow-blazed trail. From Conway, travel south on Route 16 for 0.5 mile and turn west on Route 112 (the Kancamagus Highway). Drive 2.5 miles and turn right on Passaconaway Road. The parking area is on your right.

In Franconia Notch, don't miss the 3.2-mile trail around **Lonesome Lake.** Dwarfed by the twin peaks of 4,358-foot South Kinsman and 4,293-foot North Kinsman, the lake does feel very lonely in the winter. Take the Franconia Notch State Parkway north and exit at the Lafayette Place Campground. Turn left into the parking area where an underpass will lead you to the other side of the road and the trailhead.

There are also guided tours to **Mount Washington's** summit during the brisk winter months. Call Rick Wilcox at **International Mountain Equipment Climbing School** in North Conway (☎ **603/356-6316;** www.ime-usa.com). For more information, contact the **White Mountain National Forest,** 719 N. Main St., Laconia, NH 03247 (☎ **603/528-8721**).

SWIMMING

The best remedy for an arduous hike is the crisp waters of a lake, pond, or stream. Any body of water will do. My favorite swimming hole in the White Mountains is **Perch Pond,** simply because it was sitting there after I had taken the Ridgepole mountain-bike trail. The hundreds of swimming holes and lakes include the rocks of **Lower Falls Scenic Area** on the Kancamagus Highway; **Jackson Falls** in Jackson; **Echo Lake State Park,** near North Conway; and **Rocky Branch Brook,** just off Route 302 in Glen. Up north, try **Forest Lake State Beach** in Dalton.

TENNIS

The 18 red-clay courts at **Waterville Valley Resort** (☎ **800/468-2553;** www.waterville.com) were recently ranked as one of *Tennis Magazine's* Top 50 tennis resorts in the country, and as one of the 5 best in the country for families. The tennis center offers private lessons, clinics, tournaments, junior programs, round-robins, and social events.

WALKS & RAMBLES

Rail 'n' River Forest Trail

0.5-mile loop. Allow 30 min. Access: From Conway, head west for 12.5 miles and look for the PASSACONAWAY HISTORIC SITE sign on the north side of the highway. Park here.

This half-mile walk, just off the Kancamagus Highway, is an excellent introduction to the White Mountain National Forest. With pamphlet in hand, you can make 28 stops that identify such trees as the prosaic pine, spruce, white birch, and maple; and the rarer larch, black cherry, alder, and poplar. The short trail also brings you to a swamp and the banks of the Swift River. It's ideal for young walkers.

Sabbaday Falls

1 mile round-trip. Allow 30 min. Access: From Conway, travel 16 miles west on the Kancamagus Hwy. (Rte. 112) and look for the picnic area on the south side.

Another good stroll for preschoolers along the Kancamagus Highway is this 1-mile round-trip jaunt to Sabbaday Falls. It's a simple walk through a forest of maples, birches, and beeches down the stone steps to the falls. Watch the cascading water plummet over the rocks into a pool and then walk back.

Greeley Ponds

4 miles round-trip. Allow 2–3 hr. Access: From Lincoln, take the Kancamagus Hwy. (Rte. 112) for 9.5 miles and look for the brown sign to the Greeley Ponds parking area.

One of the best parts about the Whites is that you can leave your car behind on a major thoroughfare, say the Kancamagus Highway (Route 112), and within a couple of miles you can find yourself far away in the forest at the base of some mountain. This is the case with the two Greeley Ponds, nestled snugly between Mount Osceola and Mount Kancamagus. Part of an 810-acre National Forest Scenic Area, the first waterway reached is the narrow and shallow lower pond. Soon you reach the upper pond. Both ponds are a favorite beaver haunt, so come early in the morning and have your breakfast on the shores of the upper pond.

Artist's Bluff and Bald Mountain

1.5 miles round-trip. Allow 1 hr. Access: Take the Franconia Notch Pkwy. past the Old Man of the Mountains and take the Echo Lake Beach exit. Leave your car in the parking lot on Rte. 18.

For a mere 300-foot climb, Artist's Bluff and Bald Mountain reward walkers with one of the finer views in Franconia Notch. The trail starts steeply up a gully but quickly reaches Artist's Bluff, an apt name for a cliff that overlooks the entirety of Echo Lake and Cannon Mountain on the right, Eagle Cliff and Mount Lafayette on the left. To venture even higher, walk along a carriage path and then turn right on the trail to Bald Mountain. Steps and a switchback lead to the summit with better views of the Notch. Head back down to Route 18 and turn left. The trail begins and ends near Echo Lake, which is a good swimming spot for kids.

Mountain Pond

2.7 miles. Allow 2–3 hr. Access: From North Conway, drive north on Rte. 16 and turn right in Intervale onto Town Hall Rd. After crossing Rte. 16A, the road becomes Slippery Brook Rd. and later Forest Rd. 17. From the junction of Rte. 16A, drive 6.4 miles on Forest Rd. 17; the parking area and trailhead are on the right.

Mountain Pond is one of those lost-in-the-spruce-and-fir-woods waterways in the easternmost region of White Mountain National Forest. The walk through red and striped maples to the shores and around the pond is a good jaunt for the whole family. From the parking area, follow the yellow blazes some 0.3 mile to the Mountain Pond Loop Trail. You can go around the pond either way or, for a shorter stroll, head to the shelter on the northwestern shores. Don't be surprised to find loons hiding out here as well.

Square Ledge Trail

1 mile round-trip. Allow 1 hr. Access: The trail begins across the road from the Appalachian Mountain Club's Pinkham Notch Lodge. Follow Rte. 16 north from North Conway through Glen and Jackson. The Pinkham Notch Visitors Center is on the left, 0.7 mile past the turnoff to Glen Ellis Falls.

For youngsters who want to get a taste of a short uphill climb (400-foot ascent) and the just desserts of an exquisite vista, take the easy Square Ledge Trail. The trail runs together with the Lost Pond Trail before crossing a wooden bridge and making a sharp right turn. The Square Ledge Trail then branches off and makes an abrupt left up the gradual slope. Soon you'll pass Hangover Rock, a large boulder on the east side of the path. The trail then becomes steeper until you reach the summit of Square Ledge. Look directly across the valley to the face of Mount Washington and Pinkham Notch as you focus in on Huntington Ravine. Kids will no doubt feel good about their accomplishment.

Campgrounds & Other Accommodations

CAMPING

The vast array of New Hampshire campgrounds ranges from primitive sites with few amenities to full-service areas with all the modern comforts of a hotel room. State and White Mountain National Forest campgrounds operate on a first-come, first-served basis. However, several of the **National Forest sites** accept reservations 240 days or less in advance, but 14 days before arrival is the minimum time (☎ **800/280-2267**). Those campgrounds are **Campton, Waterville,** and **Russell Pond** off I-93; **Covered Bridge** off the **Kancamagus Highway; Sugarloaf I and II** in Twin Mountain; **Dolly Copp** in Pinkham Notch; **Basins, Cold River,** and **Hastings** in Evans Notch; and **White Ledge** in Conway. For more information, write or call the **New Hampshire Campground Owners' Association,** P.O. Box 320, Twin Mountain, NH 03595 (☎ **603/846-5511;** www.ucampnh.com) for their directory of 140 private, state, and national forest campgrounds.

Backcountry camping is permitted in most areas of the White Mountain National Forest; the usual exclusions are within 200 feet of streams, lakes, or trails, and within a quarter mile of roads and designated campsites.

If you want to upgrade from tents to bunk beds, the **Appalachian Mountain Club,** P.O. Box 298, Gorham, NH 03581 (☎ **603/466-2727;** www.outdoors.org) has two lodges in Pinkham and Crawford Notch, in addition to their eight high huts. The rustic **Pinkham Notch** facility accommodates 106 guests and offers family-style meals in the Main Lodge. The **Shapleigh Hostel** in Crawford Notch accommodates 24 people and is complete with self-service kitchen. Bring sleeping bags or sheets and food.

Lake Francis State Park

From Pittsburg, travel north on Rte. 3 for 7 miles to the campground sign. Turn right on River Rd. to the campground entrance. ☎ **603/538-6965.** 41 sites, no hookups, flush toilets, tables, fire rings.

Occupying the northeastern shores of pristine Lake Francis, this is the ideal North Country getaway. Swim; fish for trout and salmon; or simply hang with the beavers, ospreys, and moose.

Umbagog Lake

Access: From the junction of Rte. 16 and 26 in Errol, head 7 miles southeast on Rte. 26. ☎ **603/482-7795.** 59 sites, some on small islands that can be reached by canoe or boat. 30 sites with water and electricity, 29 with no hookups, public phone, limited grocery store, ice, tables, fire rings, wood.

Canoe over to the western side of the lake to see the pair of nesting bald eagles (see "Canoeing," above); fish for salmon, trout, perch, and pickerel; or simply lounge on the shores of this massive 8,000-acre lake and wait for the next moose to arrive. Half of the sites are located on the southern shores of the lake; the other half on islands. Canoes can be rented at the campground.

Mollidgewock State Park

From Errol, travel 3 miles south on Rte. 16 to the campground. ☎ **603/482-3373.** 42 sites, no hookups, pit toilets, piped water, ice, wood.

A popular hangout for white-water canoers, these primitive sites are located on the banks of the Androscoggin River. Part of the Thirteen Mile Woods Scenic Area, the region also has its share of fly-fishing anglers.

Dolly Copp Campground

From the junction of Rte. 2 and 16, go 6 miles southwest on Rte. 16. ☎ **603/466-2713.** 176 sites, no hookups, toilets, piped water, tables, fire rings.

One of the largest campsites in the entire national forest system with as many as 1,000 people camping here in high season. It's location is ideal for hikers making jaunts into the Presidential Range.

Dry River Campground

From the junction of Rte. 302 and 16 in Glen, travel northwest on Rte. 302 for 16 miles. The campground is on the right side of the highway. ☎ **603/374-2272.** 30 sites, no hookups, pit toilets, piped water, tables.

Strung along the Dry River in Crawford Notch State Park, these sites are close to the hike at Arethusa Falls and the rock climbing at Cathedral and Whitehorse Ledges.

Sugarloaf I and II and Zealand

From the junction of Rte. 3 and 302 in Twin Mountain, head 2.3 miles east on U.S. 302. At Zealand Recreation Area, follow signs for 0.5 mile. ☎ **603/869-2626.** 72 sites. No hookup, toilets, piped water, fire rings, tables, grills.

These campgrounds are conveniently located for hikers, snowmobilers, and cross-country skiers who want to venture into the Pemigewasset Wilderness or take the hike to the Appalachian Mountain Club's Zealand Notch Hut (open in winter).

Lafayette Campground, Franconia Notch State Park

Located off I-93; no northbound access. Exit at sign for Lafayette Campground. ☎ **603/823-9513.** 97 sites are located in the heart of Franconia Notch. No hookups, wheelchair-accessible rest rooms, public phone, limited grocery store, ice, tables, grills, wood. No services Oct–May.

Located near the Pemigewasset River at the base of the Notch, these sites arguably have the best mountain views in the Whites. It's also the starting point for the Mount Lafayette, Lonesome Lake, and Basin-Cascades hikes.

INNS & RESORTS

Tall Timber Lodge

231 Beach Rd., Pittsburg, NH 03592. ☎ **800/83-LODGE;** www.talltimber.com. Rooms range from $31 nightly in the Main Lodge to $260 nightly at one of the luxury cottages.

Founded in 1946, this is one of New England's most popular sporting camps. Many guests return year after year to relax in this wilderness setting on Back Lake, swimming at the beach and fishing to their heart's content. The lodge maintains more than 25 rental boats and sells fishing tackle as well. Up here in the Connecticut Lakes region this is fishing paradise, with copious amounts of brook, brown, and rainbow trout, along with landlocked salmon. In winter, hundreds of snow-mobiling trails weave off in every direction like spokes on bike. Bring your machine or rent one of Tall Timber's supply.

The Balsams

Dixville Notch, NH 03576. ☎ **603/255-3400;** www.thebalsams.com. Rates start at $110 per night per person during the winter, $205 in the summer, including lodging, meals, and all sports amenities—even the golf course and skiing.

There are so many reasons why The Balsams is in a class by itself that I have to list them:

- **Location.** 15,000 acres stare up at jagged Dixville Notch, one of the most majestic sights in New England.
- **History.** The 132-year-old resort is one of the last Grand Dames in existence.

- **Sports.** The Panorama golf course, the clay and all-weather tennis courts, and the 75-plus kilometers (46.9 miles) of ski trails all consistently gain high marks in sports magazines.
- **Food.** Rating four stars from the Mobil Guide, the food is exceptional, service impeccable. The copious amount of food includes a large breakfast, lunch buffets, and six-course dinners.
- **Grounds.** Manicured lawns and colorful gardens slope down to the swimming pool and Lake Gloriette. Hummingbirds whiz by on their way to the bird feeders.

I could go on and on, but that's another book. The downhill slopes have few lines, the resort bottles its own spring water, and it has even found a way to eradicate black flies in order to make hiking and biking enjoyable in the summer. Like a fine wine, this resort just gets better with time.

Inn at Thorn Hill
Thorn Hill Rd., Jackson, NH 03846. ☎ **603/383-4242;** www.innatthornhill.com. 19 rooms. Rates start at $190, including breakfast and dinner for two.

Tucked away in a small valley, not far from the slopes of Mount Washington, lies the quintessential New England village of Jackson, New Hampshire. The white clapboard inns surrounding the village green of this small town do a brisk business year-round, but the best time to venture here is during the winter months. This area of the White Mountains features the Jackson Ski Touring Foundation for cross-country skiing fanatics and Wildcat Ski Area for downhillers. After your day outdoors, relax at this shingle-style home, designed by Stanford White in 1895. Surrounded by dense woods, the 19-room inn has sitting parlors, fireplaces, piano, and all the other requisite Victorian touches that make you feel as if you've just entered an Edith Wharton novel.

Snowy Owl Inn
Waterville Valley, NH 03215. ☎ **603/236-8383;** www.waterville.com. Rates start at $69 in the summer, $89 during ski season.

The game rooms, breakfast buffets, spacious rooms, and reasonable price make this an excellent choice for families traveling to the White Mountain area. The three-story hotel is centrally located, close to Waterville Valley's ski slopes and mountain-biking paths.

Index

A

B

D

E

N

O

P

Q

R

T

Y

Z

NOTES

NOTES

NOTES

NOTES

FROMMER'S® COMPLETE TRAVEL GUIDES

Alaska
Amsterdam
Arizona
Atlanta
Australia
Austria
Bahamas
Barcelona, Madrid & Seville
Beijing
Belgium, Holland & Luxembourg
Bermuda
Boston
British Columbia & the Canadian Rockies
Budapest & the Best of Hungary
California
Canada
Cancún, Cozumel & the Yucatán
Cape Cod, Nantucket & Martha's Vineyard
Caribbean
Caribbean Cruises & Ports of Call
Caribbean Ports of Call
Carolinas & Georgia
Chicago
China
Colorado
Costa Rica
Denmark
Denver, Boulder & Colorado Springs
England
Europe
European Cruises & Ports of Call
Florida
France
Germany
Greece
Greek Islands
Hawaii
Hong Kong
Honolulu, Waikiki & Oahu
Ireland
Israel
Italy
Jamaica
Japan
Las Vegas
London
Los Angeles
Maryland & Delaware
Maui
Mexico
Montana & Wyoming
Montréal & Québec City
Munich & the Bavarian Alps
Nashville & Memphis
Nepal
New England
New Mexico
New Orleans
New York City
New Zealand
Nova Scotia, New Brunswick & Prince Edward Island
Oregon
Paris
Philadelphia & the Amish Country
Portugal
Prague & the Best of the Czech Republic
Provence & the Riviera
Puerto Rico
Rome
San Antonio & Austin
San Diego
San Francisco
Santa Fe, Taos & Albuquerque
Scandinavia
Scotland
Seattle & Portland
Shanghai
Singapore & Malaysia
South Africa
Southeast Asia
South Florida
South Pacific
Spain
Sweden
Switzerland
Thailand
Tokyo
Toronto
Tuscany & Umbria
USA
Utah
Vancouver & Victoria
Vermont, New Hampshire & Maine
Vienna & the Danube Valley
Virgin Islands
Virginia
Walt Disney World & Orlando
Washington, D.C.
Washington State

FROMMER'S® DOLLAR-A-DAY GUIDES

Australia from $50 a Day
California from $60 a Day
Caribbean from $70 a Day
England from $70 a Day
Europe from $70 a Day
Florida from $70 a Day
Hawaii from $70 a Day
Ireland from $60 a Day
Italy from $70 a Day
London from $85 a Day
New York from $80 a Day
Paris from $80 a Day
San Francisco from $60 a Day
Washington, D.C., from $70 a Day

FROMMER'S® PORTABLE GUIDES

Acapulco, Ixtapa & Zihuatanejo
Alaska Cruises & Ports of Call
Bahamas
Baja & Los Cabos
Berlin
California Wine Country
Charleston & Savannah
Chicago
Dublin
Hawaii: The Big Island
Las Vegas
London
Los Angeles
Maine Coast
Maui
Miami
New Orleans
New York City
Paris
Puerto Vallarta, Manzanillo & Guadalajara
San Diego
San Francisco
Sydney
Tampa & St. Petersburg
Venice
Washington, D.C.

FROMMER'S® NATIONAL PARK GUIDES

Family Vacations in the National Parks
Grand Canyon
National Parks of the American West
Rocky Mountain Park
Yellowstone & Grand Teton
Yosemite & Sequoia/ Kings Canyon
Zion & Bryce Canyon

FROMMER'S® MEMORABLE WALKS

Chicago
London
New York
Paris
San Francisco
Washington, D.C.

FROMMER'S® GREAT OUTDOOR GUIDES

New England
Northern California
Southern California & Baja
Southern New England
Washington & Oregon

FROMMER'S® BORN TO SHOP GUIDES

Born to Shop: France
Born to Shop: Italy
Born to Shop: London
Born to Shop: New York
Born to Shop: Paris

FROMMER'S® IRREVERENT GUIDES

Amsterdam
Boston
Chicago
Las Vegas
London
Los Angeles
Manhattan
New Orleans
Paris
San Francisco
Seattle & Portland
Vancouver
Walt Disney World
Washington, D.C.

FROMMER'S® BEST-LOVED DRIVING TOURS

America
Britain
California
Florida
France
Germany
Ireland
Italy
New England
Scotland
Spain
Western Europe

THE UNOFFICIAL GUIDES®

Bed & Breakfasts in California
Bed & Breakfasts in New England
Bed & Breakfasts in the Northwest
Bed & Breakfasts in Southeast
Beyond Disney
Branson, Missouri
California with Kids
Chicago
Cruises
Disneyland
Florida with Kids
Golf Vacations in the Eastern U.S.
The Great Smoky & Blue Ridge Mountains
Inside Disney
Hawaii
Las Vegas
London
Miami & the Keys
Mini Las Vegas
Mini-Mickey
New Orleans
New York City
Paris
San Francisco
Skiing in the West
Southeast with Kids
Walt Disney World
Walt Disney World for Grown-ups
Walt Disney World for Kids
Washington, D.C.

SPECIAL-INTEREST TITLES

Frommer's Britain's Best Bed & Breakfasts and Country Inns
Frommer's Britain's Best Bike Rides
The Civil War Trust's Official Guide to the Civil War Discovery Trail
Frommer's Caribbean Hideaways
Frommer's Adventure Guide to Central America
Frommer's Adventure Guide to South America
Frommer's Adventure Guide to Southeast Asia
Frommer's Food Lover's Companion to France
Frommer's Gay & Lesbian Europe
Frommer's Exploring America by RV
Hanging Out in Europe
Israel Past & Present
Mad Monks' Guide to California
Mad Monks' Guide to New York City
Frommer's The Moon
Frommer's New York City with Kids
The New York Times' Unforgettable Weekends
Places Rated Almanac
Retirement Places Rated
Frommer's Road Atlas Britain
Frommer's Road Atlas Europe
Frommer's Washington, D.C., with Kids
Frommer's What the Airlines Never Tell You